Flags over the Warsaw Ghetto

The Untold Story of the Warsaw Ghetto Uprising

Moshe Arens

gefen
publishing house
JERUSALEM ◆ NEW YORK   Est. 1981

Cover Design: Pini Hamou
Typesetting: David Yehoshua

Originally published in Hebrew as Degalim me-al ha-geto: Sipuro shel mered
Geto Varshah © Miskal-Yedioth Ahronoth, Sifre Hemed, 2009
The map entitled "Warsaw Ghetto during the Uprising" appears in Moshe
Arens, The Warsaw Ghetto Uprising — A Reappraisal, Yad Vashem Studies,
vol. 33 (2005), p. 121.

ISBN: 978-965-229-527-9
3 5 7 9 8 6 4

Gefen Publishing House Ltd.
6 Hatzvi Street
Jerusalem 94386, Israel
972-2-538-0247
orders@gefenpublishing.com

Gefen Books
11 Edison Place
Springfield, NJ 07081, USA
1-800-477-5257
orders@gefenpublishing.com

www.gefenpublishing.com

Printed in Israel

Send for our free catalogue

Library of Congress Cataloging-in-Publication Data

Arens, Moshe.
[Degalim me-'al ha-Geto. English]
Flags over the Warsaw Ghetto : the untold story of the Warsaw Ghetto uprising / Moshe Arens.
p. cm.
Includes bibliographical references.

ISBN 978-965-229-527-9

1. Warsaw (Poland)–History–Warsaw Ghetto Uprising, 1943. 2. World War, 1939-1945–
Jewish resistance–Poland–Warsaw. 3. Holocaust, Jewish (1939-1945)–Poland--Warsaw.
4. Jews–Poland–Warsaw–History–20th century. I. Title.

D765.2.W3A854513 2011   •   940.53'1853841--dc23   •   2011018123

This book is dedicated to the memory of

Pawel Frenkel and Mordechai Anielewicz,

who led a few hundred Jewish youngsters in a desperate battle against far superior German forces in the Warsaw Ghetto Uprising in April 1943, the first uprising against the German conquerors during World War II.

They fought for the honor of the Jewish people.

Acknowledgments

The inspiration for this book came from the late Haim Lazar. Lazar, a member of the Jabotinsky-led Betar Zionist youth movement, had been a member of the United Resistance Organization (FPO) in the Vilna ghetto. On orders from the organization, he left the ghetto to join a Jewish partisan group in the nearby forests and participated in sabotage operations against German targets in the area. On arriving in Israel after the war, he dedicated himself to writing books that dealt with the activities of members of Betar and the Irgun Zvai Leumi. One of his books, *Muranowska 7*, published first in Hebrew in 1963, was devoted to the Warsaw Ghetto Uprising. In the book he emphasized the important part played by the resistance organization ZZW led by members of Betar in the uprising, in parallel to the role played by ZOB, the resistance organization led by Mordechai Anielewicz. The book broke new ground but did not attract much attention, and the generally accepted narrative of the uprising, which essentially ignores the part played by members of Betar, has remained in place to this day. On rereading his book many years later, and sensing that an injustice had been done to the fighters from Betar, I decided to research the uprising, so important in the history of World War II and the history of the Jewish people. David Landau, the former editor of the *Haaretz* daily in Tel Aviv, suggested that my research on the Warsaw Ghetto Uprising be published as a book. This is that book.

I owe a debt of gratitude to the libraries and archives that house the documents and books relating to the Warsaw Ghetto Uprising. Yad Vashem in Jerusalem, the Jewish Historical Institute (ZIH) in Warsaw, the Jabotinsky Institute in Tel Aviv, and Beit Lohamei Hagetaot in Kibbutz Lohamei Hagetaot. At the Jewish Historical Institute in Warsaw I was assisted by Dr. Eleonora Bergman, the current director, while at the Jabotinsky Institute, whose archives are ably directed by Amira Stern, I was the beneficiary of unlimited help by Daniela Osacky, the granddaughter of Haim Lazar. The head of the archives at Beit Lohamei Hagetaot, Yossi Shavit, was most helpful in searching for material I needed.

At Yad Vashem I had the opportunity to conduct long conversations with Professor Yisrael Gutman, himself a fighter in the Warsaw Ghetto Uprising, and a renowned expert on the Warsaw ghetto.

Dr. Havi Ben-Sasson of the Hebrew University in Jerusalem, an expert on the Warsaw ghetto, generously shared with me her encyclopedic knowledge of the source material dealing with the ghetto.

I met with surviving members of the uprising from both resistance organizations that fought in the Warsaw ghetto in order to glean every bit of additional information I could on the preparations for the uprising, the uprising itself, and the relations between the two resistance organizations in the ghetto.

Two surviving fighters of the Betar-led resistance organization ZZW, Juta Hartman and Fella Finkelstein, met with me for many hours. Of the surviving fighters of ZOB living in Israel, I met with Simha (Kazik) Rotem, Aharon Carmi, and Stefan Grayek, now deceased. On a trip to Warsaw I spent a number of hours with Marek Edelman, who had been a member of ZOB Command and chose to remain in Poland after the war. Shoshana (Emilka) Rosenzweig, a member of Betar in her youth, who went through the war as a Pole working as a courier for the Polish underground (AK), granted me a number of interviews. She had been a frequent visitor to the ghetto, smuggling weapons to ZZW and ZOB, and got to know Pawel Frenkel, the commander of ZZW.

The composite picture of Pawel Frenkel, of whom no photograph has survived, was drawn by the artist Gil Gibli, based on information provided by Fella Finkelstein, who had been sworn into

ZZW by Frenkel, and Yisrael Ribak, who as a youngster was under Frenkel's command in a branch of Betar in Warsaw before the war.

Shlomo Nakdimon, the Israeli journalist, called my attention to an interview given to him over forty years ago by Dr. David Wdowinski, a prominent Zionist-Revisionist, who survived the Warsaw ghetto and who was associated with ZZW there. It was in this interview that I noticed the reference to the ZZW fighter Stefan Wladislaw, who fell in a gunfight with the Germans and was buried by his comrades in the Warsaw Jewish cemetery, which was located next to the ghetto and has been preserved to this day. The present director of the cemetery, Przemyslaw Yisroel Szpilman, was kind enough to locate Wladislaw's grave and send me a photograph. The inscription on the tombstone throws important new light on the early formation of ZZW. The photographs of the German war cemetery near Warsaw, which also contains the graves of German soldiers who fell during the Warsaw Ghetto Uprising, were obtained with the help of Marian Turski, the chairman of ZIH in Warsaw.

I am grateful to the prominent Holocaust historian Saul Friedlander of UCLA, who took the time to read some of my research papers on the Warsaw Ghetto Uprising and comment on them.

I am also grateful to Ita Olesker and Deborah Meghnagi Bailey for scrupulously editing the original manuscript.

The Hasten Foundation of Indianapolis and the Reuven and Edith Hecht Foundation of Haifa provided support for some of the work.

And last, but certainly not least, my wife Muriel read and reread the manuscript, providing frequent valuable advice.

Contents

Introduction

Six million Jews – men, women, and children – were slaughtered by the Germans and their associates during World War II, gassed, shot, beaten, and starved to death. Unarmed and undefended, they were led like sheep to slaughter. Resistance against the *Einsatzgruppen*, the special death squads of the SS, against their many collaborators among the nations of Europe, and against the might of the Wehrmacht, the German army, was next to impossible. Nevertheless, in a few instances, it became possible. As partisan fighters in the forests and swamps of White Russia and the Ukraine, Jewish fighters ambushed German units and blew up German installations. And in the Warsaw ghetto there was an uprising, the first uprising against the Germans in the areas occupied by their conquering armies during World War II.

Organized resistance within the walls of the ghetto needed the support of the ghetto's inhabitants. As long as most of them still lived with the hope that they and their families might yet survive the war, and feared that the least sign of resistance would bring about draconian punishment by the Germans that would lead to the total extermination of all those who had managed to survive, a Jewish uprising in the ghetto could not take place. In the Warsaw ghetto, only after more than 270,000 Jews had already been sent to the Treblinka gas chambers in the summer and fall of 1942, did it finally become clear to those who remained that they were *all* destined for extermination. At that point, in what was left of the ghetto, which at one time had been populated by more than 400,000 Jews, the stage was set for the uprising.

The Warsaw Ghetto Uprising was a lonely battle. The fighters were cut off from the rest of the world, and the uprising went almost

1

unnoticed in the capitals of the Allied powers. During the desperate combat in the streets of the Warsaw ghetto, they were not offered any assistance, nor did they receive any words of encouragement. As far as Roosevelt, Churchill, and Stalin were concerned, they did not exist. Only years later did the world begin to appreciate the courage of the Jewish fighters in the Warsaw ghetto, who, outnumbered and outgunned, were the first in Hitler's Europe to rise up against the German conqueror.

The Warsaw Ghetto Uprising was a momentous event in the history of the Jewish people, and one of the key events of World War II. It has been commemorated in numerous books and articles, in Holocaust museums, in annual memorial meetings, in statues and street names in Israel and in Warsaw. It has become an integral part of the history of World War II, and has over the years become a part of the collective memory of people around the world. Fictionalized versions – *Mila 18* by Leon Uris and *The Wall* by John Hersey – have been read by millions. And yet the full story of what really happened during the ten days of combat against the German forces, between April 19 and April 28, 1943, is not generally known. Who were the Jewish fighters who dared oppose the armed might of the SS troops and their Ukrainian auxiliaries under the command of SS General Juergen Stroop? Who commanded them in battle? What were their goals? The generally accepted version of these events is far from the whole story.

It is the purpose of this book to set the story straight. It is a story of daring and courage and sacrifice that should be known as accurately as we can reconstitute it after all these years – out of respect for and in homage to the fighters who rose against the German attempt to liquidate what remained of the Warsaw ghetto, and made a last-ditch fight for the honor of the Jewish people. And also, for the sake of historical truth.

The truth about the Warsaw Ghetto Uprising begins with the existence of two resistance organizations in the ghetto that did not unite despite the desperate battle they were facing. The rivalry between these two organizations – the Jewish Fighting Organization (ZOB), led by Mordechai Anielewicz, and the Jewish Military Organization (ZZW), led by Pawel Frenkel – was rooted in past ideological differences that had become completely irrelevant in the ghetto. Nevertheless, these ideological differences prevented the two organizations from uniting even after most of the Jews from the Warsaw ghetto had been sent to the Treblinka gas chambers, and they also continued to influence the narrative of the uprising as related by some of the survivors. In their reminiscences, the surviving members of the ZOB recorded their personal experiences and almost totally suppressed mention of the existence of ZZW in the ghetto. The leaders of the political organizations to which members of ZOB belonged were intent on getting credit for the valor of their members, and had no interest in drawing attention to the part played in the uprising by members of rival organizations. As for the ZZW, all of its senior commanders fell in battle with the Germans. There was, in effect, nobody left to tell their story. And yet, the facts were there – they only needed to be examined.

The most detailed description of the fighting in the ghetto was provided by SS Police General Juergen Stroop, the man charged by the head of the SS, Heinrich Himmler, to liquidate what remained of the Warsaw ghetto after the mass deportations to Treblinka in the summer and fall of 1942. Daily, and sometimes twice daily, he issued reports to his superior, SS Police General Friedrich-Wilhelm Krueger in Krakow, reports that were passed on to Himmler. There is little reason to doubt the accuracy of these reports, although on occasion they were embellished in order to exaggerate the courage of his troops, and certain details that seemed to him to be embarrassing at the time appeared only in his summary report, after he had "declared victory" over the Jewish uprising. His mission was to bring about the extermination of the Jews in the Warsaw ghetto and to destroy the ghetto itself, as ordered by Hitler. As he fanatically pursued this mission he became aware of the existence of two Jewish resistance organization, to whom he sometimes referred by the initials of their Polish names – ZZW and ZOB – but he was completely "neutral" between them in his determination to root out all resistance in the ghetto.

Stroop considered the suppression of the uprising and the subsequent destruction of the Warsaw ghetto a great achievement, as did his superiors. Praise was heaped on him by Himmler, and he was awarded the Iron Cross. In commemoration of his achievement, Stroop put a collection of his daily reports, covering the period from April 19 to May 16, 1943, together with his summary report of May 16, 1943, into a fancy album, together with a series of photographs he had had taken during the action there. The album, entitled *Es Gibt Keinen Juedischen Wohnbezirk in Warschau Mehr* – The Jewish Quarter in Warsaw No Longer Exists – also included a list of the names of the casualties the Germans sustained during the fighting, who had "fallen for the Fuehrer and their country." One copy of the album was presented to Himmler, another to Stroop's immediate superior, Krueger, and one Stroop kept for himself. That copy was admitted as evidence at the Nuremberg war crimes trials. It has since been widely published and is available in a number of languages.[1] It is the primary source for material about the Warsaw Ghetto Uprising and about the resistance to the German forces by the two Jewish resistance organizations. In his daily reports Stroop does not usually

---

1   Yosef Kermish, ed., *Mered Geto Varsha be-einei ha-oyev: Ha-dochot shel Juergen Stroop* [The Warsaw Ghetto Uprising in the eyes of the enemy: The Juergen Stroop reports] (Jerusalem: Yad Vashem, 1966), 121–92. Also, Juergen Stroop, *The Stroop Report: The Jewish Quarter of Warsaw Is No More!* ed. Sybil Milton (New York: Pantheon Books, 1979).

identify the names of the resistance organizations that were engaging his troops, but from the locations of the battles, as indicated by him, together with eyewitness reports, in most cases there is no doubt regarding the specific organization that was involved in each of the major engagements of the Warsaw Ghetto Uprising.

Stroop was taken prisoner at the end of the war by the U.S. Armed Forces in western Germany. Once his identity became known to his captors, he was ordered to write a report describing the action in the Warsaw ghetto. This report was composed by Stroop in Wiesbaden on May 1, 1946, three years after the uprising. In it Stroop refers to the raising of the Zionist (now Israeli) and Polish flags by the Jewish fighters over Muranowski Square, first mentioned in his summary report of May 16, 1943.[2]

Stroop was sentenced to death at the Dachau International Military Tribunal for the execution of captured U.S. air crews, but before the sentence was carried out he was extradited to Poland to stand trial in Warsaw for war crimes committed in the Warsaw ghetto.

While awaiting trial in the Mokotow prison in Warsaw, Stroop replied in writing to forty-two questions submitted to him about the Warsaw Ghetto Uprising. In his reply to a question regarding the battle at Muranowski Square, Stroop wrote:

> Muranowski Square (I do not remember the name anymore) was the place that the ghetto fighters defended with the greatest stubbornness. This square was controlled by a building (built of concrete), which protruded into the square. Fire from

2   A copy of the Wiesbaden report as handwritten by Stroop in Gothic script is in the Yad Vashem Archives, no. 1539, tr. 3. It appears in English translation in Haim Lazar Litai, *Muranowska 7: The Warsaw Ghetto Rising* (Tel Aviv: Massada P.E.C. Press, 1966), 309–15. Also in German in Wolfgang Scheffler and Helge Grabnitz, *Der Ghetto-Aufstand Warschau 1943* (Munich: Goldman Verlag, 1993), 174–81.

submachine guns and machine guns prevented entry into this square. The day before SS-Untersturmfuehrer Dehmke, known as a very capable officer, fell, I received an order to capture the above-mentioned building with an assault unit. Strong fire, supported by grenades and Molotov cocktails, blocked the action. Only the following day did they succeed in penetrating the building. The defenders retreated in the direction of the roof of the building. SS-Unterstrumfuehrer Dehmke fell later, in the attic. In the building there were a number of rooms reinforced by concrete walls. If I remember correctly, it seems that the defenders escaped by way of the roofs, aside from a few who were killed.[3]

Three survivors of the Warsaw ghetto were given the opportunity to question Stroop in prison, and their questions and his answers were recorded. The three were Marek Edelman, who had been a member of the Command of ZOB, Mordechai Anielewicz's organization, and commander of the ZOB forces in the Brushmakers' Workshop area; Rahel Auerbach, who had worked with Emmanuel Ringelblum, the Warsaw ghetto chronicler, in the ghetto; and Stefan Grayek, an active member of the Socialist Zionist party Po'alei Zion in the ghetto. To one of Edelman's questions Stroop replied: "The strongest defense was at Muranowski Square." When Edelman persisted and asked: "In which locations aside from Muranowski Square was there fierce fighting?" Stroop replied: "Today I cannot say with the same exactness as about Muranowski Square. I also remember the Brushmakers' Workshop, but I cannot describe the matter precisely."[4]

When these replies are analyzed in the context of Stroop's daily reports and his summary report sent from the ghetto during the up-

---

3   Kermish, *Mered Geto Varsha be-einei ha-oyev*, 200–201.
4   Ibid., 211–35.

rising, the centrality of the battle at Muranowski Square – "the battle for the flags," which was fought by the ZZW fighters led by Pawel Frenkel and the important role played by ZZW in the uprising – are apparent.

While in prison awaiting his trial, Stroop and another German prisoner shared a cell with a Pole, Kazimierz Moczarski, imprisoned by the Polish Communist regime. Moczarski had been a member of the right-wing Polish underground (AK). Stroop regaled his cellmates with stories about the Warsaw ghetto. These were later published by Moczarski in his book *Conversations with the Executioner*.[5] They are consistent with Stroop's operational reports, adding details here and there, and reflecting Stroop's personal feelings while he was committing heinous crimes against the Jews in the ghetto.

Stroop's testimony at his trial in Warsaw adds some additional evidence to the mass of data already available. From it all stands out the major role played in the uprising by ZZW, the resistance organization commanded by Pawel Frenkel and his deputy Leon Rodal. They and the senior commanders of ZZW are known to have been members of Betar, the Zionist-Revisionist youth organization founded by Ze'ev Jabotinsky.

The years preceding World War II were a time when Socialists throughout the world were preaching the "class struggle" and "solidarity of the proletariat." Many of them, not only avowed Communists, saw the Soviet Union as the pioneer and leader of this "struggle." This was also true in Palestine, where the Socialist Zionists had achieved a dominant position in the Jewish community. They saw the Zionist Revisionists of Betar, who believed in market economics and free enterprise, as Fascists and enemies of the working classes. The Socialist Zionist movements in the Diaspora religiously followed

---

5   Kazimierz Moczarski, *Gespraeche mit dem henker* [Conversations with the executioner] (Frankfurt am Main: Fischer Taschenbuch Verlag, 1982).

the line laid down by their parent organizations in Palestine. Even during the war years, German occupation and suffering in the ghetto did not make a significant dent in the rivalries among Jewish political movements that were in large part the product of this anachronistic ideology. Under the desperate circumstances of the Warsaw ghetto, the Socialist Zionist movements were able to include the other "proletarian" movements – the Socialist anti-Zionist Bund (the Jewish Socialist Union) and the Communists – in the ZOB fighting organization, but still could not reconcile themselves to uniting with members of Betar, a group they considered Fascist.

It is notable that the Jewish resistance organization that was formed in the Vilna ghetto at the beginning of 1942, after the German mass executions of Vilna Jews in the Ponar forest, the United Partisan Organization (Fareingte Partizaner Organizciye – FPO), included in its ranks members of Betar, members of the Socialist Zionist youth movement Hashomer Hatzair, and Communists. There, the leaders of Betar and Hashomer Hatzair, Yosef Glazman and Abba Kovner, fully grasping the dimension of the tragedy facing the Jews in the areas of German conquest, decided to put all the rivalries of the past behind them in order to create a common framework to resist the Germans. In the Warsaw ghetto this did not happen.

The differences that prevented unity between ZOB and ZZW in the Warsaw ghetto carried over into the narrative of the uprising as it was related after the war by the surviving members of ZOB, who insisted in claiming for their organization the primary role in the uprising. This narrative was promoted in Israel, governed for the first twenty-nine years of its existence by the Socialist Labor party.

The generally accepted narrative of the Warsaw Ghetto Uprising assigns the major role to ZOB, the resistance organization led by Mordechai Anielewicz. If ZZW is mentioned at all, it is assigned only a marginal role. It is made clear in this book that this narrative strays considerably from the actual facts as we can reconstruct them from the wealth of available evidence. Recognition of the role of ZZW in the uprising in no way belittles the courageous and daring fight waged by the fighters of ZOB.

The primary source material about ZOB, its founding and development, is Yitzhak Zuckerman's voluminous recorded reminiscences, which were published after his death.[6] "Antek" Zuckerman, the leader of the Socialist Zionist youth movement Dror in the ghetto, and the moving spirit in the organization of ZOB, was, as would be expected of a leader of a youth movement, strongly ideologically oriented. As mentioned earlier, he saw the natural partners for the organization of a resistance organization only in the "proletarian" camp – the Socialist Zionist movements, the non-Zionist Socialist Bund, and the Communists.[7] Jabotinsky's Zionist-Revisionists were certainly not among the candidates he chose for the resistance organization he was attempting to form. It was this political orientation that led to the exclusion of the Revisionists from ZOB, and precluded unity between ZOB and ZZW at a later stage.

Zuckerman was sent to "Aryan" Warsaw a few days before the uprising to make contact with the Polish underground on behalf of ZOB, and was unable to return to the ghetto once the uprising had begun. Even though he did not participate in the uprising, he became the foremost spokesman about the Warsaw Ghetto Uprising in later years, because he was the most senior of the ZOB members

---

6   Yitzhak Zuckerman (Antek), *A Surplus of Memory* (Berkeley, CA: University of California Press, 1993). Originally published in Hebrew as *Sheva ha-shanim ha-hen 1939–1946* [Those seven years] (Tel Aviv: Hakibbutz Hameuhad–Beit Lohamei Hagetaot, 1990).

7   See the description of Zuckerman's initial efforts to form a resistance organization, by his wife Tzivya Lubetkin, in *Biymei chilayon u-mered* [In the days of destruction and revolt] (Tel Aviv: Hakibbutz Hameuhad–Beit Lohamei Hagetaot, 1979), 67.

to have survived. The generally accepted narrative of the uprising is essentially the story as he told and retold it over the years.

Zuckerman assigns to ZOB the primary role in the organization of the uprising and the fighting in the ghetto. He limits ZZW to a marginal role. Contrary to the evidence provided by Stroop's operational reports that the fighting at Muranowski Square lasted four days, Zuckerman claimed that ZZW fought on "part of Muranowska Street" for two days but then could hold out no longer, and that its fighters escaped the ghetto on April 20.[8] He also ignored the presence of ZZW fighters in other areas of the ghetto, even though eyewitness reports of ZZW and ZOB fighters make it clear that ZZW fighters were involved in the fighting in other parts of the ghetto. Zuckerman's tone regarding ZZW was generally disparaging.

Even though a number of eyewitness accounts corroborate Stroop's reports testifying to the length and intensity of the fighting at Muranowski Square,[9] they have not influenced the generally accepted narrative nor the exhibits devoted to the Warsaw Ghetto Uprising at the Yad Vashem Museum in Jerusalem or the Holocaust Museum in Washington, D.C. Eyewitness accounts substantiating the participation of ZZW fighters in resistance to the Germans in other localities in the ghetto[10] have similarly been generally ignored. The

---

8   Yitzhak Zuckerman, *Ba-geto u-va-mered* [In the ghetto and in the revolt] (Tel Aviv: Hakibbutz Hameuhad–Beit Lohamei Hagetaot, 1985), 146.

9   See Ryszard Walewski, *Jurek* (Tel Aviv: Moreshet and Sifriat Poalim, 1976), 67–74; and Jack Eisner, *The Survivor* (New York: William Morrow & Co., 1980), 177–97.

10 For testimony on the activity of ZZW fighters in the Toebbens-Schultz Workshop area, see Simha Korngold's diary (Yad Vashem Archives O33/1566) and Fella Finkelstein-Shapchik's testimony in Lohamei Hagetaot Archives, no. 9648. For the activity of ZZW fighters in the Brushmakers' Workshop area, see Juta Hartman-Rutenberg's testimony in Haim Lazar Litai, *Matzada shel Varsha* [Masada of Warsaw] (Tel Aviv: Jabotinsky Institute, 1963), 255–59.

attempt to portray the Warsaw Ghetto Uprising as an achievement of the "working classes" has survived to this day, despite the vast political changes that have taken place in the intervening years.

Two young men in their early twenties led the uprising: Mordechai Anielewicz and Pawel Frenkel. Anielewicz, who commanded one of the two Jewish armed resistance organizations, ZOB, is generally known as the commander of the Warsaw Ghetto Uprising. Frenkel, commander of the other Jewish armed resistance organization, ZZW, is almost unknown.

The true story of the Warsaw Ghetto Uprising needs to be told. *Veritas vincit*, the truth conquers.

Chapter 1

Warsaw

Warsaw was the largest Jewish community in Europe before World War II, and the second largest in the world, after New York. Close to 370,000 Jews lived there, constituting a third of the city's population and more than 10 percent of the over 3.3 million Polish Jews. Many of them lived in poverty, finding it difficult to make a living under the economic conditions imposed by the government of Poland, which aimed at reducing Jewish participation in the Polish economy. Some survived only with the help of assistance they received from the American Jewish Joint Distribution Committee.

The authoritarian leader of the Second Polish Republic, Józef Piłsudski, generally pursued a policy of respect for Poland's minority population, including the Jews, but things took a turn for the worse after his death in 1935. Anti-Semitic laws limited the entry of Jewish students into universities, while frequent anti-Jewish riots by Polish hooligans were apparently condoned by the government. Most Polish Jews would have preferred to leave Poland – the Zionists for Palestine, the others to any country prepared to admit them – but the British Mandatory Administration in Palestine provided only a yearly trickle of visas for Jews, and those wishing to emigrate to other countries found that after Hitler's rise to power in Germany, most countries preferred to keep Jews out. The followers of the Jewish Socialist Bund placed their hopes in their fellow Polish Socialists, anticipating that one day, in a Socialist Poland, everything would come right. While Zionist parties urged Jews to leave and immigrate to Palestine, the Bund took up the call for *Doikeyt* (Living Here and

Now). According to the Bund, the critical problems of Jewry needed to be resolved not by escaping from the hard realities of everyday life, but by addressing them, "here and now," in Poland, by means of an energetic political and cultural program. Meanwhile, deep in the underground, Jewish youngsters who belonged to Communist cells expected redemption to come from the Soviet Union. And even in this period of great distress, the many Orthodox Jews, led by great rabbis, kept their faith with the Almighty.

Jewish Warsaw was a beehive of cultural, political, social, and religious activity. All political movements – religious, Zionist, non-Zionist, and anti-Zionist – were represented there. It boasted two large Yiddish dailies, *Haynt* and *Der Moment*. In addition to many religious educational institutions, an extensive network of schools, with instruction in Yiddish, Hebrew, or Polish, provided education to Jewish youngsters.

Many of the youth were organized within a framework of youth groups that provided both social activity and ideological indoctrination for their members, and generally commanded their fierce loyalty. There were the three Socialist Zionist youth movements: Hashomer Hatzair, Dror-Freiheit, and Gordonia. Hanoar Hatzioni and Akiva were oriented toward general Jewish Zionist education. And there was Betar, the Zionist youth movement founded and headed by Ze'ev Jabotinsky, which provided paramilitary training for its members; it was the largest Zionist youth movement in Poland. The Bund's youth movement, Tsukunft, like its parent organization, was Socialist and anti-Zionist; unlike the Zionist youth movements, which promoted the Hebrew language, it concentrated on secular Yiddish culture. All of them had their headquarters in Warsaw.

The profound ideological differences between the different sectors of the Jewish community led to unbridgeable schisms, leaving little room for cooperation. A wide gulf separated the Bund from the Zionists. The relations between the Zionists and Agudat Yisrael, the anti-Zionist Orthodox religious party, were especially bad. Yitzhak Gruenbaum, leader of the Polish General Zionists, editor of the Yiddish daily *Haynt*, and leader of the Jewish faction in the Polish parliament, was especially adamant in his opposition to Agudat Yisrael, and the rift between the parties continued after he left for Palestine in 1933, where he joined the Jewish Agency Executive. The voting in the 1936 elections for the Warsaw Jewish Community Council resulted in a three-way tie between the representatives of the Zionists, the Bund, and Agudat Yisrael. The refusal of the Zionists to enter into a coalition with Agudat Yisrael made it impossible to establish a functioning coalition supported by a majority on the council. This stalemate meant that the Polish government was compelled to dissolve the council and appoint in its stead a group of Jews not affiliated with any of the parties. The appointed council was headed by Maurycy Mayzel, a partly assimilated Jew with connections to the Polish government, and included Adam Czerniaków, an engineer, who in time would become the head of the *Judenrat* in the Warsaw ghetto. The Warsaw Jewish community was left without an elected leadership in the tragic days that were to follow.

This was only one instance of the rivalry and even animosity that characterized the relations of different elements of the Warsaw Jewish community, torn as they were between opposing ideologies: religious against Zionists, Zionists against anti-Zionists, Jewish nationalists against assimilationists, and almost all against the Communists. But the various Zionist movements, as well as the Bund, concentrated their primary antagonism toward the Zionist Revisionist movement of Ze'ev Jabotinsky. This movement preached militant Zionism, and believed that the leadership of the World Zionist Organization was passively acceding to Britain's backtracking on its commitments undertaken in the Balfour Declaration and defined in the League of Nations Mandate for Palestine. The movement had been steadily gaining strength in the bi-yearly elections to the World

Zionist Congress, to the point that it was threatening the leadership of Chaim Weizmann and his coalition partners, the Socialist Zionists.

At the Zionist Congress in Basel in 1931, Jabotinsky introduced a motion declaring that the aim of the Zionist movement was the establishment of a Jewish State in Palestine with a Jewish majority. The Congress refused to put the motion to a vote, leading to a declaration by Jabotinsky, backed by his followers, that "this is not a Zionist Congress."[1] It was the start of the rift that ultimately led to the withdrawal of Jabotinsky's movement from the World Zionist Organization.

A dramatic worsening in the relations between Jabotinsky's movement and the rest of the Zionist camp came with the murder of Chaim Arlozoroff, the Socialist Zionist leader, in Palestine, in June 1933. Arlozoroff, a leading figure in the Socialist Zionist movement and head of the Political Department of the Jewish Agency, was murdered by two unknown persons while walking with his wife on the Tel Aviv beach. The incident was exploited by Labor Zionist circles in Palestine and abroad to launch an attack on the Revisionists as being responsible for the murder. The arrest by the British police in Palestine of two Revisionists, accusing them of the murder, and their subsequent trial, brought the internecine strife to a fever pitch, even though the accused were eventually found not guilty after a long trial.

This incident and the accusations that followed created a chasm between Jabotinsky's followers and most other Zionist movements – a chasm that lasted for many years due to the accusations of political assassination and the counter-accusations of a fabricated blood libel. A broad anti-Revisionist coalition was formed, which included

---

1   Joseph Schechtman, *Fighter and Prophet: The Vladimir Jabotinsky Story* (New York: Thomas Yoseloff, 1961), 152.

not only the Socialists but also the General Zionists. Under their combined signatures appeared a statement calling for the wholesale outlawing of the entire Jabotinsky movement. It read: "We declare that the moral responsibility for this brutal assassination falls upon the entire Revisionist movement, which has produced such a murderer.… Whoever is still concerned about the fate of Zionism must shake himself clear of the Revisionist past. No intercourse whatever with Revisionism! Let our motto be: 'Expel the Revisionist gangs from Jewish Life!'"[2]

The resulting animosity immediately spread to Poland, the most active arena of Zionist politics outside of Palestine and a stronghold of the Revisionists. There, the influential General Zionist mass-circulation daily, *Haynt*, a paper to which Jabotinsky had contributed articles until 1932, joined the anti-Revisionist campaign. In response, Jabotinsky began writing for *Der Moment*, the rival Warsaw daily. At the Zionist Congress later that same year, the Revisionist delegation was maligned and ostracized, paving the way for their break with what had until then been a common organizational framework.

An additional source of friction between the Revisionists and the Socialist Zionists, who by that point were the dominant force in the World Zionist Organization, was the continuing labor disputes in Palestine. The Revisionists opposed waging a class struggle between Jewish workers and Jewish employers in Palestine and the resulting strikes, which were supported by the Palestine Federation of Labor (the Histadrut), dominated by the Socialist Zionist camp. They felt that such a policy would be harmful to the Zionist enterprise in Palestine, and called for compulsory arbitration to resolve labor disputes there. This ideological split resulted in the Revisionists forming another labor federation in Palestine, the National Labor Federation (Histadrut Ovdim Leumit) in 1934. They, in turn, were

---

2   Ibid., 185–86.

accused of being strike-breakers, and the results were frequent violent confrontations between the two camps. This too was reflected in
the strife between the Revisionists and the rest of the Zionist camp in
Poland, and made the Revisionists anathema to all Socialists, Zionists, and non-Zionists alike.

In 1935, the Revisionists finally withdrew from the World Zionist Organization and founded the New Zionist Organization. With
the establishment of an independent political framework, the Revisionists were not bound anymore by the restraints placed on member organizations of the World Zionist Organization, and they began
launching their own political initiatives. In June 1936, at a mass
meeting in Warsaw, Jabotinsky sounded the call for the evacuation of
the Jews of Eastern Europe to Palestine. Facing the distress of these
communities and fearing an impending catastrophe, Jabotinsky saw
in such a move the only constructive solution to their problems,
which, if implemented, would also mean attaining a Jewish majority
in Palestine in a very short time. This call was followed by meetings
with Polish government representatives, as well as the representatives of other Eastern European governments, in an effort to enlist
their support for the evacuation plan.

The evacuation proposal brought down another avalanche of
criticism on the heads of Jabotinsky and his followers. The Histadrut
daily in Palestine, *Davar*, ridiculed "the Fuehrer Jabotinsky, who all
these years had been busily distorting every sound idea in Zionism."
It went on to accuse him of having concluded a pact with the Polish
government to deport Jews from Poland in yearly installments.[3] *Der
Moment* in Warsaw also joined the opposition to Jabotinsky. The
battle over his evacuation proposal in the Polish Jewish community
continued to rage until the outbreak of World War II. Jabotinsky's
contacts with the Polish government, which was widely viewed as

---

3   Ibid., 341.

anti-Semitic and Fascist, seemed to accord with the accusation that Jabotinsky and his followers were themselves Fascists. The brown-colored uniforms worn by the members of the Revisionist youth organization, Betar, only helped the comparison between the Revisionist youth and the brown-shirted Nazis in Hitler's Germany. But the greatest fury against Jabotinsky's evacuation plan came from the Bund. Evacuation of the Jews from Poland was diametrically opposed to the Bund's ideal of Jewish integration in a Socialist Poland, an aim that was to be achieved by the combined efforts of the Jewish and Polish working classes. On the occasion of Jabotinsky's visit to Vilna, the Bund there issued a manifesto calling Jabotinsky's evacuation plan a base and criminal scheme, and referred to him as the spiritual father of Jewish Fascism.

In 1937 an additional divide opened between the Revisionist movement and the rest of the Zionist camp. A wave of Arab terror against the Jewish community of Palestine had begun in 1936, and the Haganah, the Jewish military organization in Palestine charged with defending the Jewish community against Arab attacks, became divided in its response to the situation. Some were prepared to accept a policy of restraint, but others saw a need for retaliatory action. The split led to the existence of two Jewish military organizations – the Haganah, accepting the policy of restraint set by the Histadrut leadership and supported by most of the Zionist parties, and the Irgun Zvai Leumi (IZL), which looked on Jabotinsky as its commander-in-chief. As the IZL began retaliatory actions against Arab targets, relations between the two groups deteriorated, and accusations were leveled against Jabotinsky that he had set up his own militia in Palestine which was refusing to accept the discipline imposed by the established Zionist leadership. Warnings were issued that force might have to be used by the Haganah to restrain the IZL.

Meanwhile, the creation of the IZL in Palestine also had a great impact on the Revisionist youth movement, Betar, in Poland, ultimately leading to considerable friction within the ranks. Members of Betar in Poland were enthusiastic in their support of the IZL's actions in Palestine, and saw themselves as future soldiers in the ranks of the IZL. To them the IZL was the realization of Betar's militant ideology. The IZL leadership in Palestine saw in the large Betar organization in Poland a reservoir of recruits to their ranks. Not prepared to wait until such time as they would arrive in Palestine, IZL emissaries were sent to Poland to organize IZL cells among Polish members of Betar. In the spirit that characterized the conspiratorial organization of the IZL in Palestine, those inducted into these cells were sworn to secrecy. They were given basic military training that was intended to prepare them for eventual service in the ranks of the IZL in Palestine.

One such emissary was Avraham (Yair) Stern, a member of the IZL high command in Palestine. He arrived in Warsaw in the summer of 1937, and thereafter visited Warsaw frequently to oversee the creation of a network of IZL cells in Poland and to establish contacts with Polish government officials, with the aim of obtaining Polish support for the IZL. These contacts were based on the relations that Jabotinsky had already established with the Polish government, and eventually led to Polish agreement for the IZL to conduct military courses in Poland for its members, for Polish army officers to provide instruction in these courses, and for arms from Polish army stores to be shipped to the IZL in Palestine.

Natan Friedman-Yellin (Yellin-Mor), a member of the Polish Betar leadership, was the first in Betar to fall under the spell of "Yair." During Yair's visit to Warsaw, he asked Friedman-Yellin to represent the interests of the IZL in the "travel agency" for illegal immigration to Palestine, run by Avraham Stawski, one of the men who had been accused and then exonerated of the murder of Arlozoroff. In addition, Yair charged him with another task – the organization of the planned underground IZL cells in Poland. IZL cells had to be organized in every city and town that had a Jewish population. They would be the skeleton of a future army.

Using the small budget that Yair put at his disposal, Friedman-Yellin bought two-week unlimited railroad tickets. For months he spent a good part of his time in Polish railroad cars and stations, passing from one end of the country to another, from city to town and from town to city. He used his connections with Betar members, and every place he went he would turn to the person who seemed most prepared and most ripe ideologically. Generally, that would not be the head of the local Betar chapter. With this fellow he would have a first conversation, beginning with a careful exploration of his opinions, and he would go on to ask him to establish an IZL cell in his town.[4]

The admiration Polish Betar felt for the exploits of the IZL in Palestine, and the attractive nature of the secretive underground cells being established, made it easy for the IZL to recruit the most capable Betar members. Before long, friction began to develop between the Polish Betar leadership in Warsaw and the parallel IZL leadership that was developing within its ranks. People were heard saying that the IZL was the only serious expression of true Betar ideology, while meanwhile the Betar leadership was insisting that there was no need for this parallel organization within Betar. Efforts being made by Jabotinsky himself to arrive at an agreed common hierarchy for the two frameworks were only partially successful. Those members of the Polish Betar who joined the IZL viewed their IZL commanders as the ultimate authority.

The organizational friction in the ranks of Betar took on an ideological flavor as IZL emissaries and some of their new recruits began expressing impatience with Jabotinsky, insisting that at this juncture

---

4   Natan Yellin-Mor, *Shnot be-terem* [The preceding years] (Tel Aviv: Kinneret, 1990), 16.

the time for diplomacy had passed, and that major emphasis had to be placed on military operations that would lead to the establishment of a Jewish State in Palestine. As expressed by Menahem Begin at the world conference of Betar in Warsaw in September 1938, shortly before he became the head of Polish Betar, the period of practical Zionism, which had been replaced by political Zionism, must at this time be followed by "military Zionism."[5] Begin eloquently expressed the views held by the IZL, even challenging Jabotinsky on this subject at the conference. However, he unequivocally accepted Jabotinsky's authority and supported Jabotinsky's efforts to establish a unified Betar-IZL hierarchy. This brought him into conflict with Stern and the IZL emissaries working in Poland.

Under Stern's direction and aided by Natan Friedman-Yellin, the IZL had by this point established a political presence in Warsaw. In addition to the network of IZL cells, which included thousands of Betar members, Stern had been successful in mobilizing a circle of Jewish-Polish intellectuals, who were caught up by his idea of the "fighting Jew," and became fervent supporters of the IZL. This circle was led by a couple, Henryk and Lili Strassman. Henryk Strassman was a senior official in the Polish Ministry of Justice, a lecturer of criminology at Warsaw University, and a reserve officer in the Polish army, and he used his connections to assist Stern in his negotiations with the Polish government. Lili Strassman became the editor of a Polish IZL weekly, *Jerozolima Wyzwolona* (Jerusalem Liberated).

---

5   H. Ben-Yeruham, *Sefer Betar* [The book of Betar], vol. 2, part 2 (Tel Aviv: Havaad Lehotzaat Sefer Betar, 1975), 862–63. "It is our impression," Begin said, "that we stand before the third period of Zionism. The Jewish national movement started with 'practical Zionism,' afterwards came 'political Zionism,' now we are on the threshold of 'military Zionism.'" For a description of the work of IZL emissaries among Betar in Poland and the resulting friction with the Betar leadership, see pp. 841–44. Also see David Niv, *Ma'arachot ha-Irgun ha-Zvai ha-Leumi* [The battles of the Irgun Zvai Leumi], part 2 (Tel Aviv: Mosad Klausner, 1965), 163–96.

For the Yiddish-reading public, the IZL began publishing a weekly newspaper, shortly to become a daily, *Di Tat* (The Action), which was edited by Friedman-Yellin.[6]

The IZL presence in Poland was strengthened by emissaries that arrived from Palestine to organize the transport of immigrants to Palestine, many of them Betar members. They would enter the country on ships bought and leased by the IZL, and thereby bypass British restrictions on Jewish immigration to Palestine. This "illegal" immigration to Palestine was encouraged and directed by Jabotinsky. It also met a specific need of Revisionist youth, who felt that they were not receiving their fair share of the small quota of annual visas issued by the British administration in Palestine and given to the Jewish Agency for distribution to potential immigrants.

In May 1939, the Neville Chamberlain government issued the MacDonald White Paper, announcing severe restrictions on Jewish immigration to Palestine. It was the beginning of Britain's attempt to prevent the establishment of a Jewish State in Palestine, a confrontation with Zionism that was to last until Britain's withdrawal from Palestine in May 1948. These restrictions on Jewish immigration, enforced by a British fleet blockading the shores of Palestine, would prevent the escape of Jews fleeing from Hitler's Europe throughout the war.

Jabotinsky was undoubtedly motivated by his sense of an approaching catastrophe for European Jewry. A year earlier, addressing a mass meeting in Warsaw on August 7, 1938, which on the Hebrew calendar was the Ninth of Av, the anniversary of the destruction of the Temple in Jerusalem, he said:

"It is now three years that I plead with you, Jews of Poland, the crown of world Jewry. I warn you without respite that the catastro-

---

6   Shmuel Katz, *Jabo*, vol. 2 (Tel Aviv: Dvir, 1993), 1057–59; and Schechtman, *Fighter and Prophet*, 455–56.

phe approaches. My hair has turned white and I have grown old during those years since my heart bleeds, dear brothers and sisters, because you do not see the volcano which will soon begin to erupt with the fire of destruction. I see a terrible sight, time is short when one can still save oneself.

"I know you do not see because you are busy and worried with your day-to-day cares. Listen to my words at this twelfth hour: For God's sake, let everyone save his soul while there is still time – and time is short!"

And then he added: "And I want to say to you one more thing today, the Ninth of Av: those who will succeed to escape the calamity will live to see a festive moment of great Jewish joy: the renewal and establishment of the Jewish State! I don't know if I myself will live to see it – but my son will see it! Of that I am certain, just as I am certain that tomorrow the sun will shine. With all my heart I believe in it."[7]

The MacDonald White Paper gave added impetus to the Revisionist attempts to organize illegal immigration to Palestine, while in protest against the White Paper, the IZL began attacking British targets in Palestine. The success of "illegal immigration," which brought about twenty thousand Jews from Europe to the shores of Palestine in the years preceding World War II and during the first months of the war, gave rise to the idea that in time an armada of thousands of armed Betar members from Europe could be brought to the shores of Palestine to launch a military insurrection by the IZL that would wrest control of Palestine from the British. To discuss this possibility, Jabotinsky met with senior members of the IZL in August 1939, at the French Alpine resort of Vals-les-Bains. The delegation was composed of Haim Lubinsky, Hillel Kook, and Alex Rafaeli. Although Jabotinsky had hesitated in the past, at that meeting he gave his ap-

---

7   Ibid., 1068–69.

proval for the planned landings in Palestine and the IZL insurrection against British rule.

The war was to put an end to that plan. Lubinsky returned with the message to Palestine, only to find that the entire IZL Command had been arrested by the British. Kook and Rafaeli went on to the U.S., where for the ensuing years they were part of the IZL delegation there, headed by Kook, who went by the name Peter Bergson.[8]

By August 1939, twenty thousand members of Betar, many of them also members of IZL cells, had been registered at Betar headquarters in Warsaw in anticipation of leaving for Palestine on one of the ships chartered by the Revisionist movement. At the beginning of August, a convoy of twelve hundred members of Betar, especially selected as reinforcements for the IZL in Palestine, left Warsaw on a train to Bucharest, expecting to board a ship for Palestine at a Romanian Black Sea port. They were led by Menahem Begin, who intended to accompany them to the Polish-Romanian border. Transit visas through Romania had been arranged for them in Warsaw. However, the British policy of preventing European Jews from reaching Palestine was not limited to the Royal Navy patrolling the Palestine coast; it also included British Intelligence disrupting the activities of those engaged in chartering ships and organizing transports toward Black Sea ports. They also used their diplomatic missions to exert pressure on European governments to impede the movement of those attempting to leave Europe for Palestine. Therefore, when the Betar convoy reached the town of Shniatyn on the Romanian border, they found that the Romanian border guards would not honor their transit visas and refused them entry into Romania. The British diplomatic mission in Bucharest had pressured the Romanian government to deny them transit through Romania.

---

8   Alex Rafaeli, *Dream and Action* (Jerusalem: Private publication, 1993), 80.

The twelve hundred members of Betar set up camp next to the railway line on the Polish-Romanian border while pressure was brought to bear on Romanian officials in Bucharest and bribes were being offered, in an attempt to reverse the ruling that had cancelled the transit visas – but to no avail. Some two hundred of the group managed to steal across the Romanian border, eventually reaching the Revisionist-chartered ship *Neomi Julia*, which sailed from Constanza on the Black Sea on August 29 and reached Palestine on September 19, 1939, nineteen days after the outbreak of World War II. The others continued to wait at the border. As war tensions between Germany and Poland rose, the Romanians closed their border with Poland, and the Polish provincial governor ordered all those encamped at the border to return to Warsaw. They had missed their last chance to leave Poland before it was overrun by the Germans. The escape route for the Jews of Europe to Palestine was blocked by the British government.[9]

The last World Zionist Congress before the war was held in August 1939, in Geneva. One of the delegates at the Congress, a member of the youth movement Dror, and representing Po'alei Zion, the Socialist Zionist party from Poland, was twenty-five-year-old Tzivya Lubetkin, who was to play a key role in the Warsaw Ghetto Uprising a few years later. As he closed the Congress, Chaim Weizmann, the president of the World Zionist Organization, said: "I have no prayer but this – that we will all meet again alive."[10] That prayer would not be answered.

---

9   Ben-Yeruham, *Sefer Betar*, 965. See also Yitshaq Ben-Ami, *Years of Wrath, Days of Glory* (New York: Robert Speller & Sons, 1982), 260. Also William R. Perl, *The Four Front War* (New York: Crown Publishers Inc., 1979), for a description of the "illegal immigration" to Palestine organized by the Revisionists during those years.

10   The Jewish Agency for Israel, *Zionist Congresses under the British Mandate* (Jerusalem: The Pedagogic Center, the Department for Jewish Zionist Education, 2000).

The threat of war only served to intensify the activities of the Zionist youth movements. August was the time for the movements' summer camps, and among the participants of the annual summer camp of the North-Warsaw branch of Betar, one of the eight Betar branches in Warsaw, were Pawel Frenkel, Simha Witelson, Alek Halberstein, and Pinhas Toib, young leaders of Betar.[11] All of them were already members of IZL cells. They would constitute the nucleus of the IZL resistance organization in the Warsaw ghetto, headed by Pawel Frenkel.

As the war clouds gathered over Europe in August 1939, the Jews of Warsaw were in a turmoil of political activity that pitted the Bund against the Zionists, the Bund and the Zionists against the religious, the Bund and most of the Zionists against the Revisionists, and the Revisionists themselves split between those accepting the authority of the official party hierarchy and those taking their orders from their IZL superiors. The war and the tragic fate of Warsaw's Jews would not dispel these divisions.

---

11 Lazar Litai, *Matzada shel Varsha*, 48.

Chapter 2

Between Warsaw and Vilna

September 1939–November 1940

On September 1, 1939, the German army invaded Poland and quickly advanced eastward. By September 8, the Germans had reached the outskirts of Warsaw, and by September 13, Warsaw was surrounded and under siege. The leaders of all the Jewish political groups fled Warsaw before the arrival of the Germans. Among them were Moshe (Sneh) Kleinbaum and Moshe Kerner of the General Zionists, Anshel Reiss and Avraham Bialopolski of the Socialist Zionist Po'alei Zion, Yitzhak Leib and Nathan Buksbaum of the Marxist Zionist Left Po'alei Zion, Zerah Warhaftig and Aaron Weiss of the religious Zionist Mizrahi, Yitzhak Meir Levin of the ultra-Orthodox religious Agudat Yisrael, and Henryk Ehrlich and Victor Alter of the Bund.[1] The emissaries of the Zionist youth movements from Palestine who had been working with their counterparts in Poland left to return to Palestine, as did the IZL emissaries. One of them was Hillel Tzur, with whom members of IZL in the Warsaw ghetto unsuccessfully attempted to make contact in May 1942.

The leadership of the Zionist youth movements also left Warsaw. This included almost the entire leadership of Betar: Menahem Begin, Natan Friedman-Yellin (Yellin-Mor), Yisrael Sheib (Eldad), Yisrael Epstein, and David Yutan;[2] the leadership of Hashomer Hatzair:

---

1   Yisrael Gutman, *The Jews of Warsaw 1939–1943: Ghetto, Underground, Revolt* (Bloomington, IN: Indiana University Press, 1982), 121.

2   Yisrael Eldad (Sheib), *Ma'aser rishon* [The first tithe] (Tel Aviv: Hamatmid, 1950), 40. Another member of the Betar leadership, Peretz Lasker, had

Chaim Holtz (Alon), Zelig Geyer, Yosef Shamir, Yitzhak Zalmanson, and Tosya Altman, who succeeded in reaching Vilna;[3] and the leadership of Dror: Yitzhak (Antek) Zuckerman and Tzivya Lubetkin, who fled eastward and, with the entry of Soviet armed forces into Poland from the east on September 17, in accordance with the Molotov-Ribbentrop pact, soon found themselves in the Soviet occupation zone, which included more than a third of pre-war Poland.[4]

Warsaw was under heavy bombardment. Lili Strassman, who had founded the group of Polish-Jewish intelligentsia in Warsaw who supported the IZL, was in a bomb shelter, her husband Henryk away in the Polish army. (Ultimately he became one of the Polish officers who were executed on Stalin's order during the Katyn massacre). As the bombs fell, all she could think of were the weapons the Polish government had transferred to the IZL that had not yet been shipped to Palestine. They were stored somewhere in Warsaw. Under the circumstances, she thought that those weapons had to be made available to the Polish army. Despite the constant bombardment, she made it to the headquarters of the commander of the defense of Warsaw, General Walerian Czuma. Unable to see him, she convinced an officer to accompany her to the weapons storehouse, and she turned the weapons over to the Polish army. She received a receipt for the weapons and felt that the IZL had repaid a debt of honor to the Poles in their hour of need.[5]

---

been serving as an officer in the Polish army and returned to Warsaw after the fighting was over.

3   Levi Dror and Yisrael Rosenzweig, eds., *Sefer ha-Shomer ha-Tzair* [The book of Hashomer Hatzair], vol. 1, 1913–1945 (Merhavia: Sifriat Hapoalim, 1956), 455.

4   David Gotesfurcht, Aharon Richman, and Haim Harari, eds., *Sefer Dror* [The book of Dror] (Ein Harod: Hakibbutz Hameuhad, 1947), 446.

5   *Sefer Ayala (Lili) Lubinsky* [The Book of Ayala (Lili) Lubinsky] (Tel Aviv: The Committee to Mark the Memory of the Late A.L. Lubinsky, 1960), 130–31.

During the siege of Warsaw, the mayor, Stefan Starzynski, was appointed by General Czuma as civilian commissar of Warsaw. On September 23, he appointed Adam Czerniaków head of the Warsaw Jewish council in place of Maurycy Mayzel, the former head of the council, who had fled the city. "I have been appointed to fulfill a historic role in a besieged city. I will try to live up to it," Czerniaków noted in his diary.[6] Four days later Warsaw surrendered to the Germans, and on October 1, the Wehrmacht entered the city.

Jabotinsky, in London, saw Polish Betar, the largest and strongest Betar branch in the world, in which he had placed so much hope, disappear in a matter of days. On September 25, he wrote to Shimshon Yunichman, the leader of Betar in Palestine: "The Polish Betar is in ruins. There is no need to explain the magnitude of this loss. The fate of the other Betar branches in Europe is as yet unknown. But one thing is clear – maybe only in Eretz Yisrael can the spirit of Betar endure. This places a responsibility, unprecedented in the annals of our movement, on you.... At this time it is difficult to lead the Betar in Eretz Yisrael and I demand of you to fulfill this difficult task."[7]

On October 5, Hitler reviewed a victory parade of German troops along Ujazdowskie Avenue in Warsaw. Thousands of Wehrmacht soldiers marched by saluting him, tanks rolled by, and Luftwaffe aircraft flew overhead.

The day before the parade, Czerniaków was taken to the Police and Gestapo headquarters in Warsaw. There he was questioned for two days and ordered to furnish the names of rich Jews, lists of Jewish institutions, and the employees of the Jewish community. After

---

6   Adam Czerniaków, *The Warsaw Diary of Adam Czerniaków*, eds. Raul Hilberg, Stanislaw Staron, and Josef Kermisz (New York: Stein & Day, 1979), 76.

7   Jabotinsky Institute Archives 101-6/3-פ.

subjecting him to anti-Semitic sermons, the Gestapo informed him that he was being designated as the *Aelteste* (elder) of the Jewish community, the head of the *Judenrat* (Jewish council). He was ordered to provide a list of twenty-four Jews who would become the membership of that *Judenrat*. He was informed that the *Judenrat's* sole task would be to execute the orders given to Czerniaków by the Gestapo.

Adam Czerniaków was then fifty-nine years old. An engineering graduate of the Warsaw Polytechnic Institute, with a second degree from the University of Dresden, he had been chairman of the Organization of Jewish Craftsmen and had represented them in the Warsaw Jewish Community Council. Few of Warsaw's Jews had heard of him. He now had this position thrust upon him: to represent Warsaw's Jews under German occupation.

The first meeting of the *Judenrat*, called into session in accordance with these instructions, took place in the middle of October. Gerhardt Mende, a Gestapo official, participated in the meeting. He delivered a lecture, for which they were required to remain standing, addressing the *Judenrat* members as if they were criminals. He declared that the fate of the Jewish community was in the hands of the Gestapo, and the community had no right to address any other German authority. There would be no room for the least objection or discussion.[8]

A month later, Czerniaków was informed by the Gestapo that within three days a ghetto would be set up for the Jews of Warsaw.

---

8   Nathan Weinstock, "*Sur Shmuel Zygielbojm*" [About Shmuel Zygielbojm] (II), *Le Monde Juif* 158 (Sep.–Dec., 1996): 130–31. Zygielbojm, a leading member of the Bund, was one of the first members of the *Judenrat*; this is his record of the early days of the German occupation of Warsaw. A few months later he managed to leave Poland and join the Polish government-in-exile in London. In May 1943 he committed suicide in a desperate attempt to call attention to the extermination of Polish Jewry.

However, the German military commander of Warsaw acceded to a request from Czerniaków and deferred the establishment of the ghetto. It was another eleven months before the Jews of Warsaw were enclosed behind ghetto walls.

Czerniaków had not been one of the leaders of the Jewish community before the war. The leaders, almost to a man, had fled Warsaw. Among those that remained, there were only those who had held secondary positions. Among the Revisionists there was Dr. David Wdowinski, a psychiatrist and senior member of the Revisionist movement in Poland, and Peretz Lasker, a member of the Polish Betar leadership and a reserve officer in the Polish army, who was at the front when the leadership of Betar left Warsaw. Among the General Zionists, there was Menahem Kirshenbaum, who had represented the Zionists in the Warsaw Jewish Community Council. And there was Dr. Emmanuel Ringelblum, a lecturer in Jewish history and an active member of the Marxist-Zionist Left Po'alei Zion, who was a part-time worker for the Joint Distribution Committee; David Guzik, one of the heads of the Joint in Warsaw; and Dr. Yitzhak Schipper, a prominent Zionist and professor of history at Warsaw University. Among the many rabbis who stayed behind there were Zysha Fridman and Menahem Ziemba, leading members of Agudat Yisrael. None of them joined the *Judenrat*.

From the first days of the occupation, the Jews were subjected to attacks and discrimination, such as being pulled from food lines, seized for forced labor, and violated because of their traditional clothing and hairstyles. At random, Jews were targeted on the streets, forced to do calisthenics, beaten, spit at, and humiliated. Teachers, craftsmen, professionals, and members of welfare and cultural institutions lost their positions. It was only the beginning.

On October 7, Joseph Goebbels, the German propaganda minister, recorded in his diary: "The Jewish problem will be the most difficult to solve. These Jews are not human beings anymore...they have to be rendered harmless."[9] "Rendering harmless" was a Nazi euphemism for putting to death.

On October 10, the Soviets announced that Vilna and the surrounding region, occupied by Soviet forces, would be transferred to Lithuania. This set in motion a stream of some fifteen thousand Jewish refugees from German- and Soviet-occupied Poland to Vilna. The city was handed over to Lithuania on October 28, 1939. Most of the leaders who had fled Warsaw succeeded in reaching Vilna, and the holders of certificates for entry into Palestine or visas to other countries expected to be able to leave the city, now part of independent Lithuania, for Palestine or other destinations. Those who were not in possession of such documents hoped to be able to obtain them during their stay there. In any case, Vilna seemed a lot better for the moment then either German- or Soviet-occupied Poland.

In Vilna, the members of the various Zionist youth movements who had arrived from Poland began organizing themselves within their movement frameworks under the guidance of their leaders from Warsaw. Dormitory housing and soup kitchens were established for their members who had found refuge in Vilna, and educational and cultural work was resumed.

The Polish leadership (*Hahanhagah Haroshit*) of Hashomer Hatzair established itself in Vilna and began discussions regarding the future of their movement in German-occupied Poland. Seeing their movement primarily as an educational instrument for Jewish youth, they concluded that as long as there was a Jewish community in

---

9   Joseph Goebbels, *Die Tagebücher von Joseph Goebbels* [The Diary of Joseph Goebbels] (Munich, 1998), part 1, vol. 7, p. 141.

Poland, the movement must be there as well, and that therefore the flight of its members from Poland should be stopped. They were aware of the fact that due to the anti-Zionist policy of the Soviet Union there was no real possibility of continuing their movement's activities in the Soviet occupation zone. However, in the German occupation zone, despite the difficult conditions, the movement seemed to be free to continue its activities. Therefore they decided to send senior members of Hashomer Hatzair who had fled to Vilna back to Warsaw.[10]

It was a fateful decision, requiring great courage, to leave the seeming safety of Vilna and voluntarily return to areas ruled by the Germans. The first to go was twenty-one-year-old Tosya Altman, who succeeded in crossing the lines on her second attempt, arriving in Warsaw at the end of 1939. After her went twenty-six-year-old Yosef Kaplan and twenty-year-old Shmuel Breslaw, who arrived in Warsaw in February 1940. Twenty-year-old Mordechai Anielewicz volunteered to return to Warsaw from Vilna and was accompanied by his girlfriend Mira Fruchner. Crossing the demarcation line between Lithuania, the Soviet zone, and the German zone was still relatively easy at the time, and they all made it to Warsaw. They were to become founders and leading members of one of the Jewish armed resistance movements in the ghetto, eventually commanded by Anielewicz. The rest of the leadership, in due time, received certificates for entry to Palestine and left Vilna before the Germans reached that city.

The Dror youth movement leadership faced the same issue. Assembled in October in the city of Kovel, in the Soviet zone, in a building that was directly under the nose of the Soviet security service, they decided on a three-pronged approach: some would begin underground organizational work in the Soviet zone, others would

---

10   Dror and Rosenzweig, *Sefer ha-Shomer ha-Tzair*, vol. 1, 432, 445.

return to the German zone, and the rest would try to make it to Palestine. Like the Hashomer Hatzair leadership, they assigned great importance to the continuation of educational work among the Jewish youth, even under occupation. Within a few weeks, however, it became apparent to them that it was not possible to carry out Zionist educational work under Soviet rule, and that Dror could continue to function only in the German zone. On December 31, they met again in Lvov, in the Soviet zone. It was decided that twenty-five-year-old Tzivya Lubetkin would return to Warsaw. She was followed in April by Yitzhak (Antek) Zuckerman, twenty-five years old, and Tuvia Borzykowski, twenty-nine years old, and the Dror organizational work in Warsaw commenced.[11] Zuckerman in time became the initiator of the establishment of an armed Jewish resistance organization in Warsaw, and Lubetkin, who became Zuckerman's life-long companion and comrade, together with Tuvia Borzykowski, would be among the mainstays of this organization.

The Revisionists, who were established in Vilna, saw things differently. They were divided into two groups – those who had also become members of the IZL, and those who had not. The IZL members took their instructions from Friedman-Yellin. He organized an IZL framework in Vilna that included the IZL members from occupied Poland and those among the Betar members in Vilna, all of whom operated in great secrecy. He located Avraham Amper in Ludmir in the Soviet zone and ordered him to come to Vilna. Amper had had direct organizational responsibility for the IZL cells in Poland. He remembered the names and addresses of the IZL cell commanders and, using the Soviet postal service, dispatched telegrams to those in the Soviet zone, ordering them to make their way to Vilna; it was more difficult to establish contact with IZL members in the German

---

11 Gotesfurcht, Richman, and Harari, *Sefer Dror*, 446; and Zuckerman, *A Surplus of Memory*, 36–40.

occupation zone. Nonetheless, IZL members were arriving in Vilna from all over Poland, cells were organized, and weapons' training was resumed. All this was in the expectation of finding ways of moving on to Palestine and joining the IZL struggle there.[12]

No long discussions were needed to adopt this approach. The IZL members saw themselves as soldiers in the IZL; as far as they were concerned, the front was in Palestine, and it behooved them to make their way to the front in the most expeditious manner possible. Those who had managed to get to Vilna were hoping to make it to Palestine from there. Those who had remained in Poland were considered as having been cut off from the front and, at least for the time being, could not be utilized. Little priority was assigned to educational work among the Betar members that had been left behind. All eyes were on Palestine.

Begin and the rest of the Betar leadership were in a more ambivalent position. They were the leaders of a large youth movement with thousands of members still in Poland who were now almost leaderless, except for Peretz Lasker in Warsaw. They too realized that there was no possibility of organized activity in the Soviet occupation zone – but was the continued functioning of the movement in the German zone their responsibility, and did it require that at least some of them follow the example set by the leaders of Hashomer Hatzair and Dror, and return to Warsaw? Their dilemma was made more difficult by the fact that they also considered themselves members of the IZL, and were fully aware of the IZL's approach. Indeed, under Amper's instruction, Begin and the rest of the Betar leadership had been given an elementary IZL course during their time in Vilna. So should they follow the line taken by the IZL leadership in Vilna, as determined by Friedman-Yellin and Amper, or should their

---

12 Eldad, *Ma'aser rishon,* 40; and Yellin-Mor, *Shnot ba-terem,* 133.

responsibilities to the movement in Poland, which they had led up until the outbreak of the war, take priority?

To this dilemma an additional consideration had to be added. Would Begin, who was well known in Poland and easily recognizable, be able to function there for any length of time before being arrested, or worse? Begin's predicament was made more difficult by letters he received from world Betar headquarters in London, not signed by Jabotinsky but no doubt approved by him, that suggested in no uncertain terms that he should have remained with the Betar movement in Poland. He received similar letters from Shimshon Yunichman, the leader of Betar in Palestine, making it clear that "the captain should not have been the first to abandon ship."[13]

Begin was hurt by the accusations leveled against him and tried his best to justify his departure from Warsaw. "Do you really assume that I did not have all these thoughts…before I decided to leave Warsaw?" he wrote to Yunichman from Vilna in January 1940. "After all, we believed then that Poland would resist for months, that a hundred kilometers beyond Warsaw it would already be safe… therefore we decided to move eastward…but nobody imagined that the country would collapse in a matter of days…and that the Russians would advance from the east."[14]

13　This was quoted by Begin in his reply to Yunichman's letter. See Begin's second letter to Yunichman, from Vilna, written on February 4, 1940, Jabotinsky Institute Archives 1/3/106-פ.

14　Letter written by Begin in Vilna on January 8, 1940 to Shimshon Yunichman, in the Jabotinsky Institute Archives Tel Aviv, 1/3/106-פ. From the letter it is clear that Begin was in contact with Peretz Lasker, the one member of the Polish Betar leadership still in Warsaw. Most of the letter is devoted to the situation in Palestine and contains Begin's opinions on the situation there and advice on what should and should not be done by his comrades there. The criticism of Begin's leaving Polish Betar behind as voiced by Mordechai Katz, the secretary of the world Betar headquarters in London, as referred in Begin's second letter to Yunichman, most probably reflected

Yosef Glazman, the head of Lithuanian Betar, in close contact with Begin and the Polish Betar leadership in Vilna, also took it upon himself to justify the decision of the Polish Betar leadership to leave Warsaw. In a letter to Yunichman in January 1940 he argued that the Polish Betar membership had not been abandoned by their leadership, because activities carried out from Lithuania would be more effective than what could have been done in the occupation zone. He reported that there were now five hundred Polish Betar "refugees" in Vilna, most of them of high caliber, who could contribute significantly to the movement in Palestine, but at that point this was no more than a dream for them since the way to Palestine was not open; the number of visas allocated to them by the Jewish Agency were minimal.[15]

Begin was in contact with Lasker in Warsaw, as well as a number of others who had stayed behind, and learned that Betar activity was possible under German occupation. The Germans, unlike the Soviets, took no particular interest in the political or cultural activities of the Jews under their control. Begin considered returning, and at one point even announced to the Betar leadership in Vilna that he was going back to Warsaw, but finally decided to stay in Vilna.[16]

From his letter to Yunichman it is clear that Begin's thoughts were focused on the MacDonald White Paper and Britain's role in Palestine. It was the time of the "phony war" on the western front, and Begin had to consider the possibility that the war might come to a close with an agreement between England, France, and Germany without Britain changing its anti-Zionist policy. Therefore, enlisting on Britain's side in the war at this time, as advocated by Yunichman, seemed to him not likely to advance the cause of Zionism, while

the opinion of Jabotinsky, who was in London at the time.

15 Jabotinsky Institute Archives 1/1/33-ב.
16 Eldad, *Ma'aser rishon*, 97.

organizing resistance to the German occupation in Poland was certainly not in his thoughts then. The front, as far as he was concerned, was in Palestine.

Lasker had decided to stay in Warsaw and not to go to Vilna. Since at that time the Germans were not preventing Jews from leaving areas under their occupation, it was possible for Jews possessing entry permits to non-belligerent countries to leave the German occupation zone, and via Italy, then still neutral, to proceed to their destination. Lasker was busy trying to promote this route for Betar members. He asked Begin to ask Yunichman to intervene with the Jewish Agency in Palestine and persuade them to give him visas to Palestine for members of Betar in German-occupied Poland. But the number of visas was very limited, and members of Betar were as usual placed at the bottom of the list of candidates, so the efforts of Yunichman and the Revisionist organization in Palestine in this regard produced only minimal results. Still, a few succeeded in making it to Palestine. One of them was Lili Strassman, who reached Palestine via Trieste. Lasker also thought he might be able to organize "illegal immigration" from German-occupied Poland to Palestine, but nothing came of these plans.

On December 1, 1939, the Germans declared that all Jews above the age of ten in the *Generalgouvernement* area,[17] which included Warsaw, had to wear a white armband with a blue Star of David on their right arm. This was a clear indication of the direction of German plans for the Jews.

---

17 The administration of German-occupied Poland was divided in October 1939 almost equally, with the western part being annexed to Germany, while the eastern part, containing the cities of Warsaw, Cracow, and Lublin, was established as the *Generalgouvernement*, governed from Cracow by Hans Frank.

By February 1940, Begin was fully aware of the worsening conditions of Jews under the German occupation, and in his second letter to Yunichman, sent on February 4, 1940, he informed him that some Zionist dignitaries in German-occupied Poland had been able to leave for Trieste after receiving visas for Palestine. He pleaded with him to try to arrange certificates for Lasker and some of the senior Revisionists in the German zone so that they would be able to "get out of this hell." He emphasized that to do so was a sacred duty.[18]

The German blitzkrieg victories in Denmark, Norway, Holland, Belgium, and France in April and May 1940 dashed all hopes of an early German defeat, which might have brought the Jews relief from German oppression. They could only look with foreboding into the future. Meanwhile, with the world's attention focused on the German victories, the Soviets utilized the opportunity to begin the process of occupying the Baltic countries – Lithuania, Latvia, and Estonia.

From their vantage point in Vilna, Begin and Glazman, the head of Lithuanian Betar, could sense the approaching danger. On June 6, 1940, they wrote to Jabotinsky in New York, asking if he could transfer some funds for a last-minute effort to assist the endangered members of Betar: to arrange for safe hideouts for those that might shortly be hunted by the NKVD (the Soviet secret police), and to help those under German occupation in Poland, most of whom were in great need. "We are in contact with Lasker in Warsaw," they wrote, "and he is asking for assistance for our comrades there. It is possible to send parcels from Lithuania to them, and we hope that 'our delegation in America' can channel some resources to these urgent needs."[19] They could not know that Jabotinsky, who would die two months later, was not in a position to assist them financially.

---

18 Begin's letter from Vilna to Yunichman of February 4, 1940, Jabotinsky Institute Archives.

19 Jabotinsky Institute Archives 1-2/22/3-א. Jabotinsky was in the U.S. at the

On June 15, Red Army tanks rolled into Vilna and the Soviet takeover of the Baltic countries began. By August 3, Lithuania formally became a member republic of the Soviet Union. This spelled the end of all overt Zionist activity in the Baltic countries. On that same day, Jabotinsky died in New York. During the previous eleven months he had witnessed the almost total destruction of the Eastern European branches of the movement he had founded and led. The news of his death reached Vilna, but no public memorials were held. On the seventh day after his death, many of his followers assembled in the Vilna Jewish cemetery to mourn, under the guise of attending a rabbi's funeral.

The members of Betar in Vilna left the communal dormitory and dispersed, in the hope of avoiding the attention of the Soviet secret police. Menahem Begin and Yisrael Sheib (Eldad) moved to a house in the Vilna suburbs; Natan Friedman-Yellin went into hiding in a small village. Despite these attempts to avoid detection, on September 20, Begin was arrested by the NKVD and, after interrogation, sentenced to penal servitude in Siberia. Surprisingly, however, the Soviets were still allowing "refugees" in Vilna to leave, if they had visas to another country. This unexpected good news meant a desperate search by refugees for any visas they could obtain. Chiune Sugihara, the Japanese consul in Kaunas, went against instructions and spent his last weeks in Lithuania issuing as many Japanese visas he could, saving more than six thousand lives. Another method of escape was the mass forging of British visas for Palestine; the Soviet authorities recognized them and allowed bearers to leave. Hundreds left Vilna, many with forged documents, some of them making their way to Palestine.

---

time trying to gain support for the creation of a Jewish army to participate in the war against Germany. The delegation of the IZL in the U.S. was headed by Hillel Kook (aka Peter Bergson).

Friedman-Yellin left Kaunas by train for Moscow in December 1940, continuing via Odessa and Turkey to Palestine. He and Sheib were to become members of the command of the Stern group, which under Avraham Stern's leadership insisted on continuing the fight against British rule in Palestine and had broken away from the IZL. Among the "Vilna refugees" who made names for themselves in the Palestine underground were Yisrael Epstein, a member of the Betar leadership in Poland and later a member of the IZL command in Palestine; Yaacov Banai, the operations officer of the Stern group; and Avraham Amper, who was killed in an encounter with the British police not long after arriving in Palestine and joining the Stern group. The leading members of Polish Betar, who had left tens of thousands of their charges in Poland, were finally moving to the front in Palestine.

The news of Jabotinsky's death also reached Peretz Lasker and his Betar comrades in Warsaw. Like all of Jabotinsky's disciples and admirers throughout the world, they mourned the loss of the man who had been their teacher and guiding light. Lasker arranged for a meeting of senior Betar members in Warsaw in his apartment on the seventh day after Jabotinsky's death, and then on the thirtieth day, sixty members of Betar assembled at Betar's secret meeting place on Leszno Street. Another gathering devoted to Jabotinsky's memory took place at the Warsaw Jewish cemetery on August 8, 1940, the Ninth of Av. Many of those who had been members of IZL cells before the war went to that meeting. Contacts made that day were the starting point of the IZL underground in the Warsaw ghetto.[20]

---

20 This is evident from information in Peretz Lasker's letter to the editor of *Herut* printed on August 8, 1961, as well as the reminiscences of Moshe Poznerson, who had been recruited into the IZL before the war, which were published in the publication of Muzeon ha-Lohamim ve-ha-Partizanim, Tel Aviv, April 1983.

That summer, the rumor began to spread that the Germans were planning to enclose the Jews of Warsaw in a ghetto. Peretz Lasker had set up a new Betar leadership, and at a council held that summer, Binyamin Shohat, who had commanded an IZL cell before the war, suggested the establishment of an organization to fight the Germans. It was the first suggestion of armed resistance to the Germans, and it met with general approval. The idea was in line with the Betar ideology of militant Zionism, put forth by one who had training in the use of weapons. He saw himself as a soldier of the IZL, but now with little chance of joining the IZL in Palestine, he felt the need to resist the humiliations the Germans were imposing on the Jews. Although nobody could have imagined the horror of the campaign of extermination the Germans would later wage against the Jews, Lasker and his comrades did realize that concentrating the Jews in a ghetto meant depriving thousands of any possibility of a livelihood, forcing them into a limited area in which many of them would most likely starve. Ironically, though, within the confines of a ghetto it would be easier to establish a secret network for eventual armed action.

Subsequently, more meetings were held to discuss the organization of a fighting unit. One of those that participated was Leon (Leibale) Rodal, a journalist who had written for *Der Moment* and the IZL's *Di Tat*, as well as for the New York Yiddish dailies *Der Tog* and *Morgenzhurnal* before the war. His participation was considered of particular value because of his good relations with the General Zionists, and especially with Menahem Kirshenbaum, who was the chairman of the *Koordinatsia*, the coordinating committee of the Zionist parties in Warsaw, which excluded the Revisionists.[21] He was twenty-seven years old at the time, the son of a wealthy Jewish fam-

---

21 Peretz Lasker, "Ha-Irgun ha-Zvai ha-Leumi herim rishon et nes ha-mered be-Varsha" [The Irgun Zvai Leumi was the first to raise the banner of revolt in Warsaw], *Herut*, April 24, 1962.

ily in Kielce, and had headed the Revisionist chapter in Kielce before coming to Warsaw to pursue a career as a journalist. He would go on to become one of the leaders of the Revisionist-led fighting organization during the uprising.

There were a number of suggestions regarding how to proceed in such a way as to ensure absolute secrecy for the organization. It was decided not to attack individual Germans who entered the ghetto, so as not to endanger the Jews in the ghetto. Experience with the Germans since the occupation had shown that they would have no compunction about applying large-scale collective punishment if any harm came to a German. The exact nature of the military action to be taken and what the targets would be was left open, to be determined by circumstances at the appropriate time. It was decided to organize members in groups of five for weapons training, to begin the acquisition of weapons, and to locate a place to store them. The next step was to obtain the financial means to implement the program. Lasker set up his headquarters at a secret location, on Leszno Street in the Jewish section of the city. Feverish activity began to implement the plans; places were located to store weapons and the first money was collected.

The Socialist Zionist youth movements and the Bund gave no thought to the possibility of armed resistance to the Germans at that time. They concentrated on educational and welfare activities among their members. The Socialist Zionist movements, attached to Marxist ideology, saw the war between Germany and the West as a struggle between imperialist powers that would eventually lead to a victory for Socialism.[22] The Bund saw itself wedded to the Polish Socialists and would consider only actions that were taken in concert with them. The Revisionists were not burdened by such ideological constraints.

---

22 Gutman, *The Jews of Warsaw 1939–1943*, 126.

On October 12, Czerniaków, the German-appointed head of the *Judenrat*, was informed of the decision to establish a ghetto in Warsaw. German officials presented him with a map of the ghetto and informed him that until October 31 the resettlement was to be voluntary, and after that, compulsory. The ghetto was officially sealed on November 16, 1940. Some 380,000 Jews were now cut off from the world. They did not yet know that the Warsaw ghetto was a deathtrap.

Chapter 3

In the Ghetto

November 16, 1940–July 22, 1942

With the establishment of the ghetto, a Jewish police force was organized, supposedly operating under the authority of the *Judenrat*. The Jewish policemen were distinguished by their police caps, special armbands, high boots, and rubber truncheons. Czerniaków appointed Jozef Szerynski, a convert to Catholicism and former officer in the Polish police, to head the Jewish police. Szerynski had severed all ties to the Jewish community after his conversion, but now found himself subject to German racial laws and therefore in the ghetto. Soon enough the Jewish police began taking their orders directly from the Germans. The gates to the ghetto were manned by Jewish, Polish, and German police, who checked all those entering or leaving to assure that they had a valid reason.

Events in the ghetto were chronicled assiduously by the historian Emmanuel Ringelblum and a team of assistants, and the information was assembled in an archive, codenamed "Oneg Shabbat." The archive contained documents and summaries of ghetto life, as well as information that reached Warsaw from other regions in Poland. The archive was hidden in three milk cans buried underground, but only two of the cans were recovered after the war.

"I started gathering documents on our times in October 1939," wrote Ringelbum. He continued, "As a leader of the Social Self-Help, I had vivid daily contact with life around me.... I noted down all I heard during the day, adding my remarks to it.... From these daily notes, I later produced weekly and monthly reviews, after the staff of the Oneg Shabbat had been enlarged...besides adults, young people and even children were also enlisted in the work of Oneg Shabbat. Oneg Shabbat was anxious to give a many-sided picture of Jewish life during the war. It wanted to produce a photographic copy of all that the Jewish masses experienced, thought, and suffered...."[1]

Not long after the ghetto was established, it became apparent that there would not be enough food for all its inhabitants; its numbers were growing daily due to the transfer of Jews from the provinces, and the overcrowded conditions were creating a breeding ground for epidemic diseases. The lack of food became catastrophic in March 1941, and thousands began dying from starvation and disease. As long as contact with the U.S. was still possible, help was provided by the Joint Distribution Committee.

The youth movements took it upon themselves to try to care for their members and assure their physical survival. They established cheap soup kitchens, which also provided opportunities for ideological and educational activities. Peretz Lasker, the senior Betar leader in the ghetto, also turned his attention to "assuring the existence of our people." Writing after the war about that period in the ghetto, he said, "It was clear that the Nazis were achieving their goal and the Jewish population would decrease quickly."[2]

---

1 Emmanuel Ringelblum, *Ktavim aharonim* [Last documents], *Jan. '43–April '44* (Jerusalem: Yad Vashem, 1994), 3–22. Ringelblum was discovered by the Germans hiding out in Aryan Warsaw after the uprising and was executed, together with his wife and son. His legacy, the part of his archive that was discovered after the war, left an invaluable picture of events in the ghetto and ghetto life.

2 Lasker, "Ha-Irgun ha-Zvai ha-Leumi herim rishon et nes ha-mered be-Varsha."

The leaders of the Zionist youth movements in the ghetto felt isolated from their home base in Palestine. Who was to guide them, advise them, assist them? Much thought and great effort was invested by all the youth movements in Warsaw in establishing contact with the outside world.

The leaders of Betar, including Pawel Frenkel, hoped to be able to establish contact with IZL headquarters in Palestine. As IZL members, they still saw themselves as soldiers of the IZL. Now they were held captive behind a double barrier: the walls of the ghetto, and the war raging on land and sea that barred their way to the front in Palestine. Although they were focused on using their strength against the German enemy, they also saw it as their duty, as prisoners of war, to break out of the walls that enclosed them and to find an escape route to the home base, at least for a few of them. Every effort and risk seemed justified in their eyes in order to establish this contact, even if only to notify the command in Palestine of their determination to fight in their place of captivity. Already in August 1940, shortly after the Jabotinsky memorial meeting at the Jewish cemetery, Moshe Poznerson, a member of an IZL cell, was sent by his commander, Binyamin Shohat, on a mission to reach the Hungarian border, cross into Hungary, and establish contact with the IZL in Palestine. Poznerson managed to reach the vicinity of the Hungarian border in October of that year, but he fell sick, was compelled to cross into Soviet territory, and was arrested there.[3] Other similar attempts were unsuccessful.

The leaders of the Socialist Zionist youth movements in the Warsaw ghetto, in contrast, did succeed in contacting the leadership of their movements in Palestine. Hehalutz, the roof organization of the Socialist Zionist youth movements Dror, Hashomer Hatzair,

---

3   Poznerson's reminiscences were published in the publication of Muzeon ha-Lohamim ve-ha-Partizanim, Tel Aviv, April 1983.

and Gordonia, had a liaison office in Geneva, Switzerland. Natan Schwalb, a member of Gordonia, headed the Geneva office and was in frequent contact with Tzivya Lubetkin, who headed the Hehalutz "center" in Warsaw. From Geneva, Schwalb maintained postal communications with members of the Hehalutz youth organizations in areas under German control, and he used the meager funds that had been put at his disposal by the Histadrut, the Jewish Agency, and the Joint to send food parcels and money to them. He was instructed to apportion the assistance in accordance with a "party" key: half for Dror, and the rest evenly split between Hashomer Hatzair and Gordonia; the other movements, including Betar, were left out.

The Jewish Agency, the World Jewish Congress, and the Joint also had representatives in Geneva, who relayed information they received from the German occupied territories to the Jewish leadership in America and Palestine.[4] Nevertheless, these contacts could not assuage a feeling of abandonment among the youth leaders in the ghetto. In December 1940, Tzivya Lubetkin wrote to Palestine: "More than once I have decided not to write to you anymore.... I will not describe here what I am going through, but I want you to know that even one word of comfort from you would have sufficed.... To my regret, however, I have to accept your silence, but I will never forget it."[5]

In the spring of 1941, Lasker met with the secretary of the *Judenrat* of Hrubieszow, which was in the Lublin region. Yulek Brandt, a leading member of Betar in that region, had come to Warsaw and seen the conditions in the ghetto; Brandt suggested that he might be able

---

4   For the activity of the Hehalutz liaison office in Geneva, see Raya Cohen, *Bein "sham" le-"khan"* [Between "there" and "here"] (Tel Aviv: Am Oved, 1999), 78–112.

5   Quoted by Saul Friedlander in *The Years of Extermination* (New York: Harper Collins, 2007), 126.

to arrange places of work in the agricultural farms of the Hrubieszow region for some young men and women. After consultation with the head of Hrubieszow's *Judenrat*, in a meeting of Revisionists and the Betar leadership a few days later, Brandt put forth a detailed proposal for the gradual transfer of hundreds of Betar members, based on the requests of farm owners and the approval of the German *Arbeitsamt* (employment office) in Hrubieszow. The plan was implemented in the summer of 1941. The surroundings there were almost idyllic. Betar members were allowed to hold meetings, attend lectures, receive periodic visits from Lasker, and, after working hours, engage in military training with the weapons at their disposal.[6]

When on June 22, 1941, the Germans launched their attack against the Soviet Union, there was no immediate change in the Hrubieszow region, nor for that matter in Warsaw. For the Jewish population already under German occupation, the attack at first raised hopes of a quick Soviet victory, but those hopes were dashed in a matter of days, as the speed of the advance of the German army into the Soviet Union and the extent of its initial victories over the Red Army were reported. As the Wehrmacht penetrated into the Soviet Union, they were followed by the SS *Einsatzgruppen* (special operations units), charged with the mission of exterminating Jews, and the mass indiscriminate murder of Jews began.

On June 24, the German army entered Vilna, which had a Jewish population of about 57,000 at the time. The systematic killing of the Jews of Vilna started on July 4. By the middle of December 1941, the Germans – with the help of Lithuanian collaborators – had massacred 33,000 of the Jews of Vilna, including women and children, after taking them to an execution site in the Ponar woods

---

6   Lasker, "Ha-Irgun ha-Zvai ha-Leumi herim rishon et nes ha-mered be-Varsha."

nearby.[7] That winter, the ultimate purpose of the German killings became clear to a group of youngsters from the Zionist youth movements in Vilna. They understood what those in the many ghettos did not, and what had not yet been comprehended by Jewish leaders in America or the leadership of the Jewish community in Palestine. The Germans were still trying to hide the truth from the Jews they had not yet killed, but Abba Kovner, the twenty-three-year-old leader of Hashomer Hatzair in Vilna, saw through their machinations. He had been hiding in a monastery near the city, under the protection of Catholic nuns, and though he had not been a direct witness to the horrors of the murder in Vilna, the reports he received from his comrades were enough. He saw it all. "Hitler is planning to destroy all of European Jewry, and Lithuanian Jewry is fated to be the first in line," he declared.[8]

Kovner and other leaders of Zionist youth movements in Vilna saw the mass killings as part of a planned German campaign for the extermination of the Jewish population in the regions under their control. That same month, discussions were held about setting up a united Jewish resistance organization in the Vilna ghetto. With the German atrocities directed indiscriminately at all elements of the Jewish population, they decided to try to bring representatives of all the groups in the Vilna ghetto into an underground organization.[9] The FPO (*Fareinigte Partizaner Organizacje*, United Partisan Organization) was established on January 21, 1942, and from inception it included most of the Zionist youth groups, as well as the Communists. Shortly thereafter the anti-Zionist Socialist Bund

---

7   Dina Porat, *Me'ever la-gashmi* [Beyond the physical] (Tel Aviv: Am Oved, 2000), 88.

8   Dina Porat, "The Vilna Proclamation of January 1, 1942 in Historical Perspective," *Yad Vashem Studies* 24 (1996).

9   Nisan Reznik, *Nitzanim me-afar* [Buds from the ashes] (Jerusalem: Yad Vashem, 2003), 75.

joined. Itzik Wittenberg, the thirty-four-year-old leader of the Communist underground in the Vilna ghetto, was chosen to command,
and his deputies were Yosef Glazman of Betar and Abba Kovner of
Hashomer Hatzair. Later, the FPO Command was joined by representatives of Hanoar Hatzioni and the Bund.[10] Thirty-three-year-old
Glazman had been the head of Betar and the IZL cells in Lithuania
and had done compulsory military service in the Lithuanian army,
so had military training. He had been a well-known figure in Kaunas
and had moved to Vilna after the Soviet takeover of Lithuania to try
and avoid arrest by the NKVD.

Glazman and Kovner had dominant personalities, commanding
authority among their followers. This facilitated the establishment of
the united resistance organization, especially since the Bund, a bitter
ideological opponent of the Revisionists, joined only after the FPO
had already been established. Wittenberg was chosen to head the
FPO on the assumption that, through his Communist connections,
it would be possible to obtain assistance from the Red Army. The
youth of Vilna proved that it was possible to bridge the ideological
divides of pre-war years in the face of common danger.

The organizers of the Vilna Jewish underground were intent on
bringing the news of the massacres at Ponar to the world, and especially to the Jewish communities in Poland. They hoped to inspire
them to follow their example and set up resistance organizations that
would unite the entire spectrum of Jewish movements. Even before

---

10 Ibid., 75–81. Anshel Shpielman, who headed the IZL cell in Zofjowka in
    eastern Poland, answered the IZL call to come to Vilna after the Soviet
    occupation of eastern Poland. He was in contact with Yosef Glazman, the
    head of the Lithuanian Betar, during his stay in Vilna (ultimately he ob-
    tained an exit permit and left for Palestine). According to Shpielman, an
    exit permit was obtained for Glazman, but Glazman chose to stay with the
    members of his movement, eventually becoming one of the leaders of the
    FPO; see Anshel Shpielman, *Adam ve-lohem* [Man and fighter] (Tel Aviv:
    Yair Publications, 1995), 82.

the formal establishment of the FPO this was their goal. To that end, in December 1941, a month before the establishment of the FPO, four messengers from Vilna arrived in the Warsaw ghetto. They had been spirited out of the Vilna ghetto in a German army truck by Sergeant Anton Schmidt. Sergeant Schmidt was serving with the German army in Vilna, but he had decided to try and help the Jews of Vilna and was in touch with the founders of FPO. The messengers were Shlomo Entin of Hanoar Hatzioni, Edek Boraks of Hashomer Hatzair, and Yehuda Pinczewski and Yisrael Kempner of Betar. They were charged with contacting their respective youth movements in the Warsaw ghetto, alerting them to the mass killings that had taken place in Vilna, explaining to them that this was part of a wider German plan for the extermination of the Jewish people, and convincing them to organize an armed resistance movement that would embrace all Jewish groups in the Warsaw ghetto.[11]

Yitzhak (Antek) Zuckerman, the head of Dror, the Socialist Zionist movement in Warsaw, was one person who was cognizant of the real danger. Originally from Vilna, he had already received news of the mass killings by November. A Polish gentile who had been sent to Vilna to report on events there had returned to Warsaw with the terrible news. Years later Zuckerman recalled: "I was stunned by the story of Ponar…this was not a pogrom anymore! For the first time, the news that Ponar was death sliced through me like a razor…I realized this was total death."[12]

---

11 Ibid., 75. However, according to Yitzhak Arad, "this was not a combined delegation for the purpose of a common appearance in Warsaw, but rather a group that traveled together, and in Warsaw everyone was to contact the members of his respective movement," in Yitzhak Arad, *Vilna ha-Yehudit be-maavak u-ve-khilayon* [Jewish Vilna in struggle and destruction] (Jerusalem: Yad Vashem, 1976), 192.

12 Zuckerman, *A Surplus of Memory*, 149.

However, those who held leadership positions in the political parties in the Warsaw ghetto were not convinced. When Shlomo Entin returned to Vilna from the mission to Warsaw, he recounted that the comrades he spoke to about the idea of resistance answered that this was possibly needed in Vilna, since it was a "peripheral, Communist" city, but in Warsaw, "the center of the world," mass killings of the Jewish population by the Germans were not possible. Wdowinski, the leading Revisionist in the ghetto, described the mood in the ghetto after the arrival of the four messengers from Vilna: "The news brought gloom and anxiety upon the ghetto.... But soon people consoled themselves with the thought that the eastern districts were recognized as Russian territory, but other laws prevailed in the *Generalgouvernement* and that the Jews in this part of Poland would therefore be saved. Many believed that it would be impossible to exterminate the half million people in the Warsaw ghetto."[13]

"Our idea of resistance to the Germans, and revolt against them, has not as yet succeeded in penetrating the minds of the members of the Halutz movements in Warsaw. The people in Warsaw have not yet made up their minds," reported Entin on his return, "they do not see the situation as we do. They interpret the events differently." Edek Boraks, another of the messengers from Vilna, when he finally returned from Warsaw, also reported that "in Warsaw they still do not want to believe; the truth has not yet penetrated their hearts and minds."[14]

Twenty-five-year-old Shlomo Entin was not prepared to give up. He was determined to return to Warsaw, still hoping to convince the

---

13 David Wdowinski, *And We Are Not Saved* (New York: Philosophical Library, 1963), 53.
14 Reznik, *Nitzanim me-afar*, 83. Also Reyzel Korchak, *Lehavot ba-afar* [Flames in the ashes] (Merhavia: Moreshet and Sifriat Hapoalim, 1965), 69.

leadership there that this was a time for resistance and unity. "This is our most important mission today," Nisan Reznik, one of the initiators of FPO in Vilna, reports him saying upon his return from his first mission.[15] Entin braved the danger of another trip to Warsaw from Vilna, and repeated his plea for resistance and unity with the leadership there, but evidently his efforts bore no fruit. From Warsaw he continued his mission to the ghetto in Bialystok, intending to return thereafter once more to Warsaw. On his way there he was caught by the Germans and executed.[16]

The Betar emissaries that went to Warsaw from Vilna, Kempner and Pinczewski, did not need to convince the Betar leadership in Warsaw of the need to prepare for armed resistance against the Germans; they were already actively engaged in such preparations. However, since the other groups in the Warsaw ghetto lacked the conviction that this was the call of the hour, there was simply no partner for the establishment of a united resistance organization at that time. Kempner remained with his Betar comrades in Warsaw, while Pinczewski continued on to Lodz to bring the message from Vilna to the ghetto there.[17]

Tosya Altman had been sent by the leaders of Hashomer Hatzair in Warsaw to visit the movement in Vilna. She arrived at the end of December and heard the report of the massacre that had taken place there. Aghast at what she heard, her reaction was that the movement's members should come to Warsaw. They would escape the dangers still threatening them in Vilna and strengthen the ranks of the movement there. She still considered Warsaw a safe haven.

"Listen, Tosya," she was told, "you say that you are prepared to receive us in Warsaw with open arms. That you will be happy to be

15 Reznik, *Nitzanim me-afar*, 83.
16 Ibid., 85.
17 Lazar Litai, *Matzada shel Varsha* , 84.

with us, that we would strengthen the ranks of your activists. You and Yosef Kaplan and all the other comrades are prepared to care for us, to accept us.... Do you understand Tosya? We here are already at the peak of evil, while you, even if for the past two years you have received blows, you are still on the way up. The peak is still ahead of you. This peak, Tosya, is total destruction. We have already tasted it – your turn has not yet come. Your situation is better and also more dangerous. Better – you have time to prepare for the confrontation, step by step; to lay the foundation of political thought and afterwards to build action upon it. While we have to do everything at the same time.... Tomorrow you may find yourself facing extermination like us."

"I have no right to tell you what to do," Tosya replied. "You have lived with death...we live a different reality. I will report everything in Warsaw. I will also report your views on Warsaw and its surroundings. I admit that you have raised a question that has not as yet been raised before us so acutely."

Tosya told them about Edek Boraks, who had been sent from Vilna to Warsaw. "He arrived in Warsaw, and it is good that he came. We had him meet the representatives of the Jewish community in the ghetto, with the people from the Joint, with representatives of the political parties. What he said made a tremendous impression. And indeed he was the first messenger that brought the terrible truth. He described in simple and graphic language the whole horror. Of course, the majority did not believe him, or they believed, but were sure that in Warsaw this will not happen. That the Germans would be afraid of the reaction in Europe."[18]

Tosya was present in the Vilna ghetto on New Year's eve, December 31, 1941, when, in the guise of a New Year's party, an as-

---

18 Hayka Grossman, *Anshei ha-mahteret* [The people of the underground] (Tel Aviv: Moreshet and Sifriat Hapoalim, 1965), 48.

sembly of Zionist youth was held to commemorate those who were murdered at Ponar, and where Abba Kovner, the leader of Hashomer Hatzair in Vilna, read out his call: "Let us not go like sheep to the slaughter!... Hitler is planning to destroy all of European Jewry, and Lithuanian Jewry is fated to be the first in line.... The only worthy response in this situation is resistance, and the choice of death as free men." Kovner's declaration in Yiddish was followed by Tosya Altman reading it in Hebrew.[19]

On her return to Warsaw, Tosya informed the Hashomer Hatzair leadership there that their comrades in Vilna believed that what had happened in Vilna was going to happen, sooner or later, throughout all the areas under German occupation, and that armed Jewish resistance embracing all Jewish groups must be organized. But the mood in the Warsaw ghetto at the time, where no mass killings had taken place, was not conducive to accepting this message.

In January 1942, another courier from Vilna arrived in Warsaw. Twenty-two-year-old Hayka Grossman, a member of Hashomer Hatzair and more recently a member of the FPO in Vilna, used her Polish looks to serve as an underground courier. Able to move freely from city to city in Poland, she had been sent to Bialystok and Warsaw to bring the message of the FPO to the ghettos there. In her book, *Anshei Hamahteret*, Grossman writes about arriving in Warsaw after a visit to Bialystok:

"I told them [her comrades from Hashomer Hatzair in Warsaw] about Vilna. Since the time that Edek left for Warsaw, the movement has developed significantly. The defense is organizing into a united underground movement. United and closely knit...the main problem is shortage of weapons and shortage of money...the object of my visit, as decided by the Command of FPO, in addition to obtaining information and awakening public opinion, is obtaining

---

19 Porat, *Me'ever la-gashmi* , 91–92.

money. In Vilna there is no Joint, there are no institutions. There is no contact with the outside world. I also have to bring back Edek. Abba [Kovner] complains about his absence...."

She saw Mordechai Anielewicz, her comrade from Hashomer Hatzair, who guided her through the ghetto. "What do we need to do tomorrow to get things moving?" she asked him.

"I suggest we organize a meeting with the community leaders. We will do it through Kirshenbaum. The political parties have to be invited. You will speak there about the situation in Vilna, in Lithuania, and White Russia. Push them to the wall, let them draw their conclusions themselves," he answered.

The meeting took place in the home of Menahem Kirshenbaum, the General Zionist who chaired the Coordination Committee of the Zionist parties. The Revisionists were not invited – they were still boycotted, even in the ghetto, and thus not included in the committee. In addition to representatives of Zionist parties, representatives of the Bund were invited.

In the comfortable surroundings of Kirshenbaum's living room, faced by a group of middle-aged political leaders, Hayka Grossman did not know where to start. "My story seemed to sound somewhat strange at this table with its upholstered chairs," Hayka Grossman recalled. "Outside it was a cold, rainy, January day. In our host's home, it was warm and comfortable." After she told the story of the massacre in Vilna and the decision of the youth movements to set up an armed resistance organization, tea was served. Then a lively debate ensued. "Only a few wanted to draw logical conclusions from what I had said. I was taken aback by what was said by the people of the Bund. Their representative, Maurycy Orzech, announced that he was fully confident that what happened in Vilna could not happen in Warsaw."[20]

---

20 Grossman, *Anshei ha-mahteret*, 80–83.

This was the first direct confrontation between the middle-aged second-tier leadership of the political parties in the ghetto (the top leadership having left Warsaw in September 1939), and the younger leaders of the youth movements, represented by Hayka Grossman, a twenty-two-year-old, regarding the possibility of resistance to the Germans in the ghetto. The adult leadership preferred to continue to live with the hope that what happened in Vilna could not happen in Warsaw.

Afterwards, at her meeting with members of Dror, led by Zuckerman, Grossman found more common ground. They had been influenced by the news brought by the emissaries from Vilna, in addition to news that had recently reached Warsaw about an extermination camp at Chelmno, some 70 kilometers from Lodz, where the Germans had begun large-scale extermination of Jews from the Lodz region using exhaust gas introduced into hermetically sealed vans. Yet an understanding with leaders of Dror in the ghetto was not sufficient for the establishment of a resistance organization. Grossman returned to Vilna not having convinced the leaders in the Warsaw ghetto to follow the example of the FPO in Vilna. She did not meet with any representatives of the Revisionists.

On her return to Vilna, she reported, "It seems that in Warsaw the decision has not yet been taken about setting up an organization for resistance common to all the political groups. My stories about the FPO make a big impression, but it is strange. The community life of the Warsaw ghetto flows in the old and tried ways of many years, and it is difficult to awaken them and change them. A change that must come while there is still time…the radical change, the basic change of values, the turn – where is it? As compared to what happened in Vilna and Belorus, things in Warsaw are unclear, missing content and substance, and it will be bad if to the construction of the underground, the last brick will not be added: unison of the forces and preparation for armed combat."[21]

The Revisionists, meanwhile, were continuing with their plans for a resistance organization. Peretz Lasker was still heading operations in Warsaw, although he was also concerned with the Betar members working on the farms in the Hrubieszow region. Throughout the fall and winter of 1941, the Betar members working on those farms were not disturbed by the Germans. In December 1941, Lasker set out from Warsaw for another visit to the area in order to explore the possibility of transferring more groups of Betar members from the ghetto to the farming estates. This plan was never realized. Lasker discovered that the Betar members on one of the farms had been organized by Pawel Frenkel as an IZL unit and no longer accepted Lasker's authority. He realized that the IZL had continued its separate activity even in the ghetto. Shortly thereafter, in February 1942, Lasker left Warsaw for Czenstohowa, leaving Pawel Frenkel in the leadership position of the Revisionist underground in the ghetto.

Frenkel was twenty-one years old at the time. He had been a member of Masada, a Revisionist youth movement for high school students attending Jewish-Polish and Polish state schools. Masada had developed with the goal of attracting intellectual youth that ordinarily were not likely to join Betar. The Masada leadership claimed that Masada would potentially produce intellectual leadership for Betar. Frenkel bore this claim out. In 1938, leading a group of Masada members, he joined Betar, and before the outbreak of the war he had become head of the division for young members in the Betar branch in north Warsaw (*ken tzafon*). By that time he had also been drawn into the IZL framework and was heading an IZL cell. Trying to maintain a low profile, Frenkel had remained aloof from the early

---

21 Ibid., 83.

organizational activity of Betar in the ghetto, but in the winter of 1941–1942, influenced by the news from Vilna, he began actively recruiting former members of Masada and members of IZL cells for an underground organization. He required of his recruits that they leave their families and be quartered in housing exclusively inhabited by members of the underground group.

He attempted to build his organization primarily with those who had been members of IZL cells before the war, depending on their past experience in underground military activity and their prior allegiance to the IZL. Frenkel saw the resistance organization he was forming in the ghetto as an arm of the IZL in Palestine and a direct continuation of the IZL framework that had been established in Poland before the war. As a Polish name for the organization, he adopted Zydowski Zwiazek Wojskowy, or ZZW – The Jewish Military Organization (Irgun Zvai Yehudi). The ZZW also continued collecting weapons – including those that Polish soldiers had discarded. When Joseph Grienblatt, who had been an IZL member and served as an officer in the Polish army, returned to Warsaw after escaping from a German prisoner-of-war camp, Frenkel showed him a store of such weapons that he had accumulated.[22]

Frenkel was highly suited to being a commander of an active fighting underground. His great intelligence served him in his relationship with his subordinates and with the other fighting organization in the ghetto, his energy and steadfastness made it possible for him to coordinate and control small fighting units in different

---

22 Testimony given by Adam Halperin to Haim Lazar in the Jabotinsky Institute Archives 7,1-ב. Halperin had been the deputy head of the northern branch of Warsaw Betar before the war, and Frenkel had been one of its leaders; Halperin maintained contact with Frenkel in the ghetto. See also Lasker, "Ha-Irgun ha-Zvai ha-Leumi herim rishon et nes ha-mered be-Varsha"; and Joseph Grienblatt's videotaped testimony in the Jabotinsky Institute Archives.

parts of the ghetto, and his manner charmed all those who came into direct contact with him. He was, according to Wdowinski, a man of exceptional character, honest and modest – the very personification of "*hadar*", the dignified behavior that Jabotinsky demanded of members of Betar.[23]

Leib Rodal, who worked at Frenkel's side from the start, was also a young man, but older than Frenkel by about eight or nine years. Before the war he had been head of the Kielce branch of the Revisionists, and was a well-known personality at the party's conferences. He was a successful writer in the party's press and in *Der Moment*, and had also written for Yiddish dailies in New York. He was a vibrant personality, not easily daunted despite seeing obstacles clearly. He combined the open-eyed realism of a Jewish merchant with the sharpness of a Talmud scholar, and was able to analyze events and situations and reach logical conclusions. He had many contacts and was appreciated by all who knew him, and he knew how to make friends even among opponents, which was a trait that served him well in times of stress and trouble. Above all, he had a natural enthusiasm for the Jewish national ideal, faith in the Jewish people, and unswerving loyalty to the Jabotinsky movement.

Friedman-Yellin, who had been the editor of the IZL Warsaw daily *Die Tat* before the war, wrote about him some years later: "Editor of the Warsaw column was Leibel Rodal, about thirty, son of a wealthy family in one of the provincial towns, Kielce. He had been a correspondent for daily papers since an early age. Always well dressed, elegantly, but not ostentatiously, he loved life and its pleasures, big and small. He enjoyed them without neglecting his journalistic work, which was for him the first priority. As a member of the Revisionist movement from an early age, he grew close to the IZL when the paper was founded. I felt that the paper was closer

23 Wdowinski, *And We Are Not Saved*, 77.

to him than the political themes it advocated. I was not sure that a person like him, who had never been in need and was used to everything being available for him in good measure, would be capable of sacrificing his comforts if it was required, or sacrificing even more than that. I was wrong about him. As it turned out, during the German conquest Leibel Rodal entered the ghetto, even though with the means available to him he could have saved himself by passing as a Polish "Aryan" Christian. He was a member of the Irgun Zvai Yehudi that was active in Warsaw from the first days of the ghetto. With the outbreak of the revolt in April 1943, Leibel Rodal was one of its commanders, and in one of the battles against superior German forces he fell as a hero."[24]

Meanwhile, in Hrubieszow, despite the relative isolation from the German occupation forces, the members of Betar were always in danger of being picked up for the "Osttransport" – forced labor battalions ruthlessly run by the SS, in which the laborers were kept digging antitank trenches and constructing a defense line in the east for no clear military purpose. It was well known that nobody returned from the Osttransports. At a meeting of unit commanders in November 1941, it had been decided that as soon as Germans were sighted at any of the farms looking for laborers, the Betar members there would withdraw to the neighboring Lublin forests. They would resist by force any attempt at transfer to the Osttransport. This decision was put into practice in April 1942, when the Germans began liquidating the Jews in the Lublin area. The Betar members on the farms fought back, among them leading members of Betar from Warsaw, including Binyamin Shohat, Falek Langleben, Asher Frenkel, and Hayim Haus. They all fell in battle.[25]

---

24 Natan Yellin-Mor, *Shnot ba-terem*, 39.
25 Lasker, "Ha-Irgun ha-Zvai ha-Leumi herim rishon et nes ha-mered be-Varsha."

Other Betar members who had been at Hrubieszow found ways to return to Warsaw. Among them were Salek Hasenshprung, Eliyahu (Alek) Halberstein, and Yosef Bilawski, who joined Frenkel and Rodal, and together constituted the command of the IZL resistance organization, the ZZW.[26] Lasker's initiative to send a few hundred members of Betar to the farms in Hrubieszow had provided these youngsters with a year of respite from ghetto life, but it resulted in some of Betar's best and most devoted members not being present to participate in the Warsaw Ghetto Uprising.

Outside of the Revisionist organizations, Antek Zuckerman, the head of Dror, was still the only person who was taking Hayka Grossman's appeal seriously. He continued trying to persuade the political leadership of the ghetto of its importance. He met repeatedly with some of the leading personalities in the ghetto, discussing with them the danger facing the ghetto, and proposed setting up an armed resistance organization. Their reactions were negative. He was accused of being irresponsible and spreading panic that could bring a catastrophe upon the ghetto.

Next, Zuckerman turned to the Bund, reasoning that it was the key element needed for the establishment of a resistance organization. Outside assistance in weapons and training would be needed, and the only potential ally outside the ghetto who might supply them he assumed were the Polish Socialists. The Bund, whose ideology was based on maintaining a united front with the Polish Socialists, could be the link to them. The Bund, therefore, seemed to be the lifeline which Zuckerman needed.

---

26 Adam Halperin, *Helka shel Betar be-Mered ha-Geto* [Betar's part in the Ghetto Uprising], in *Ha-emet al Mered Geto Varsha* [The Truth about the Warsaw Ghetto Uprising] (Information Department of Betar Headquarters in Eretz Yisrael, 1946), 16.

Zuckerman reasoned that the Bund would only be prepared to establish a resistance organization with those who shared a common Socialist ideological basis. Therefore, on March 23, 1942, Zuckerman convened a meeting of the "proletarian" parties – the Bund, Po'alei Zion, Left Po'alei Zion, and Dror, in the communal kitchen run by Dror at Orla Street. In attendance were Maurycy Orzech and Abrasha Blum, the leaders of the Bund, Lezer Levin and Yohanan Morgenstern of Po'alei Zion, Hersh Berlinski and Melech Feinkind of Left Po'alei Zion, and of course Zuckerman himself, representing Dror. There was no representative from Hashomer Hatzair, who at this point were not expected to bridge the ideological gap with the anti-Zionist Bund. No invitations were issued to representatives of the "non-proletarian" Revisionists. Cooperation with them was evidently anathema to the Socialist Zionist parties and the Bund.

Zuckerman opened the meeting by describing the situation of the Jews in Poland in general, and the situation in the Warsaw ghetto in particular. He proposed selecting a leadership that would be charged with preparing the defense of the ghetto. This leadership would determine the structure of the organization and the means to be used in defense of the ghetto population. Everything seemed to depend on the response of the Bund.

After listening to Zuckerman's proposal, the Bund's Orzech launched into a tirade. He stated that the Bund had always been for defense, and the history of the Bund provided adequate testimony to that position. Establishing his distance from the other parties present, he declared that had it not been for the circumstances in the ghetto he would not be sitting at the same table with them. Then he continued with a reminder that the ghetto was not a world unto itself. Defending the ghetto was dependent on external political factors, and the Bund was tied to external political factors. The Bund had a commitment to the Polish Socialists, and therefore the Bund would not join an organization whose actions might be inconsistent with the Bund's obligations to its allies, the Polish workers. His conclusion, therefore, was that the Bund would not join a common fighting organization. Abrasha Blum, the other representative from the Bund, spoke somewhat more moderately, but ultimately expressed his agreement with Orzech's views.

The representatives of Po'alei Zion and Left Po'alei Zion were prepared to go along with Zuckerman's proposal, but in Zuckerman's view everything depended on the participation of the Bund, since he had set his hopes on establishing contact with the Polish underground through them. As it turned out at a later stage, the Bund's commitment to the Polish workers was far stronger than the commitment of the Polish workers to the Bund, and these connections ultimately proved to be of little value.[27]

Whereas the shock of the mass killings at Ponar had swept aside the barriers that separated the political groups in the Vilna ghetto and focused everyone on the immediate goal of united armed resistance, the same could not be said of Warsaw. Tzivya Lubetkin had heard of the mass murder at Ponar from one of the Betar emissaries from Vilna, and Zuckerman was aware that the Revisonists supported armed resistance to the Germans. It is possible that he

---

27 For a description of Zuckerman's attempts to set up a resistance organization at this time, see Lubetkin, *Biymei chilayon u-mered*, 66; Zuckerman, *A Surplus of Memory*, 171; Zuckerman, *Ba-geto u-va-mered*, 102; and Hersh Berlinski, *Zichroines* [Remembrances] in *Drei* [Three] (Tel Aviv: Ringelblum Institute, 1966), 156–58. From Berlinki's detailed description of the meeting convened by Zuckerman, it is clear that the ideologies prevalent before the war among the Jewish movements in Warsaw still dominated the thinking of their leadership in the ghetto. The framework for the resistance movement envisioned by Zuckerman at the time was to be the "proletarian" parties, while the "proletarian" but anti-Zionist Bund believed that joining such a resistance organization was contrary to its ideological commitment to the Polish Socialists. There would have been no room for the Revisionists in such a setup.

believed that the other Socialist parties, and especially the Bund, would refuse to join a framework that included the Revisionists, but even after his meeting with them ended in failure, he did not approach the Revisionists.

On the night of April 17, 1942, a Friday, the ghetto received a terrible shock. Over fifty Jews were dragged from their homes and shot in the street for no apparent reason.[28] It became known as "the night of blood." The ghetto was stunned and terrified. Could it be that the men who had been shot were suspected of some illicit activity, and the murders that night were meant as a warning, and no more? Or was this a sign of things to come?

The shock of the "night of blood" was followed shortly by more horrifying news: the mass killings of the Jews of the Lublin ghetto. In the spring of 1942, the Germans set up three "killing centers" in the Lublin district – Sobibor, Belzec, and Majdanek. On March 16, the transport of the Jews of Lublin to Belzec began, and in late spring the gas installation in Belzec was upgraded so as to increase its killing capacity. The Polish underground estimated that 130,000 Jews had been sent to the Belzec camp. At the end of April 1942, the news reached the Warsaw ghetto via two Betar members, the brothers Zvi and Moshe Zylberberg, who had escaped from Lublin.[29]

The brothers reported what had happened to the leading Revisionists in the ghetto, among them Dr. Wdowinski, Leon Rodal and his brother Avraham Rodal, and Dr. Michael Strykowski. In effect,

---

28 Gutman, *The Jews of Warsaw 1939–1943*, 176.

29 Moshe Zylberberg, *Keitzad noda'a be-Varsha ha-emet al Treblinka* [How the truth about Treblinka became known in Warsaw] (Tel Aviv: Muzeon ha-Lohamim ve-ha-Partizanim, April 1969), no. 7a. Moshe Zylberberg, one of the two brothers who managed to escape the German massacre in Lublin, survived the Holocaust. A similar version appears in the article *"Ver Ferfelsht di Geshichte?"* [Who falsifies history?] by Zylberberg in *Unzer Velt*, published in Munich in June 1948.

the ghetto in Lublin had been liquidated. Over the course of several days, more than forty thousand Jews in Lublin had been shot or burned to death. The same had already happened to the Jews in the smaller districts around Lublin. To the Revisionists who listened to their report, the situation was clear. The extermination of the Jews had nothing to do with this or that region, or with this or that German administration. The wave of extermination had already swept into the territory of the *Generalgouvernement*, which had been under German control before the attack on the Soviet Union in June 1941. This terrible news would surely convince the ghetto leadership that Warsaw might very well be next in line, and that the time had come to create a united organization for armed resistance. They suggested that the Zylberberg brothers go and see the head of the *Judenrat*, Czerniaków, and tell him what had happened in Lublin. Wdowinski accompanied the Zylberberg brothers to the *Judenrat*, where the two refugees repeated their news.

After the war, Moshe Zylberberg described the meeting with Czerniaków: "We reported to him about the deportations to the death camp, that we were among the very few who succeeded in escaping the deportations...for more than two hours we described to him the horrible sights we had witnessed." Czerniaków's response was to reply that he thought they were exaggerating. Then he said that he had the personal assurance of the Governor of the *Generalgouvernement*, Hans Frank, that three large ghettos in Poland would remain – Warsaw, Radom, and Krakow. So there was no reason for concern in Warsaw.

The Zylberberg brothers turned next to Menahem Kirshenbaum, the head of the Zionist Coordination Committee in the ghetto, in the hope that the Zionist leadership would believe their report and understand the implications for Warsaw. After greeting them in his apartment, Kirshenbaum turned to Moshe Zylberberg and asked,

"Mr. Zylberberg, what is happening in Lublin? Is it true that things are already quiet there?"

"Yes, in the cemetery it is quiet," Moshe Zylberberg replied, and started reporting what he and his brother had witnessed.

Kirshenbaum did not want to hear him out, and interrupted him, "Do not spread such horror stories in the ghetto. The Jews of Lublin were not liquidated in Belzec and Sobibor as you claim. They are in Rovno and in Pinsk. Letters have been received that report that the heads of the community made appropriate arrangements for them. I have received a letter from a friend, a well-known Zionist, who reports that it is quiet now and that most of the Jews will remain in Lublin."

In reply, Zylberberg explained to Kirshenbaum that seven thousand of the fifty thousand Jews in Lublin were transferred to Majdan-Matareski, a poor workers' quarter on the eastern outskirts of the city, while the rest were not in Pinsk or Rovno, but had all been murdered. "A similar fate awaits the Jews of Warsaw," warned the two brothers, "and you must use the time that remains to prepare for armed resistance on the day of liquidation."

Hearing this, Kirshenbaum cried out, "This is the opinion of Revisionist hotheads – such acts could bring about a catastrophe on the entire ghetto."[30]

Seeing the Zylberberg brothers' message being met with such refusal to understand or act, Dr. Wdowinski decided to approach some of the other Zionist leaders in the ghetto himself. The Zylberberg brothers themselves, disbelieved and denied by almost all they approached, joined the IZL resistance.

Although Wdowinski was a highly respected psychiatrist and a prominent Zionist within Revisionist ranks, as a Revisionist he did not command authority with Zionists in other organizations. He met

---

30 Ibid.

with Dr. Yitzhak Schipper, a leading Zionist, well-known historian, and former member of the Polish Parliament, and also with David Guzik, the director of the Joint Distribution Committee. He told them what had happened in Lublin and demanded the immediate organization of a united resistance organization in preparation for the threat that so clearly hung over the Jews of Warsaw. Dr. Schipper, an intelligent and highly educated man, looked at Wdowinski as if he were suffering from a high fever and talking in delirium. "You Revisionists were always hotheads," he told him with a friendly smile. "It is impossible to liquidate a population of half a million souls. The Germans will not dare exterminate the largest Jewish community in Europe," he argued. "They will still have to reckon with world public opinion. And we have the assurance of Governor-General Frank that Warsaw, Radom, and Krakow will remain." Next Wdowinski went to see Kirshenbaum, as he had not accompanied the Zylberberg brothers to their meeting with him – but he met with a similar reception. Kirshenbaum warned that the least sign of armed resistance would bring down a catastrophe upon the Jews in the ghetto.

It seemed that nothing could penetrate the armor of self-denial. All the leading personalities in the ghetto reacted the same way. They did not want to believe what they heard of Vilna, and were convinced that even if what they were told was true, the Jews of Warsaw were not facing that kind of danger. Only the young people, those organized within the framework of the Zionist youth movements, saw the approaching danger and wanted to prepare for it.

Wdowinski was frustrated. He had achieved nothing. "On my own responsibility, as head of a political party, I could do nothing," he wrote after the war about this period. "We, the Revisionists, could not take upon ourselves as a single party the organization of the resistance. Such a resistance had to have the backing of the great majority of the population. We did not have it. It was clear that the

German answer to the least resistance in the ghetto would be a blood bath. That onus we could not take upon ourselves."[31]

Antek Zuckerman, speaking about this period, said: "While the spring months of 1942 passed in Warsaw, great attempts were being made to create a united Jewish force for defense. But all the attempts led nowhere. The indifference of one section of the population, the lack of faith of another section, and the opposition of another section brought all our efforts to nothing. After the Vilna episode came the gas trucks of Chelmno. The *Generalgouvernement* burned on both sides, in the east and in the west – while in the center there was still relative quiet. The Poles had no faith in a Jewish fighting organization. Openly, they claimed 'the ghetto is Communist and serves as a spring-board for the Soviet Union. To internal enemies it is impossible to give arms.'"[32]

During those months, two Communists in the ghetto approached Zuckerman with a suggestion to organize a "united bloc of workers and democratic forces" in the ghetto. The two were Andrzej Shmidt and Yosef Finkelstein-Lewertowski. Shmidt, whose original name was Pinhas Kartin, had fought with the International Brigade in Spain, and was reported to have been parachuted into German-occupied Poland from the Soviet Union. Finkelstein-Lewertowski had at one time been a member of Po'alei Zion and held important positions with them, but had left them to join the Communists. Now these two had been charged with the mission of organizing support for the Soviet Union in the ghetto, and recruiting the younger generation for active partisan warfare.

---

31 Wdowinski, *And We Are Not Saved*, 54–56.

32 Yitzhak Zuckerman's article "Mordechai My Comrade" in Mordechai Tennenbaum-Tamaroff's *Dapim min ha-dlikah* [Pages from the fire] (Jerusalem: Yad Vashem and Beit Lohamei Hagetaot, 1987), 221.

They met with Zuckerman and with Mordechai Tennenbaum, a leading member of Dror, and although what they proposed was not exactly what Zuckerman had in mind, by that stage he was prepared to try almost anything that might lead to armed resistance. The thought of receiving weapons and military training from the Soviet Union was certainly attractive. Zuckerman convinced Po'alei Zion and Hashomer Hatzair, at first hesitant to cooperate with the Communists, to join what would be called the Anti-Fascist Bloc. The Bund, however, stubbornly refused to cooperate with the Communists, even though Zuckerman told their representatives that it was a matter of life and death.

The Bloc was established at the end of April 1942.[33] In addition to the organization of "anti-Fascist combat divisions," its aims included the "organization of joint forces for a political and propaganda war against Fascism and reactionary forces within the ghetto."[34] The name chosen was consistent with the terminology of Soviet propaganda at the time – that the war was a war against Fascism – but it invariably opened a chasm between them and the forces in the ghetto that were labeled as Fascists, like the Revisionists. No cooperation with them could be envisaged. In any event, it did not take long for disappointment to set in. The promised weapons did not arrive, and Andrzej Shmidt and other Communists were arrested by the Germans. That was the end of the Anti-Fascist Bloc.

In June, Mordechai Tennenbaum published an article in his movement's publication in memory of the Italian Socialist leader Giacomo Mateotti and the Zionist Socialist leader Chaim Arlozoroff: "The same hand put an end to their lives. Mateotti was murdered by killers hired by Italian Fascism; Arlozoroff – by men sent by the Fascist organization that has arisen among Jews. The deaths of the

---

33 Ibid., 183; and Lubetkin, *Biymei chilayon u-mered*, 69.
34 Zuckerman, *Ba-geto u-va-mered*, 103.

martyrs, Mateotti and Arlozoroff, and the deaths of thousands of unknown fighters, cry out for retribution. And the day of reckoning will come," he wrote.[35] The years of German occupation, the news from Vilna and Lublin, and the threat hanging over the Jews of Warsaw had not dampened the hostility of Socialist Zionists to Revisionist Zionists.

Also that spring, the Revisionists issued a publication in the ghetto entitled *Magen David*.[36] It contained an article written by IZL commander Pawel Frenkel, under a pseudonym. It was an ode to Jabotinsky, the founder of the Revisionist movement and Betar, and the commander-in-chief of IZL. In his ode dedicated to Ze'ev Jabotinsky, Frenkel referred to the coming battle against the Germans:

> When your spirit is among us we do not mourn your departure from us. When your teachings are before us we are not orphaned. We are struggling on the edge of the abyss with the wave of the storm that overtakes us. We are not ruled by despair, because the wave creates the swimmer – this is what you taught us. You taught us to be the sons of kings or to die.[37]

---

35 Tennenbaum-Tamaroff, *Dapim min ha-dlikah*, 172. This sentiment in the Socialist Zionist camp that the Revisionists were Fascists is also reflected in Emmanuel Ringelblum's note describing his visit to the headquarters of ZZW in the ghetto. ZZW, he wrote, is "under Revisionist influence and tending to Italian-style Fascism" (Ringelblum, *"Oneg Shabbat" Selected Documents* [Jerusalem: Yad Vashem, 1987], 596).

36 Ringelblum Archives, ring 1, no. 744. The publication was in Yiddish. When recovered it was in poor shape. It was deciphered by Haya Lazar and translated into Hebrew. It contents appear in Lazar Litai, *Muranowska 7*, 333.

37 An allusion to the Betar anthem written by Jabotinsky. In it appear the lines: "You were born the son of kings, crowned with the crown of David," and "To die or to conquer the mountain, Yodefet, Masada, Betar."

We know how to die. Therefore we will also know how to be beautiful when we die.

In the stormy sea, in the darkness of the storm, your teachings light the way for us, they lead us with an unseen hand, and hold us securely in the storm.

We knew you as Samson,[38] as a fighter and tragic hero, whose people did not understand him, his life was tragic and his fight was glorious.

Then you began telling us of David – the spirit of Samson became the spirit of David. We saw the transmigration of the souls. We looked for its realization in your lifetime.

We awaited the kingdom, and we still await it.

You are not with us anymore but your spirit is with us.

You live among us. Your voice is in our ears, every one of your gestures is traced in our memory, accompanying our lives and our battle.

Together with you we will change our situation, together with you we will go into battle. Together with you we will realize the legend of King David, the redeemer.

In May 1942, the IZL underground in the Warsaw ghetto decided to make yet another attempt to establish contact with their comrades in Palestine. They decided to try to send a telegram to Hillel Tzur. Tzur had been one of the IZL emissaries from Palestine organizing IZL cells in Poland before the war; he had returned to his hometown of Netanya in September 1939. The only way to reach him was through the Red Cross office in Warsaw. Stefan Wladislaw was picked for the daring task of leaving the ghetto and presenting himself at the Red Cross office. Wladislaw, an IZL member, was of "Aryan" appearance and was fluent in Polish. Even though Tzur's exact address was

---

38 An allusion to Jabotinsky's novel, *Samson*.

not known, it was expected that addressing the telegram to Netanya would be sufficient. Since Netanya at the time was a small town, they hoped Tzur would be located by the postal authorities there. Since the message had to pass German censorship, it would have to be completely innocuous. It would be signed "Binyamin Esgani." This had been Binyamin Shohat's pseudonym. He had held the rank of *segan* (deputy) in the IZL, and it was hoped that Tzur would recognize the signature, as he had known Shohat during his stay in Warsaw.

Armed in case of interception, Wladislaw arrived at the Red Cross office on May 17, 1942 and sent the cable without difficulty. It duly arrived in Palestine on August 31, 1942, and was delivered to Tzur. The message read: "I work as a clerk for the Mutual Public Assistance. I live under the most difficult circumstances. I have no material means. I also miss you a lot. Write how you are doing."[39] The rest was blocked out by the German censor.

When the letter was delivered to Tzur he could not identify the sender and did not understand the meaning of the coded message, nor was he or any of the Jewish community in Palestine aware at that time of the Nazis' mass murder of Jews. Even if the telegram had been understood, it is doubtful that the IZL in Palestine would have been in a position to help. The IZL there had split between the supporters of Raziel, commander of the IZL, who had declared a truce in the fight against the British in Palestine, and Stern, who insisted on continuing the fight against British rule in Palestine. Raziel subsequently had fallen while on a mission for the British in Iraq, while Stern, the leader of the splinter group Lehi, had been killed by the British police in Palestine. With the IZL in such a state of disarray

---

39 The letter can be seen in the Jabotinsky Institute Archives 10/1-כרב. Also in the publication of Muzeon ha-Lohamim ve-ha-Partizanim, Tel Aviv, April 1983.

it would hardly have been in a position to issue instructions to its soldiers in the Warsaw ghetto.

Jabotinsky's followers, and the many who cherished his memory, assembled on July 13, 1942 at the Tlomacki Synagogue, on the second anniversary of Jabotinsky's death. The synagogue was packed with people who had come to pay their respects to the memory of the man who had warned the Jews of Poland of the impending catastrophe. Among the organizers of the memorial were Wdowinski and Leon Rodal. It might, perhaps, have been a suitable occasion for a display of unity bridging past ideological divides. But it was not to be. Past differences could not be forgotten. The leaders of the Zionist movements in the ghetto were conspicuous by their absence.[40]

Nine days later, on July 22, the eve of the ninth day of the Hebrew month of Av, the Germans began the systematic extermination of Warsaw's Jews.

---

40 Wdowinski, *And We Are Not Saved*, 58–59.

Chapter 4

The Great Deportation

July 22, 1942–September 24, 1942

The pace of the extermination of Polish Jewry was determined by how fast the Germans could build their death camps, and the capability of the German-managed railroad system to transport Jews to these camps at a time when the transportation requirements of the German army advancing deep into the Soviet Union put great stress on the system. The Treblinka death camp was built for the Jews of the Warsaw and Bialystok districts at Malkinia, on the Bug River, 125 kilometers from Warsaw, and was completed in July 1942. Now the Germans were ready to begin the extermination of Warsaw's Jews at an "accelerated tempo."

In the middle of that month, rumors spread through Warsaw that the Germans were planning large-scale deportations of the Jews of the ghetto. These rumors, coming as they did after the news of the massacres at Ponar and the gassing of Jews at Chelmno, and after the arrival of survivors of the massive liquidation in Lublin, were enough to arouse a sense of panic among the Jews of the ghetto. The news from the front was also not encouraging. The German army was advancing deeper into Russia by the day.

Adam Czerniaków, the head of the *Judenrat*, had told all those who warned him of impending disaster that he had the assurance of Hans Frank, the governor of the *Generalgouvernement*, that the ghettos of Warsaw, Krakow, and Radom would remain. Early in the morning of July 20 he hurried to Gestapo headquarters hoping to put his mind at ease. The Gestapo officials he questioned regarding the rumors of impending deportations all replied that they had no knowledge of such deportations, and that it was nonsense.[1]

Of course, they knew much more than they claimed. In mid-July, Hermann Hoefle, the main deportation and extermination expert of the Lublin district, having completed his mission there, had arrived in Warsaw. He was accompanied by a group of extermination specialists. SS units in Warsaw had been reinforced by Polish "police" and Ukrainian, Lithuanian, and Latvian auxiliary troops. The stage had been set for the great deportation of Warsaw's Jews to the gas chambers of Treblinka. The day after Czerniaków's visit to the Gestapo, several members of the *Judenrat* were arrested by the Germans and held as hostages, in case the *Judenrat* didn't cooperate.

The Germans called it Die Grosse Umsiedlungsaktion – the Great Resettlement Operation. True to their demonic tradition, the Nazis had chosen to begin the deportations on the eve of the Ninth of Av, the anniversary of the destruction of the Temple in Jerusalem: a day of Jewish mourning. On the morning of July 22, Hoefle, accompanied by a retinue of Gestapo officials, arrived at Czerniaków's office in the *Judenrat* and dictated the instruction to "prepare for resettlement of non-productive elements," beginning that very day. The people affected by the order were to report voluntarily at the *Umschlagplatz* (collection point) at the northern end of the ghetto, near the railway siding and the waiting freight cars. The quota was six thousand people a day, and the deportation would be limited to a total of sixty thousand "non-productive persons." Exempt were all Jews who were employed and fit for work, plus their wives and children, Jewish policemen and their wives and children, Jewish hospital and sanitation personnel and their wives and children, and all Jews who were patients in hospitals and were not fit for removal. The "resettlement" was to start that day at 11 a.m. The *Judenrat* was

---

1   *The Warsaw Diary of Adam Czerniaków*, entry for July 20, 1942.

held responsible for the delivery of six thousand persons daily, to arrive no later than 4 p.m.[2]

The Germans had designed their instructions so as to create the impression that the deportation, although massive, was nevertheless going to be limited to only sixty thousand people and to those Jews who were "non-productive," thus lulling the rest of the population into believing that as long as they were engaged in "productive work" in the German workshops in the ghetto, they and their families would be safe. Why then would the able-bodied "productive workers" engage in resistance to this order, and arouse bloody German vengeance on everybody in the ghetto, when they and their families had been "promised" their lives?

On the first two days, the *Judenrat* used the Jewish police to deliver the required quota. Those selected for deportation were the inhabitants of the old age homes and the ghetto prison, as well as people from the provinces who had only recently arrived in the Warsaw ghetto. When, on July 23, Czerniaków was ordered to provide ten thousand people the following day, including children, he realized that it was the Germans' intention to use him, the *Judenrat*, and the Jewish police to organize the orderly assembly of tens of thousands of men, women, and children for deportation from the ghetto. That night he returned to his office, asked for a glass of water, closed the door behind him, and swallowed potassium cyanide pills. When the *Judenrat* workers entered his office they found him dead. On his desk he had left two short notes. In one he bade farewell to his wife, asking her to forgive him. He wrote, "To act in any other way is impossible." On the other he had written: "Ten thousand are demanded for tomorrow, and then seven thousand each time...."[3]

---

2 Ibid., entry for July 22, 1942.

3 Jonas Turkow, *Azoy Iz Es Geven*, [That is who it was] as quoted by Philip Friedman in *Martyrs and Fighters* (London: Routledge and Kegan Paul, 1954), 148–49.

Czerniaków was replaced by Marek Lichtenbaum, a colorless member of the *Judenrat* who used the *Judenrat* bureaucracy and the Jewish police to implement the German instructions. Thus began the great deportation from the Warsaw ghetto, during which 270,000 Jews were transported to the gas chambers in Treblinka in the space of seven weeks. The overall command of the operation was in the hands of SS-Oberfuehrer (Colonel) Ferdinand von Sammern-Frankenegg, who had been the SS and Police commander of Warsaw since 1941.

The management of the railroads also succeeded in doing their part. In recognition of their contribution to the extermination of Warsaw's Jews, Karl Wolf, chief of Himmler's personal staff, addressed the following letter on August 13, 1942, to Dr. Theodor Ganzenmueller of the German Transport Ministry:[4]

> Dear Party Member Ganzenmueller:
> For your letter of July 28, 1942, I thank you – also in the name of the Reichsfuehrer-SS [Himmler] – sincerely. With particular joy I noted your assurance that for two weeks now a train has been carrying every day 5,000 members of the chosen people to Treblinka, so that we are now in a position to carry through this population movement at an accelerated tempo. I, for my part, have contacted the participating agencies to assure the implementation of the process without friction. I thank you again for your efforts in this matter and, at the same time, I would be grateful if you would give to these things your continued personal attention.
> With best regards and
> *Heil Hitler!*
> Your devoted,
> W.

---

4   Raul Hilberg, *The Destruction of the European Jews* (Chicago: Quadrangle Books, 1961), 313–14.

The immediate reaction of the ghetto's population was to seek safety in documents that would prove that they were "productively employed." Any employment would do, and people were prepared to pay for the "privilege" of being listed on the employment roll of a workshop. Attempts were made to establish private workshops that would provide contract labor for existing workshops. Premium prices were offered for a sewing machine around which a small workshop could be established.

While this feverish activity was consuming the ghetto's population, the representatives of the political parties and movements in the ghetto met in an emergency session to discuss the situation and decide on what action to take. By default, they were the leaders whose decisions would influence the course of events in the ghetto at that fateful and tragic moment. Would there be resistance to the deportations? Would the Warsaw Jewish community be the example to all Jews under German occupation not to submit to German orders? Did they have the authority to take such a fateful decision, and would the population of the ghetto follow whatever decision they would take?

Sixteen men took part in the deliberations, representing a wide spectrum of the Jewish community. The representatives of the Zionist political parties were Yosef Sack of Po'alei Zion; Shachna Sagan, Adolf Berman, and Emmanuel Ringelblum of Left Poalei Zion; and Menahem Kirshenbaum, Yitzhak Schipper, and Lipa Bloch of the General Zionists. The representative of Agudat Yisrael, the religious party, was Rabbi Zisha Friedman. Maurycy Orzech was there to represent the Bund, and Josef Lewertowski-Finkelstein to represent the Communists. The representatives of the Socialist Zionist youth movements were Shmuel Breslaw and Yosef Kaplan of Hashomer Hatzair and Yitzhak (Antek) Zuckerman of Dror. The directors of the American Joint Distribution Committee in Warsaw, Daniel Guzik and Yitzhak Giterman, also attended, as did Alexander Landau, the

Jewish owner of one of the larger workshops in the ghetto. They met on July 23, the day after the beginning of the deportation and the day of Czerniaków's suicide.[5]

There was no representative of the Revisionists at this assembly. Despite the terrible threat hanging over the Jews of Warsaw, the Revisionists were still not invited, were still ostracized. The Revisionist view was well known – they were for active resistance against the Germans. Wdowinski had made his views clear in his meetings with Kirshenbaum, Schipper, and Bloch, and they in turn had told the rest. They had all heard the rumor that the Revisionists had already organized an armed underground. That was another reason for those opposed to active resistance to keep them away from the deliberations.

The discussions began, and went on for many hours. All felt the great burden of responsibility resting on their shoulders. Dr. Yitzhak Schipper, the fifty-eight-year-old historian and former member of the Polish parliament who had made a name for himself researching the history of the Jews in medieval Poland, took the historical perspective. He argued that from a historical point of view, a case could be made both for resisting the Germans, and for submitting to the German orders and not resisting the deportation. But then he came down on the side of submission: "We are in the midst of a war. Every nation sacrifices victims; we too are paying the price in order to salvage the core of our people. Were I not convinced that we can succeed in saving the core, I, too, would come to a different conclusion. There are times in the history of a people," he said, "when they cannot and should not fight, when fighting in unfavorable conditions would lead to the loss of what could have been rescued otherwise. It

---

5   Meilech Neustadt, *Hurban u-mered shel Yehudei Varsha* [The destruction and revolt of the Jews of Warsaw] (Tel Aviv: The General Federation of Jewish Labor in Palestine, 1947), 137–38.

is better to write off those being sent away and at that price save the others. We have no moral right to endanger the lives of all the Jews of Warsaw. We have to save what can be saved," he concluded.

Rabbi Friedman put his faith in the Almighty: "The Lord has given and the Lord has taken away. We have no right to endanger the lives of Jews since we know that the enemy is applying the principle of collective responsibility. We have no right to raise our hands against the Germans because it may bring disaster to hundreds of thousands of Jews. I believe in God and in miracles. God will not allow His people, Israel, to be destroyed. We must wait and the miracle will happen," he concluded.

Although most of those present were not religious, Rabbi Friedman's words made a great impression. His conclusion was the same as that of Professor Schipper, even though based on entirely different considerations.

To some it seemed no more than a theoretical discussion. No preparations had been made for resistance to the Germans, other than by the Revisionists, who were not part of the conversation. The Bund representative, Maurycy Orzech, stuck to his known position, that resistance to the Germans was predicated on forming a united front with the Polish Socialists, and that as long as the Polish Socialists were not prepared to join in resistance against the Germans, the Bund would not participate in separate Jewish resistance.

The younger members of the group, the representatives of the youth movements Hashomer Hatzair and Dror, Yosef Kaplan, Shmuel Breslaw, and Yitzhak Zuckerman, made the case for resistance, but they were in the minority. To the majority they seemed like impetuous youngsters who lacked the wisdom that came with age and experience. The majority did not support resistance. Their opinion was that the Germans would deport perhaps sixty thousand, but not all of the Jews in the ghetto. It was felt that by resisting, the ghetto's doom would be hastened and that, for the acts of a few, the many would suffer death.[6]

It was all too easy to engage in wishful thinking and assume that the Germans would stick to the plan they had announced. The Germans had succeeded in dividing the Jews of the ghetto into two groups – those destined for deportation, and those hoping to evade the danger. The assembled representatives had also fallen into that trap. At that point the ultimate destination and fate of those being deported was not known. Just how and where were they going to be resettled? Nobody knew. But that inconclusive meeting, which did not end with a call to the population of the ghetto to resist the deportation, meant that 270,000 of Warsaw's Jews were led off to the gas chambers of Treblinka without resistance.

During the first week of deportations, over sixty thousand men, women, and children were sent to Treblinka by train. This first phase of deportations, from July 22 till July 30, was handled primarily by the Jewish police force, under the supervision of the Germans. The trains returned empty to Warsaw the following day.

David Landau, a ZZW fighter, described the routine that was established for herding Jews to the *Umschlagplatz*:

> Szerynski [the head of the Jewish police] had trained his Jewish forces to perform their part: a block of streets would be closed off in the morning; the Jewish police would call out that the street had been surrounded and no one was to leave his dwelling; the caretakers of the buildings would immediately close the building gates and anybody found in the street would

---

6 Zuckerman, *A Surplus of Memory*, 193, and *Ba-geto u-va-mered*, 105. See also Adolf-Avraham Berman, *Mi-yemei ha-mahteret* [From the days of the underground] (Tel Aviv: Menorah, 1971), 46, on the rumors that the Revisionists had a group of fighters in the ghetto at that time.

be either shot on the spot or handed over to the police guarding those to be taken to the *Umschlagplatz*. The Germans and their assistants would then go from building to building and the Jewish policemen would call to the trapped inhabitants: *Alles herunter* [Everybody come down]. Pressure was applied to hurry: *schnell, schnell!* It would be the duty of the Jewish police to go in first to check the open apartments in case anybody had disobeyed the orders. Walls would be tapped, wardrobes opened, searches made to make sure nobody had hidden under the beds. The cellars and attics were searched for those perfidious ones who failed to obey the German order. The police would drag down those found hiding, to be dealt with by the Germans or their helpers....

When all the tenants were assembled in the yard the selection started. In theory, those who had valid working cards (*Arbeitskarten*) were to be released unharmed, to return to their apartments. But theory was of no use. The fate of the Jewish individual trapped in a closed-off area was more a matter of luck. It depended on the whim of the German selector. He decided who went and who stayed. Those selected for deportation were handed over to the Jewish police. Together with their Aryan colleagues they led the victims off to the *Umschlagplatz* on foot or in carts.[7]

On July 28, the leaders of the Socialist Zionist youth movements, Dror and Hashomer Hatzair, met at the Dror center on 34 Dzielna Street.[8] Frustrated by the passivity of the political leadership, they were not prepared to passively accept the massive deportation from the ghet-

---

7   David Landau, *Caged: The Landau Manuscript* (The Landau Family, 1999), 120.

8   Zuckerman, *A Surplus of Memory*, 197, 219.

to. Two years earlier, Yosef Kaplan and Shmuel Breslaw, members of the Hashomer Hatzair leadership in Poland, had come to Warsaw from Vilna to lead Hashomer Hatzair in German-occupied Poland, and Yitzhak Zuckerman and Tzivya Lubetkin had done the same, returning to Warsaw from the Soviet zone to lead the Dror movement. They had come to provide social and welfare activities and ideological training for their youngsters. Now they decided to lead their movements in resistance to the Germans. They were joined by Yisrael Kanal of the General Zionist youth organization, Akiva. They were not going to wait for the approval of the adult political organizations. At that time they had no military training and no weapons, but still they would begin – to acquire weapons, to train, to establish contact with the Polish underground. They named their organization the Jewish Fighting Organization (*Irgun Yehudi Lohem*). It came to be known by the initials of its Polish name, Zydowska Organizacja Bojowa – ZOB. They hoped to enlist others in the underground organization they were forming, but not the Revisionists, at least not yet. Five were chosen to command the organization: Yosef Kaplan and Shmuel Breslaw of Hashomer Hatzair, and Yitzhak Zuckerman, Tzivya Lubetkin, and Mordechai Tennenbaum of Dror. Tosya Altman, Frumka Plotnicka, Lea Perlstein, and Arye Wilner were chosen to make contact with the Polish underground outside the ghetto and begin the acquisition of weapons.[9]

Michel Mazor, who had been active in social welfare activity in the ghetto, was frustrated by the passivity with which the Jews were accepting the deportations. He told Ringelblum and Sagan of Left Poalei Zion, both of whom had participated in the fateful assembly at the beginning of the deportations, that he believed it was necessary to warn the people of the fate awaiting them, and that lacking any other

---

9   Ibid.

means of defense, hundreds of thousands should overrun the gates of the ghetto, force their way through the guards, and then disperse on the "Aryan" side. The great majority would probably be slaughtered, he thought, but it was still probable that a number would manage to escape and go into hiding. After all, there was nothing to lose, since they were all destined for extermination. Ringelblum and Sagan maintained their belief that there was still hope of saving part of the population; that it was not certain that the Germans were intent on total extermination, and they were likely to respect the documents of the "productive workers" in the selections.[10]

This had been Sagan's and Ringelblum's opinion during the discussion held on the day that Czerniaków committed suicide; it remained their view, and it reflected that of the majority. This rationalization of passive acceptance of deportation was the insurmountable obstacle to any attempts at resistance. After the great deportation, Ringelblum lamented: "Why did we allow ourselves to be led like sheep to the slaughter? Why did everything come so easy to the enemy? Why did not the hangmen suffer a single casualty? Why could fifty SS men (some people say even fewer), with the help of some two hundred Ukrainian guards and an equal number of Latvians, carry out the operation so smoothly? The resettlement should never have been permitted. We ought to have run out into the street, have set fire to everything in sight, have torn down the walls, and escaped to the other side. The Germans would have taken their revenge. It would have cost tens of thousands of lives, but not 300,000."[11]

The second phase of the great deportation lasted from July 31 until August 14. During that period, the SS and its Ukrainian, Latvian, and Lithuanian helpers were actively involved in hunting

---

10 Michel Mazor, in *Le Monde Juif*, no. 46, pp. 9–10.
11 Emmanuel Ringelblum, *Notes from the Warsaw Ghetto* (New York, 1958), entry for October 15, 1942.

and beating Jews in the streets of the ghetto, chasing them from their homes to the *Umschlagplatz* and loading them into the waiting freight cars. Some were killed in the streets before they even arrived at the *Umschlagplatz*. On August 5, the Germans deported the orphans from the Jewish orphanage run by the well-known physician and author of children's books, Janusz Korczak. His orphanage had operated for many years in Warsaw and was moved into the ghetto when the ghetto was established. Throughout the years in the ghetto Dr. Korczak continued caring for the orphans. Now the sixty-four-year-old educator was ordered to send the children to the *Umschlagplatz*.

Hillel Seidman, the ghetto archivist, wrote the following in his diary entry for August 12, 1942:

> Today Korczak's orphanage is to be "evacuated"...Korczak himself may remain, physicians are needed. They are not marked for deportation, and the *Judenrat* has still the power to protect him and, as a matter of fact, it has protected him. Thus, he is safe.
>
> But Korczak refuses to stay behind. He will not abandon "his" children, he will go with them.
>
> And so a long line is formed in the front of the orphanage on Shliska Streeet. A long procession, children, small, tiny, rather precocious, emaciated, weak, shriveled and shrunk. They carry shabby packages, some have schoolbooks, notebooks under their arms. No one is crying.
>
> Slowly they go down the steps, line up in rows, in perfect order and discipline, as usual. Their little eyes are turned towards the "doctor," they are strangely calm, they feel almost "well." The "doctor" is going with them, so what do they have to be afraid of? They are not alone, they are not abandoned.

Dr. Korczak busies himself with the children with a sober earnestness. He buttons the coat of one child, ties up a package of another, or straightens the cap of a third. Then he wipes off a tear which is rolling down the thin little face of a child....

Then the procession starts out. It is starting out for a trip from which – everybody feels it – one never comes back. All these young, budding lives, innocent souls in which who knows what forces slumber, opportunities and talents, and maybe even the powers of a genius? Who knows? And all this, marching quietly and orderly to the place of their untimely doom.

The children are calm, but inwardly they must feel it, they must sense it intuitively, otherwise how could you explain the deadly seriousness on their pale little faces? But they are marching quietly, in orderly rows, calm and earnest, and at the head of them, Janusz Korczak.

On all sides the children were surrounded by Germans, Ukrainians, and also Jewish policemen.[12]

Nahum Remba, the secretary of the *Judenrat* who was present at the *Umschlagplatz*, reported to Ringelblum: "This was no march to the cattle cars, but rather a mute protest against this murderous regime...a procession the like of which no human eye has ever witnessed."[13]

Korczak and the two hundred orphans were among the 100,000 Jews shipped to Treblinka from the Warsaw ghetto during that phase of the deportation.

---

12 Hillel Seidman, *Yoman Geto Varsha* [Warsaw Ghetto Diary] (New York: The Jewish Week, 1957), 57–59.

13 Ringelblum, *Notes from the Warsaw Ghetto*, entry for October 15, 1942.

During August, the news spread through the ghetto that those deported were being sent to their death. This terrible news came from Polish railroad workers and from a few Jews who managed to escape from the trains and from Treblinka. The Bund dispatched one of its members, the Aryan-looking Zalman Friedrych, to obtain exact information on what was happening. A Polish railroad worker advised Friedrych which route to investigate. When he reached Sokolow, he learned that the Germans had constructed a small branch railroad to the village of Treblinka. Each day trains packed with Jews were switched onto the new spur. At Treblinka, he was told, there was a large camp divided into two sections, one for Jews and one for Poles. According to the residents of Sokolow, terrible things were happening in Treblinka. While in Sokolow Friedrych ran into a Jew who had escaped from Treblinka and was told about the gassing of the Jews upon their arrival in Treblinka. He returned to Warsaw with this information.[14] Still, every day thousands who were on the verge of starvation voluntarily reported to the *Umschlagplatz*, unable to resist the cunning German offer of bread and jam to those who reported of their own volition.

For weeks, people still clung to the hope that the deportations were going to be limited, and that a certain number of Jews would be allowed to remain in the ghetto. As the deportations proceeded, estimates of that number decreased from day to day, until it became clear that the deportations were actually limitless.

The third phase of the deportation lasted from August 15 to September 6, and included an intermission of six days, from August 28 to September 2, during which the Germans deported Jews from some of the towns surrounding Warsaw to Treblinka. During this third phase the Germans had greater difficulty in meeting their

---

14 Bernard Goldstein, *The Stars Bear Witness* (New York: Viking Press, 1949), 118.

daily quotas, and the brutality of the Germans and their helpers had no limit. Many Jews were shot in the streets of the ghetto during the roundup, and "productive workers" from the workshops were frequently included in the shipments. About 55,000 Jews were sent to their deaths in Treblinka during this period. By that time the Germans had emptied large parts of the ghetto, leaving only the area of the workshops and a part of what used to be the Central Ghetto inhabited.

Accurate reports were sent to Berlin on the progress of the deportation of Warsaw's Jews to Treblinka. On August 21, 1942, Joseph Goebbels noted in his diary that he had received information from Friedrich-Wilhelm Krueger, the Higher SS and Police Leader of the *Generalgouvernement*, that "at this time Jews were being evacuated in vast numbers and pushed to the East." Adding his own observation, Goebbels commented that "all this is happening on quite a significant scale. Here the Jewish question is handled in the right way, without sentimentality and without much consideration. That is the only way to solve the Jewish problem."

August 20 saw the first use of firearms by a ZOB fighter, directed against the head of the Jewish police force, Jozef Szerynski, who had made the Jewish police force a willing tool of the Germans. Yisrael Kanal, one of the founding members of ZOB, went to Szerynski's apartment wearing a policeman's cap, and as Szeryinski approached, shot him in the face. Szeryinski was lightly wounded.[15] The Germans paid no attention to this incident, as the life of a Jew was of no importance to them.

Toward the end of August there was another leadership meeting chaired by Kirshenbaum to discuss the situation and the possibility of resistance to the deportations. After long discussion it was decided to postpone a decision because it was rumored that on the

---

15 Zuckerman, *A Surplus of Memory*, 202–3.

first of September the deportations were going to end. And so it went – every time the subject was discussed, there was a rumor that the deportations were about to end.

Alexander Landau's carpentry shop, OBW, had served as a hiding place for Yosef Kaplan, Shmuel Breslaw, and many others from Hashomer Hatzair. Landau's daughter, Margalit, was an active member of that organization. During the manhunts in the ghetto, the workshop provided a measure of protection to the men, women, and children crowded there, some posing as workers and others simply hiding there.

On the morning of September 3, Shmuel Breslaw ran into the Dror center at Dzielna 34, where Yitzhak Zuckerman was staying, with the news that Kaplan had been arrested by the Gestapo. They had come looking for him at Landau's carpentry shop while he was away, and when he returned they whisked him away in their car. Frantic efforts began to try and free him by organizing bribe money. Breslaw was rushing through the streets of the ghetto on this mission when he was stopped by a passing German car, and after being searched, was shot on the spot. On the very same day, ZOB suffered a further blow. Reginka Shneiderman was transferring the meager weapons store that ZOB had assembled during the previous few weeks, from its hiding place at Mila 63 to Dzielna 34. She was stopped in the street, the weapons were discovered, and she was shot.[16] Kaplan was shot after being held in the Pawiak prison for a few days.[17] Little over a month after its foundation, ZOB was crippled. Part of its leadership was dead, including the two leaders of Hashomer Hatzair in the ghetto, and its weapons were gone. ZOB had fallen apart, and the deportations continued.

---

16 Lubetkin, *Biymei chilayon u-mered*, 85–86.
17 Zuckerman, *A Surplus of Memory*, 199–201.

During the fourth phase of the deportations, which lasted from September 6 to September 10, the Germans adopted a new method. Each workshop was allotted a quota of workers who would be immune from deportation, and all Jews still in the ghetto were ordered to assemble in a few of the streets adjoining the *Umschlagplatz* for a giant selection. Jews were chased out of their homes into the *"kessel"* (cauldron), as the selection area came to be called, where the "non-productive elements," doomed to extermination, were separated out and sent off to Treblinka. Close to 40,000 men, women, and children were picked out of the *"kessel"* for shipment to Treblinka during those five days.

A day before Kaplan's arrest, he had received an urgent visit from Irena Adamowicz. Adamowicz was a thirty-eight-year-old Polish woman who had been associated with the Polish Scout movement. She had been closely linked to the Hashomer Hatzair movement in Poland before the war, and volunteered to do courier work for them during the years of German occupation. A few months earlier, Kaplan had sent her to visit the ghettos of Vilna, Shavli, and Kaunas, to bring news from the Warsaw ghetto and messages of encouragement from the Hashomer Hatzair leadership there. She had a working understanding of Yiddish, so it was easy for her to establish contact as she moved from ghetto to ghetto.

In Vilna, Adamowicz met with Abba Kovner and also with Yosef Glazman, the two deputy commanders of the FPO. She reported to them on the establishment of the Anti-Fascist Bloc in the Warsaw ghetto. She was struck by the fact that the Vilna underground, the FPO, had included the Revisionists, whereas the Anti-Fascist Bloc in Warsaw had deliberately excluded them – a detail she shared with Glazman and Kovner. From Vilna she proceeded to Kaunas, where again she found that the underground resistance there included the Revisionists. Thereafter she traveled to Shavli, and then she returned

to Vilna. Everywhere she encouraged organizing resistance to the
Germans. Before her departure for Warsaw, in the middle of August
1942, she met with Glazman and was entrusted by him with a letter
to Dr. Wdowinski in the Warsaw ghetto. She delivered this letter to
Yosef Kaplan when she met him, a day before he was arrested, asking him to pass it on to Wdowinski. In case the letter was lost or
not delivered, Glazman made Irena Adamowicz commit the letter's
contents to memory. The letter never reached Wdowinski.

Glazman's letter, as recounted by Adamowicz, addressed to "the
Revisionist comrades" in the Warsaw ghetto, called for unity in the
ranks of the Revisionists, and the creation of a united framework
with the other movements in the ghetto.

These were the main points of Glazman's letter, as remembered
by Adamowicz after the war:

1. *Unity in the ranks of the Revisionist movement.*
You should strengthen yourselves internally [*Zollen zich in-
erlich shterken*].

You must examine yourselves regarding the questions: Are
you acting in accordance with your ideology, the real and true
one, which realizes the idea of Trumpeldor? Are you going to
the limit, achieving in your actions all that is possible? Are
your actions characterized by determination and clear thinking [*inerliche feier*, internal fire]? Do you avoid splitting of the
ranks [*zershpliterungen*, splintering] and personal rivalry in
the movement?

After self-examination the conclusions must be drawn, to
arrive at solidarity of thought, human closeness, comradeship,
and mutual assistance – as if you are members of a single family. You must be united not only on an ideological basis and in
light of action in the public interest, but also with an internal
unity that evolves in the crucible of daily work and mutual as-

sistance. These principles must be applied in facing the daily challenges that confront you, and when facing matters of the highest importance; but always in all situations people must be drawn closer together....

2. *It is imperative to turn to other movements and offer them cooperation and assistance.*

Your people have to approach other movements in the Zionist camp. The achievements and the uniqueness that are typical of you must become part of the entire nation, as happened in Lithuania, where more than once we became a "fist of steel" of the people, a fist that not only defended a particular group, but everybody (for example, the Jewish police in Kaunas, the movement of partisans). Of course this does not involve "surrender" by the Revisionist camp, rather on the contrary, strengthening its position among the people. Because you will enrich all the values that exist among the people by the addition of our strengthened and crystallized views.

There is no need to wait until somebody proposes some kind of agreement, but rather after you have strengthened yourselves internally, take the initiative and be the first to turn to other movements with a proposal for cooperation and mutual assistance [*aroisgeen zu den anderen bewegungen*, reach out to the other movements].[18]

Pawel Frenkel, the commander of ZZW, had judiciously established himself in a multi-story apartment building that bordered on the northern ghetto wall, at 7 Muranowska Street. In a building that seemed to have been abandoned, hidden from the outside world, he and his fighters remained untouched by the great deportation.

---

18 Lohamei Hagetaot Archives no. 94 (3507).

Many of them were armed and were prepared to kill anyone coming after them. They remained unhurt during the entire deportation operation.[19]

Frenkel knew that the IZL would need access to the world outside the ghetto, and therefore a tunnel would have to be dug under the ghetto wall. During the days of the great deportation his fighters dug a fifty-meter-long tunnel from the cellar of the building at 7 Muranowska Street, under Muranowska Street, to the cellar of the building at 6 Muranowska Street, which was on the other side of the ghetto wall. They also took control of a fourth-floor apartment in that building. The tunnel and the apartment would serve as a lifeline and hideaway for the ZZW in the months to follow.

Cezary Ketling, an officer in the Polish underground who entered the ghetto through the tunnel, provided a description:

> Cutting across Muranowska Street, it connected the ghetto with the "Aryan" side. Its beginning was in the cellar of house number 7 of that street, its end, across the street, in house number 6. On the side of the uneven numbers, just next to the sidewalk, a high wall made of red bricks, covered on top with broken glass and cut wires, separated in a totally mechanical way two quarters of the same city, two living organs of one organism. A tram line ran through the middle of the street; further on there were only a few blocks of houses. Beyond them, the "free" wide world, so close, but strange; free, but deceiving in its appearance of freedom.
>
> That was the world to which the tunnel on Muranowska Street, dug with the utmost self-sacrifice and effort, was supposed to lead. That free world, threatening in its foreignness, was the

---

19 For precautions taken by ZZW during the great deportation see Landau, *Caged*, 123.

one to which the hopes of the young fighters were directed. Their motto was: to eradicate the passivity and inactivity of their own community, and to stand up to the impending threat of destruction with bravery and fortitude.

The work of digging the tunnel had to be well hidden from the crowds of people who were constantly milling about the yard of the house. The terrible overcrowding of the Jewish population in the ghetto resulted in masses of people constantly flowing through the streets and houses like a river that had overflown its banks. The digging of the tunnel in these conditions involved thousands of difficulties. Only a limited number of people could have access to the tunnel's one-meter diameter entrance, and speed was a dire necessity. Every day, ever more threatening news of the imminent total liquidation of the ghetto was heard.

In the beginning, the work was directed by specialist engineers. The rubble and water flowing into the tunnel were taken out with buckets under the cover of night. The hard pavement of the street, deeply pressed into the ground, was unyielding. Since it was impossible to use modern digging methods because of the necessity to keep quiet, the earth had to be cleared away by hand. And in the middle of the work the diggers came upon a real obstacle: a water pipe. The specialists declared that the work could not be continued. It was impossible to get around the water pipe since it obstructed the tunnel in its center. The road on top might collapse, and underneath, it was filled with subsoil water. The specialists therefore discontinued their work.

But those who measured their might according to their goals, and not their goals according to their might, did not stop. There were about sixty of them. The soul of the group and the initiator of the building of the tunnel was Szlamek. Extremely talented and resourceful, he was only about twenty years old. His fervor, enthusiasm, energy, and self-sacrifice influenced everyone around him. He was inexhaustible in his work, a poet without the knowledge of the art of writing, a self-taught man – a virtuoso. He composed songs and played the piano beautifully. Szlamek, although a layman, had better technical knowledge than the engineers. He was an outstanding human being who ultimately became the hero of the tunnel. None of the obstacles could break him. He continued, and completed the building of the tunnel. The tunnel was the crown of his short and beautiful life, which came to an end in his heroic fight against the Germans during the April 1943 uprising in the ghetto.

This was the tunnel through which I entered the ghetto for my appointment that I had made in December 1942 with the representatives of the Jewish organization. Those were the first days of January 1943. The tunnel could only be used under the cover of night. For that purpose, it was necessary to be in the house of the yard watchman before the police curfew, and to wait for an opportunity to go down into the cellar. It was necessary to walk across quite a large yard, at dusk or even later, when none of the inhabitants would be descending into their cellars. The entrance to the tunnel was from one of the cellars, which had been transformed into a bunker. After lifting the cover of the entrance to the tunnel (it was covered with earth to hide its location), you would enter the tunnel on all fours. It was lit with electrical light and padded with blankets.[20]

---

20   Lazar Litai, *Matzada shel Varsha*, 173–75.

It was during the great deportation that Jan Karski, the Polish resistance fighter, decided that he had to see the ghetto himself before leaving for London as a courier for the Polish underground to the Polish government in exile, so that his description of Poland under German occupation would be complete. But how was he going to enter and leave the ghetto? If he was to avoid being caught by the German dragnet as he entered the ghetto, he would have to use the ZZW tunnel under Muranowska Street. David Landau was chosen to lead Karski into the ghetto through the tunnel.

This is his story:

> On the second day without deportation [August 29], I received the order to present myself immediately to the administration of ZZW at Muranowska 7–9. I was not told why I had been called up; I was told to wait and was in the meantime introduced to a man who had, like me, been called to Muranowska. He must have belonged to an underground group but I did not know him, and he was introduced to me only by his first name, Marek. I never met him again. I do not recall if it was Rodal [Frenkel's senior assistant] or one of the Lopata brothers [ZZW fighters] who told us to be patient and make ourselves comfortable. He warned us that we may be waiting many hours for nothing. There was an unusual coming and going of people who were not known to me. In the small office of our leader Frenkel, every quarter of an hour someone would come, the door would close for some minutes, the door would open, the messenger would leave, to be replaced after a short interval by another messenger. We sat and waited.
>
> Some time in the early afternoon, after a messenger had been closeted with Frenkel for more than the usual minutes, Frenkel called us to the door of his cubicle: "Has either of you a personal weapon?" he asked. I had a Belgian revolver, which

was my personal property. I do not recall if my companion had a weapon or not. "Give them each a light automatic and two grenades," Frenkel ordered the store man, "and send them out to me." With these words he locked up his office and left for the outside. We received a light automatic pistol each with loaded magazines, a spare magazine for each and two hand grenades. Frenkel was waiting for us in the passage of the building: "You'll take up positions across the road on the 'Aryan' side, in the street on both sides of number six." Pointing to me he continued: "You'll take up your position on the corner of Muranowska and Sierakowska streets, and you," he turned to my companion, "will take the Przebieg and Muranowska corner. At those corners you will wait for two people. One of them will look like an aristocrat with a newspaper in his hand and a pipe in his mouth and the other will be dressed rather poorly. Whoever sees them coming will signal to the other about it. From that moment on, the one who sees the two men will pay attention only to the visitors, while the other will guard the area to make sure that it is safe to lead the visitors to the bunker entrance, and watch out that there is not some unexpected danger coming from somewhere. If anything should look suspicious you'll go towards your guests and in passing give them a sign to ignore you and go on. If the area is clear it will be the duty of the one on whose side they come to bring them through the tunnel from the 'Aryan' side to the ghetto. That's all." Frenkel did not repeat his instructions and, not even asking if we had understood, he turned and left us.

We went back to the interior of Muranowska 7–9, down the steps of a cellar, opened the trapdoor to the tunnel and began to crawl towards the Aryan end. After the first few steps, my companion called back to me to bend down. The tunnel became a narrow passage not much more than a meter high

and not wide enough for two people to crawl side by side...
the project had been undertaken out of desperation for some
safe passage. It had involved a number of city engineers who
knew what lay under the surface. Unfortunately one of the
larger sewer pipes ran right along the street and the tunnel
had to be dug in a bend down under it. To make it easier to
crawl through, the tunnel had to be elongated as it bent.... At
one stage the engineers had been ready to abandon the work
but on the insistence of the Jewish side and the help of children aged twelve to fourteen years who became human moles,
the tunnel was finished. Now we were supposed to bring our
guests through this tunnel into the ghetto and, obviously, back
out again.

...They came from the street I was observing. I recognized
the face of Dr. Feiner whom I had already seen once.... His
companion was a tall, rather slim-looking younger man, not
much older than I.... Nobody spoke throughout the whole
time we were making our way through the tunnel, except
when I called back instructions.... When we reached the ghetto side, the difficulty of the journey showed on their faces.[21]

Karski and Feiner were led to a meeting with Menahem Kirshenbaum
in one of the abandoned buildings in the ghetto, where Karski
received a briefing about the deportations and the condition of the
remaining Jewish population in the ghetto. After the war, Karski
wrote: "What I learned at the meetings, and later, when I was taken
to see the facts for myself, was horrible beyond description.... Never
anywhere in the history of mankind, never in the realm of human

---

21 Landau, *Caged*, 132–34.

relations, did anything occur to compare with what was inflicted on the Jewish population of Poland."[22]

When Karski arrived in London, and thereafter Washington, and met with Allied leaders, his report of the extermination of Polish Jewry was met with disbelief that bordered on indifference.

On August 8, Gerhart Riegner, who worked in the office of the World Jewish Congress in Geneva, received information from a German industrialist about plans discussed "in Hitler's headquarters for the extermination of all Jews in Nazi-occupied lands." He sent this news in a telegram to Sidney Silverman in London, a member of parliament and the head of the British section of the World Jewish Congress. Silverman sent the cable on to Rabbi Stephen S. Wise in New York, head of the World Jewish Congress. The news also reached the offices of the Jewish Agency in Jerusalem. The American Undersecretary of State, Sumner Welles, who had also received the cable through the U.S. consul in Geneva, asked Wise not to release the information until an attempt could be made to confirm its contents. Wise, the leading American Zionist of the time, decided to withhold the terrifying news from the public. Only in November 1942, three months later, did Wise inform the press of the Riegner cable. During those months hundreds of thousands of Jews were being killed, month by month.

Warsaw's Jews had believed that the world was unaware of what was happening to them, and that if the world only knew, the Germans would not be able to continue with their mass murder. Now they knew better. In the Warsaw ghetto, Chaim Kaplan wrote in his diary: "A joke is making the rounds: Rabbi Stephen S. Wise is help-

---

22 Jan Karski, *Story of a Secret State* (Boston: Houghton Mifflin, 1944), 320–21.

ing. He has ordered the American Jews to say the memorial prayer for the departed souls of the Polish Jewry. His foresight is accurate."[23]

On the evening of September 15, leading members of Dror and Hashomer Hatzair gathered to mourn the loss of Kaplan and Breslaw. They assembled at Mila 63, the apartment building in which the workers of Landau's carpentry shop were lodging. One of those present was Miriam Heinsdorf, who had been Kaplan's companion during the previous few years. The tragic events had brought the leadership of the two youth movements closer to each other – they were now a single bereaved family. Miriam Heinsdorf sang a melancholy Russian song in memory of her beloved.

Their thoughts turned to the future. The feeling was one of desperation and hopelessness. Two of their leaders had been slain, their few weapons were gone, and the daily roundups of men, women, and children were continuing amid complete passivity. Was there still a chance for organized resistance to the Germans, or had they missed the opportunity? Did they have the strength to begin all over again? Ideas that arose from despair were put forth; some suggested attacking the Germans with their bare hands the following day – at least they would die fighting. But ultimately more sober views prevailed, and they decided that an attempt must be made to rebuild a united resistance organization.[24]

For the last day of the deportation, the Germans chose September 21, which was Yom Kippur, the Day of Atonement – the holiest day of the Jewish year. The final victims were members of the Jewish police and their families. Between July 22, the Ninth of Av, and September 21, Yom Kippur, approximately 270,000 of Warsaw's Jews

23 Chaim A. Kaplan, *Scroll of Agony: The Warsaw Diary of Chaim A. Kaplan* (New York: Macmillan, 1965), 287.
24 Zuckerman, *A Surplus of Memory*, 214–16, and *Ba-geto u-va-mered*, 80–81.

had been sent to the Treblinka gas chambers. Most of the great Jewish community of Warsaw was exterminated during that period.

On September 24, 1942, SS-Untersturmfuehrer Karl Brandt proclaimed the end of the "Resettlement Action" in the Warsaw ghetto. Only 50,000 Jews remained, anticipating the next action that would put an end to the Warsaw ghetto.

Chapter 5

Two Resistance Organizations

ZOB had lost two of its leaders – Yosef Kaplan and Shmuel Breslaw – during the deportations. Another, Mordechai Tennenbaum, had left for Bialystok to organize resistance there. Their meager store of arms had been lost, but the decision had been made by those that remained of the decimated ZOB to reconstitute their Jewish Fighting Organization. They were reinforced by Mordechai Anielewicz, who had been away from Warsaw on a mission for his movement, Hashomer Hatzair, during the time of the deportations, and had now returned to the ghetto. After the loss of Kaplan and Breslaw, and in the absence of Arye Wilner, who had been delegated to work on the "Aryan" side to make contact with the Polish underground, Anielewicz was now accepted as the senior leader of Hashomer Hatzair in the ghetto. Wilner had in the meantime successfully made contact with the Polish underground and was hopeful about receiving assistance from them.

Yitzhak Zuckerman of Dror, the other movement involved in ZOB, thought it might be possible to bring Left Poalei Zion into ZOB, as it was ideologically close to Hashomer Hatzair and Dror. At the end of October, he initiated a meeting at the Hashomer Hatzair headquarters at Mila 61, with Anielewicz and three members of Left Po'alei Zion, Hersh Berlinski, Pola Elster, and Hersh Wasser. It was around the core of these three movements – Dror, Hashomer Hatzair, and Left Po'lai Zion – that he planned to rebuild ZOB.

Berlinski, Elster, and Wasser were a few years older than Zuckerman and Anielewicz. Feeling themselves more mature, even more responsible, they faced the enthusiasm and determination of the younger generation, their orthodox Marxist thinking giving rigidity to their arguments. Sitting in the decimated ghetto, most of whose population had been sent to Treblinka, they launched into discussions and intricate arguments still true to their traditional ideological positions that dated from pre-war times.

They discussed the situation in the ghetto and plans for its defense. They agreed that a fighting organization should be established to defend the ghetto, and that measures should be taken against the Jewish police and other collaborators with the Germans. However, sharp differences of opinion arose when it came to the suggested structure of leadership. Left Po'alei Zion was a political party rather than a youth movement, and their representatives insisted that a political committee representing the political parties and youth movements in the ghetto be formed to oversee the military organization and make the principal decisions. Anielewicz and Zuckerman were strongly opposed to having two levels of leadership. The memory of the ill-fated assembly of political representatives when the deportations began, on the day of Czerniaków's suicide, was still fresh in their minds. The outcome of that meeting had been passive acceptance of the deportations to Treblinka. Anielewicz and Zuckerman had little respect for the polical parties and felt that involving their leadership would just lead to a repetition of what happened before the deportation, when the parties argued endlessly and ultimately did nothing. They maintained that two levels of leadership would result in useless discussions and only obstruct the work of the organization. And they felt that the parties had no right to tell them what to do. Only the youth could be counted on; only they would do what needed to be done. There had to be a single military leadership, they argued. There was no more time for discussion and argument, they had to get started.

Berlinski and his comrades stood their ground, insisting that Zuckerman and Anielewicz were mistaken. The political parties might have made some mistakes in the past, they argued, but it was not for the youth movements to judge them. The political parties were responsible for leading the political struggle; it was not the job of the youth movements. The Jewish masses had not placed their trust in the youth movements, and would not do so in the future. "Don't imagine that just because you have two broken revolvers you can become so presumptuous and ignore everybody else," Berlinski argued. "A group that has weapons and trains in their use will be striving to use them at the first opportunity; it is just such a desire which could lead to irresponsible actions, which have to be prevented. A political authority will correctly judge the appropriate time for military action. There must not be an ill-timed action that will bring about an early liquidation of the ghetto. Even if we assume that the ghetto will be destroyed, and we shall die, that does not mean that we are accountable to no one. We are responsible for our actions to the Jewish masses in the world and to our comrades abroad. We do not want our graves stoned because we took irresponsible actions. If you do not agree that the political parties should control the fighting organization, then you are setting conditions that will prevent us from taking part." It was finally agreed that they would return to consult with their party's institutions.[1]

When they resumed negotiations, the representatives from Left Po'alei Zion reported that the party had confirmed their demand for the establishment of a political committee to oversee the activity of the military organization and to take the principal decisions. They were about to part on that note, when Zuckerman and Anielewicz realized that if this was the position of Left Po'alei Zion, it would also

---

1   See Berlinski, *Zichroines*, 168–71; and Zuckerman, *A Surplus of Memory,* 247–49.

be the position of the other political parties, and if they did not give in to this demand it would be impossible to set up a broad-based resistance organization, so they capitulated. They agreed to the establishment of a two-tier leadership that would include a political committee in addition to a military command. The political committee would be called the Jewish National Committee (Zydowski Komitet Narodowy – ZKN). At that meeting, the foundation was laid for the reconstituted Jewish Fighting Organization, ZOB, which would eventually come to include almost all the political parties and youth movements in the ghetto, excepting only the Revisionists and the Orthodox religious groups. It was agreed that the Bund should be approached to join ZOB, but the inclusion of Revisionists was not even discussed. Moreover, it was clear that once the Bund joined, they would veto the inclusion of the Revisionists.

The Bund had lost many of its members in the deportations. One of its leaders, Maurycy Orzech, had left the ghetto for "Aryan" Warsaw during the great deportations. It was Orzech who, in previous discussions about resistance in the ghetto, had insisted that the Bund was committed to joint action with the Polish Socialists and would therefore not join a Jewish resistance organization. With him outside of the ghetto, the Bund was prepared to show greater flexibility – the influence of its younger generation, which supported joining a united resistance organization, became dominant. On October 15, at a meeting of Bund activists in the ghetto, the principal decision was taken to join a united fighting organization.[2]

At about that time, the first good news began arriving from the war fronts. On November 4, 1942, Montgomery had broken through at El Alamein and was chasing Rommel's Afrika Korps across Libya. On November 8, 1942, the Allies had landed forces in Morocco and

---

2   Marek Edelman, *The Ghetto Fights* (New York: American Representation of the General Jewish Workers' Union of Poland, 1946), 28.

Algeria, while the Red Army had halted the German army's advance at Stalingrad. The turning point in the war seemed to have come – what Churchill called the "end of the beginning." What remained of the Warsaw ghetto was ripe for resistance.

The decision taken by the Bund leadership in October to join a united resistance organization was implemented the following month. In November 1942, the organizers of ZOB met with representatives of the Bund. Mordechai Anielewicz, Yitzhak Zuckerman, and Hersh Berlinski, now joined by Yohanan Morgenstern of Po'alei Zion, explained the organization of ZOB, its aims and missions, and proposed that the Bund join the ZOB. The Bund was represented by Abrasha Blum and Berek Shneidmill. A lengthy discussion ensued, and finally the Bund representatives gave their agreement to join ZOB, to be integrated as Bund units alongside the others. However, they were not prepared to take their place in the political committee, the ZKN, which was to guide the ZOB in its actions. This, they explained, would be contrary to their commitments to the Polish working class. To overcome this problem they suggested that a committee be set up that would coordinate political matters between the Bund and the ZKN. Each member of this Coordinating Committee (called Zydowsi Komisja Koordinacyja, or ZKK) would be entitled to veto decisions taken by the ZKN. Abrasha Blum felt that this would make things look right – the Bund's ideological constraints would be satisfied. It was something he thought they could justify to their Polish Socialist colleagues and, at the same time, be workable.

Thus, after lengthy and intricate negotiations, a rather cumbersome organizational superstructure was agreed on that would provide the Bund with the appearance of acting independently. The Coordinating Committee, ZKK, charged with coordinating between the Bund and ZKN, would be composed of one representative of the Bund and a representative of the ZKN. The Bund representative would have veto power over its decisions. ZOB, the military organization, would be responsible to this political superstructure, in which the Bund would, in effect, have veto power. Aside from permitting the Bund to join ZOB, this arrangement had the additional advantage of allowing Arye Wilner, when contacting the Polish underground in "Aryan" Warsaw, to pretend that ZOB was an organization that included all the political parties in the ghetto. This was important since some in the Polish underground had voiced concerns that he represented no more than a small group that might be dominated by Communists.[3]

The time had come to staff the leading positions in the political committees, the ZKK and ZKN, and the fighting organization, the ZOB. Since the structure was political, based on the parties and youth movements participating, the committees and the ZOB command had to be staffed so as to be representative of these groups. The principal committee, the Jewish National Committee (ZKN), was headed by Menahem Kirshenbaum of the General Zionists, Yitzhak Zuckerman of Dror, and Yohanan Morgenstern of Po'alei Zion. Kirshenbaum was also appointed to the Coordinating Committee (ZKK), where he met with the Bund's senior official, Abrasha Blum, while Zuckerman acted as its secretary.

A number of sub-committees were established for both the Coordinating Committee and the Jewish National Committee, giving all parties, including the Communists, the impression that they would participate in making the important decisions. As it turned out, these cumbersome committees were left with almost nothing to do as the hour for the uprising approached.

The really important decisions concerned the staffing of the Command of the ZOB, the military organization. Here too political considerations were the determining factor. In any case, the lead-

---

3   Berlinski, *Zichroines*, 172; and Zuckerman, *A Surplus of Memory*, 221.

ing personalities had no prior military training or experience that would qualify them for the positions. Unlike Betar, the Socialist Zionist youth movements had in past years not accented the need for military preparedness or provided any military or paramilitary training to their members. Political considerations thus determined that leading representatives of the main participating groups constitute the ZOB Command: Yitzhak Zuckerman of Dror, Mordechai Anielewicz of Hashomer Hatzair, Berek Shneidmill of the Bund, Yohanan Morgenstern of Po'alei Zion, Hersh Berlinski of Left Po'alei Zion, and Michael Rosenfeld of the Communists.[4]

When the ZOB was first founded on July 28, 1942, the founders had not seen the need to appoint a commander. It was assumed that decisions would be taken collectively by the members of the Command, who were all considered equal. Zuckerman had been no more or less important than Kaplan or the other members of the Command. This seemed quite natural to them as members of Socialist youth movements, who had no military tradition and looked with disdain on the paramilitary organization of Betar and its military hierarchy. Now, however, with the addition of the political parties, the Bund, and the Communists, there suddenly seemed to be a need to appoint a commander of the ZOB. Although, at the time, the assumption was that decisions would be taken collectively and therefore not too much attention should be given to the selection of the person to fill the position of commander, ultimately it was that position that would prove of great importance.

Zuckerman had been a driving force in the establishment of a resistance organization in the ghetto, was one of the organizers of the Anti-Fascist Bloc, and had been a member of the original ZOB Command set up in July. It was natural that he be chosen to command the reconstituted ZOB. But Anielewicz wanted the job, and he

---

4   See Zuckerman, *Ba-geto u-va-mered*, 108, and *A Surplus of Memory*, 222.

proposed himself for it at a meeting of the Command. Zuckerman was disappointed, convinced that he was the natural candidate for the position, but decided not to make an issue of it. In any case, Zuckerman was on both the Coordinating Committee with the Bund and on the Jewish National Committee, and felt confident that he would be able to make his influence felt.[5] Since none of the other four saw themselves taking the position, Anielewicz was chosen as commander.

The members of the Command were assigned areas of responsibility. Zuckerman was given the responsibility for the weapons store, which gave him control of any planned action. Berlinski was put in charge of planning, Shneidmill of intelligence, and Morgenstern of finance, while Rosenfeld was left without any specific responsibility. The Bund replaced Shneidmill in due time with Marek Edelman. But it was an inner circle that took the important decisions; they met frequently and consisted of Zuckerman, Lubetkin, and Anielewicz, sometimes joined by Miriam Heinsdorf, who had been Yosef Kaplan's companion.[6] Arye Wilner of Hashomer Hatzair, who for the past few months had been attempting to establish contacts in "Aryan" Warsaw, was appointed to represent ZOB outside of the ghetto; Adolf Berman, of Left Po'alei Zion, was to represent the Jewish National Committee there. Leon Feiner, a member of the Bund, who had not been living in the ghetto, was going to continue to represent the Bund in "Aryan" Warsaw.[7]

Mordechai Anielewicz was twenty-three years old at the time of his appointment as commander of ZOB. He was of medium build, with a narrow face and long hair. Together with his girlfriend, Mira

---

5 Zuckerman, *A Surplus of Memory*, 228–29.

6 Zuckerman, *Ba-geto u-va-mered*, 108, and *A Surplus of Memory*, 229.

7 Zuckerman, *A Surplus of Memory*, 220; and Berman, *Mi-yemei ha-mah-teret*, 103.

Fruchner, some years younger than he, he had returned to Warsaw from the seeming safety of Vilna in 1940 to take up a leadership position in Hashomer Hatzair in German-occupied Poland. He had been a member of the Hashomer Hatzair leadership in the city of Warsaw before the war, but in the ghetto his Hashomer Hatzair comrades Kaplan and Breslaw were recognized as senior to him. But now they were gone.

Born to a poor family in Warsaw, Anielewicz had joined Betar at the age of twelve. Some years later, while in high school, he left Betar and joined Hashomer Hatzair, preferring their Marxist approach to Zionism. Among his comrades he was considered a "leftist," with considerable rhetorical skills in debating questions of ideology. He was a voracious reader, and during the early years in the ghetto he used to come to Ringelblum to ask for books on Jewish history and economics. During the first three years under German occupation, he devoted himself to intense educational and cultural activities among the Hashomer Hatzair youth. Although seemingly quiet and restrained, he was nevertheless ambitious and determined. When ZOB was reconstituted in October, he made it clear that he saw himself as commander of the organization, even though he was four years younger than Zuckerman and had not participated in the previous ZOB organization. After having become the commander of ZOB he expressed his regret for the years invested in cultural and educational activities. "We should have trained the youth in the use of weapons and educated them to take revenge on the greatest enemy of the Jews and the human race," he said.[8] He was about the

---

8   Ringelblum, *Ktavim aharonim*, 45–52. Also Zvi Lichtenberg and Sarah
    Yutan, *Mordechai Anielewicz ke-hanich Betar* [Mordechai Anielewicz as a
    member of Betar], no.4 (Tel Aviv: Pirsumim Muzeon ha-Lohamim ve-ha-
    Partizanim, 1968), 11.

same age as Pawel Frenkel. These two youngsters were destined to lead the Warsaw Ghetto Uprising.

The ZOB at that time consisted of about a hundred members, organized in groups of five, each group composed of members of the same political organization or youth movement. Its arsenal of weapons was made up of sticks, knives, brass knuckles, chemicals for the manufacture of explosives, and two pistols.[9] Neither the ZOB Command nor the two political committees and their various sub-committees included Revisionists. No thought was given by the leaders of ZOB at that time to include the Revisionists or to coordinate ZOB's actions with them.

The ZOB's structure was based on combat units organized according to the political affiliations of the units' members. This lent coherence to the organization and guaranteed mutual trust among its members, but in effect it excluded not only the Revisionists, but all those who wanted to participate in the resistance to the Germans but were not affiliated with a specific party or youth movement.

On the other hand, the IZL leadership opened its ranks to all those eager to fight the Germans, whether or not they were affiliated with any party or movement, especially if they already had acquired weapons of their own. They adopted the Polish name Zydowski Zwiazek Wojskowy (ZZW) for their organization, and as their weapons' store increased, they began recruiting new members. By that time, there were various small groups in the ghetto who had sprung up, succeeded in finding weapons, and were intent on defending themselves should they be cornered by the Germans. They came to be known as *vilde,* "wild" – unaffiliated groups that were not under any central control.

The ZZW was commanded by Pawel Frenkel, assisted by Leon Rodal. They had been strengthened by members of Betar who had

---

9   Berlinski, *Zichroines,* 172–73.

returned to the ghetto from Hrubieszow in June. Three of them, Alek Halberstein, Salek Hasenshprung, and Yitzhak Byelewski, joined Frenkel, Rodal, and Natan Shultz to constitute the ZZW Command. Rodal had been active in the Revisionist organization; the others had been senior leaders of Betar before the war. Though enlistment of non-affiliated fighters had considerably strengthened the organization, its leadership continued to be made up of men and women who had grown up in the Revisionist movement. Unlike ZOB, ZZW did not have a political committee to supervise the military organization, but there was an advisory group led by Dr. David Wdowinski, which included Leon Rodal, and Dr. Michael Strykowski, who had been among the leaders of the Revisionist-affiliated youth organization, Masada, before the war.[10]

Had there been a leading personality in the Warsaw ghetto, capable of inspiring the people, rising above past ideological rivalries and enmities that had become completely irrelevant by now – with the charisma to mobilize followers from all parts of the ghetto's society – he might have been able to lead resistance to the Germans during the great deportation. But the leading personalities in Jewish life had all left Warsaw as the German army approached in September 1939. Under these circumstances it was inevitable that the initiative for organizing resistance to the Germans would come from the youth movements and their leaders. Unlike the vast majority of the ghetto's inhabitants, these movements had an organized, devoted, and disciplined membership and recognized leaders. They commanded the fierce loyalty of their members. Until the great deportation, the young men and women who led these movements were looked upon by the adult representatives of the parties and movements in the ghetto as brash and immature, and their ideas for organizing

---

10 Halperin, *Helka shel Betar be-Mered ha-Geto,* 16.

resistance were not taken seriously. But when the failure of the established adult leadership in the ghetto became obvious during the great deportation, the leadership of the youth movements gradually came to the fore.

The youth movements were wedded to the ideological concepts on which they were founded many years previously, and persisted in ideological rivalries and animosity from past years. The divide between the Socialist-oriented movements, whether Zionist or Bund, and the Revisionists could not be bridged in the Warsaw ghetto, even as it became clear that the Germans were out to kill each and every Jew, paying no heed to their political affiliation. Although the IZL in Palestine, already in the days of David Raziel, tried to establish itself as a military organization not attached to any political movement, as far as the Socialist Zionists in Palestine were concerned, it was just another Revisionist organization. In the Warsaw ghetto, as well, the leadership of the Bund and the Socialist Zionist groups insisted on regarding it as a Revisionist group. And so, almost inevitably, two resistance organizations developed in the ghetto: ZZW, led by Pawel Frenkel, and ZOB, led by Mordechai Anielewicz.

After the great deportation they were fully aware of each other's existence. Desultory meetings were held to see if the two organizations dedicated to a common cause could find a way to unite their forces. But the ideological differences of past years, completely irrelevant under present circumstances, prevented it. The hostility of the Bund toward the Revisionists, whom they considered as Fascists, was particularly fierce. The Bund would probably not have joined ZOB had the Revisionists been among its members. Once the Bund was represented in the Command of ZOB and held veto power on principal decisions in the Coordinating Committee – specially set up to accommodate their ideological constraints unity – between ZOB and ZZW had become nearly impossible.

In Vilna, Yosef Glazman, the Betar leader, together with Abba Kovner of Hashomer Hatzair, had been among the founders of FPO, the United Partisan Organization. After the massacres at Ponar, Kovner insisted that there was no difference anymore between Jews belonging to different organizations and movements, and that the Germans were out to kill them all. There, the Bund had only later joined an already existing organization. But in Warsaw, because of the aversion of the Socialist Zionist parties, Dror and Hashomer Hatzair, to including the Revisionists in their original plans for a Jewish resistance organization, the sequence had been reversed. There was an added structural problem in that the ZOB was organized as a collection of fighting units, each composed of members of the same political party or youth movement. ZZW had accepted into its ranks men and women who were eager to fight the Germans but were not affiliated with any movement, in addition to the core that had come from Betar or the Revisionists. How would they all be integrated into the ZOB organizational structure? Moreover, the ZOB leadership was concerned that among such unaffiliated members of ZZW there might be Gestapo agents who would find their way into ZOB.

The leaders of each organization viewed the other critically. ZOB saw itself as being composed of the elite of Jewish youth in the ghetto, of those who had gone through years of ideological indoctrination, imbued with the ideals of Socialism. They saw in ZZW Fascists, or those inclined to Fascism, to whom had now been added a motley crew of "porters, smugglers, and thieves."[11] There was little enthusiasm for mixing their ideological purity with these people, even though they were facing a common enemy.

---

11   Marian Apfelbaum, *Retour sur le Ghetto de Varsovie* [Return to the Warsaw Ghetto] (Paris: Editions Odile Jacob), 21, quoting Marek Edelman in an interview with Anka Grupinska in 2000.

The leadership of ZZW saw themselves as fighters who had received years of military training and indoctrination in Betar and IZL, and who had begun preparing themselves for resistance to the Germans long before the others had even entertained the thought. They felt that the fighters of ZOB were no more than amateurs when it came to military matters, and that their organization was based on political representation rather than on military experience and ability. They were better trained and better armed than ZOB. Uniting the forces of ZZW and ZOB under a command made up of those most experienced and capable in military matters seemed the right way to go. But to put themselves under the authority of the ZOB "politicians" and their political committees was likely, in their opinion, to prejudice the very cause they were preparing for.

ZOB, commanded by Anielewicz, was a strong, coherent organization by virtue of its organizational structure. The fighters in each combat unit trusted each other and were loyal to their unit commander. In the ZOB Command were represented the largest youth movements and parties that constituted ZOB, and their members had the feeling that they had a voice in running the organization. This was ZOB's strength, but it also served as a serious constraint in its development. The majority of the ghetto's inhabitants were not affiliated with any party or organization, and many of those who wanted to participate in resistance to the Germans felt that this was a matter for all Jews, regardless of political affiliation. After the great deportation, many among the remaining Jews in the ghetto, seeing the end approaching, began preparing to resist the Germans. Not only did many prepare subterranean bunker hideouts throughout the ghetto, but some also began acquiring weapons and ammunition for themselves, their families, and friends. When they sought to join ZOB, they generally found that the party-oriented structure of ZOB was unable to accommodate them.

Some of those who had organized on their own eventually found their way to ZZW, which, although led by Revisionists, did not restrict membership to members of Betar or the Revisionist organization. In time ZZW, commanded by Frenkel, became a resistance organization led by members of Betar, but many of its members had had no prior affiliation with the Revisionists or any other movement.

Among those who had had no prior affiliation with the Revisionists who joined ZZW were Dr. Ryszard Walewski and the group he led; Jack Eisner and his friends, who during the uprising participated in the fighting at Muranowski Square; and the group led by Simha Korngold in the Toebbens-Schultz Workshop area, who accepted the ZZW invitation to join its ranks.

Chapter 6

Preparing for the Uprising

The Jewish resistance to the German program to exterminate the Jewish people pitted an essentially unarmed civilian population – men, women, and children – against the SS and their Ukrainian, Latvian, and Lithuanian auxiliaries, and the German army. They, in turn, were backed by Hitler's government bureaucracy, dedicated to the extermination of the Jews at all costs and right until the last day of the war. Meaningful resistance required an organization and leadership. Even where such organization and leadership existed or was formed on the spot, German superiority in force and weapons was in any case overwhelming. Only fierce determination by the members of an organized group, not burdened by concern for the fate of families and led by men of stature, was essential for resistance to take place.

All leading personalities of the Polish Jewish community had left Poland at the outbreak of the war. The Warsaw *Judenrat* was no substitute for this leadership. It quickly revealed itself as the servile executor of the orders of the Gestapo. Avraham Levin, one of the Warsaw ghetto diarists, wrote about them shortly before the great deportation: "In our small isolated world, men who are unqualified and were never meant to head a Jewish community – the largest community in Europe – in these terrible times pushed their way to the top. That is one of the insipid consequences of war: the tragedy of the 'elite sinking and the rabble rising;' the tragedy of leaders who were not anointed to their thrones."[1]

The Jewish police in Warsaw, unlike the Jewish police in the ghettos of Kaunas and Riga, which became centers of resistance to the Germans, did the bidding of the Germans with callousness and brutality, and showed no sign of resistance. The youth organizations continued their pre-war organizational and ideological existence, their leadership maintaining their authority and commanding the loyalty of the membership. Among them, first and foremost, were the two Socialist Zionist youth movements, Hashomer Hatzair and Dror, the Revisionist youth movement Betar, and the Bund youth movement Tsukunft. Whereas the direction for the Bund youth came from the adult Bund leadership, Maurycy Orzech and Abrasha Blum, the leaders of Hashomer Hatzair in the Warsaw ghetto, Yosef Kaplan and Shmuel Breslaw, had been independent in their decisions, and Yitzhak Zuckerman was essentially not dependent on the leaders of Dror's parent organization, Po'alei Zion. The elite of the Revisionist youth in the ghetto saw themselves as soldiers in the IZL, and gave unquestioning obedience to their superiors and to Pawel Frenkel, the youngster who assumed command of the IZL in the ghetto.

The Polish underground answered to the Polish government in exile in London. That government appointed its representatives in Poland, the *delegatura*, and the military leaders, to lead the Polish underground army. No similar chain of command existed for the Jews in Poland.

The Jewish authority that might have been expected to organize rescue efforts and give guidance and instructions to Jewish resistance organizations in German-occupied Europe was the leadership

---

1   Avraham Levin, *Mipinkaso shel ha-moreh mi "Yehudiya"* [The journal of the teacher from "Yehudiya"] (Tel Aviv: Hakibbutz Hameuhad–Beit Lohamei Hagetaot, 1969), 43.

of the Jewish community in Palestine, and specifically the Jewish Agency Executive in Jerusalem, headed by David Ben-Gurion. At the beginning of the war the Jewish Agency had set up the Committee of Four – Yitzhak Gruenbaum, Eliyahu Dobkin, Moshe Haim Shapira, and Emil Shmorak, headed by Yitzhak Gruenbaum, a former leader of Polish Jewry – charged with the task of gathering information on the fate of European Jewry during the war years.

Natan Schwalb, the Geneva representative of Hehalutz, the roof organization of pioneer youth movements in the Histadrut in Palestine, was in postal communication with Tzivya Lubetkin, who headed the Hehalutz "center" in Warsaw, and with other members of Dror, Hashomer Hatzair, and Gordonia in occupied Poland; he received letters from them and sent them letters, food packages, and occasionally money. Schwalb was the only direct contact between the Jewish establishment in Palestine and the Warsaw ghetto. His extremely limited budget, provided by the Joint and the World Jewish Congress, was woefully inadequate to meet the needs of the youth movements that were in contact with him. When postal communications with Warsaw ceased with the onset of the great deportation, the news from Warsaw was relayed to him by members of youth movements in other Polish cities. In the letters from Poland, which went through German censorship, he received succinct reports in dissimulated language of the conditions prevailing there – the deportations and mass killings, and the preparations for armed resistance by ZOB. The letters were relayed to Eliyahu Dobkin, the head of the Aliyah department of the Jewish Agency in Jerusalem, and to the Histadrut executive in Tel Aviv.[2]

But neither Schwalb nor those in Palestine to whom he forwarded the letters understood fully the desperate messages that were

---

2   For a description of the activity of the Jewish liaison offices in Geneva during the war, see Cohen, *Bein "sham" le-"khan"*.

encoded in them. The feeling of those in Poland who saw in their contact with Schwalb the connection to the Zionist leadership in Palestine, was a sense of frustration, anguish, and abandonment. It was expressed in a letter to Schwalb by Tosya Altman, one of the leaders of Hashomer Hatzair in Poland, written in 1942 during the period of the deportations from the Warsaw ghetto. "You have erased us from your memory," she wrote, and continued, "I am restraining myself so as not to express the bitterness that has accumulated toward you and your friends because you have completely forgotten us. I resent the fact that you did not even help me with a few words.... It is only the certainty that we will never see each other again that brought me to write this letter.... I have only one desire: to let the world know that Israel is so sick."[3] Although the letter is phrased in personal terms and refers to "Israel who is so sick" in order to get by the German censor, it is clear that she was addressing the leadership in Palestine and describing the fate of Polish Jewry.

In August 1942, at a time when a million and a half Jews had already been killed, and at the height of the great deportation from the Warsaw ghetto, Gerhart Riegner, the World Jewish Congress representative in Geneva, sent a cable that reached Stephen Wise, president of the World Jewish Congress and the leading American Zionist, in New York. Riegner cabled that he had learned from a reliable source that Hitler had ordered the extermination by gassing of all European Jews. It was only in November, after having kept this information from the public for three months at the request of the U.S. State Department, that Wise publicly confirmed the reports of the systematic extermination of the Jews in Europe. Another million Jews were killed during this period.[4]

---

3   See Bracha Habas, *Michtavim min ha-geta'ot* [Letters from the ghettos] (Tel Aviv: Am Oved, 1943), 42–43.

4   Hilberg, *The Destruction of the European Jews*, 718–19. Also see Louis

The IZL delegation in the U.S., headed by Hillel Kook (known in the U.S. at the time as Peter Bergson) – which included Yitzhak Ben-Ami, Arye Ben-Eliezer, Shmuel Merlin, Alex Rafaeli, and Eri Jabotinsky – had concentrated on promoting the establishment of a Jewish army to fight the Germans alongside the Allies. Already in September 1942, they decided to direct their efforts to rescuing Jews caught in the German trap in Europe. This decision was based on the sporadic news coming out of Europe regarding mass killings of Jews by the Germans. When Wise finally released the contents of the Riegner cable in November, their activity to make the American public aware of what was happening to the Jews of Europe and to pressure the U.S. government to take action to help save Europe's Jews moved into high gear. In addition to full-scale advertisements in the largest newspapers in the U.S., they staged the pageant "We Will Never Die," written by the well-known writer Ben Hecht, who had been enlisted by the IZL delegation. It played in Madison Square Garden to an audience of 40,000 on March 9, 1943; the pageant thereafter toured the U.S. Many members of Congress and other prominent personalities agreed to publicly endorse the call for rescue efforts.

But here too the old political rivalries' came to the fore. The Zionist establishment, headed by Wise, was not only unwilling to combine their rescue efforts with those of the IZL delegation, but insisted on launching vicious attacks against them.

In Palestine, the Committee of Four had received reports of German acts of mass extermination, including the use of gas chambers and crematoria, but they had been skeptical of the truth of these reports and did not disseminate them publicly. Until the beginning of

---

Rapoport, *Shake Heaven and Earth* (Jerusalem: Gefen Publishing House, 1999), 64–66, for the initiatives taken by the IZL delegation in the U.S. under the leadership of Hillel Kook (aka Peter Bergson).

November 1942, the Zionist leadership and the Jewish community in Palestine were primarily concerned with the possibility of the advance of Rommel's Afrika Korps through Egypt to Palestine and the measures that needed to be taken to deal with such an eventuality.

But two events in November changed all that. At the beginning of November, Montgomery defeated Rommel at El Alamein and began chasing Rommel's forces westward, and the threat that hung over the Jewish community in Palestine was suddenly lifted. Also in November a group of sixty-nine Jews from German-occupied Europe arrived in Palestine. They were holding Palestinian British passports or certificates entitling them to enter Palestine and had been exchanged for a group of German citizens in Allied hands. Some of them had left Poland after the great deportation from the Warsaw ghetto, when the ultimate fate of those sent to Treblinka was already known. On their arrival in Palestine, they brought living testimony of the atrocities committed by the Germans against the Jews, which confirmed earlier reports of German mass killings. Face-to-face meetings with them and their testimonies finally made the Jews of Palestine fully aware of what was happening to their brothers and sisters in Europe, and aroused extreme concern and anxiety. They were shocked into deep mourning.

On November 22, 1942, the Jewish Agency Executive, for the first time since the outbreak of the war, held a meeting devoted almost exclusively to the fate of European Jewry. Eliyahu Dobkin, a member of the Committee of Four, reported on his meetings with the recent arrivals from Europe. He concluded that their reports should be accepted as true. At the end of November 1942, the Jewish Agency issued a public announcement confirming that the Germans were engaged in the systematic and methodical extermination of the Jews of Europe. A month of mourning and a fast-day were declared, and demonstrations were held. Now accusations were leveled against the Jewish Agency Executive, and specifically against

Gruenbaum, who had kept from the public reports that had arrived in the past about the German campaign to exterminate the Jews of Europe. The ensuing debate in the Jewish community in Palestine focused on the size and scope of the demonstrations to be held demanding action to rescue the remnants of European Jewry. Here the more moderate views of the Jewish Agency leadership were opposed by the Revisionists and Agudat Yisrael, who felt that the situation called for extreme measures.

Even though Montgomery's victory at El Alamein and the subsequent landing of Allied forces in North Africa had removed the threat to the Jewish community in Palestine, and Zionist leaders in Palestine could now turn their full attention to the fate of the Jews under German occupation, no concrete steps were taken to establish contact with the Jews that were still alive in Poland. Whereas in the past it had been argued that the reports received from Europe of mass exterminations seemed to be exaggerations and should be treated with caution, now the pendulum had swung the other way. The argument was put forth that there may not be anybody left to be rescued. When demands began to be heard that money should be raised from the Jewish community in Palestine for rescue efforts for the Jews who had so far survived the German extermination campaign in Europe, leaders of the Jewish Agency claimed that there was probably hardly anyone left to be saved. They argued that in any case nothing effective could be done, that the British administration prohibited the transfer of funds to Axis-occupied areas, and that under no circumstances should money be deducted from the funds collected for Zionist activities in Palestine.

Funds for rescue in Europe suddenly came into "competition" with funds needed for work in Palestine. The Histadrut leadership, attuned to the clamor of the public, appealed to the Jewish Agency Executive to permit the launching of a drive to collect funds specifically for rescue efforts in Europe, but they met consistent obstruction from the Agency leadership. Even Gruenbaum, the head of the Committee of Four, which was supposed to be directing the Zionist rescue effort in Europe, insisted that nothing should be done that might in any way detract from the Zionist enterprise in Palestine, and that "Zionism was above all." At a meeting of the Zionist Executive on January 18, 1943, he declared: "When I was asked about the possibility of allocating funds from Keren Hayesod [the fund for support of the Zionist enterprise in Palestine] toward the rescue of Jews in the lands of the Diaspora, I said no, and I say again – no."[5] The Zionist leadership in Palestine did not view itself as leaders of the Jewish people, but rather as leaders of the Socialist Zionist movement.

In January 1943 a small amount of additional funds from Palestine were made available to Schwalb in Geneva. They were to be distributed to members of the Socialist Zionist political parties, Poalei Zion and Left Poalei Zion, in addition to members of Hehalutz. Schwalb was going to be joined in the decisions regarding their disbursement by two members of Poalei Zion in Geneva, Haim Posner and Alfred Silbershein. When a trickle of money finally began to be transferred to Warsaw from Palestine, it was too late to be of any assistance in the uprising.[6]

Although the IZL and the Zionist youth movements in the ghetto recognized the authority of the leadership of their movements in Palestine, they received no direction from them – even after Rom-

---

5   See Dina Porat and Yehiam Weitz, eds., *Bein Magen David la-tlai ha-tzahov* [Between the Star of David and the yellow badge] (Jerusalem: Yad Vashem, 2002), 128–29.

6   See Dina Porat, *Hanhagah be-milkud* [A leadership entrapped] (Tel Aviv: Am Oved, 1986), 65–76, and 117–51 for a description of the debate among the Jewish leadership in Palestine on this issue at the time. Also Hava Eshkoli, *Ha-Yishuv ha-Yehudi be-Eretz Yisrael nochah ha-Shoah* [The Jewish Community in the Land of Israel facing the Shoah] (Jerusalem: Yad Yitzhak Ben Zvi, 1993).

mel's defeat at El Alamein and after the the magnitude of the German murder campaign had become well known in November 1942. After the split in the ranks of the IZL in 1940, the death of David Raziel while on a mission for the British in Iraq in May 1941, and the killing of Avraham (Yair) Stern by British police in Tel Aviv in February 1942, the IZL in Palestine was itself in disarray and lacking any financial resources. The young men and women in the Warsaw ghetto were practically isolated from their home base in Palestine, receiving no guidance from there, and left to take their own decisions.

In the areas of German occupation, attempts were made on the spot to provide overall guidance, assistance, and encouragement to some of the youth movements and underground groups. Hashomer Hatzair and Dror used couriers to maintain contact between the Warsaw ghetto and other ghettos. Yosef Kaplan had sent money to the FPO in the Vilna ghetto with Hayka Grossman and Irena Adamowicz. Mordechai Anielewicz was sent to Zaglembie as an emissary of Hashomer Hatzair. ZOB, after its initial formation in the Warsaw ghetto, sent a member of its Command, Mordechai Tennenbaum, to Bialystok to organize resistance there. The senior Betar leader in the German zone of occupation, Yosef Glazman in Vilna, deputy commander of FPO, attempted to provide guidance to Revisionists in the Kaunas and Warsaw ghettos. But the form and timing of acts of Jewish resistance remained determined by local conditions and circumstances. There was no central Jewish resistance movement.

In the ghettos, those preparing to fight the Germans had to choose between fighting in the ghetto or joining the partisans in the forests. Joining the partisans seemed the easier way. Whereas in the ghetto they were destined to face the Germans totally outnumbered and outgunned, in the forests it would be possible to hide from the Germans, conduct sabotage operations of German facilities, and ambush German units, with a far higher probability of local success and survival than in the ghetto. In addition, in the forests they expected to receive the assistance of Polish and Communist partisan forces, whereas in the ghetto they had to be prepared to fight alone.

Those who chose to fight in the ghetto were not counting on military success or physical survival. Their motivation was to write a page in history for the honor of the Jewish people. Therefore in the ghetto, the fighters were dependent on the moral support of the ghetto's population. As long as the Germans were successful in deceiving many of the Jews and convincing them that they had a chance of surviving the war – that only some of the Jews were destined for deportation or even extermination – there was bound to be objection, rage, and even betrayal against those who, by their resistance to the Germans, were likely to bring catastrophe on all those who had survived so far. Without the moral support of those living in the ghetto, resistance against the Germans within the confines of the ghetto was destined to be senseless and self-defeating.

Nevertheless, the fighters in the Warsaw ghetto – the ZOB and the ZZW – chose to conduct resistance to the Germans in the ghetto. They understood that, unlike the contribution they might make to partisan warfare against the Germans, resistance in the ghetto would be uniquely identified with Jewish resistance against the Germans, a battle for the honor of the Jewish people. It would be a desperate battle, a battle in which militarily they were bound to be defeated, but one whose historic impact would reverberate for generations. Choosing the time for this battle, however, was a horrendously difficult decision.[7]

The fighters in the ghetto awaited the moment when they would have the moral support of the ghetto's population. That moment came only after the great deportation had sent 270,000 men, wom-

---

7   Zuckerman, *A Surplus of Memory*, 181–82.

en, and children to the gas chambers of Treblinka. The mass deportations ended on September 21, 1942.

Yehoshua Perle, the well-known Yiddish writer, who survived the great deportation, wrote in the Warsaw ghetto in October 1942: "Three times 100,000 people lacked the courage to say: No. Each one of them was out to save his own skin. Each one was ready to sacrifice even his own father, his own mother, his own wife and children."[8] These words were written six months before the Warsaw Ghetto Uprising.

It was a bereaved people that were left in the ghetto after the last day of transports to Treblinka. Fathers had lost wives and children, wives their husbands, whole families had been destroyed. On Yom Kippur, the last day of the deportations, some of the survivors gathered to attend prayers in the ghetto, wherever possible. In workshops and small apartments, Jews gathered to hear the cantor recite the Yom Kippur prayers. All those attending the services had lost family and friends during the past eight weeks. In one of the workshops, the famous cantor Gershon Sirota led the prayers. For years he had been the cantor of the great Tlomacki Synagogue in Warsaw, had won world renown in his many appearances in Europe and America, and become known as "the Jewish Caruso." Sirota's voice broke when he came to the last prayer "Our Father, Our King," and sobbing was heard from the small assembled congregation, as he intoned "Our Father, our King, have compassion on us, on our children, and on our infants. Our Father, our King, act for the sake of those who were slain for Thy holy name. Our Father, our King, avenge the spilt blood of Thy servants."[9] But just how was the murder of hundreds

---

8   Quoted by Friedlander, *The Years of Extermination*, 528.
9   Seidman, *Yoman Geto Varsha*, 108.

of thousands to be avenged, and what would the New Year bring to those who had survived so far?

The deportations had emptied whole sections of the ghetto. Three isolated sectors now constituted the ghetto – what had remained of the Central Ghetto, the Toebbens-Schultz Workshop area, and the Brushmakers' Workshop area. The Germans gave the population of the ghetto until September 27 at 2:00 p.m. to move into the newly defined areas. Between the inhabited areas there were now large abandoned blocks of houses. The survivors were mostly workers in the workshops, employees of the *Judenrat* and others who were in possession of documents that had proved acceptable to the Germans, and those who had hidden in workshops and pre-arranged bunkers and hiding places during the daily roundups. Many of them had lost their immediate families.

The mood in the ghetto had changed. There was now no doubt that death awaited those who were being deported and that it was the Germans' intention to eventually liquidate the Warsaw ghetto. There were no more illusions that the Germans would not dare to do in Warsaw what they had done in Vilna and Lublin. The workers in the workshops still clung to their "productive labor," but many of them were also preparing for the worst. Bunkers and other hiding places were being built, and arrangements were being made by those who had the means or "Aryan" looks to leave the ghetto and attempt to hide in "Aryan" Warsaw. Some bought pistols, and the idea of resistance to the Germans the next time they began deportations gained adherents.

Both ZOB and ZZW, without coordinating with each other, decided on the very same steps to strengthen and prepare themselves for the coming battle: to assassinate officers of the Jewish police force and other collaborators with the Germans in the ghetto, so as to weaken the authority of the *Judenrat* and establish their own authority in their place, while discouraging collaboration with the

Germans; to force the *Judenrat* to contribute funds and extort such funds from wealthy Jews in the ghetto; and to use these funds to acquire weapons on the "Aryan" side, smuggle them into the ghetto, and build an arsenal of weapons with which to equip their fighters.

Szerynski was the first to be targeted for assassination. Jacob Lejkin, who had succeeded Szerynski as head of the Jewish police, was the next target. On October 29, a team of three members of Hashomer Hatzair, directed by Anielweicz, tracked Lejkin on his way home from the police station, and shot and killed him. The ZOB issued a typewritten statement announcing that the sentence against Jacob Lejkin had been carried out on October 29 at 6:10 p.m. A month later, on November 29, 1942, under the direction of Zuckerman, Yisrael Fuerst, an official of the *Judenrat* who had co-operated with the Gestapo, was shot and killed by a ZOB unit that had followed him to his home in the ghetto.[10] ZZW fighters entered the home of Jurek Fuerstenberg, one of the high-ranking officers of the Jewish police, and after reading a list of his crimes to him, shot and killed him. This was followed by the execution by ZZW fighters of Anna Milewicz, a former member of Hashomer Hatzair, who had turned informer for the Gestapo. A number of Gestapo agents in the Brushmakers' Workshop area were executed by ZZW.

One by one, fighters of ZOB and ZZW were picking off officers of the Jewish police and officials of the *Judenrat*, and others who were cooperating with the Germans, undermining the authority of the *Judenrat* and the Jewish police. Avraham Levin, like most of the Jews in the ghetto, did not know at the time who the executioners were. He noted in his diary: "It is assumed that this is an act of revenge and punishment for Jews who bloodied their hands with the blood of their brothers, hunting hundreds of thousands of Jews

---

10 Zuckerman, *A Surplus of Memory*, 244–47.

to the *Umschlagplatz* and to Treblinka."[11] On November 30, 1942, referring to the execution of Jewish collaborators, he wrote: "[It] made a great impression on the Jews and frightened those whose conscience is not clean and who have on their hands the blood of the victims."[12]

The Germans did not concern themselves with the killing of Jews by Jews in the ghetto. They had set up an organization of their agents in the ghetto, Zagiew, which posed as an underground resistance organization, with the intention of trapping Jews planning resistance into their ranks. When they were unmasked, most of their members were liquidated by ZOB and ZZW fighters.

In the atmosphere created by the punitive assassinations, it had become easy to bribe members of the Jewish police and the Polish police that stood guard at the entry to the ghetto. This made it possible to smuggle weapons and ammunition into the ghetto. Substantial smuggling of pistols and grenades into the ghetto ensued, carried out by ZOB and ZZW, as well as by unaffiliated individuals and groups. All that was needed was money to buy weapons in "Aryan" Warsaw. Smuggling in weapons also became a thriving business for those intent on profiting from this situation.

But where was the money to buy the weapons and ammunition going to come from? No assistance had been forthcoming from the Jewish Agency in Palestine, but ZOB did receive some financial assistance from Yitzhak Gitterman and David Guzik, the representatives of the Joint in the ghetto, who had access to funds transferred to the ghetto from abroad by the Joint. ZZW was not a beneficiary of these funds, which were reserved for organizations connected with the establishment. Most of the money for weapons, however, was obtained by raids on wealthy Jews – those who had found ways

---

11 Levin, *Mipinkaso shel ha-moreh mi "Yehudiya,"* 134.
12 Ibid., 153.

to profit from the situation in the ghetto through connections with the *Judenrat*, with smugglers, or with the Germans. The *Judenrat* treasury also became a target for the impounding of funds for the resistance. ZOB and ZZW carried out such expropriations, referred to as "execs." The *Judenrat* was pressured and humiliated by fines that were levied against it and its head, Marc Lichtenbaum. The ZOB even kidnapped his son and threatened to kill him if he did not pay the fine they demanded.

The ZOB and ZZW were not the only ones to sieze funds in the ghetto. Gangs of thieves, even Polish robbers who entered the ghetto, sometimes masquerading as ZOB or ZZW fighters, used the lawless state of the ghetto at that time to steal whatever they could. Jewish Communists, members of the Polish Communist party (PPR), sometimes operated on their own, extracting money from Jews in the ghetto, even though they had joined ZOB and were supposedly subject to ZOB discipline.

The bulk of the money obtained through expropriations, however, was obtained by ZOB and ZZW. But since the two groups did not coordinate their operations, they frequently found themselves at cross purposes, demanding money from the same person, or pressuring a person who, in the opinion of the second fighting organization, should be better left alone. ZOB claimed that although Fuerstenberg had deserved the death sentence meted out to him by ZZW, they had been in the middle of negotiations with him for weapons he promised to obtain for them in an attempt to ransom his life. When ZZW killed some German plainclothesmen who were cruising through the ghetto, ZOB considered the action mistaken, concerned that it might bring about immediate German reprisals. But it seemingly went unnoticed.

On occasion their members came to blows over these differences. This happened at Leszno 74, the apartment of one of the rich Jews in the ghetto. When Zuckerman learned that ZZW was about to enter the man's apartment, he sent a ZOB unit to the area to abort the expropriation. In another incident, ZZW demanded money from Avraham Gepner, head of the supply authority of the *Judenrat*. But Gepner insisted that he would only deal with Tzivya Lubetkin, and it was she who finally received money and supplies from him for ZOB.[13]

Twenty-one-year-old Feygale Peltel, whose code name was Wladka, was a member of Tsukunft, the Bund youth movement; she had an "Aryan" face and worked as courier for ZOB. One of her tasks was purchasing weapons in "Aryan" Warsaw and smuggling them into the ghetto. "First you had to find arms. You'd risk your life, but you'd get them. Then you had to smuggle them into the ghetto," she wrote after the war.[14]

David Landau, a member of Betar before the war, had an "Aryan" face and spoke perfect Polish, and thus was able to move around Warsaw when leaving the ghetto, posing as a Pole and looking for arms to purchase and smuggle back into the ghetto for the ZZW arsenal. When leaving the ghetto he would hide a roll of banknotes to be used to purchase weapons or ammunition. Sometimes he had specific orders for certain types of ammunition for arms they had in stock. Generally he would buy whatever arms he could find, with a few bullets to go with them. Later he would order larger quantities of bullets to fit the weapons he had purchased. He had become one of the key buyers of arms in "Aryan" Warsaw.[15]

A number of ZZW fighters left the ghetto each morning to work at the Warsaw Praga railroad station, together with others who were assigned by the Germans to work outside the ghetto. Many German

---

13   Zuckerman, *A Surplus of Memory*, 323–24.
14   Feygale (Wladka) Peltel, *Fun Beyde Zaytn Ghetto Moyer* [From Both Sides of the Ghetto Wall] (New York: Workmen's Circle, 1948), 121.
15   Landau, *Caged*, 148.

and Italian soldiers returning from the Stalingrad front arrived at the train station. Some were only too eager to trade in their weapons for cash. These weapons made their way to the ZZW arsenal.[16]

Twenty-year-old Shoshana (Emilka) Kossower, a member of Betar in Radzymin before the war, had decided to move to Warsaw in 1942 when the executions in her region began. There she went to work for Olgierd Rudnicki-Ostkiewicz, an officer in the AK, passing as a Polish girl. She became a courier for the AK, distinguishing herself by her courage and ingenuity. But she did not forget her roots and visited the headquarters of ZZW in the ghetto at Muranowska 7 frequently, each time bringing some arms with her that she had smuggled into the ghetto. On one occasion she entered Frenkel's office and brought him some pistols. Looking at Frenkel, she said: "You know, you look like a Pole and speak prefect Polish. You could leave the ghetto and live in relative safety on the other side, and help your organization from there."

"I will stay here until the end," he replied.

Emilka had known that, but still she could not keep herself from saying to Frenkel: "So you want to die as a hero."

"No," Frenkel replied, "I don't want to live at any price. I want to die as a man."[17]

Not all of the weapons for ZZW had to be smuggled into the ghetto past the guards at the ghetto gates. Two tunnels under the ghetto walls had been constructed by ZZW – one at Muranowska 7 in the Central Ghetto area and the other at Karmelicka 5 in the Toebbens-Schultz Workshop area – and they served to bring weapons into the ghetto.

---

16 Seidman, *Yoman Geto Varsha*, 171; and Lazar Litai, *Matzada shel Varsha*, 183.

17 Lazar Litai, *Matzada shel Varsha*, 179 and 191–92. Also, videotaped interview with Shoshana Rosenzweig (Kossower) in the Jabotinsky Institute Archives.

Frenkel realized that the pistols and hand grenades that were being smuggled into the ghetto might be effective in encounters at short range, but were going to be of little use in engagements with German soldiers equipped with standard field equipment. Weapons with longer range, such as rifles and machine guns, were going to be needed. But such weapons could only be obtained from the Polish underground.

Frenkel had been searching for a connection with the Polish underground, hoping that the pre-war relationship between the Revisionists and the Polish government could be renewed under the present circumstances. He succeeded in reaching Janusz Cezary Ketling-Szemley, code-named "Arpad." Ketling was one of the leaders of a Polish underground group called PLAN (Polska Ludowa Akcja Niepodleglosciowa – Polish People's Action for Independence), which was associated with the Armia Krajowa (AK), the main Polish underground.

Ketling was not going to reach any decisions before meeting face-to-face with the leader of the Jewish underground seeking his assistance. A meeting was arranged on a cold wintry morning at 11 a.m. in Targowek, a distant working-class district of Warsaw in the area of the Brodno cemetery. Ketling had serious doubts about going to the meeting. The appointed place was far and isolated, and could well turn out to be trap. There were many German patrols on the roads, making the trip precarious. Nevertheless, Ketling could not resist the temptation to meet Jews who, he was told, were determined to fight the common enemy. Carrying his weapon, and accompanied by three armed bodyguards, Ketling carefully approached the designated place for the meeting.

The building in which the meeting was to take place was isolated from the other buildings in the area. It was a primitive one-story shack, hardly suitable for living quarters. Entering the building, Ketling found a low, dark room filled with wooden planks on which a large number of hand grenades, ammunition, and pistols had been stored. Standing in the room were a few young men in their twenties, whom he identified as Jews, dressed in simple clothes and wearing boots. Pistols and hand grenades were stuck in their leather belts. To Ketling their bearing gave them away as members of a military organization. They were Pawel Frenkel and some of his comrades from the ZZW.

There was no place to sit down; the group stood during the conversation, hands in their jacket pockets in the freezing cold. After cursory handshakes all around, Frenkel, in fluent Polish, proceeded to describe the nature and aims of his organization. Frenkel, knowing the Poles well, knew what was most likely to engage their interest. "We would like to be a part of the Polish underground and participate in actions against the Germans outside the ghetto," he told Ketling. "We also expect our military capability in the ghetto to be utilized in the case of an uprising against the Germans. We declare our loyalty to Poland and to the leadership of the Polish underground," he continued. Ketling listened patiently. Now came the time for Frenkel to enumerate ZZW's requests. "We want to purchase weapons from you and have your instructors come to the ghetto to instruct our fighters."

As the conversation developed, Ketling learned that a number of attempts had already been made by Frenkel to receive assistance from the Polish underground, but they had all been unsuccessful. "We assumed that the problem was the individuals we dealt with, rather than the official policy of the Polish underground, so we decided to try one more time."

"We are followers of Jabotinsky," Frenkel explained, and described the special relations that had developed between Jabotinsky and the pre-war Polish government, and the assistance his movement had received from the Polish army at that time, including military instruction for members of their organization who had come to

Poland from Palestine. "Although conditions are different today, we hope that we can establish a similar relation now. We are counting on the Polish people and its leaders," Frenkel concluded.

Ketling replied that he did not have the authority on behalf of AK or the *delegatura* to reply to their requests or even negotiate with them. Then he added, "But I am prepared to take upon myself the task of trying to arrange for the assistance that you are requesting." They set a time and place for their next meeting, and Ketling received an invitation to visit them in the ghetto.

"But how am I going to get to you in the ghetto, and how did you succeed in getting out of the ghetto to this distant place?" Ketling asked. Frenkel explained to Ketling that the ZZW had built a tunnel that led out of the ghetto, that they had left the ghetto at night through this tunnel a few days ago and come to this shack, which they had rented from a Polish tram driver. Here they concentrated weapons and food they had obtained in Warsaw, to be returned to the ghetto through the tunnel. On the day of the meeting they had acquired a large quantity of weapons and ammunition, which they must now bring back to the ghetto as soon as possible. The group of ZZW fighters was well armed, and they felt confident of their ability to defend themselves if they were to be intercepted by the enemy. They had posted guards around the shack and were prepared to defend it if they were discovered.

Although it was freezing in the shack, the ice had been broken between the two parties: the Jewish youngsters and the Polish underground leader. Ketling was impressed. These boys seemed intent on fighting the Germans, seemingly not caring about the danger they were facing. They struck him as dedicated and responsible. Ketling told Frenkel that he would do everything in his power to assist them in carrying out their plans. As they parted, both felt that a bond of trust had been established between them, and that they were not going to disappoint each other.

In the beginning of January, Ketling entered the ghetto through the Muranowska tunnel to meet again with Frenkel and his men. The tunnel could only be used at nighttime. In order to use it, one had to go into the house at Muranowska 6, on the other side of the wall surrounding the ghetto, before the curfew, and then enter the tunnel through the cellar after dark. The tunnel was lit with electric lights and padded, and Ketling had to crawl through it on all fours. Emerging from the tunnel, Ketling entered the cellar of Muranowska 7 where he was greeted by Frenkel, who took him up to his head-quarters. There stood a unit of armed ZZW soldiers for his inspec-tion, and Fenkel proceeded to give him a report on the situation in the ghetto and their preparations. Ketling was greatly impressed by the military bearing of the ZZW fighters and the precision of Fren-kel's report.

Now it was Ketling's turn to report. He excused himself for not having as yet obtained a reply from AK, since there had not been enough time to arrange that. However, he had brought with him ex-plosives and Molotov cocktails and was prepared to train ZZW fight-ers in their use. He spent the whole night providing instructions on the use of the material he had brought into the ghetto, and at dawn he left, as he had come, through the tunnel.

Ketling returned to the ghetto a number of times, and close links of cooperation were established between him, his organiza-tion, and ZZW, although he did not obtain the approval of the AK leadership for this cooperation. When the watchman of the house at Muranowska 6 refused to cooperate regarding the use of the tunnel, Ketling replaced him with one of his men.[18]

Arye (Jurek) Wilner was born in 1917 in Warsaw and had been an active member of Hashomer Hatzair there. Together with many of

---

18 Lazar Litai, *Matzada shel Varsha*, 180–82.

his comrades, he fled to Vilna as the German army approached Warsaw and was in Vilna when the Germans began the mass executions at Ponar. In October 1941 he managed to reach the Warsaw ghetto from Vilna. He had a Polish appearance and it was easy for him to move around outside the ghetto. ZOB had chosen him to represent them in "Aryan" Warsaw for the acquisition of weapons for ZOB. His initial attempts to make a connection to AK had produced no results. "We don't believe you Jews are going to fight – you are going like sheep to the slaughter," he was told by AK representatives. In desperation, Wilner turned to the Communists, who were more friendly, and through them he managed to purchase a few old pistols and hand grenades, which were smuggled into the ghetto at the beginning of September 1942. It was these weapons that were discovered by the Germans while they were being transferred from one hiding place in the ghetto to another on September 3.

It was not the number of Jewish fighters but the number and quality of weapons in their hands that was going to determine the nature of the upcoming battle with the Germans.

Frenkel had been fortunate in making the contact with Ketling, for Wilner was having no end of trouble trying to obtain the assistance of AK for ZOB. In his first meeting with them he was asked who were the members of the organization he represented. It was made clear to him that a condition for AK assisting the ghetto underground was that it be representative of all parties and movements in the ghetto. After the agreement with the Bund in November and the establishment of the committees to oversee the actions of ZOB, Wilner was able to report to them that all parties were represented in ZOB. He even included the Revisionists, aware that the relations the Revisionists had with the pre-war Polish government and Polish army were known in AK. He judiciously omitted mention of the Communist membership in ZOB, in deference to the hostility of AK

to the Communists and their suspicion that the Socialist Zionist organizations were close to the Communists.

But now the AK handed ZOB a dilemma. They told Wilner that
as a condition for their support, they required a declaration that in
case of war between Poland and the Soviet Union, ZOB would be
prepared to fight for Poland against the Red Army. This demand
regarding a future hypothetical situation, difficult to envisage at that
time, nevertheless created great turmoil among some of the ZOB
member organizations, who clung to their ideologies fashioned in
pre-war days. Rather than dismissing the issue as irrelevant and telling the AK what they wanted to hear, a long drawn-out discussion
ensued. Hashomer Hatzair and Left Po'alei Zion felt that such a declaration would mean betraying their "most sacred ideals." The Bund
representatives would not express an opinion on the matter. The
ZOB meeting to discuss the Polish demand could reach no conclusion.

The following day they met again, and Berlinski came up with
an idea for how to wiggle out of this dilemma. He suggested that,
rather than ZOB, the Jewish National Committee, ZKN, transmit
a declaration to the Poles which would state that: "As citizens of
Poland we are bound by the decisions of the Polish government."
Then Berlinski, on behalf of Po'alei Zion Left, cleared his conscience
by giving the following speech: "Dear Comrades! In case of a conflict between Poland and the Soviet Union we will do everything
to weaken the fighting ability of Poland. Our place is in the ranks
of the Red Army, and we will do all in our power to help it gain
victory. November 1917 taught us that many of our friends today
will become bloody enemies at a decisive moment of the battle for
control of the workers. We have united to fight against the German
occupier, against the liquidation of the Jewish masses in the Warsaw
ghetto. It cannot be ruled out that the weapons we will acquire by a
common effort will be turned one against the other at the time of the

fateful determination of the future nature of the world, if the political interests of the working class and its avant-garde will require it of us." The Hashomer Hatzair representative nodded his agreement, and the Bund representative held his peace. After receiving the ZKN declaration AK made no further demands of a political nature.[19]

The attitude of General Stefan (Grot) Rowecki, the commander of AK at the time, was clearly negative in regard to supplying weapons to the Jews in the ghetto. In a telegram to the Polish government-in-exile, he wrote on January 2, 1943: "Jews from all kinds of groups, including Communists, have turned to us lately asking for arms, as if we had depots full of them. As an experiment I took out a few revolvers. I have no assurance that they will use these weapons at all. I shall not give out any more weapons."[20] To make their position clear beyond doubt, Ketling was put on trial in an AK military court because of the assistance he had rendered to ZZW.

Wilner, assisted by Tosya Altman, was not able to obtain any significant assistance from AK, and had to resign himself to occasional purchases of weapons that were then smuggled into the ghetto through the entrance gates.

Toward the evening of December 24, 1942, a snowy Christmas eve, David Landau received a summons to attend a meeting at ZZW headquarters at Muranowska 7. The date for the meeting had been judiciously chosen by the leaders of the organization, assuming that on that evening the Germans would be too busy celebrating to appear in the ghetto. While waiting for their leaders to appear, those assembled took their places on long benches in the largest room and exchanged views on the developments since the end of the great deportation, and the current situation in the ghetto.

---

19 Berlinski, *Zichroines*, 177–81.
20 Gutman, *The Jews of Warsaw 1939–1943*, 256; and Jabotinsky Institute Archives 2-ב, 7-כ.

It took a while before the leadership arrived. Four entered the room. They were Frenkel, Rodal, and the Lopata brothers – Jan and Yuzek Lopata, the sons of the baker Lopata. Frenkel rose to speak. He warned that a new attempt by the Germans to liquidate the ghetto might come at any moment. The heavy losses they were suffering at Stalingrad, the quarter of a million men who had been cut off, and the impending defeat, might well lead them to take out their frustration on the remaining Jews of Warsaw. Coupled with the advances of the Allied armies in North Africa, the German debacle at Stalingrad may well portend the eventual defeat of the Germans. "Yes, comrades," he continued, "the end of Hitler's Germany is in sight, but we will not live to see it."

Frenkel went on to say that that the extent of the German extermination campaign against the Jews was now well known in London and Washington, but no steps had been taken to put a stop to the killings. "We are on our own," he declared. "We will have to fight alone for the honor of the Jewish people and for the right to die in dignity, and inflict as many casualties as possible on the Germans."

Then Frenkel described the relations between ZZW and ZOB. On matters relating to collecting funds in the ghetto for the purchase of arms, coordination had been achieved with ZOB so as to avoid the same person being approached by both groups. The difference of opinion on the organizational structure continued – ZOB insisting on accepting only members of youth movements and political parties, and organizing its combat units according to party affiliation, while ZZW had now opened its ranks to men and women who were not affiliated with any party or movement.

When Frenkel had finished, it was time for questions. The recurring question was when would they begin to fight the Germans? Would the battle start the next time the Germans renewed deportations? Many were not satisfied when Frenkel evaded the question by saying that it would depend on the conditions at the time. He had to explain that the fight against the Germans would have to be part of a general uprising, which meant that they would have to be certain that ZOB would join the battle. Many refused to accept this answer, and the atmosphere in the room became tense.

"Why do we have to wait for them? And what if they do not order their people to attack the Germans?" some called out.

Frenkel remained calm but firm: "We are independent as far as the order to take up arms against the Germans is concerned. Should we decide that the time is ripe tomorrow, that would be our own decision. Nobody can tell us what we can or cannot do, it will be our decision." Frenkel explained that although ZZW was at this time better equipped than ZOB, ZOB did represent almost all the parties and movements in the ghetto, and it was therefore important that resistance to the Germans be a combined effort of the two organizations. That means that ZZW would await the decision of the ZOB Command on when to begin the uprising. "If we determine that they have failed to start fighting at the right moment, we will be justified to act on our own," Frenkel concluded.

Not everybody was satisfied with Frenkel's explanation, but Rodal called them all to order. "You are soldiers, you have to accept military discipline and follow the orders of our commander," he said, and with that the discussion was closed.

Yuzek Lopata had at one point left the room, and when Frenkel called on him to return, to the amazement of those present, he was dressed in an SS uniform. Frenkel explained that ZZW had acquired such uniforms and intended to use them to sow confusion in the ranks of the Germans when the time came. For the time being this had to remain completely secret, he emphasized. Then the ZZW fighters were told that they were free to go.[21]

---

21 Landau, *Caged*, 165–73.

Menahem Kirshenbaum, the chairman of the Jewish National Committee (ZKN), understood that it was essential to unite the two resistance organizations. He, a General Zionist, did not harbor hostility to the Revisionists like his Socialist Zionist colleagues on his Committee. To explore the matter, he chose two men who had good relations with the Revisionists, Nahum Remba and Hillel Seidman. Nahum Remba, the highly respected secretary of the *Judenrat*, was the brother of Aizik Remba, who had been one of the leaders of Betar in Poland before leaving for Palestine, and now held a leading position among the Revisionists there. Hillel Seidman, a pre-war journalist and ghetto archivist, was close to the religious leadership in the ghetto and had many friends among the Revisionists.

Kirshenbaum thought that considering their background, it should be possible for Remba and Seidman to find a common language with the Revisionists. But by the same token they were not representative of the Command of ZOB, all of whose members belonged to movements with a long history of antagonism to the Revisionists. What they might bring back might very well not be acceptable to ZOB. Moreover, the ZKN did not include the Bund, whose representative in the Coordinating Committee had the power to veto any agreement that might be reached.

On January 7, 1943, after dark, Remba and Seidman made their way to a large building on Zamenhofa 21, to which the *Judenrat* had moved its offices after the great deportation. After climbing to the attic, they descended through an opening in the floor of the attic into a hidden room whose doors had been sealed, leaving only a small peep-hole. It was a hiding place that some of the Revisionists were using in the ghetto. As Remba and Seidman entered the room they recognized among the assembled Revisionists Leon Rodal and Zvi Zylberberg, who, with his brother Moshe, had brought the news of the killings in Lublin to the Warsaw ghetto in April 1942. Also there was Dr. Michael Strykowski, one of the leading Revisionists in the ghetto.

When they had sat down, after some introductory conversation, Remba asked what their resistance organization was doing at the present time. He was told that ZZW was accumulating arms, and that they had members who were part of work details which left the ghetto each morning for work at the eastern railroad station, where they were able to buy arms and then smuggle them into the ghetto.

Remba and Seidman raised the suggestion that the weapons they were bringing into the ghetto should be transferred to a common store of weapons as part of a process of uniting the two resistance organizations. In response, some of the Revisionists present raised concerns about the contacts that the Bund, a member of ZOB, maintained with Polish Socialists, which might lead to leakage of information that would compromise the resistance organization.

Remba made light of these concerns. Firstly, he said, the Bund people are keeping themselves busy writing reports to the Polish government-in-exile in London. Secondly, he does not believe that they have any real contacts with the Polish Socialists – they just brag about such contacts. Seidman, for his part, was more cautious. He conceded that his meetings with Polish Socialists had left him with a bad impression regarding their attitude to Jews.

After a lengthy discussion, Remba and Seidman suggested that Dr. Wdowinski and another Revisionist attend the meetings of the ZKN as a first step toward uniting ZZW and ZOB. But unity between the two groups was a long way off. Only if Frenkel and Anielewicz could put their heads together, and Anielewicz could overcome the stumbling block of the Bund, could the two organizations unite.

Seidman used the opportunity to collect some stenciled ZZW publications for the archives. He noticed the title of one of the articles: *Morituri te salutant* (Those who are about to die salute you), the greeting of the gladiators going to their deaths in Roman times.

Then he and Remba climbed back up into the attic and down to the street, congratulating themselves on having achieved a step toward unity of ZOB and ZZW. However, more formal negotiations between the parties would be required if anything substantial was going to be achieved.[22]

On January 9, SS-Reichsfuehrer Heinrich Himmler arrived in Warsaw. He met with Colonel Freter, head of the Armament Command in Warsaw, and the SS and Police Commander of Warsaw, Oberfuehrer Ferdinand von Sammern-Frankenegg. "I have come to Warsaw," Himmler announced, "in order to confirm whether the Fuehrer's order to liquidate the ghetto by the end of 1942 has been carried out." He was informed that there were still 40,000 Jews in the ghetto, and that most of them were employed in the workshops, producing goods for the German war effort. As far as Himmler was concerned, this was far too many. The question for him was what was the minimum number of Jews that were needed to be left alive for the time being for work in the workshops to continue? That was Colonel Freter's department. All the rest should be exterminated as quickly as possible, Himmler ordered.

Himmler had little faith in some of the German businessmen like Walter Toebbens and Fritz Schultz, who were using Jewish slave labor in their workshops in the ghetto and enriching themselves. "These are war profiteers operating fictitious 'armament industries,'" he insisted. Their books should be examined with a microscope, and they should be inducted into the army and sent off to the front. "If I am not mistaken," Himmler vituperated, "a man who had no property three years ago has become a well-to-do man here, if not a millionaire, and only because we, the state, have driven cheap Jewish labor into his arms." After rambling on like this for a while, he instructed Sammern-Frankenegg that 8,000 Jews were to be deported

---

22 Seidman, *Yoman Geto Varsha*, 170–74.

at once, and from the remainder he was to send 16,000 to forced labor camps. Actually, there were over 50,000 Jews in the ghetto at the time, all preparing themselves for the German move to liquidate the ghetto. They were convinced that this was not far off.[23]

It was on the following day, January 10, 1942, that Seidman received an invitation to visit a bunker, one of the many that were springing up all over the ghetto. These bunkers, built under the ground, were intended to provide hiding places for an extended period of time, so as to permit Jews to outlive the next deportation, and maybe even survive until the end of the war.

Two yeshivah students told him to appear that day at 5 p.m. at Nalewki 35. "Come by yourself," he was told, no questions asked. There was a military air in the order issued by these boys dressed in the traditional Orthodox attire, which had become rare in the ghetto. At the designated hour, at Nalewki 35, Seidman was met by another yeshivah student who told him to follow him. Passing through numerous passageways and three courtyards, they finally entered a cellar two levels below street level. Continuing through the cellar, they emerged at Kopiecka 11. They climbed the stairs to the top floor. There, in a small room, there was a ladder that lead to the attic. They climbed the ladder and then continued through passageways, twisting themselves through small openings, till they finally came out in the attic of Zamenhofa 38. There they descended. The building was completely sealed. On entering one of the rooms they faced an oven. The yeshivah student climbed into the oven and disappeared. "Follow me," he called out to Seidman. Seidman crawled after him into the oven to find an opening that led into a cellar.

After climbing down a rope ladder, Seidman finally stood on solid ground. Looking around, he saw a large room, lit by electric

---

23 Raul Hilberg, *The Destruction of the European Jews*, 323. Also Gutman, *The Jews of Warsaw 1939–1943*, 328–29.

bulbs. In a small room to the side he saw a kitchen with an electric stove and a gas stove, and a cupboard full of food. To his question as to how long this supply will last, he was was told that that depended on the number of people using the bunker, but for a hundred and twenty people it should last for eight months. "That should be enough, the situation should not last longer than that," he was told.

The bunker was located under a bombed-out building. Above ground there was only rubble and no sign of life. But in the bunker there were all the conveniences – electric lighting, water, gas, a special water reservoir, toilet facilities, and a plentiful food supply. In addition there was a supply of coal in case the electricity would be cut off, and a supply of candles.

The many bunkers being built in the ghetto were designed by diligent and creative Jewish engineers and technicians that came up with ingenious ideas. According to Seidman, the bunkers were one of the technological achievements of the war. After the war, Seidman thought, they would surely arouse the astonishment of the world. But by the time the Germans finished with the ghetto there would be no more bunkers left. None were able to resist the methodical German methods used to discover them and ferret out their inhabitants.

Seidman was led into the next room where a Gemara lesson was in progress. The yeshivah students were being allowed the use of the bunker by the engineers who built it. Some of them approached Seidman and told him that they were joining the Revisionist resistance movement, but were in need of funds for the purchase of weapons. "We have to be prepared for war," they told him. Sixty-year-old Rabbi Menahem Ziemba, one of the great rabbis of Poland and one of the leaders of Agudat Yisrael in the ghetto, had encouraged his students to prepare for resistance to the Germans. Encouraged by their rabbis, the yeshivah students, who until now had kept apart from the resistance organizations, were now joining the resistance. Seidman promised to try to obtain the assistance they requested. Then he went out, traversing the same tortuous path as when he came in.

A few days later, Seidman was present at a discussion at which Rabbi Ziemba was also in attendance. Rabbi Ziemba said that, looking back on the period of the great deportation, it had been a mistake to go willingly to the *Umschlagplatz* – the Jews should have resisted. "But we deluded ourselves. A clever and intelligent people had lost its ability to think clearly. All the time we thought that maybe, or despite everything.... And we thought that there was reason to believe. Our enemies spoke of the Jews of great influence – Bernard Baruch, Henry Morgenthau, Hore-Belisha. Why did they not remember us, their brothers who were destined to be exterminated? We hoped and believed that in time help would arrive. Was it not for this illusion, we might have behaved differently. And in addition we were greatly mistaken when we thought our enemy was stupid, while we were the smart ones. We should have understood from the beginning that this evil enemy is out to destroy us. And now we must resist and not give ourselves up willingly to the enemy."

And then Rabbi Ziemba added: "There are different ways to sanctify the name of God. If they demanded that the Jews convert, like in Spain in the days of the Inquisition, and one could save oneself by conversion, our death would constitute the sanctification of the name of God. Today the only way to sanctify the name of God is to offer armed resistance." On hearing Rabbi Ziemba's words all arguments ceased in the Orthodox community. The verdict had been given.

Seidman, listening to Rabbi Ziemba, remembered meeting in Warsaw shortly before the war Wolfgang von Weisel, the Revisionist leader who had come from Palestine to speak at meetings in Poland. "I have but one mission here in Poland," Von Weisel told him. "To repeat in every city and town, to young and old, 'Jews. Learn to shoot.'"[24]

Rumors were circulating in the ghetto about an approaching deportation, which might begin on January 15, 1943. Kirshenbaum called into session the Jewish National Committee (ZKN) to discuss the situation. In the evening they gathered at his home. Not everybody attended. Such gatherings involved a certain danger and some preferred to remain in hiding. There was Anielewicz, Ringelblum, Tosya Altman, Alexander Landau, a representative of Tsukunft, and a representative of Agudat Yisrael. Dror and Hashomer Hatzair were represented. Also Orzech, who had come into the ghetto from his hiding place in "Aryan" Warsaw, attended. Kirshenbaum raised the fateful question: should resistance begin as soon as the Germans start executing the next deportation? The representative of Tsukunft, who had been charged with making contact with Polish partisans, reported that they say it is too early to act; they are not yet ready and cannot promise assistance. Their advice is to wait. Orzech supported that position, although he did not believe in assistance from the Polish partisans, who, according to him, were very poorly organized.

Kirshenbaum reported on the arms at their disposal. They had been bought from Polish policemen and smugglers at a price of 3,000 to 4,000 zloty a pistol. The price on the market now is about 5,000 zloty a pistol. (The black market exchange rate was 50 zloty to the dollar.)

Seidman, who attended the meeting, reported on his contacts with the Polish Socialist Party (PPS). The results, he said, were zero. Nobody promised help, everyone giving different excuses. One told him the time was not yet ripe; another said that they were waiting

---

24 Seidman, *Yoman Geto Varsha*, 179–87 and 219–21.

for a signal from London. A third said quite frankly: "We cannot besmirch the resistance movement in the eyes of the Polish people by helping the Jews, because, you must know, the Poles dislike Jews." There was one Polish Socialist who Seidman met, who told him: "Start resisting, and we will immediately assist you." Orzech, who knew this man, remarked that this man had no influence among the Polish Socialists, and, in addition, he was a known liar.

Orzech only a few months ago had placed his hopes on the Polish Socialists, and had insisted that resistance to the Germans be conditioned on participation by them in an uprising. He was now very pessimistic of obtaining assistance from them. "There are reasons for that," he added mysteriously, not giving any further explanation. Kirshenbaum was of the opinion that no assistance at all was to be expected from the outside. "After all," he said, "it is well known that Poles are turning over to the Germans any Jew they discover outside the ghetto. Many Poles have found a new way of making a living like this – they threaten to turn over Jews whom they see outside the ghetto and extort money from them."

But the young representative of the Bund youth movement Tsukunft did not want to admit that there was no such thing as "proletarian solidarity." "We must find the right address, and turn to the real Socialists," he said. He claimed to know such Socialists and said his comrades were in contact with them. According to him, there was no need to despair, and efforts should continue to establish contact with proletarian forces outside the ghetto.

Kirshenbaum adjourned the meeting without reaching a decision.[25]

---

25 Ibid., 191–95.

Chapter 7

Last Months before the Uprising

January 1943–April 1943

In anticipation of a German move to liquidate the ghetto, both resistance organizations issued proclamations in January to the Jews of the ghetto. The ZOB proclamation, written in Polish, read:

> On January 22, 1943, six months will have elapsed since the start of the deportation from Warsaw. We all remember those harrowing days in which 300,000 of our brothers and sisters were transported to and brutally murdered in the Treblinka death camp. Six months of constant fear of death have passed without our knowing what the next day will bring. We received reports left and right about Jews being killed in the *Generalgouvernement*, Germany, and the occupied countries. As we listened to these terrible tidings, we waited for our own time to come – any day, any moment. Today we must realize that the Hitlerite murderers have let us live only to exploit our manpower until the last drop of blood and sweat, until our last breath. We are slaves, and when the slaves no longer bring in profits they are killed. Each of us must realize this, and always keep it in mind....
>
> Jewish masses – the hour is drawing near. You must be prepared to resist, not give yourselves up to slaughter like sheep. *Not a single Jew should go to the railroad cars. Those who are*

unable to put up active resistance should resist passively, meaning go into hiding. We have just received information from Lvov that the Jewish police there forcefully executed the deportation of 3,000 Jews.[1] This will not be allowed to happen again in Warsaw. The assassination of Lejkin demonstrates that. Our slogan must be: *All are ready to die as human beings.*[2]

The proclamation issued by ZZW in January 1942, written in Polish as well, read:

Prepare for action! Be on the alert!

We are going out to war! We are among those who have set themselves the goal of rousing the people. We want our people to adopt the slogan: *Rise up and fight! Do not despair of the chance for rescue!* Know that deliverance is not to be found in going to your death impassively, like sheep to the slaughter. It can only be found in something far more noble: War!

He who fights for his life has a chance of being saved. He who rules out resistance from the start is already lost, doomed to a degrading death in the suffocation machine at Treblinka.

Rouse yourselves to war: find the courage to indulge in acts of madness. Put a stop to the degrading resignation expressed by such statements as: "We are all bound to die." That is a lie. For we have been sentenced to live! We, too, are deserving of life. You just have to know how to fight for it!

---

1 On January 11, 1943 a Jew from Lvov arrived in the Warsaw ghetto and reported on the series of deportations that were taking place there since August 1942.

2 Nahman Blumental and Yosef Kermish, eds., *Ha-meri ve-ha-mered be-Geto Varsha* [The uprising and the revolt in the Warsaw Ghetto] (Jerusalem: Yad Vashem, 1965), 122–23.

...In the name of the fight for the lives of the helpless mass-es, whom we wish to save and whom we must rouse to action, we are rising up in revolt! We do not wish to fight for our own lives alone. We can save ourselves only after we have done our duty! *As long as Jewish life – even one, single, solitary life – is in danger, we must be prepared to fight!*

Our slogan: Not even one single Jew will ever again perish in Treblinka!

Destroy the traitors to the people!

A war for life or death with the conqueror unto our last breath!

Prepare for action!

Be on the alert![3]

January 15 came and went and there was no sign of another German deportation action. ZOB and ZZW assumed that the action had been postponed. On January 17 at 5 p.m. the ZOB command was scheduled to meet to discuss plans for defense of the ghetto, but Anielewicz postponed the meeting to January 19 at the same hour; that meeting never took place.[4] Both organizations were taken by surprise when in the early hours of a snowy, freezing cold January 18 morning – the temperature was –20°C – they found the ghetto surrounded and the daily work details, the *Placowska*, who left the ghetto each morning at 6:30 a.m. for work on the "Aryan" side, turned back at the ghetto gates.

SS-Oberfuehrer Ferdinand von Sammern-Frankenegg had assembled German SS troops and Ukrainian and Latvian auxiliaries in order to carry out the orders of Himmler to send 8,000 Jews from the ghetto to the gas chambers in Treblinka. Sammern-Frankenegg, a forty-six-year-old lawyer of Austrian origin, and a member of the SS since 1932, had assumed the duties of SS and Police Commander of Warsaw on July 22, 1942, the day of the beginning of the great deportation. That deportation had been carried out under his direction. Yet, he was not one of Himmler's favorites. According to Himmler he was "from the cavalry, very pleasant, but in no way suited to his function." Sammern-Frankenegg had advanced to his present position with the help of fellow Austrian Ernst Kaltenbrunner, who had inherited the post of head of the RSHA (*Reichsicherheitshauptamt*), the German security apparatus, after the assassination of Reinhardt Heydrich in 1942. Now he was facing a test that would, no doubt, be closely watched by Himmler. To witness the operation he had invited the commander of the Treblinka labor camp SS-Haupsturmfuehrer Theodor van Eupen-Malmedy.

The Germans' first stop was the *Judenrat* building at Zamenhofa 21, at the entrance to the Central Ghetto. There they picked up anyone they could lay their hands on, including members of the *Judenrat* who happened to be there. From there they continued to Mila, surrounding the buildings on that street, forcing the inhabitants down into the street, and marching them off to the *Umschlagplatz*. Next it was the turn of Niska Street and the workers of the *Werterfassung*, the repository of goods the Germans had stolen from the Jews destined for extermination. From there to the workshops, where those arbitrarily selected as not being "legitimate" workers were sent off to the *Umschlagplatz*. The orphanage on Stawki Street was an easy target.[5]

By now the whole ghetto was in panic. All realized that the manhunt was on. This time nobody willingly went off to the *Umschlagplatz*. Whoever could went into hiding. The bunkers that had been prepared were filled to capacity.

---

5   Seidman, *Yoman Geto Varsha*, 233–35.

On that day ZOB had been caught unprepared. It had not prepared bunkers to hide its fighters. Its stock of arms consisted of a few pistols and grenades, and improvised Molotov cocktails. Only two groups of fighters with some weapons were concentrated in different locations, but these two locations were separated from each other: Anielewicz with a group from Hashomer Hatzair at Mila 63, at the far western end of the ghetto, and Zuckerman with a group of Dror members at Zamenhofa 58, overlooking the road to the *Umschlag-platz*. The sudden deployment of troops by the Germans, blocking off certain sections of the Central Ghetto and initially concentrating on Mila Street, made it impossible for Anielewicz and Zuckerman to communicate and decide how they were going to deal with this unexpected situation. In effect, already in the early morning hours Anielewicz and his people were cut off from the other ZOB fighters.

As soon as Zuckerman realized that another action was in progress, he tried to make contact with Anielewicz, but quickly found that this had become impossible. Before long the area he was in had also been surrounded.

As Zuckerman and his comrades were looking down from one of the fourth-floor windows of the building at Zamenhofa 58, onto the street below them, at the stream of Jews being herded to the *Um-schlagplatz* by a few Germans, they were shocked to see a Hashomer Hatzair unit among the column of hundreds moving down the street. It was Anielewicz's unit which had been forced by the Germans out of the building at Mila 63 and marched off in the direction of the *Umschlagplatz* with the others. Zuckerman was at a loss as to what to do. He considered throwing grenades onto the moving column below, but realized that more Jews would be injured than Germans by such an action. While weighing his options, he was astounded to recognize Anielewicz in the crowd. As Zuckerman described it after the war:

"It happened right before our eyes. A few members of Mordechai Anielewicz's unit were afraid they were approaching the **Umschlag-platz** (it wasn't far from there). They begged Mordechai Anielewicz to give the order. When they got to the corner of Zamenhofa and Niska he gave the sign, knowing that the hope of being saved was slim. The fighters in the group began throwing their grenades. Most of them were killed. The people scattered. At first we were sure they were all killed; for three days I was sure Mordechai was killed."[6] ZOB almost lost its commander that day.

Actually, three members of the group managed to get away and hide in a little building nearby on Niska Street. There they were discovered by a Polish fire brigade that operated in the area, who turned them over to the Germans. They were killed on the spot. Anielewicz had succeeded in overpowering a German who was chasing him and taking away his rifle. While running with the rifle he was pulled into a nearby bunker belonging to some Jewish underworld characters, who were amazed to see a Jew with a gun. He stayed there for three days, not knowing what was happening above ground. After the action was over, he left the bunker and made contact with Zuckerman and his comrades, who had already given him up for lost.

Zuckerman and his group, on the fourth floor of the building at Zamenhofa 58, realized that the Germans were going to search all the buildings on the street, and that their turn was bound to come. The encounter of Anielewicz and his unit with the Germans in the street, which they had witnessed, and the seeming loss of the entire unit, led Zuckerman to the conclusion that they were unable to confront the Germans in the open, and that the preferred tactic was to try to catch them by surprise. He therefore decided to await them, rather than going down into the street. When he and his fighters heard them climbing the stairs, they were prepared for them.

---

6   Zuckerman, *A Surplus of Memory*, 281–82.

Four Germans entered the room in which Zuckerman and Zecharia Artstein were waiting. The two fired at them and the Germans fled. Then Zuckerman and his unit hastily left the building, escaping over the rooftops, knowing the Germans would return.[7]

That evening Yitzhak Gitterman, one of the directors of the Joint in Warsaw and a member of the Jewish National Committee, was intercepted at the entrance to Wolynska 21 by a team of SS soldiers and shot on the spot; thus the Jewish National Committee lost one of its members. At the *Umschlagplatz* something occurred that the Germans had not experienced before. A group of Bund members that had been caught and brought there under guard, after being harangued by one of its members to not board the trains, refused to board the railroad cars. Van Eupen-Malmedy, who was there inspecting the cargo, had them shot immediately.[8]

The action lasted for four days, from January 19–22, 1943. The Germans succeeded in shiping 6,500 Jews to Treblinka. It was mostly the elderly, the sick, the exhausted, and children. The quota of 8,000 set by Himmler had not been met, and for the first time since the ghetto was set up, a little over two years earlier, the Germans encountered some armed Jews offering resistance. The Germans had suffered a number of wounded, including a police captain. ZOB had lost many of their best people, but were encouraged that, nevertheless, the organization had survived its first encounter with the Germans.

The action had caught the Jewish National Committee by surprise. It did not have the opportunity, as their organizational concept envisaged, to meet and decide whether this was the appropriate time to offer resistance. There was no possibility for contact between ZOB and ZZW, and reaching a decision for a coordinated response.

---

7   Ibid., 282–90.
8   Edelman, *The Ghetto Fights*, 30.

The ZOB's small, as yet poorly armed units were dispersed with no contact between them. But those of its fighters who were armed and were caught up in the German manhunt decided on their own to resist and inflict casualties on the Germans. Despite the heavy losses, it was a morale booster for them and an inspiration for the ghetto's inhabitants.

ZZW, as well, had been taken by surprise. But arrangements had been made for hiding places for its members, and they were not caught up in the four-day manhunt. Frenkel and Rodal, sizing up the forces the Germans had brought into the ghetto, concluded on the first day of the action that this was not the major action they were expecting for the liquidation of the ghetto, the time for the planned uprising. Their decision was to hold their fire and not commit their troops, awaiting that action, which they felt sure was going to come.[9]

On the last day of the action, Frenkel addressed some of the ZZW fighters who had assembled at the ZZW headquarters at Muranowska 7. After reviewing the progress of the war in North Africa and at Stalingrad and the latest deportations in the ghetto, Frenkel concluded:

"Our fight when it comes and no matter how short it is, will not be forgotten! We will live in the pages of Jewish history! Children in the future Land of Israel will learn about us and we will be the model for the courage they will need. You see, it may be late, but the Jews of the ghetto have decided to resist the deportation to death. Even those with no guns and no organization are no longer afraid to resist. The murderers have already noticed it. The Germans are dispirited. Today they will leave us in peace while they prepare themselves better to finish us off. Of course we will fight with guns in our hands,

---

9   Landau, *Caged*, 181.

and most of us will fall. But – we will live on in the lives and hearts of future generations and in the pages of their history.

"Comrades! We will die before our time but we are not doomed. We will be alive for as long as Jewish history lives!"[10]

That afternoon the troops that had been brought into the ghetto to carry out the deportation were withdrawn from the ghetto. German troops did not return to continue this murderous task until April 19, 1943, the day the uprising in the Warsaw ghetto began.

Anielewicz and Zuckerman, reviewing the events of the German action, concluded that they had to reorganize. Regional commanders had to be appointed for the three disconnected parts of the ghetto – the Central Ghetto, the Brushmakers' Workshop area, and the Toebbens-Schultz Workshop area. Anielewicz would take charge of the Central Ghetto, Zuckerman the Toebbens-Schultz area, and Marek Edelman the Brushmakers' area. The unexpected German action had taught them that their meager weapons store should not be kept in a central location, but be distributed to the combat units so that they would be prepared for any eventuality.[11]

Summing up the lessons of the events in January, Zuckerman said after the war:

"The first and most important lesson was that we could not defend ourselves in hand-to- hand combat, because of the quantity and quality of our weapons. We learned that from two conspicuous incidents of self-defense: the street battle of Mordechai Anielewicz's unit and the death of most of the unit, while my unit watched what was happening from the roofs and the upper floors. That taught us not to go into the street at all, that we must not be caught outside. So we had to carry out a guerilla war from the houses…. The second

---

10 Ibid., 182–83.
11 Zuckerman, *A Surplus of Memory*, 291.

thing we learned immediately, early in the morning of January 18, was that you had to maintain total isolation between the units and to foster their independence…that in battle every unit has to stand alone, on its own, on the responsibility of its commander."[12]

Although bunkers were being built all over the ghetto, the ZOB Command decided that they would not build any bunkers or hideouts for its people. "We were afraid that it would occur to some comrades that there are hiding places and tunnels and escape through them. And that could be done even after forty-eight hours of fighting…. We were afraid of the idea that we wouldn't have to fight to the end," was Zuckerman's explanation.[13]

The ZZW Command also appointed regional commanders – Frenkel, assisted by Rodal in charge of the Central Ghetto, Samuel Luft commanding the ZZW forces in the Brushmakers' Workshop area, and Natan Shultz, who was one the Betar members who had returned from Hrubieszow, commanding the Toebbens-Schultz Workshop area. But contrary to the tactics adopted by ZOB, the ZZW Command decided to engage the Germans frontally in the Central Ghetto. At Muranowski Square, the area was to be fortified and sizable forces and the heaviest weapons in the hands of ZZW were going to be concentrated there to face the Germans in battle when the time came.[14]

ZZW prepared hideouts and bunkers for its people in case of need. The tunnels at Muranowska 7 in the Central Ghetto, and at Karmelicka 5 in the Toebbens-Schultz area, provided them with a connection to the outside world.

---

12 Ibid., 307–8.
13 Ibid., 312.
14 Halperin, *Helka shel Betar be-Mered ha-Geto*, 16–17.

Himmler was clearly not satisfied with the results of the January action. His conclusion from the resistance that had been encountered was that the Warsaw ghetto had to be completely destroyed. On February 16, 1943, he addressed the following order to the Higher SS and Police Commander of the *Generalgouvernement* SS-Obergruppenfuehrer Friedrich-Wilhelm Krueger, the superior of Sammern-Frankenegg:

"For security reasons I hereby order that the Warsaw ghetto be destroyed, after the concentration camp has been transferred elsewhere. All useful parts of the buildings, as well as all kinds of materials, are to be disposed of.

"The razing of the ghetto and the transfer of the concentration camp are necessary because Warsaw will never quiet down and its criminal deeds will never end, as long as the ghetto stands.

"A general plan for the destruction of the ghetto must be submitted to me. At least, it is necessary that the dwelling space for 500,000 subhumans available until now, which would never be fit for Germans, should completely disappear. In this way, Warsaw, that city of a million people, which has always been a center of decay and mutiny, will be reduced."[15]

Himmler had to find a compromise between his desire to kill as many Jews as possible, and satisfying the German Armaments Authority's requirements for the continued functioning of Warsaw ghetto workshops that were supplying the German war effort using Jewish slave labor. At the same time, he had to obey Hitler's orders to destroy the Warsaw ghetto. His solution was the transfer of what were, for the time being, essential workshops of the Warsaw ghetto to locations outside Warsaw – to Trawniki and Poniatowa in the Lublin region – which were to be run as concentration camps, and sending the remaining Jews of the ghetto to Treblinka.

15 Nuremberg Document NO-2494.

The experts on running concentration camps were the SS, and Himmler conceived the idea of putting the workshops under the authority of the SS. In his fiendish mind this would have the double benefit of increasing the economic resources of his SS empire, while targeting the workers for eventual extermination by the SS. For that purpose, there was no one more suitable among Himmler's subordinates than Odilio Globocnik, the Higher SS and Police Commander of the Lublin region. He had established his reputation with Himmler by putting up the extermination centers at Belzec, Sobibor, Treblinka, and Majdanek. He would take responsibility for these "workshop concentration camps" in the Lublin region. Accordingly, Himmler gave orders that Globocnik should take control of the workshops using Jewish slave labor in the Warsaw ghetto, and transfer them to the Lublin region.

The question for Globocnik was how to get thousands of Jewish workers to willingly transfer the workshops with their manufacturing equipment and move to the Lublin district. He knew that the Jews knew that the moves in the past, although advertised as transfers to work camps, had actually been transfers to the Treblinka death camp. They had meant not work but death. If Globocnik, whose murderous reputation preceded him, was seen as the man in charge of the move, it was going to be difficult to obtain the cooperation of the workers in transferring the machinery and moving the workshops. To give it the appearance of a move that was genuinely connected with a continuation of their work in the ghetto, and to try to lay to rest the fear that this was another German ruse, Globocnik decided to subcontract the task to Walther Toebbens, who owned the largest workshops using Jewish slave labor in the Warsaw ghetto.

On January 31, 1943 Globocnik signed a contract to that end with Toebbens. Toebbens would have preferred to continue running his workshops in the Warsaw ghetto, rather than coming under SS control and moving them to the Lublin region. But he had no choice but to submit to instructions, which he knew came from Himmler. Thus Toebbens became the *Umsiedlungs-Kommissar.* A thirty-four-year-old German businessman from Bremen, Toebbens had become rich by employing Jewish slave labor in his Warsaw ghetto workshop. He had shown himself to be a brutal taskmaster, notorious for whipping his workers and on occasion shooting them. He had no compunctions about defrauding them and delivering them to the SS for shipment to Treblinka whenever this suited him. However, many of the workers assumed that in this case his commercial interests would prevail and the workshops would actually be moved and continue production in the Lublin region.

Toebbens proceeded to attempt to implement the plan. He personally, and his assistants, appeared at meetings of the workshop workers, explaining that the move of the workshops would be for the benefit of the workers and their families. In the new locations, he promised, conditions would be far healthier than in the Warsaw ghetto. He gave his word of honor that the sole reason for moving the workers and their families was the continued functioning of the workshops. "Don't believe the malicious rumors, which I know are being spread in the ghetto, that deportation means death," he appealed. Those who would not make the move should expect the worst, he threatened. "I need only to press a button, and thousands of SS will come and shoot all the Jews on the spot," was his most convincing argument.[16]

On this issue the rabbis in the ghetto also decided to take a stand. At a meeting chaired by Rabbi Menahem Ziemba, the rabbis decided to advise the workers in the shops not to move to Trawniki and Poniatowa.

Both Jewish resistance organizations called on the workers not to make the move, explaining that deportation meant death, rather

---

16 Yad Vashem Archives TR/10-26 (Toebbens' file).

than survival. On the night of March 14, ZOB posted proclamations on the ghetto walls in which the shop workers were told not to cooperate with Toebbens' plans. Toebbens now realized that he was in direct competition with the Jewish underground in the ghetto. His business interests were at stake and he needed the cooperation of his Jewish workers for the move. This was one case where force was not going to be the determining factor.

On March 20, 1943, he countered the ZOB proclamation with a proclamation of his own, addressed to "The Jewish Armament Workers of the Jewish residential area." For himself and his partner Schultz, he replied to the call of the "Commando of the Combat Organization" (*Kommando der Kampforganization*). "Jewish armament workers! Do not believe those who want to mislead you. With full conviction I advise you: Go to Trawniki, go to Poniatowa, because there it is possible to live, and there you will survive the war. Believe only the German shop owners, they want – together with you – to transfer the production to Poniatowa and Trawniki. Take your wives and children with you, because they will also be cared for." It was signed Walther C. Toebbens, in charge of transferring the workshops in the Jewish residential area in Warsaw.[17]

Many of the workers succumbed to the temptation and believed his call, especially after the return to the ghetto of some of the foremen who had been sent to the new area to make the initial preparations for the move, and who reported that the plans were genuine. But they did not finally escape extermination. The SS caught up with them there a few months later.

A spirit of rebellion was beginning to penetrate many of the inhabitants of the ghetto. Most understood that following the instructions of the Germans would lead to death. Some joined the resistance organizations, some procured pistols for the defense of

---

17 Ibid.

their families, and many believed that bunkers could assure survival till the war's end. Although some of the workshops' workers had heeded Toebbens' call, the move to the Lublin area was only partially successful.

Himmler concluded that the time had come to destroy the Warsaw ghetto. The Jews in the ghetto also concluded that a German attempt to liquidate the ghetto was drawing close. Those who could afford it began the construction of bunkers in which they would be able to hide for an extended period of time. The construction of a bunker was beyond the capability of any single individual. Resources and technical know-how were required. Groups banded together to build camouflaged underground apartments, containing amenities like toilets and showers, a water supply, and a large supply of food. They were built at night in complete secrecy. If the food supply was sufficient, it was estimated that the inhabitants of the bunker could survive in them for a period of a year or a year and a half.

None would turn out to be that lucky.

The first priority for ZOB after the events of January was to acquire more weapons for its fighters. Wilner had been sent to the "Aryan" side to make contact with both AK, the right-wing underground operating under the authority of the Polish government-in-exile in London, and AL (*Armia Ludowa*), the left-wing Polish underground. These contacts had at first produced few results, but after news of the Jewish resistance in January reached "Aryan" Warsaw, AK shipped fifty pistols, grenades, and explosives to ZOB.

After the German defeat at Stalingrad, Wilner found that there was a thriving market for weapons in Warsaw and that he was not dependent on AK or AL. All that was needed was money. Aided by Tosya Altman, Michael Klepfisz, Feygele Peltel ("Wladka"), and others, he was able to obtain a fair number of pistols, which could then be thrown into the ghetto over the wall at prearranged times and places. Rifles were more expensive and far more difficult for ZOB to smuggle into the ghetto. The standard weapon of ZOB fighters became the pistol, a weapon with limited effective range.

On March 6, 1943, Wilner was arrested in Warsaw by the Gestapo as he was arranging for the purchase of a pistol. The Germans thought him to be a Polish underground member and tortured him severely, putting white-hot irons on the soles of his feet, expecting to obtain information on the Polish underground. When they discovered that he was Jewish they lost interest in him and sent him off to Pawiak prison and from there to a labor camp near Warsaw. From the camp he was smuggled back into the ghetto. He arrived, wounded and bruised, and unable to walk as a result of the torture he had undergone. He remained physically incapacitated.[18]

Wilner's arrest led to a breakdown of the contact between ZOB and AK and AL. The Poles were afraid to continue such contacts, afraid that their whole organization might be in danger of exposure after Wilner's arrest. It was only in the beginning of April that they signaled that they were prepared to resume the relations that had been broken off. Now ZOB had to decide who was going to be Wilner's replacement. It would have to be somebody senior who could continue the negotiations with AK and AL, and at the same time somebody who could pass as a Pole on the streets of Warsaw. When the inner group of ZOB – Anielewicz, Zuckerman, Tzivya Lubetkin, and Miriam Heinsdorf – met to discuss the subject, it became clear that they would have to chose between Anielewicz and Zuckerman. Zuckerman thought Anielewicz to be most suited for the task, while Anielewicz suggested that Zuckerman should take the responsibility of representing ZOB on the outside.

---

18 Lubetkin, *Biymei chilayon u-mered*, 121–22; and Zuckerman, *A Surplus of Memory*, 339.

When the issue was brought to a wider ZOB leadership forum, Zuckerman was chosen. This decision necessitated a change in the regional command structure of ZOB, since Zuckerman had been in command of the ZOB units in the Toebbens-Schultz Workshop area. To replace him, Eliezer Geller, the leading member of the Socialist Zionist youth movement Gordonia in the ghetto, was transferred from the Brushmakers' Workshop area to the Toebbens-Schultz Workshop area and put in charge of the ZOB units there. Anielewicz and Zuckerman believed that Anielewicz needed to be freed of the direct responsibility for the Central Ghetto, so that he could concentrate on the overall command of the ZOB forces in the ghetto. To fill the gap, Yisrael Kanal was appointed to head the ZOB forces in the Central Ghetto.[19]

Although ZZW did not have a permanent representation in "Aryan" Warsaw like ZOB, they had established contact with Polish underground groups who were selling them weapons and ammunition, as well as providing training for their members. Some of their members were part of the work gangs that left the ghetto each morning to work at the Warsaw eastern railroad station, where there were many opportunities to purchase weapons and ammunition. In addition, individual ZZW fighters would find ways of leaving the ghetto to arrange for the purchase of weapons in "Aryan" Warsaw.

One of them was Stefan Wladislaw, who back in May 1942 had attempted to make contact with the IZL in Palestine by sending a cable through the Red Cross to Hillel Tzur in Netanya. Wladislaw was in "Aryan" Warsaw on February 4, 1943, purchasing pistols for the ZZW, when he was intercepted by German soldiers as he returned to the ghetto. Pulling his pistol he attacked them, killing two Germans before falling himself. His body was recovered by his comrades who had been awaiting his return, and brought to burial in the Warsaw

---

19 Zuckerman, *A Surplus of Memory*, 341–44.

Jewish cemetery. His tombstone can be found there today in section 12A. The inscription reads: "Here lies buried Stefan Wladislaw ("Nesher"), God shall avenge his blood, soldier of IZL, who fell for the defense and liberation of his people, February 4, 1943, His Comrades." Nesher was his nom de guerre in the IZL.[20]

Between January and the beginning of the uprising on April 19, 1943, meetings were held between representatives of ZOB and ZZW to discuss the possibility of uniting the two organizations. Among those participating in some of these meetings were Anielewicz, Zuckerman, Lubetkin, and Edelman for ZOB, and Wdowinski, Frenkel, and Rodal for ZZW. No real progress was made in these discussions. ZZW, comparing its assessment of the military capability of the two organizations, felt that it could carry out the discussions with ZOB on the basis of equality. The fact was that it was better equipped and better trained than ZOB. ZOB, on the other hand, considered that it was by far the most important resistance organization in the ghetto, including in its ranks all youth movements and political parties except for the Revisionists. The ideological distaste that most of the ZOB membership had for the Revisionists certainly did not serve as an incentive for uniting the two organizations. Wdowinski, who represented ZZW in some of the meetings with representatives of ZOB, later wrote about these negotiations: "Right from the start I had hoped that there would be one fighting organization. But after two meetings with Tzivya Lubetkin, a representative of the extreme left Zionist Party, and Mordechai Anielewicz, who became the head of the Jewish Fighting Organization, it became obvious that this would never come to pass."[21]

---

20 David Wdowinski speaking in Tel Aviv, as reported in *Herut* on June 12, 1961.
21 Wdowinski, *And We Are Not Saved*, 78.

Two issues turned out to be insurmountable. ZZW was looking for a merger of the two organizations, with the militarily most qualified man taking command of the merged group. ZOB, on the other hand, was prepared to accept ZZW members as individuals into the ranks of ZOB, but not ZZW as a unit. That condition, in effect, made unity between the two organizations impractical; if carried out in this manner it would degrade the combined military capability of the two organizations, since it would involve ZZW disbanding its existing trained units. It was also contrary to the organizational structure of ZOB, which was based on fighting units each composed of members of a single movement or party. The ZZW demand that the overall commander should be the militarily most qualified among them – they surely had Pawel Frenkel in mind – although quite logical, could not very well be applied to the existing ZOB structure, which was based on giving movements and political parties representation in the ZOB Command.[22] In any case, it would not be approved by the political committee, or by the Bund in the Coordinating Committee.

Days before the uprising, a last attempt to unify the forces was made by Ryszard Walewski, a thirty-seven-year-old physician with left-wing views, who had assembled around him a group determined to participate in the battle against the Germans. They had succeeded in acquiring some arms and wished to join ZOB, but found that the doors there were closed to them. They were not members of any of the constituent groups of ZOB and did not fit in.

After the war Walewski described his efforts to first join ZOB and then entering the ranks of ZZW:

---

22 Ibid., 77; and Zuckerman, *A Surplus of Memory*, 226–27. Also an interview with Marek Edelman by the author on November 25, 2005, in Warsaw.

Time is growing short, we are expecting an *akciya* any day, we cannot continue for long in this organizational vacuum. In our ranks voices grow against the policy of ZOB and for the organization of a third independent military organization. I opposed it, because it meant the continuation of division in the fighting ghetto. I felt that consolidation of all the fighting forces in the ghetto within one organization was essential....

We try for the last time. We send a final ultimatum: if the ZOB will not keep to the agreement, we will break contact. And we got to the point where we break the contact....

At this decisive time, as the ghetto stands before a general confrontation, when all efforts must be directed at strengthening our fighting capability, the organizational division of the underground ghetto results in internal tension, mutual friction, and a struggle between the organizations over influence, money, and control in the ghetto.... The competitive arguments weaken the force of resistance of the ghetto. At all costs we must bring an end to these conflicts and to attain unity of the Jewish underground.

Following this line we approach the second military organization with a suggestion of cooperation, the ZZW located right near us. This time the agreement was reached quickly. We continue as an autonomous military unit under the command of ZZW while maintaining an independent organizational structure, group commanders, and area commanders....

The internal relations in the ghetto, especially between ZOB and ZZW, did not improve. ZOB is clearly aiming to attain sole control in the ghetto and ignores the fact that there are other armed organizations that are not tied to ZOB: there is ZZW and there are other armed groups not connected to ZOB. They ignore the fact that ZZW represents a serious military force in the ghetto, being better armed, very well organized, with

better connections on the "Aryan" side – for example, an instructor who is a Captain in the Polish underground comes to
ZZW; and they are established in a well-fortified area.[23]

Walewski hoped that joining ZZW would be a first step in achieving
unity between ZOB and ZZW. He was authorized by ZZW to try to
arrange a meeting between the two leaderships. After some hesitation
ZOB agreed to hold such a meeting. The meeting produced no
progress toward unity, but an agreement on a coordinated strategy.
When the Germans entered the ghetto the defense was going to be
based on a triangle, whose apex was Muranowski Square, and whose
two corners of the base were to be the Mila-Zamenhofa and the
Gensia-Nalewki intersections. ZZW was to hold Muranowski Square
and ZOB the two angles of the base. But whereas ZZW was fortifying
Muranowski Square and preparing itself for a lengthy confrontation
with German forces there, ZOB had not abandoned its earlier decision
not to take on the Germans in a face-to-face confrontation. Under
these circumstances, the triangle could not be held.

---

23 Ryszard Walewki's testimony before the Polish Commission investigating
war crimes in Warsaw, headed by Janina Skoczinska on November 25,
1948.

Chapter 8

Last Days before the Uprising

April 15–April 18, 1943

On Thursday, April 15, 1943, Himmler telephoned SS-Brigadefuehrer Juergen Stroop in Radom. "My dear Stroop," Himmler addressed him, "everything, even the most important matters, pales beside the task that I have assigned to you in Warsaw. The time for the great action has come. Report to Krueger in Krakow to coordinate certain plans; on April 17 you must be in Warsaw. From Krakow call Hahn, and he will confidentially inform you of the address of the residence that has been prepared for you."[1] April 20 was going to be Hitler's fifty-fourth birthday, and Himmler was preparing the liquidation of the Warsaw ghetto as a birthday gift for him. It might compensate for the major defeats that the German armies had been suffering during the past few months at Stalingrad and in North Africa. Stroop was performing the duties of SS-Polizeifuehrer working out of Radom, SS-Obergruppenfuehrer Friedrich-Wilhelm Krueger was the SS and Polizeifuehrer of the *Generalgovernement*, and Ludwig Hahn was head of the Gestapo in Warsaw.

Himmler did not hold von Sammern-Frankenegg in high regard, considered him soft-hearted and unreliable, and was preparing his replacement, a man he thought would be just right for this mission. Himmler knew his man. Forty-eight-year-old Stroop had been one of the early adherents of Hitler. He joined the Nazi party and the SS in 1932. During the war he had been with the SS Divi-

---

1   Moczarski, *Gespraeche mit dem henker*, 156.

sion Totenkopf on the eastern front, and lately he had distinguished himself hunting down partisans operating in the Ukraine. According to Max Jesuiter, his chief of staff during his stay in Warsaw, "Stroop had an outspoken hatred against Jews. If it had gone according to Stroop, not one train with Jews would have left Warsaw, but Stroop could have liquidated all Jews right here."[2]

In Krakow, Krueger transmitted to Stroop Himmler's orders to immediately go to Warsaw and there to oversee the deportation of the Jews from the ghetto. He arrived in Warsaw on Saturday, and Hahn led him to his luxurious quarters on Aleja Roz, whose location had been kept secret, and gave him a rundown on the situation in Warsaw and the many failings of von Sammern-Frankenegg.[3]

On April 13, ZOB received a message through one of its contacts in "Aryan" Warsaw. The message was: "If you don't want the salt to arrive after the food, you have to come now." Anielewicz and Zuckerman assumed that the message was an indication that the AK wanted to meet with Zuckerman urgently and discuss assistance to ZOB. Zuckerman quickly prepared himself to move out of the ghetto that afternoon. Outfitted with false Polish documents, dressed in a suit borrowed from someone else, considerably too small for him, and carrying a package of used clothes under his arm, he posed as a Pole who had come to do business in the ghetto. He passed through a ghetto gate whose guards had been bribed to let him through without undue inspections. A hundred meters outside the gate, he was met by seventeen-year-old pretty blonde Franya Beatus, one of the ZOB couriers in Warsaw, acting the role of a coquettish Polish young

---

2   Testimony of Georg Michalsen at war crimes trial in Hamburg, July 25, 1974.

3   Moczarski, *Gespraeche mit dem henker*, 155–58.

woman, who led him to an apartment in which arrangements had been made for his stay.[4]

Zuckerman was eager to reestablish the contact with the AK, which had been broken off when Wilner was arrested by the Gestapo. He met with Adolf Berman, the representative of the Jewish National Committee (ZKN) in Warsaw, who arranged for a meeting with Henryk (Waclaw) Wolynski, the man in charge of Jewish affairs in AK. When the two met a few days later, Zuckerman saw before him a short, bespectacled, middle-aged man. He was gravely disappointed by what he heard. The AK, Wolynski told him, proposed that AK arrange for the ghetto fighters to leave the ghetto and establish themselves as a partisan unit under their authority. It was clear that the AK did not want an uprising in the ghetto to take place. Zuckerman understood that AK was concerned that an uprising in the ghetto could precipitate fighting by Poles against the Germans outside the ghetto, a development that they considered premature at this time, and therefore harmful to their cause. Zuckerman explained to him that ZOB was determined to carry out its battle against the Germans in the ghetto. To Zuckerman's arguments Wolynski replied that he had passed on AK policy, which had been determined by higher authority, and that he was not empowered to make any changes. Zuckerman then asked to meet the head of AK, Stefan (Grot) Rowecki, and was told by Wolynski that he would get a reply to his request on April 18 or 19.[5]

Zuckerman sent a report of the conversation to Anielewicz in the ghetto through a work gang that returned to the ghetto after its day's labor in Warsaw. He also wrote him that he intended to return to the ghetto on Passover eve, April 19, to spend the Seder with his comrades. Both Anielewicz and Lubetkin in their reply urged him

---

4   Zuckerman, *A Surplus of Memory*, 344–46.
5   Ibid., 348–49.

to stay in Warsaw and to continue to pursue his contacts with the Poles. "You haven't done anything yet and you're already coming back to the ghetto?" Lubetkin wrote. But Zuckerman decided to go to the ghetto despite his comrades' advice. He felt lonely and he did not want to miss the Seder. He was determined to reenter the ghetto on April 19. When he awoke on Monday morning, April 19, the Warsaw ghetto was sealed off by German troops, and the uprising had already begun.[6]

David Landau was in "Aryan" Warsaw on Saturday, April 17, to visit his wife, Luba, who was in hiding there. He noticed unusual traffic in the streets; something seemed to be going on. On arrival at the workplace of the ghetto work gang, which he intended to join on his way back into the ghetto, the foreman looked nervous. "I have been waiting for you since the morning. You have to report to Muranowska as soon as possible," he told him. By the end of the day, the increasing military traffic in the streets made it clear that the Germans were preparing a big operation. When Landau reported to his superior at ZZW headquarters that evening, he was ordered not to leave the ghetto from now on. "We don't know if the moment of truth will be on Monday, Passover eve, or on Tuesday, Hitler's birthday. We must be able to locate you at a moment's notice," he was told.[7]

The Germans had set the date. It was going to be Monday, April 19. They expected to have the birthday gift ready for Hitler on his birthday, April 20, the next day. On Sunday morning, April 18, von Sammern-Frankenegg convened a meeting at his office on Ujazdowskie Avenue of all the officers that were scheduled to take part in the liquidation of the Warsaw ghetto the following day: Obersturmban-

---

6   Ibid., 348–50; also Zuckerman, *Ba-geto u-va-mered*, 83–90.
7   Landau, *Caged*, 185–87.

nfuehrer Dr. Ludwig Hahn, commander of the police and security services in Warsaw, the commanders of the SS units in Warsaw, the commanders of the armored and infantry battalions that had been ordered to participate in the operation, the commanders of the security police and the regular police, and the staff officers of von Sammern-Frankenegg's headquarters.

Von Sammern notified those assembled that the following day, Monday, the Jews who still remained in the Warsaw ghetto were to be transferred. Just as the discussion began about the exact time for the participation of the various units, Juergen Stroop barged into the room. His presence seemed to embarrass von Sammern. Stroop decided not to participate in the discussion, having no intention of making suggestions at this time regarding von Sammern's plan of action.

In the early afternoon of April 18, 1943, Stroop decided to take a tour of the ghetto. He had expected to find the streets crowded with people, and was surprised to find them empty. He sensed that the Jews had been forewarned of the coming operation. On his return to his quarters in the evening, he took a bath, ate a steak dinner, drank some wine, and before going to sleep asked to be woken at 4 a.m. the next morning.[8]

This time ZOB and ZZW were not going to be caught unawares; they were prepared. Yet, many meetings and long negotiations had not brought unity to their ranks, not even coordination or a common strategy. In the Central Ghetto the ZOB Command acknowledged that ZZW forces would hold the area around Muranowski Square. That is as far as it went. Although both forces had units in the Brushmakers' Workshop area and in the Toebbens-Schultz Workshop area

---

8   Moczarski, *Gespraeche mit dem henker*, 158–62.

prepared to fight the Germans as they entered the ghetto, their activities were not coordinated.

The eve of the uprising, April 18, 1943, found the commander
of ZOB, Mordechai Anielewicz, together with twenty-three-year-old
Yisrael Kanal, who had been appointed commander of ZOB forces in
the Central Ghetto so that Anielewicz would be free to provide overall direction to the ZOB forces in the ghetto, at ZOB headquarters on
Mila Street 29. When the news arrived that the Germans were planning to enter the ghetto in force the following day, ZOB units in the
Central Ghetto took up their prearranged positions, commanding the
southern entrances to the Central Ghetto – at the corner of Nalewki
and Gensia streets, and at the corner of Zamenhofa and Mila streets.
There were two squads, commanded by Zecharia Artstein and Lutek
Rotblat, at the Nalewki entrance, and four squads, commanded by
Berl Braude, Aaron Bryskin, Mordechai Growas, and Leib Gruzalc,
overlooking the Zamenhofa-Mila intersection.[9] A group of ZZW
fighters, under the command of a ZZW unit commander, Jan "Pika"
Finkel, had taken up positions in the immediate vicinity, at Mila 28
and Mila 29.[10]

The ZOB squads in the Central Ghetto were composed of between fifteen to twenty fighters. Each ZOB fighter was equipped
with a pistol and ten to fifteen rounds, four to five hand grenades,
and four to five homemade Molotov cocktails.[11] The four rifles in

9   Aharon Carmi and Haim Frimmer, Min ha-dlikah ha-hi [From that blaze]
     (Tel Aviv: Hakibbutz Hameuhad, 1961), 215–16; Tuvia Borzykowski, Bein
     kirot noflim [Between falling walls] (Tel Aviv: Hakibbutz Hameuhad–Beit
     Lohamei Hagetaot, 1964), 36; and Gutman, The Jews of Warsaw 1939–
     1943, 372.

10   Jakub Smakowski, Zichroines fun a Yidishen Geto Kemfer [Memories of a
     Jewish Ghetto Fighter], Warsaw Jewish Historical Institute, ZIH VII/145
     (dictated by Smakowski after the war).

11   Zuckerman, Ba-geto u-va-mered, 90. According to Zuckerman, the ZOB at
     the time of the uprising possessed 350 pistols and about ten rifles. They

possession of the ZOB fighters in the Central Ghetto had been split between the four squads at Zamenhofa and the two squads at Nalewki.

The Toebbens-Schultz Workshops were a relatively large area separated from the Central Ghetto, bordered on the north-west by Nowolipki Street, on the south-east by Leszno Street, and bisected by Nowolipie Street, running parallel to the above streets. Much of the area was occupied by workshops producing materiel for the German armed forces and buildings which housed the Jews employed there and their families. German units moving toward the Central Ghetto were likely to pass these workshops, providing an opportunity for the ZOB and ZZW units stationed there to harass them as they passed. The ZOB units in this area were commanded by Eliezer Geller, the senior Gordonia member in the ghetto, who was appointed to command the ZOB forces in the area when Zuckerman was sent to "Aryan" Warsaw. His fighters, organized in eight small squads, were armed with pistols, grenades, Molotov cocktails, and a single rifle. They manned eight outposts: four on Nowolipie Street, one on Smocza Street, leading into Nowolipie Street, and three along Leszno Street.[12] In that area, the ZOB fighters had broken through walls between buildings, connecting the attics of the houses so as to enable them to move freely throughout the area. Thus they could pass between positions on Leszno, Nowolipie, a section of Smocza, and part of Nowolipki without descending into the street. A tunnel was dug from the position commanded by David Nowdoworski at Nowolipie 69 to the corner of Zelezna, where the *Befehlstelle*, the Gestapo command-post at the entrance to the ghetto, was located.

---

were distributed among twenty-two ZOB squads. Also Edelman, *The Ghetto Fights*, 35.

12 Carmi and Frimmer, *Min ha-dlikah ha-hi*, 119–20; and Zuckerman, *A Surplus of Memory*, 354.

There a mine was placed, the electric wires for its detonation leading to Nowdoworski's position, to be set off at the appropriate moment.

Twenty-five-year-old Eliezer Geller, who had served in the Polish army during the German invasion of Poland, became on his return the leading activist of the Gordonia youth movement in the ghetto. He had not believed in the chances of organized resistance in the Warsaw ghetto, and had transferred many of the Gordonia members in the Warsaw ghetto to provincial cities during the months of the great deportation, something that led to rancorous relations between him and Zuckerman. On his return to the Warsaw ghetto he expressed his regret for what he held to have been "an erroneous decision."

"It is now beyond any doubt that all forces and energy…should have been directed toward preparing for self-defense and resistance," he wrote in January.[13]

Twenty-seven-year-old David Nowdoworski, a member of Hashomer Hatzair, had been picked up by the Germans and sent to Treblinka during the great deportation, but succeeded in escaping and returning to the Warsaw ghetto, bringing confirmation to the ghetto's inhabitants of the fate that awaited those deported from the ghetto. Now he was to lead one of the ZOB fighting units.

The ZZW forces in the Toebbens-Schultz Workshop area were better armed than the ZOB. Under the command of Natan Shultz, who had returned to the Warsaw ghetto from the Hrubieszow farms in June 1942, they manned eight outposts: five along Nowolipie Street, two along Leszno Street, and one at 5 Karmelicka Street, the ZZW headquarters and the location of a tunnel the ZZW had constructed to the "Aryan" side of Warsaw.[14] The leading members of the ZZW units in

---

13 Yad Vashem Archives M-20/115a.
14 Simha Korngold's diary, Yad Vashem Archives O-33/1566.

*Mordechai Anielewicz, commander of the
Jewish Fighting Organization (ZOB)*

Pawel Frenkel, commander of the Jewish Military Organization (ZZW) –
a composite picture drawn by Gil Gibli based on testimony by Yisrael Ribak
and Fela Finkelstein-Shapchik

Warsaw 1946

Yitzhak Zuckerman (Antek), deputy commander of ZOB

Leon Rodal, deputy commander of ZZW

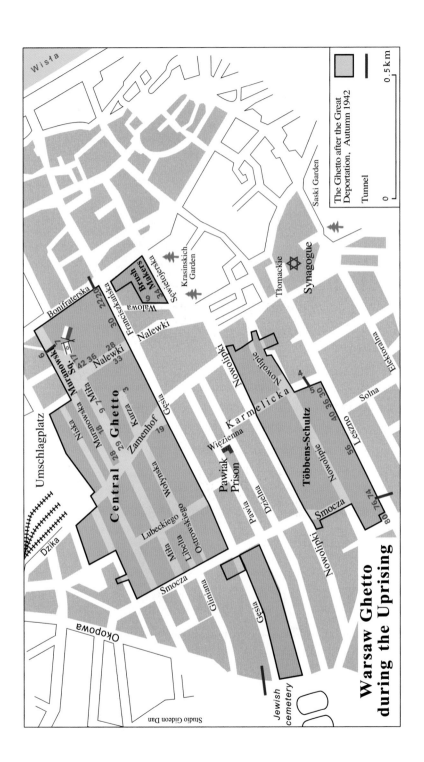

Warsaw Ghetto
during the Uprising

SS General Juergen Stroop, commander of the German forces who suppressed the uprising, at his war crimes trial

German artillery fires into the ghetto during the uprising.

Jewish girl fighters apprehended by German soldiers

The Germans set fire to the ghetto

Jews forced to leave a bunker

Jews executed by the Germans

Muranowski Square – from the archives of the
Jewish Historical Institute in Warsaw

Muranowski 3 in flames – from the archives of the
Jewish Historical Institute in Warsaw

Letter sent on May 17, 1942 through the Red Cross in Warsaw by members of the Irgun Zvai Leumi in the Warsaw ghetto, addressed to Hillel Tzur, in Netanya, Palestine, who had been their instructor in Poland before the war. It was an attempt to establish contact with the IZL in Palestine. The German censor cut away part of the letter.

DAXWANGER HERMANN ✻...
• DECKER FLORIAN ✻10.12.1921 +22.1...
• DEGEN PHILIPP ✻19.6.1908 +2.2.1...
• DEGENKOLBE HEINZ ✻28.10...
✻10.7.1941 • DEHILS HANS ✻16.10...
3.1919 +3.10.1943 • DEISS AUGUST-EMIL ✻16.12...
✻14.11.1943 • DEISS AUGUST-EMIL...
3.1899 +9.10.1939 • DEJA ARNOLD ✻18.3.1...
✻3.1914 +7.9.1939 • DELSCHEN BRUNO +20.9.1...
9.1939 • DEMMKE HANS ✻4.7.1921 +22.4.194...
+25.7.1944 • DENECHAUD RICHARD ✻23.11.19...
AS ✻18.11.1916 +23.9.1939 • DENK RUDOLF ✻29.3.19...
LO ✻3.10.1923 +5.5.1943 • VAN DER LIST WILHEL...
DER SCHULENBURG GUSTAV ✻16.4.1917 +19.9.193...
912 +28.9.1943 • DEBOEUX FRANCOIS ✻30.5.190...
M ✻9.1939 • DETZER WILHELM ✻11.8.1907 +11.6.19...
44 • DEUTSCH JOACHIM ✻30.3.1913 +20.6.194...
✻23.3.1912 +16.9.1939 • DEUTSCHER RICHARD ✻2.4.1917...

German war cemetery in Poland. It lists Hans Dehmke, who fell on April 22, 1943, on the fourth day of the battle in Muranowski Square.

The entrance to the German war cemetery in Poland

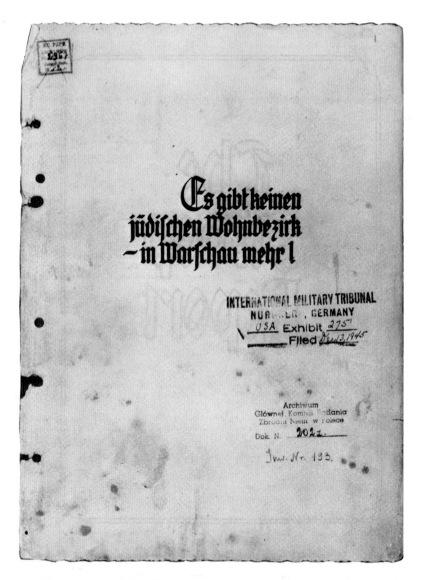

The cover page of the album prepared by SS General Juergen Stroop.
The title reads: "The Jewish residential quarter in Warsaw no longer exists!"
The album was presented as evidence in the Nuremberg war crimes trials.

The grave in the Warsaw Jewish cemetery of ZZW fighter Stefan Wladislaw, who fell in battle with German soldiers. The gravestone reads: "Here is buried Stefan Wladislaw ("Nesher"), God will avenge his blood, SOLDIER OF THE IZL, who fell in defense and for the liberty of the Jewish people, February 4, 1943, age 20. His comrades." Nesher was his nom de guerre in the IZL.

The author standing next to the grave of Stefan Wladislaw in the Jewish cemetery in Warsaw

the area, in addition to Natan Shultz, were Pinhas Toib and Simha Witelson. They and Alek Halberstein, who had been transferred to the Central Ghetto to lead a unit there, had been members of the Betar branch in North Warsaw as youngsters before the war and were well acquainted with Pawel Frenkel from those pre-war days.

There was no coordination between ZOB forces and ZZW forces in the area, but there was awareness of each other's presence. Early in the morning of April 19, a man approached the ZOB position of Gordonia members, commanded by twenty-three-year-old Yaacov Feigenblat, on Leszno 76. Feigenblat thought the man to be the ZZW commander in the area. He offered to transfer to ZOB a box of grenades and a barrel of explosives. Feigenblat eagerly accepted the offer and sent three of his men to Karmelicka 5, the ZZW headquarters in the Toebbens-Schultz area, to pick up the grenades and explosives. The grenades were distributed to the ZOB units in the area.[15]

The Brushmakers' Workshop area, separated from the Central Ghetto by Franciskanska Street, was a small walled-off block of buildings, bordered by Franciskanska, Walowa, Swientojerska, and Bonifraterska streets. It contained workshops, some making brushes for the German army, and the houses in which lived the workers and their families.

The commander of the ZOB forces here was twenty-one-year-old Marek Edelman of the Bund, who had replaced Berek Shneidmill as the Bund representative on the ZOB Command after Shneidmill's resignation. Five ZOB units were stationed in the area. Another member of the ZOB Command, Hersh Berlinski, led the Left Po'alei Zion unit there. Each of the ZOB fighters was armed with a pistol, a few grenades, and homemade Molotov cocktails. Two of the fight-

---

15 Carmi and Frimmer, *Min ha-dlikah ha-hi*, 119; and Yaakov Putermilch, *Ba-esh u-va-sheleg* [In fire and in snow] (Tel Aviv: Hakibbutz Hameuhad–Beit Lohamei Hagetaot, 1981), 75.

ers had rifles. They had dug a tunnel under the entry gate to the Brushmakers' Workshop area and placed a mine there. The electric wires for detonating the mine led to the command post of Hanoch Gutman's unit at Walowa 6, which overlooked the gate.[16]

Three ZZW units were stationed in the Brushmakers area, under the overall command of Samuel Luft from his headquarters at Swientojerska 30. The three unit commanders were Yuzek Lopata, one of the Lopata brothers, Yitzhak Bilewski, who had before the war been active in Betar in Lodz, and David Shulman, a Revisionist lawyer who had moved from the Toebbens-Schultz area to the Brushmakers area shortly before the uprising.[17] Like the ZOB fighters, they were armed with pistols, grenades, and Molotov cocktails. The units manned bunkers along Swientojerska Street. There was no contact between the forces of the two resistance organizations in this area.

The major effort by ZZW, under the command of Pawel Frenkel, to confront German troops entering the ghetto was going to be made at Muranowski Square, in the northeastern corner of the ghetto. Ryszard Walewski, who with his group had joined ZZW and was assigned to take part in the defense of Muranowski Square, has described the Square and its surroundings and the preparations for its defense:

> Blocks of tall buildings surrounded Muranowski Square. Narrow streets separated the blocks. Defensive barriers were raised. A row of houses, camouflaged passageways, cellars connected to each other, hidden garrets – made it possible to pass from house to house without going into the open square.... The topographical layout of Muranowski Square was particularly

---

16 B. Mark, ed., *Tsum tsenten yortog* [On the tenth anniversary] (Warsaw: Jewish Historical Institute, 1953), 217–18.

17 Lazar Litai, *Matzada shel Varsha*, 241.

suitable to the defense of the ghetto. To Muranowski Square were connected Muranowska and Nalewki Streets. The square faced frontally the path [that would have to be taken by the Germans] in order capture this part of the ghetto. In the front part of the houses the positions for the first line of defense were established. Two giant buildings, on both sides of the square, became fortified positions. In these buildings firing positions for machine guns were established, but in addition, the other buildings were also fortified and a network of positions for riflemen was set up there; the windows in the front of the buildings were plugged and the cellars were turned into bunkers. Thus a block of defensive positions was established in Muranowski Square.[18]

In this area Frenkel had concentrated about two hundred of his fighters, organized in four units, led by Leon Rodal, Alek Halberstein, Meir Toblos, and Yosef Goldhaber. They were armed with the best equipment ZZW possessed, including rifles and two machine guns. They were the best trained and best armed fighters in the ghetto.[19]

Emmanuel Ringelblum, the chronicler of the Warsaw ghetto, was a leading member of Left Po'alei Zion. Naturally, his attitude to the Revisionists was negative, and he considered their movement's ideology similar to "Italian-style Fascism." Yet he considered it his duty to preserve an objective record of the events in the ghetto. He knew that in addition to ZOB, there was another underground organization in the ghetto, ZZW, and that it was led by Revisionists.

Shortly before the uprising he made his way to the northeastern part of the Central Ghetto, by now an uninhabited block of build-

---

18 Walewski, *Jurek*, 67.
19 Lazar Litai, *Matzada shel Varsha*, 239. Also Alexander Donat, "Our Last Days in the Warsaw Ghetto," *Commentary*, May 1963.

ings, referred to as a "wild" area. There he entered ZZW headquarters at Muranowska 7. The headquarters was located in a six-room flat on the first floor of this abandoned building.

Some weeks later he wrote down what he had seen on this visit:

> There was a first-class radio in the command room that received news from all over the world, and next to it stood a typewriter. I talked to the people in command for several hours. They were armed with revolvers stuck in their belts. Different kinds of weapons were hung in the large rooms: light machine guns, rifles, revolvers of different kinds, hand grenades, bags of ammunition, German uniforms, etc., all of which were utilized to the full in the April "action." There was great activity in the command room, as in any army headquarters, fighters received their orders for the "barrack-points" where future combatants were being brought together and instructed. Reports arrived of expropriations of wealthy people carried out by individual groups for the sake of arming the ZZW. While I was there, a purchase of arms was made from a former Polish army officer, amounting to a quarter of a million zloty; a sum of 50,000 zloty was paid on account. Two machine guns were bought at 40,000 zloty each, and a large amount of hand grenades and bombs. In answer to my question as to why the premises were not camouflaged I was told that there was no fear of betrayal from their own followers, and in the case of an undesirable visitor, a gendarme, for example – he wouldn't leave there alive.[20]

---

20 Yosef Kermish, *To Live with Honor and to Die with Honor! Selected Documents from the Warsaw Ghetto Underground Archives "O.S." ("Oneg Shabbat")* (Jerusalem: Yad Vashem, 1986), 596. Also Ringelblum, *Ktavim aharonim*, 234.

Ringelblum was impressed by what he saw at Muranowska 7, by the military bearing of the ZZW commanders, who openly carried their personal weapons, by their self-confidence and lack of fear. He regretted the lack of unity between the two resistance organizations at these desperate times. He gave expression to these feeling some months after the uprising, while hiding in "Aryan" Warsaw, shortly before he and his family were apprehended by the Germans and shot. In a note left by him, he wrote:

> Since the war crucial questions faced the Jewish public. The former political struggles had to cease. A united political front that would embrace everybody had to be established. From the left to the right, Hitler's extermination campaign against the Jewish people was directed against all classes and all sectors. In the eyes of the enemy there is no difference between Bundists and Zionists. Both are hated and both he wishes to destroy, and therefore there was a need to change the internal struggle among the Jewish public, to set up a united national front against the forces of evil of German fascism.[21]

On Sunday, April 18, 1943, the day before the uprising, Walewski and Leon Rodal were in the ZZW headquarters at Muranowska 7, making last-minute preparations. Walewski, who survived the fighting in the ghetto, later recalled Rodal's words:

> We will all fall here. Those in battle, weapons in hand, and those as vain victims. But it is important that the memory of our battle will be retained, that the world will know that there was a battle. A tough bloody battle. And should it happen that you, of the two of us, will survive...and sometime, some-

---

21 Ringelblum, *Ktavim aharonim*, "Portrait of Shachna Sagan."

place, you were to meet my comrades, please tell them what I said, tell them that not for a moment did I doubt that Hitler's Germany would be defeated, not I, nor my comrades... that we are fighting for our people and shall die for them. That we believe that a Jewish State will arise in a struggle with our enemies there in that distant land.... During that far-off period of slavery, when the Roman legions trampled almost the entire ancient world, and the whole world kneeled before them, only one small Roman province, Judea, took up arms, rose up to fight for freedom and in defense of the honor of man, against a world of injustice. And that is the reason that Judea is inscribed in the history of man as a symbol of the fight for the spirit of man.... Maybe, some day, after many years, when the history of the struggle against the Nazi conquerors is written, we also will be remembered, and, who knows, we will become – like small Judea in its day, which fought mighty Rome – the symbol of man's spirit that cannot be suppressed, whose essence is the fight for freedom, for the right to live, and the right to exist.[22]

It was a warm, beautiful spring day. On the other side of the ghetto wall, next to the Brushmakers' Workshop area, the Easter Week Carnival was in full force in the Krasinski Garden. The music of the merry-go-round's organ grinder penetrated into the desolate streets of the ghetto.

To keep their fighters occupied, the ZZW leadership made them dismantle the rifles, machine guns, and revolvers for a last time before going into battle.[23]

---

22 Ryszard Walewski in *Kolot min ha-kever*, Givat Haviva Institute: Moreshet Archives, D2.276, pp.1, 2, and 6.
23 Landau, *Caged*, 191.

Chapter 9

Flags over the Ghetto

> *"This blue-white flag...that was*
> *unfurled over the walls of the Warsaw*
> *ghetto in the desperate uprising..."*
>
> – Israeli foreign minister Moshe Sharet at the
> ceremony when the Israeli flag was raised in
> front of the UN building in New York, 1949

April 19–April 22, 1943

Monday, April 19, 1943 – Passover eve, the first day of the uprising

The plan of SS-Oberfuehrer Ferdinand von Sammern-Frankenegg was to clear out what had remained of the Central Ghetto and ship the Jews there to Treblinka, while transferring the workers in the Toebbens-Schultz and Brushmakers' workshops and their families to the new location in the Lublin region.

His forces entered the Central Ghetto on April 19 at 6 a.m., with 850 men led by sixteen officers. The force included units of the 3rd SS Panzer Training and Replacement (T&R) Battalion, units of the SS Cavalry Replacement Detachment, units of the 22nd SS Police Regiment, a unit of "Trawniki" men (Ukrainians in the service of the Germans), and security personnel.[1] They were accompanied by a

---

1   Juergen Stroop's operational reports, report of April 20, 1943. Stroop's daily reports were originally written in German. The English translation,

light tank and two heavy armored cars. The tank was a Czech LT-38, mounting a 37-mm Skoda gun and two 7.92-mm machine guns; it was manned by men of the 3rd SS Panzer T&R Battalion.[2]

Before daybreak on April 19, it was still cold and dark. Yaacov Putermilch, a member of Yaacov Feigenblat's ZOB unit in the Toebbens-Schultz Workshop area, stood at his observation post at Leszno 76, observing the guard at the ghetto gate at the corner of Zelezna and Leszno. At a quarter to five he saw a truck approaching the ghetto gate. Six Germans jumped from the truck and took up positions along the street, and the truck continued in the direction of the Central Ghetto. As it became lighter he discerned the German and Polish guards who had been posted along the ghetto wall. His unit was prepared for battle.

At 5 a.m. he and his comrades saw a number of German units approaching. They were marching, coming from Okopowa along Leszno in the direction of the Central Ghetto. Eliezer Geller, the ZOB commander of the Toebbens-Schultz area, had joined him at his post. A grenade thrown by Geller at the Germans was supposed to be the signal for an attack on the Germans from the ZOB posts along Leszno, but Geller held back. A few SS units passed, then some ar-

---

as presented at Nuremberg, is in the public domain and retained at the National Archives.

2   French L. MacLean, *The Ghetto Men: The SS Destruction of the Jewish Warsaw Ghetto, April–May 1943* (Atglen, PA: Schiffer Publishing, 2001), 167–70. MacLean provides a detailed description of the German forces used in suppressing the uprising, naming the different units, their weapons, and their commanders. Based on research of German army personnel files, he names each of their casualties, the unit to which he belonged, and the date of injury or death. This permits identification of the German military units in some of the encounters, and estimates of German casualties in specific encounters. His casualty list is probably the best estimate of German casualties. It does not differ substantially from Stroop's casualty reports.

mored vehicles, and then some more SS soldiers. Geller stood there handling his grenade, his fighters waited impatiently, but he did not throw it. In the meantime the Germans had passed and the grenade had not been thrown.

After a short interruption more Germans appeared, then Ukrainians and Poles, then a group of Germans on motorcycles, and a number of trucks full of Germans in full battle gear. At the end of the column was a field kitchen. They passed the length of Leszno, along the ghetto wall, and then turned left on Karmelicka toward the Central Ghetto.[3] Geller had misunderstood the instructions passed to him by telephone by Yitzhak Zuckerman, the former commander of the Toebbens-Schultz Workshop area and now the ZOB's liaison in "Aryan" Warsaw, to attack the Germans in case they were to approach the Central Ghetto through Leszno Street.[4] ZZW units in the Toebbens-Schultz area, whose commander was Pinhas Toib, did not take any action either at this time.[5]

The troops approached the Central Ghetto from the south by moving along Leszno Street, passing the Toebbens-Schultz Workshop area, then turning north on Karmelicka Street, from there east on Nowolipki Street to Nalewki Street. At the corner of Nalewki and Gensia a part of their forces moved along Gensia toward the Central Ghetto gate at Zamenhofa Street, while the rest entered the Central Ghetto through Nalewki Street.

---

3 Putermilch, *Ba-esh u-va-sheleg*, 74; and Carmi and Frimmer, *Min ha-dlikah ha-hi*, 119. Carmi was in the same unit as Putermilch at Leszno 76.

4 Zuckerman, *A Surplus of Memory*, 354.

5 Lazar Litai, *Matzada shel Varsha*, 260. This is based on the diaries of Simha Korngold, a ZZW fighter stationed in the Toebbens-Schultz area (Yad Vashem Archives O33/1566). Also the testimony of Fella Finkelstein-Shapchik, a ZZW fighter stationed in the Toebbens-Schultz area at Karmelicka 5 (Yad Vashem Archives O3/5135).

At dawn on April 19, Tzivya Lubetkin joined the ZOB unit composed of members of Dror, led by twenty-year-old Zecharya "Zecharyash" Artstein, considered by Lubetkin as one of the bravest ZOB fighters. They were stationed at 33 Nalewki. Tuvia Borzykowski, a thirty-two-year-old member of that unit, was standing on a first-floor balcony overlooking the Gensia-Nalewki corner. Other groups of fighters were on the upper floors of houses overlooking the intersection and inside courtyards and in the windows of some of the apartments. On this sunny spring day, Borzykowski could see the German troops approaching from a distance. How weak we are compared to them, he thought to himself. How can we fight armored cars and tanks with pistols and a few rifles?[6]

At 6 a.m. units of the SS Cavalry Replacement Detachment entered the Central Ghetto through Nalewki Street. They came marching in formation and singing. The ZOB squads of Artstein and Lutek Rotblat were stationed at windows, balconies, and courtyards near the Gensia-Nalewki intersection. The first shots were fired from Artstein's position at 33 Nalewki Street as the Germans passed that building. These were the first shots of the uprising. They were followed by rifle and pistol shots, hand grenades, and Molotov cocktails from all sides.

Under fire the German columns fell apart, and their soldiers sought cover along the walls of houses on the street, leaving their wounded where they fell. After overcoming the initial surprise, the Germans began returning fire against the ZOB positions and evacuating their wounded. Being out in the open, they were at a disadvantage. After about two hours, the Germans retreated.[7] According to

---

6   Borzykowski, *Bein kirot noflim*, 36.
7   Lubetkin, *Biymei chilayon u-mered*, 80.

Stroop's report for that day three German soldiers were wounded in this encounter.[8] The ZOB forces had suffered no casualties.

Haim Frimmer had arrived at Anielewicz's headquarter, at Mila 29, in the evening of April 18. He took his position on an upper floor balcony of the building, overlooking Zamenhofa, and padded it with pillows for protection. From there, lying on the balcony, looking through field glasses, Frimmer could observe Zamenhofa and the entrance to the Central Ghetto. His instructions were to maintain contact with Anielewicz and Kanal, who were inside the building, inform them of what was happening below, and await their instructions. He was to throw a grenade as a signal to the fighters stationed in the area when the attack on the Germans was to begin. He was armed with a Mauser pistol, twenty bullets, a few homemade grenades, and a Polish grenade.[9]

At 2 a.m. he saw a truck enter Zamenhofa and a few Ukrainians, distinguishable by their black uniforms, get out and take up positions along Zamenhofa. One of them, armed with a submachine gun, positioned himself at the corner of Zamenhofa and Muranowska.

At 5 a.m. he saw cars entering the ghetto, stopping at the square opposite the *Judenrat* building. They came to the square, stopped, and soldiers got out. Afterwards a truck arrived and on it were tables and benches. The soldiers unloaded the benches and arranged them at right angles to one another. The distance between Frimmer and the

---

8   Stroop's operational report of April 20, 1943. Stroop reports that six SS men and six Trawniki men (Ukrainians) were wounded during the operation commanded by Von Sammern. MacLean gives the names of three *Panzergrenadiere* wounded on that day. They were obviously from the SS Panzer T&R Battalion wounded in the encounter on Zamenhofa. The other three wounded SS men must have belonged to the SS Cavalry Detachment that was attacked on Nalewki. The German casualties as reported by Jewish fighters who survived the uprising are probably inflated due to the excitement and enthusiasm that accompanied the fighting.

9   Carmi and Frimmer, *Min ha-dlikah ha-hi*, 216–18.

square was about two hundred meters, and he could make them out clearly through his field glasses. He saw the soldiers string telephone cables and connect them to telephones that had been placed on the tables. The Germans were setting up a command post for their coming operation. Additional trucks arrived with soldiers armed with submachine guns. Then motorcyclists, a few ambulances, and then a tank and armored cars stopped at the gate. They were soldiers of the 3rd SS Panzer Training and Replacement Battalion and their vehicles, under the command of SS-Obersturmbannfuehrer Walter Bellwidt. What Frimmer saw he reported back to Anielewicz without leaving his post, through a fighter who lay not far from him.

The Ukrainians who had been posted along Zamenhofa during the night were now transferred as one group in the direction of the *Umschlagplatz*. At 6 a.m. a column of infantry entered. A part of the column turned to Wolynska Street and the other part stayed, as if waiting for an order. It did not take long, and through the gate Jewish police entered. They were aligned on both sides of the street and, upon receiving the order, began advancing along the street.

When the column of Jewish police reached the corner of Mila and Zamenhofa, Frimmer asked whether this was the time to signal the attack. He was told to wait until the Germans arrive. After the Jewish police had passed, a German motorized column approached. Frimmer was ordered to throw his grenade when the middle of the German column was under his balcony, but when he attempted to light the matches around the fuse of his homemade grenade, the wind blew out the matches. The column was long so he thought he had time to try again, but again no luck. When he reported his problems to Anielewicz, another fighter stationed near a window was ordered to throw a grenade. This one worked. The signal had been given and the ZOB fighters opened fire from the surrounding buildings. The Germans tried to run for cover and return the fire, but they had been caught out in the open, and building entrances offered only partial cover. Now the battle was joined by Jan (Pika) Finkel's ZZW unit, which had been stationed on Mila Street.[10] The battle had lasted about half an hour when the Germans retreated.

Frimmer stayed at his position on the balcony, and after a while he saw armored vehicles approaching followed by a column of foot-soldiers. Von Sammern had decided to send his tank and two armored cars into the battle followed by soldiers of the Panzer Battalion. As they passed the Zamenhofa-Mila corner, the tank and armored vehicles were attacked by the ZOB fighters with Molotov cocktails. The tank was set aflame and got out of the way, while burning, in the direction of the *Umschlagplatz*. Both armored cars were damaged and some of the soldiers in the armored cars were wounded. The soldiers of the Panzer Battalion retreated. German ambulances arrived to pick up the wounded. When they had gone, the Germans began shelling the Jewish positions with artillery.[11] At this point Anielewicz gave the order to retreat and the ZOB fighters began leaving the area. Frimmer was still lying on the balcony when Anielewicz called to him: "get up, we are leaving." They went down the stairs to the courtyard of Mila 29 and entered the cellar from which there was an entry into an underground bunker. There the ZOB fighters who had participated in the battle assembled.[12]

This last encounter had lasted about ten minutes. The entire battle on Zamenhofa Street had lasted about forty minutes. One ZOB fighter was killed in the battle,[13] while Jan (Pika) Finkel's unit lost

---

10 Smakowski, *Zichroines fun a Yidishen Geto Kemfer*.

11 Carmi and Frimmer, *Min ha-dlikah ha-hi*; and Stroop's operational report of April 20, 1943. See also the testimony of Haupsturmfuehrer Georg Michalsen of Odilo Globocnik's staff, who was present at the German command post on Zamenhofa during the battle, in Scheffler and Grabnitz, *Der Ghetto-Aufstand Warschau 1943*, 198–99.

12 Carmi and Frimmer, *Min ha-dlikah ha-hi*.

13 Blumental and Kermish, *Ha-meri ve-ha-mered be-Geto Varsha*, 219. In his letter of April 23, 1943, to Zuckerman, Anielewicz mentioned the single

several fighters.[14] His unit made their way to Nalewki 42 and Muranowska 17, in the heart of the area fortified by ZZW.[15] Three SS *Panzergrenadiere* and six Ukrainians had been wounded in that battle.[16]

Stroop had stayed in his quarters that morning, together with a staff he had assembled since he arrived in Warsaw, receiving reports by telephone on the ongoing operation in the ghetto. At 7:30 a.m., von Sammern appeared in Stroop's quarters and announced that everything in the ghetto was lost, that there were already casualties, and that his forces were retreating. He intended to contact Krakow and request that Stuka dive bombers be sent to bomb the ghetto and thus break the back of the uprising. Stroop told him not to contact Krakow and that he himself intended to inspect the situation on the ground.[17]

When the news of the blows the German and Ukrainian units had suffered at the hands of the Jewish fighters became known, Stroop's telephone did not stop ringing. Three times he spoke to Krueger, and then Himmler himself telephoned. Both of them were raging mad. Krueger yelled and cursed, insisting that it was a disgrace and a military defeat. "It is a stain on the honor and good name

---

casualty and estimated the length of the battle on Zamenhofa as forty minutes. In the same letter he writes: "The pistol is of no value, we almost did not use it. We need grenades, rifles, machine guns, and explosives."

14 Smakowski, *Zichroines fun a Yidishen Geto Kemfer*. Smakowski describes the participation of his unit in the fighting.

15 Landau, *Caged*, 193. Landau describes the arrival that evening of two young fighters who had participated in the fighting near Zamenhofa. He assumed that they were not associated with any organized underground.

16 Stroop's operational report of April 20, 1943.

17 Kermish, *Mered Geto Varsha be-enei ha-oyev*, 211. Yosef Kermish, Stefan Grayek, Rahel Auerbach, and Marek Edelman had an opportunity to question Stroop while he was in the Warsaw prison. A stenographic record was kept of the questions and his answers.

of the SS," he bellowed into the phone. Von Sammern, "this Tirolean idiot, this blockhead, should be immediately arrested," he insisted. He ordered that after regrouping the troops and giving them a short break, all of the Waffen-SS troops in Warsaw be thrown into the battle in the ghetto. In response to Stroop's concern that the Poles might decide to participate in the resistance, he ordered that all German units in the area be put on alert. Himmler, after giving vent to his anger by a series of curses, ordered that von Sammern be immediately removed from command of the ghetto operation and released from his position as SS-Polizeifuehrer of Warsaw, but that he should not be arrested. He ordered that all units be withdrawn from the ghetto so that the operation could be renewed in two hours under Stroop's command. There was no need to order von Sammern to withdraw, however, since he and his forces had already retreated in haste from the ghetto.[18]

Stroop mobilized the entire armed forces available to him: The 3rd SS Panzer T&R Battalion, the SS Cavalry Replacement Detachment, the 1st and 3rd Battalions of the 22nd SS Police Regiment, one battalion of Trawniki men, and security police personnel. All in all, about 1,300 officers and men. They were allocated a tank and an armored car. In addition, Stroop had 100-mm howitzers and three batteries of 22-mm anti-aircraft guns at his disposal. To boost the spirits of his troops, they were treated to a glass of *shnaps* or wine before being sent into action.[19]

---

18 Moczarski, *Gespraeche mit dem henker*, 164–65. Moczarski, who had been a member of the Polish underground AK, which had been under the authority of the Polish government-in-exile in London, was arrested by the Polish Communist government after the war and shared a prison cell at the Mokotow prison in Warsaw with Stroop. Stroop regaled his cellmates with stories about how he suppressed the ghetto uprising, hunted down the Jews there, and destroyed the ghetto. Moczarski's book deals with his conversations with Stroop.

19 Ibid., 165.

The ZOB fighters at the Nalewki-Gensia intersection, who had held their positions, had had about a three-hour respite since their first encounter with the German troops that morning. At 11 a.m. they were assaulted by German forces, now under Stroop's command, that included a tank. Using mattresses taken from the *Werterfassung* storehouse at Nalewki 28, the Germans set up a protective barricade from which they fired at the ZOB positions. The Jewish fighters set fire to the barricade with Molotov cocktails. Upon meeting resistance, Stroop ordered an interruption in the fighting and brought up his artillery units and flamethrowers to pulverize and incinerate the buildings in which resistance fighters were located.[20] In the firefight that lasted about one hour, the Germans managed to set the building at Nalewki 33 on fire. At this point the ZOB fighters decided to abandon their positions. They had been there for six hours. Now they found their way to a bunker at 3 Kurza Street.[21]

The abandonment of the ZOB positions at the Zamenhofa-Mila intersection and the Nalewki-Gensia intersection put an end to the possibility of the Jewish fighters in the ghetto holding a "defensive triangle," with the ZZW positions at Muranowski Square and its environs serving as the apex of the triangle, while the two ZOB positions serve as the base. Maintaining Jewish control of these positions would have prevented the Germans from creating a "kettle" in the Central Ghetto into which they could herd the Jewish population for transfer to Treblinka, as they had done in September 1942 during the days of the great deportation. But the ZOB positions could not withstand the German assaults. Now the Germans were free to begin their "hunt" for the Jews of the Warsaw ghetto.

During this initial hunt Stroop's troops caught 200 Jews. Then he sent raiding parties looking for bunkers whose locations were

---

20 Ibid., 166.
21 Borzykowski, *Bein kirot noflim*, 40.

known to him; he directed his troops to pull the Jews out of the bunkers and thereafter destroy the bunkers. This led to the capture of 380 Jews. When he was informed that Jews might be hiding in the sewers, he ordered that they be inundated.[22]

Now the Germans could advance into the Central Ghetto. At 5:30 p.m., as their troops entered the Central Ghetto, they came up against very heavy resistance, including machine-gun fire, from the area of Muranowski Square.[23] Here the ZZW had prepared its main defensive positions. Stroop sent a special combat group into the block of buildings that seemed to him to be the center of resistance. In his report of April 19, 1943, describing the subsequent fighting, he writes, "...they [his troops] defeated the enemy but without capturing the enemy himself. The Jews and the criminals resisted from base to base and escaped at the last moment by flight across lofts or through subterranean passages."[24] While awaiting trial in Warsaw, Stroop related to his cellmate Moczarski that it took his troops "a long time to break the resistance," that afternoon. In the evening Stroop withdrew all his forces from the ghetto.[25] If Stroop assumed that he had put an end to resistance at Muranowski Square, he was to find out differently during the coming days.

The ZZW leadership had chosen the buildings on the south side of Muranowski Square at the corner of Nalewki Street as their main line of defense. The buildings there were mostly four- to six-story dwellings. Their roofs afforded an unobstructed view of the square and provided good cover for the two approach streets of Mila and Muranowska. Walls blocked the streets to the northeast. Accessible only from the rooftops, the Nalewki Street buildings were strategically favorable. They were easy to defend, and they gave protection from the rear.

---

22 Stroop's operational report of April 20, 1943.
23 Ibid.
24 Ibid.
25 Moczarski, *Gespraeche mit dem henker*, 167.

On April 19, 1943, as the German troops entered the ghetto, the commanders of the ZZW, Pawel Frenkel and his deputy Leon Rodal, were at ZZW headquarters on Muranowska 7. They decided to hoist the Zionist flag on the roof of the tallest building in the area, Muranowska 17. The following day they raised the Polish flag next to the Zionist flag.[26]

Poles standing on the roof of the building at Muranowska 6, outside the ghetto wall, discerned people holding weapons moving around the roofs of the houses in the ghetto opposite, disappearing and reappearing again. Suddenly they saw that a blue-and-white flag had been raised on one of the roofs. A shout went up: "Look, look, the Jewish flag! Muranowski Square is in the hands of the Jews!" They could see two very young people trying to fasten the flag securely in the wind. They were risking their lives standing on the roof – after all, they could be reached at any moment by the bullets of the enemy. In the end they succeeded in fastening the flag and it fluttered in the wind.[27]

Walewski reports that Leon Rodal said to him: "You see these flags? Seemingly of little importance, and yet a great symbol of immeasurable importance. They are a symbol of unity of the Jewish-Polish struggle against the brutal aggressor. Let the world see them and know what is happening here!"[28]

---

26 Eisner, *The Survivor*, 181.
27 Alicja Kaczynska, *Obok Piekla* (Gdansk: Marpress, 1993), 67–68.
28 Walewski, *Jurek*, 72. The reaction of the Polish underground press to the raising of the flags in the ghetto varied, depending on the political affiliation of the publishers. See Andrzej Krzysztof Kunert, ed., *Polcy-Zydzi 1939–1945* (Warsaw: Instytut Dziedzictwa Narodowego, 2001). The underground journal of the extreme right, *Miecz i Plug*, *Nurt Mlodych*, wrote on April 30, 1943: "In the first days of the actions Jews hung a Polish and a Zionist flag on Plac Muranowski. This emphasis on Polish patriotism, is at least humorous if not cynical...we do believe that the 'chosen nation' [linked] its ideology, sympathy, or hope and interests with the red banner

It was a sunny spring day, and the flags were seen far and wide in Warsaw. To the Polish population, as well as the Jewish population, they became the symbol of the Warsaw Ghetto Uprising. "If only we had a camera," Frenkel remarked, "what a picture the world would see." The Germans were enraged by this sign of open rebellion. Stroop considered the flags of great political and moral importance. He thought "they reminded hundreds of thousands of the Polish cause; they incited them and united the population of the *Generalgouvernement* – Jews and Poles. Flags and national colors are an instrument of combat just as weapons are." Himmler telephoned Stroop and ordered him "to bring down those two flags at all costs."[29]

Ten SS men and two Polish policemen were wounded, and one Polish policeman was killed during the fighting in the ghetto after Stroop took command that day, in addition to the twelve reported as wounded in the period before Stroop assumed command. They included six soldiers of the SS Cavalry Detachment, and three men of the 22nd SS Police Regiment.[30]

---

of the Volga region rather than with the Polish White Eagle" (p. 244). On the other hand *Nowe Droge* wrote on June 20, 1943: "...in the occurrence of Holy Week in Warsaw and in the succeeding acts of resistance there is meaning deeper than the irony, a political and moral sense. The Polish flag flew on the walls of the fighting ghetto and it was torn down by the enemy but each time it was replaced. The Jews had taken up the September [1939] tradition of the capital, fight with honor, under the symbol of the Republic. The national minority produced squadrons of soldiers who willingly decided to fight the common enemy" (p. 282). And on the first anniversary of the Warsaw Ghetto Uprising, the information bulletin of AK wrote: "Raising the Polish banner in the fighting ghetto the Jews confirmed their link with the Republic and their consciousness of the joint struggle with the enemy..." (p. 309).

29 Moczarski, *Gespraeche mit dem henker*, 181.

30 Stroop's operational report of April 20 mentions only that six SS soldiers and six Trawniki men were wounded during the fighting on April 19 be-

ZOB fighters in the Toebbens-Schultz Workshop area had another chance that day when they noticed German troops returning from the Central Ghetto on Smocza Street. In the afternoon of April 19, Geller, the ZOB commander of the Toebbens-Schultz area, gave an urgent order to his men. He had been told that the Germans were returning from their operations in the ghetto and an appropriate welcome must be prepared for them. The objective would be to attack the Germans while they were marching outside the ghetto wall from David Nowodworski's position at 69 Nowolipie Street. From there the mine that had been laid previously at the corner of Nowolipie and Zelezna should be actuated as the Germans marched by.

The observers on the roof announced that the Germans were approaching. They were marching from the Central Ghetto, through Smocza Street, and nearing the place where the mine had been buried. Great tension seized the fighters as the wires leading to the mine were connected, but to their disappointment the mine did not explode. The Germans continued marching and singing in the direction of the *Befehlstelle*, the German command center in the area. By the time the order was given to attack the Germans with Molotov cocktails and grenades, they were already out of range.[31]

After having given the order for the troops to withdraw from the ghetto, Stroop returned to his luxurious quarters. The Warsaw Gestapo chief Hahn awaited him there and dined with him. After dinner Stroop took a bath, changed his clothes, and telephoned

---

fore Stroop took command. The additional casualties that the Germans incurred that day after Stroop took command are listed in the opening pages of the album Stroop prepared, which includes all his operational reports. (See *The Stroop Report* [NY: Pantheon Books, 1979]). That day the Germans incurred twelve wounded during the fighting at the Nalewki-Gensia intersection and at the Zamenhofa-Mila intersection. Twelve wounded and one killed resulted from the fighting at Muranowski Square that afternoon. All in all, there were twenty-four wounded and one killed that day.

31 Putermilch, *Ba-esh u-va-sheleg*, 76.

Krueger and Himmler to report on the day's events. Himmler expressed his satisfaction, and said that Stroop had not disappointed him. However, he warned Stroop not to be overly optimistic regarding the following days. "Dear Stroop," he said, "difficult days are still ahead of you, even very difficult ones. Be careful and consult with Hahn. I empower you to use all available means, but only when it will be absolutely necessary. Try not to destroy or burn down the houses in the ghetto until such time as the workshops, especially those producing armaments, have been evacuated."

After drinking a glass of wine, Stroop went to bed; but before he fell asleep Himmler was on the phone again. "Having read your and Krueger's reports for the day, I wanted to call your attention to the fact that you have only completed the opening phase of the *Grossaktion*. April 19 is only the prelude to a historic event that one day will be referred to as the *Grossaktion* of Warsaw. This prelude you have so far managed in an excellent manner, especially after the miserable attempts of von Sammern. Just continue and the Fuehrer and I will never forget it."[32] Now Stroop could go to sleep.

Stroop had withdrawn his troops from the ghetto for the night, and the Jews of the Warsaw ghetto were able to celebrate the Passover Seder – some in underground bunkers, others in abandoned apartments, and some of the fighters standing guard.

It is the irony of history and testimony to the world's indifference to the tragic fate of the Jewish people during the war, that on the very same day that the Warsaw Ghetto Uprising began, April 19, 1943, the Anglo-American Conference on Refugees opened in Bermuda. The conference's organizers refused to speak openly of the German program to exterminate the Jewish people, cloaking their deliberations behind the indeterminate terminology of concern for

---

32 Moczarski, *Gespraeche mit dem henker*, 169–70.

"refugees." In his opening speech the head of the British delegation, Richard Law, said that victory in the war provided the only real solution of the refugee problem and the persecuted people "should not be betrayed...into the belief that aid is coming to them, when, in fact, we are unable to give them immediate succor." It was a self-fulfilling prophecy.

Tuesday, April 20, 1943 – the first day of Passover, the second day of the uprising

Early in the morning of April 20, German and Ukrainian troops marched singing in the direction of the Central Ghetto along the side of Leszno Street, bordering the Toebbens-Schultz Workshop area, outside the ghetto wall, while others entered Nowolipie Street from Smocza Street moving in the direction of Karmelicka Street. This time the ZOB and ZZW units were ready for them. The ZOB units at 76 and 74 Leszno Street lobbed grenades over the ghetto wall and fired their pistols from upper story windows at the passing troops. As the troops continued to advance they were attacked again from ZZW positions at 40 and 30 Leszno Street and the ZOB unit at 36 Leszno Street. The troops marching along Nowolipie Street came into the direct line of fire of ZOB and ZZW positions along that street.[33] Despite the harassment by Jewish fighters, the German troops continued advancing toward the Central Ghetto.

At 7 a.m. that morning, Stroop sent nine raiding parties, each composed of thirty-six men and led by one officer, into the Central Ghetto to hunt for Jews hiding out there. He put Police Major Sternagel in charge of the operation. Stroop expected the operation to

---

33 Putermilch, *Ba-esh u-va-sheleg*, 75; and Lazar Litai, *Matzada shel Varsha*, as quoted from Korngold's diary.

be completed within four hours. But when two of his raiding parties reached the area of Muranowski Square they were met by a hail of fire by ZZW forces from machine guns, submachine guns, and rifles. To deal with this unexpected center of resistance, Stroop threw into the battle two assault units, aided by armored vehicles and a tank. ZZW forces quickly put the tank out of action. In their attempt to withdraw the damaged tank, two Waffen-SS soldiers were wounded.[34]

Stroop had decided that demolition experts and flamethrowers were needed to deal with the many bunkers he now realized were in the ghetto. He turned to the Railroad Armored Train Replacement Detachment of the Wehrmacht at nearby Rembertow and requested that an engineering unit be sent to the Warsaw ghetto. Oberleutnant Hermann Hoppe of Detachment 1, at the head of his thirty-man demolition and flamethrower platoon, reported to Stroop that day. Stroop explained to him that the Jews were fiercely resisting deportation and many of them were hiding in bunkers, which Hoppe was ordered to open with the use of explosives. His men, in groups of five or six, were assigned to SS units and put under their command. But it quickly became clear that ZZW's forces at Muranowski Square and their attacks on the German forces were the major problem facing the Germans in the ghetto; and Hoppe's men, instead of being sent to explode bunkers, were thrown into the battle there. Hoppe, after the war, described what happened at Muranowski Square:

> We had here the mission to overcome a number of resistance points that were established in a number of floors and the attic of a big residential block. This residential block was combed through by us, starting with the ground floor, the resistance being broken by hand grenades and gunfire. When we reached

---

34 Stroop's first report for April 20; and Moczarski, *Gespraeche mit dem henker*, 173.

the attic the resistance became so strong that we – also the SS
operated with us – because of our own losses had to retreat.
Here in the attic, at my side, Feldwebel Josef Siegert was severely wounded by a shot through the lungs. I still remember
well that we had great difficulty to bring Feldwebel Siegert to
safety.[35]

Walewski describes the fighting at Muranowski Square:

A block of defensive positions was established in Muranowski
Square, that the enemy was unsuccessful in capturing in the
first days of the battle, despite his superiority in weapons and
trained manpower. The main regions of deficiency were in
the areas behind Muranowski Square, from the side of Bonifraterska, with its old houses, whose walls, which were falling
apart, could not withstand sustained fire from the enemy. The
Germans could exploit this weakness in the rebel's defenses
and attack Muranowski Square from Bonifraterska Street. As
it turned out the parallel attacks from Muranowska and Bonifraterska streets caused great difficulties for the defense of the
square.... The group of fighters under my command was positioned at the front of the square.... Two machine gun positions, on both sides of the square, cover our fighters. They spit
uninterruptedly fire and lead, against the attacking German
columns. The Germans retreat and run for their lives. The
square empties. It is not the first and not the last time. A shell
bursts. The machine gun flies apart. There are wounded. The
order is given: to evacuate the wounded under fire. To transfer
them to the "Aryan" side, to a hospital. The evening of the first

---

35 Hoppe's testimony at a war crimes trial held in Hamburg is given in Scheffler and Grabnitz, *Der Ghetto-Aufstand Warschau 1943*, 379.

day of battle fell. The Germans gathered their casualties and left the ghetto.[36]

In a supplementary message for April 20, 1943, Stroop reported that he had crushed the resistance at Muranowski Square with the aid of Wehrmacht engineers and flamethrowers, and then sent his raiding units searching for bunkers. According to him they had found and blown up nine bunkers, caught 505 Jews, and sent the able-bodied to be transferred to the newly located workshops at Poniatowa.[37] The flags were still flying over Muranowska 17. ZZW lost many of its fighters that day, including Alek Halberstein, one of ZZW's senior commanders, who had manned one of its machine guns.

Stroop's problems at Muranowski Square were far from over. The battle against the ZZW forces continued in the following days. Stroop in his daily reports makes no mention of the flags the ZZW had hoisted on the building at Muranowska 17, even though their removal, as ordered by Himmler, became his primary objective dur-

---

36 Walewski, *Jurek*, 67. Alexander Donat, a survivor of the Warsaw ghetto, wrote about the resistance in the battle of ZZW fighters at Muranowski Square, in "Our last days in the Warsaw ghetto," *Commentary*, May 1963: "The resistance men there were under the command of Pawel Frenkel and Leon Rodal, and were the best armed and best trained fighters in the ghetto." Arye Najberg, a survivor of the Warsaw ghetto, wrote about the battle for the flags in *Ha-aharonim* [The last ones] (Tel Aviv: Sifriat Hapoalim, 1958), 89: "During the first three days of the revolt, a battle was fought there for every floor, for every room, for every corner of a stairway. The Germans fought with rage to conquer the flags that flew on the roofs. Here heroically fought a group under the command of Pawel [Frenkel] (it was said that he belonged to the Revisionists)." Ringelblum followed the battle in the hours of the afternoon from the fourth floor of the building at Nalewki 32. Though not mentioning that the fighters belonged to ZZW, he wrote afterwards: "They fought from the rooftops as Polish flags and Zionist flags (blue-white) flew over their heads" (Ringelblum, *Ktavim aharonim*, 254).

37 Stroop's supplemental report for April 20, 1943.

ing the coming days. They evidently constituted too much of an embarrassment for him at the time to be mentioned in his daily operational reports. Only in his summary report to the assembled SS leaders in Krakow on May 16, 1943, after he had "declared victory," does he refer to what became known as "the battle for the flags."

Calling the ZZW forces at Muranowski Square "the main Jewish combat group," he reports that "it had already retired during the first and second day to the 'so-called' Muranowski Square. There it was reinforced by a considerable number of Polish bandits. Its plan was to fortify itself in the ghetto by all means in order to prevent us from invading it. The Jewish and Polish standards were hoisted at the top of a concrete building as a symbol of the war against us." Considering the fierce resistance he encountered at Muranowski Square, Stroop, quite naturally, assumed that he had now come up against "the main Jewish combat group."[38]

In his conversation with Moczarski in the Warsaw prison while awaiting his trial, he recounts this battle:

> Already during the first two days of the *Grossaktion* the numerically strongest Jewish combat-unit included Polish 'franctireurs.' They withdrew in the direction of Muranowski Square where it was sizably reinforced by Aryans. The Jews maintained constant contact with the AK.... At Muranowski Square it came to a fierce battle.... Our intelligence had reported for

---

38 Stroop's summary report, May 16, 1943. Although Poles had sold weapons to the ghetto fighters, and ZZW had brought Poles into the ghetto at various times to provide instruction to its fighters, no Poles took part in this battle at Muranowski Square. Stroop considered Jews to be "subhumans," and either found it difficult to believe that the fierce resistance he was encountering was being offered by Jewish fighters without outside help, or else he deliberately falsified his report so as to provide some excuse for the difficulty he was encountering at Muranowski Square.

some time that the AK already on the day that the ghetto was established, began setting up various resistance points, delivering weapons and instructions, and teaching the Jews streetfighting, engineer operations, the manufacture of explosives, grenades, etc. As visual proof of these facts, the Jewish rebels raised on a high building next to the Jewish white-blue flag also the white-red Polish flag. These flags were the signal to fight against us Germans.[39]

Stroop had expected, based on instructions he had issued to the German managers of the workshops engaged in supplying materiel for the German army using Jewish slave labor, that two sectors of the ghetto – the Toebbens-Schultz shops and the Brushmakers' shops, both geographically isolated from the Central Ghetto – would be evacuated willingly by the Jewish workers, who were promised by their German managers an orderly transfer to new shop locations in Poniatowa and Trawniki. But in both sectors there were ZOB and ZZW fighting units, whose members urged the Jewish workers not to report for shipment.

In the Brushmakers' area, commander of the ZOB forces was Marek Edelman, and commander of the ZZW forces was Samuel Luft. Each ZOB fighter was armed with a pistol and a few grenades and Molotov cocktails. Two of their fighters had rifles. The ZZW fighters were armed with pistols, grenades, and Molotov cocktails. Both groups manned positions along Swientojerska Street and held bunkers along that street. There was no coordination, or even contact, between the fighters of the two organizations. Edelman in his

---

39 Moczarski, *Gespraeche mit dem henker*, 179. The intelligence reports referred to by Stroop are probably based on information he received regarding the assistance provided to ZZW by some Polish underground groups.

reminiscences of the Warsaw Ghetto Uprising does not even mention the existence of ZZW in the ghetto.[40]

While the battle at Muranowski Square continued that day, Stroop sent troops to the Brushmakers' Workshop area at 3 p.m. in an attempt to get the Jewish workers there to report for shipment.[41] The workshop area, separated from the Central Ghetto by Franciskanska Street, was a small walled-off block of buildings, bordered by Franciskanska, Walowa, Swentojerska, and Bonifraterska streets. The German troops entered the Brushmakers' compound through the gate at 6 Walowa Street. At the gate, buried below ground, the ZOB had placed a mine. Simha (Kazik) Rotem was at the ZOB observation post overlooking the gate. As he saw the Germans approaching, he reached for the electric contact to detonate the mine. But Hanoch Gutman, his unit commander, snatched the contact out of his hands and detonated it. This was the signal for Gutman's unit to attack the German soldiers with pistols and grenades. The Germans withdrew.[42] When they returned, the Jewish workers still refused their call to come out peaceably, and a four-hour battle ensued between the German forces and the ZOB and ZZW fighters in the area.[43]

Now Stroop employed his artillery. His 20-mm anti-aircraft guns and his 100-mm howitzers, stationed outside the ghetto walls, began blasting the buildings in the Brushmakers' Workshop area. Flame-

---

40 Edelman, *The Ghetto Fights*.
41 Stroop's operational report for April 20, 1943.
42 Simha Rotem (Kazik), *Memoirs of a Warsaw Ghetto Fighter* (New Haven, CT: Yale University Press, 1994), 34.
43 *Relatzia fun an Anteilnemer in Geto Oifstand* [Report from a participant of the ghetto uprising], published in Mark, *Tsum tsenten yortog*, 218. This is a description of the fighting in the Brushmakers' Workshop area by an anonymous ZOB fighter, fragments of whose notes were found in Warsaw after the war and are to be found in the Jewish Historical Institute (ZIH) there. B. Mark, director of ZIH at the time, assumes that the author was the ZOB fighter Zygmunt Fryderych.

throwers were used to set fire to the buildings.[44] The ZOB fighters took cover in their bunkers.[45] The ZOB lost one of its fighters there that day. It was Michael Klepfisz, a member of the Bund, who was an engineer and had been active in smuggling weapons into the ghetto and producing homemade grenades and Molotov cocktails there.[46]

In a direct act of participation of Polish underground fighters in the uprising, a ten-man team of the Armija Ludowa (AL), the left-wing Polish underground, that afternoon attacked one of the 20-mm anti-aircraft guns firing on the Brushmakers' Workshop area from a position outside the ghetto walls. It succeeded in killing the two-man Wehrmacht crew manning one of the guns.[47]

Stroop was unable to occupy the Brushmakers' Workshop area that day and withdrew his forces from the ghetto for the night. That day two Wehrmacht soldiers were killed and six Waffen-SS and one Trawniki man were wounded in the fighting. Five hundred Jews had been hunted down during the day's operation. "It was not an easy day," Stroop complained. In his conversations with Krueger that evening, considering the uncertain situation he claimed he was facing, he received authorization to burn down and completely destroy the Brushmakers' Workshop area. That he intended to do the following day.[48]

That night Frenkel sent the first contingent of ZZW fighters, eight men and six women, including those wounded during the fighting that day at Muranowski Square, through the Muranowksa tunnel to the building at Muranowska 6. From there they were

---

44 Stroop's operational report for April 20, 1943. Also Moczarski, *Gespraeche mit dem henker*, 174.

45 Mark, *Tsum tsenten yortog*, 220.

46 Edelman, *The Ghetto Fights*, 36–37.

47 Mark, *Tsum tsenten yortog*, 241.

48 Stroop's operational report for April 20, 1943. Also Moczarski, *Gespraeche mit dem henker*, 176.

driven by ZZW's Polish contacts to the Otwock region, about thirty kilometers southeast of Warsaw, with the task of setting up a base for partisan operations against the Germans. Two days later they were discovered there by a unit of German gendarmes and fell in a gun-battle with the Germans.[49]

Wednesday, April 21, 1943 – the second day of Passover, the third day of the uprising

At 7 a.m. on April 21, 1943, Stroop resumed his attack against the ZZW positions under Pawel Frenkel's command at Muranowski Square. It was to be the third day of fighting in what came to be known as "the battle for the flags." It was to Muranowski Square that he sent "the main body of the forces." Simultaneously, he ordered a thirty-seven-man "battle group reinforced by engineers and heavy arms" to complete cleaning out the Brushmakers' Workshop area, that he had begun the previous day.[50]

Jack Eisner, a ZZW fighter, describes in his book *The Survivor* the fighting that day:

> On Wednesday, April 21, the Germans, in battalion strength began to assemble their armed might on Muranowska Street. They had deployed their infantry all along the walls of the

---

49 Adam Halperin, *Helka shel Betar ba-Mered ha-Geto* (Tel Aviv: Information Department of the Betar headquarters in Eretz Yisrael, *Teshuvah le-mesal-fim* [An answer to the falsifiers], 1946), 22; and Yitzhak Zuckerman and Moshe Basok, eds., *Sefer milhamot ha-getaot* [The book of ghetto wars] (Tel Aviv: Hakibbutz Hameuhad, 1956), 177.

50 Stroop's operational report for April 21, 1943. Throughout most of the fighting, Stroop followed a policy of withdrawing his forces from the ghet-to with nightfall and reentering the following morning, while keeping the ghetto cordoned off during the night.

houses. Their vehicles were in the center of the street. A half-track with signal equipment surrounded by three armored vehicles was set up a short distance from the square and would serve as mobile headquarters.... Precisely at 9 a.m. the tanks, armored cars and howitzers opened a merciless assault. They were after the buildings on the south side of Muranowski Square, number seven in particular, where the Jewish and Polish flags were flying. By noon, the ZZW fighters decided to counterattack from the rear.... About twenty-five young Jews, some in SS uniforms, crossed the Mila Street buildings to the south side of Muranowska. One by one they moved toward the attics and roofs. The SS troops, anticipating such tactics, aimed bursts of machine gun fire at the buildings behind them. Nevertheless, the Jewish fighters, armed with Molotov bottles and some Sten and submachine guns, managed to get through. At a given signal, they bombarded the street below. Havoc hit the SS. Several vehicles, including a Panzer half-track, caught fire.... After a while the SS regrouped. Two snakelike columns of Germans swarmed down the street, hugging the buildings. Simultaneously, the SS machine gunners directed heavy fire at the upper floors of the Muranowski Square structures. Some of them were burning.

Now the SS began an assault on the street-level stores and the lower floors. A fierce battle developed. The Jews threw all they had at the SS. In several buildings the Germans managed to reach the first floor. Each time they were driven back behind the Panzers. In such close fighting the entrenched Jews had the upper hand. Even though various floors were burning, they still managed to attack from the windows and attics....

By late afternoon General Stroop ordered a withdrawal. The Germans pulled back into the safety of the Aryan world. The battle was temporarily halted. In growing darkness, we climbed down from the roof. Muranowski Square, although still smoldering, was overflowing with excited ZZW fighters.

On the third evening of the uprising, the ghetto was still fighting in high spirits, with most of its population unharmed and still in their bunkers....[51]

Most of the ZOB fighters in the Brushmakers' Workshop area, together with their commander, Marek Edelman, had taken shelter from the German shelling on the evening of April 20 in the bunker at Swentojerska 34 to plan their operations for the next day. But conditions in the area became so intolerable, as the result of German shelling and the heat generated by the many buildings that had been set aflame by the Germans, that they concluded that they had to leave the Brushmakers' Workshop area and try to make their way to the ZOB bunkers at Franciskanska Street 22 and 30, in the Central Ghetto. On the night of April 21 they made their escape.

This is how Edelman describes the passage of his forces from the burning Brushmakers' area to the Central Ghetto:

The flames cling to our clothes which now start smoldering. The pavement melts under our feet into a black gooey substance. Broken glass, littering every inch of the streets, is transformed into a sticky liquid in which our feet are caught. Our soles begin to burn from the heat of the stone pavement. One after another we stagger through the conflagration. From house to house, from courtyard to courtyard, with no air to breathe, with a hundred hammers clanging in our heads, with

---

51 Eisner, *The Survivor*, 183. Eisner was under the impression that the flags were raised on the roof of the building at Muranowska 7, while according to Landau they were raised on the roof of the building at Muranowska 17. He pointed this out to Eisner when the two visited Warsaw after the war. See the footnote in Landau, *Caged*, 203.

burning rafters continuously falling over us, we finally reach the end of the area under fire. We feel lucky just to stand here, to be out of the inferno.

Now the most difficult part remains. There is only one possible way into the Central Ghetto – through a small breach in the wall [around the Central Ghetto] guarded from three sides by Gendarmes, Ukrainians, and "navy-blue" police [Polish police in the service of the Germans]. Five battle groups have to force their way through this breach. One after another, their feet wrapped in rags to stifle the sound of steps, under heavy fire, tense to the utmost, Gutman's, Berlinski's, and Grynbaum's groups force their way through. Success! Jurek Blones' group covers from behind. While the first of this group emerge on the street, a German searchlight illuminates the entire wall section. It seems as if not a single person more will be able to save his life here. Suddenly Romanowicz's single well-aimed round puts out the searchlight and, before the Germans have time to collect their wits, our entire group manages to cross over to the other side.[52]

But fighting by ZZW forces against German troops in the area continued that day. The fighting was "bitter" according to Stroop, the Germans being attacked by grenades, explosives, pistols, and Molotov cocktails. After repeated attacks, Stroop reports, his troops succeeded in "clearing part of the buildings of the subhumans" who were resisting. Then his engineers blew up the buildings from which fire had been directed against his troops, and set fire to blocks of

---

52 Edelman, *The Ghetto Fights*, 37–38; and Rotem, *Memoirs of a Warsaw Ghetto Fighter*, 39. Also the reminiscences of Hersh Berlinski, leader of the Left Po'alei Zion unit in the area, as they appear in Joseph Kermish, ed., *To Live with Honor and to Die with Honor* (New York: Holocaust Publications, 1986).

houses in the area. He managed to catch 5,000 Jews who were taken to the *Umschlagplatz* and shipped to Treblinka, but admitted that there still remained a number of bunkers, deep below the earth, that he could not locate.[53]

At night, part of the ZZW fighters, under the command of Samuel Luft, succeeded in breaking out of the area and joining their comrades at Muranowski Square. The rest, under the leadership of the ZZW commanders Avraham Rodal and Yuzek Lopata, took shelter in the bunker at Swientojerska 38, in which a wounded ZZW fighter had been placed.[54] This was the end of the fighting in the Brushmakers' Workshop area.

The previous day Stroop had given orders that the workshops in the ghetto would have to be prepared to move out the following morning with all their equipment and personnel, holding the German workshop owners responsible. They at first remonstrated with Stroop, insisting that this was not their responsibility, but after Stroop drew his pistol and threatened them they quickly fell in line. The German workshop owners and Walter Toebbens, the owner-manager of many of these shops in the ghetto, then promised to carry out this order.[55] Instructions appeared, under Toebbens' signature, for the Jewish workers in these shops to assemble at 6:00 the following morning at designated locations prepared to be transported to Trawniki and Poniatowa. His instructions included the warning

---

53   Moczarski, *Gespraeche mit dem henker*, 176–77.

54   Lazar Litai, *Matzada shel Varsha*, 258, as reported by Juta Rutenberg-Hart-man, a ZZW fighter in the area, and a supplementary interview with her by the author. She recalled that a number of ZZW fighters were killed and wounded in the fighting. She was ordered to stay with one of the wounded in the bunker at Swientojerska 38.

55   Stroop's operational report for April 20, 1943. Also Moczarski, *Gespraeche mit dem henker*, 176.

that anyone found in the area after the transfer had been completed would be shot on sight.

In the Toebbens-Schultz Workshop area, the assembly areas were on Leszno and Nowolipie Streets.[56] That morning German SS and Ukrainian units established themselves at the *Befehlstelle*, the Gestapo command center at Leszno 80, and in the surrounding streets of the workshop area, prepared to implement Stroop's orders. ZOB and ZZW fighters hurled grenades and Molotov cocktails at the troops from their positions on Nowolipie and Leszno streets, and ZZW fighters succeeded in setting fire to the O. Schilling Workshop at Nowolipie Street. Their positions were attacked by the Germans and their auxiliaries, and the Jewish fighters withdrew to bunkers in the area.[57] They had no chance of interfering with the transport of Jewish workers. According to Stroop's report for that day, 5,200 Jewish workers obeyed Toebbens' call.

On that day many of the ZOB fighters from the Central Ghetto had gathered together with Anielewicz in the bunker at Mila 29. It was one of the best furnished bunkers in the ghetto, with a water supply and electricity and a plentiful supply of food, whose wealthy owners welcomed the ZOB fighters.[58] Those who had come over from the Brushmakers' Workshop area had assembled in the bunkers at Franciskanska 22 and 30.

In addition to ZOB fighter Michael Klepfisz, who fell in the fighting in the Brushmakers' Workshop area, a number of ZZW fighters fell and many were wounded that day in the heavy fighting at Muranowski Square and also in the Brushmakers' Workshop area. German casualties that day were five wounded – one from the Cavalry

---

56 Blumental and Kermish, *Ha-meri ve-ha-mered be-Geto Varsha*, 349–50.
57 Simha Korngold's diary, Yad Vashem Archives O33/1566. Also Putermilch, *Ba-esh u-va-sheleg*, 81.
58 Borzykowski, *Bein kirot noflim*, 44–45.

Replacement Detachment, two from the 22nd SS Police Regiment, and two Ukrainians.[59] These German casualties were sustained during the fighting at Muranowski Square. Stroop claims to have killed 230 Jews that day.[60]

Thursday, April 22, 1943 – the third day of Passover, the fourth day of the uprising

This was the fourth day of the battle at Muranowski Square, and the flags on the roof of Muranowska 17 were still fluttering in the April breeze. Stroop again threw the main body of his troops into the battle to remove these flags, and reported that at 12 noon the "operation was still in progress."[61]

In his supplementary report that evening, he reports that Untersturmfuehrer [Hans] Dehmke, an officer in the SS Cavalry Replacement Battalion, had been killed later in the day. A grenade he was holding exploded when he was fired upon by ZZW fighters. In addition, Dehmke's body was riddled by bullets, some of which hit his throat. Dehmke was hit as he attempted to climb to the roof of the building on which the flags were flying. Stroop had known him personally. He was shaken by his death and sent a long condolence letter to his mother. Another German, a member of the 22nd SS Police Regiment, received a bullet in the lungs during the fighting at Muranowski Square. Stroop was so incensed by the death of Dehmke that he ordered the immediate killing of two hundred Jews in revenge. At his war crimes trial in Warsaw in 1951, when confronted

---

59 MacLean, *The Ghetto Men*, 167.
60 Stroop's operational report for April 21, 1943.
61 Ibid., April 22, 1943, up to 1200 hours.

by the prosecutor with this murderous act, Stroop excused himself by saying that "these are the laws of war."[62]

Eisner reports on the fighting that day:

> Early Thursday morning, General Stroop returned with more troops, heavier artillery, and more armor. German guns pounded Muranowski Square for hours. At noon, the infantry assault resumed. Shells exploded. Walls collapsed. Windows shattered. Debris rained into the streets. Some floors in each building were burning. The roof next to the flags was smoldering.... Still our flags were flying. Shells had torn them. Bullets had pierced them. Their edges were charred. Their fabric was shredded. But despite everything, our colors were up there, defiantly challenging the Germans.
>
> Now the SS were fighting their way into the buildings.... Everyone on the roofs opened fire. Most of our fighters were scattered through the blazing buildings. They were firing from rooms, from windows, from attics, from stairs.
>
> But the German artillery fire and machine-gunning took their toll. A number of Germans reached the third and fourth floors. They were waving small flags to their command cars in the street.
>
> Late in the afternoon General Stroop called the battle off again. The Germans left the ghetto once more.... Most of our positions were in ruins. The day's fighting had resulted in a heavy toll of wounded and killed. Those not hurt were busy tending to those who were. Also, our reserve supplies in the

---

62 Stroop's second report of April 22, 1943; Moczarski, *Gespraeche mit dem henker*, 180–81; and the proceedings of Stroop's trial in Warsaw, published by the Jewish Historical Institute Warsaw (ZIH) on April 19, 1953.

bunkers were running low. We were especially short of long-range weapons....

Our fighters were exhausted. They desperately needed rest.[63]

Walewski describes the day's fighting in the square:

Muranowski Square shook. The walls moved. The street was cut into ribbons. The infantry advanced. Muranowski Square was filled with black and green uniforms. To capture the flags – at all costs. "We will not give up the flags," said the young [Leon] Rodal. "We will try to surprise the Germans again!"

...The Germans introduced new forces again and again into the battle. Their uninterrupted assaults weakened us. There was nobody to replace the wounded, and those that were not injured had reached the end of their strength. It was impossible to receive additional deliveries of weapons from the "Aryan" side. At the end only a single machine gun was left for the defense of the entire square. It looked like Muranowski Square was lost.

We improvised a plan: To retreat from our positions, to cease firing the machine gun that was positioned to defend the building on which the flags flew. The enemy's assault groups would surely storm into the labyrinth of buildings of Muranowska Street, and penetrate through the supposedly undefended square to the building with the flags so as to wipe out as quickly as possible the "disgrace" of the flags that the rebels had raised for all of "Aryan" Warsaw to see; and while the Germans are in the Square to open fire on them from all sides.

---

63 Eisner, *The Survivor*, 183.

The machine gun ceased firing. Quiet settled on the square. Everyone waited with bated breath for the next move.

But what happened was unexpected.... Their commanders decided to delay the attack on the positions "abandoned" by us and the German soldiers stayed in place and did not advance toward us. It seemed that the enemy did not underestimate us.... Suddenly young [Leon] Rodal appeared in the uniform of an SS officer...with him came four others, all dressed in SS uniforms, all having "Aryan" looks. "I will go," said Rodal, "and bring the Germans straight opposite our positions, straight under the flags. They will smell our weapons and find out that our flags are not just rags on wooden poles. For the ghetto, they have to pay with life and blood." Then he left.

He entered Muranowski Square, sure of himself as a real SS officer, and with him the other four. They mixed among the Germans. Suddenly, he yelled with full force: "Why are you standing there, monkeys? Why are you staring at these miserable flags?" He pulled his pistol from his holster, raised it, and ordered, "Forwards after me! *Jude Verecke!*" ...The Germans followed him.... Rodal stopped and ordered the Germans to halt and wait. He himself will go to find the best way to get to the cursed flags. He will take only a few with him – his four comrades. They entered a stairway, reached a window, and from there threw grenades on the Germans massed in the courtyard. The rest of us opened fire from nearby windows and stairways.... Muranowski Square continues to defend itself. The rebels' flags fly over Warsaw. The struggle continues.[64]

The fighting had by now spread to Bonifraterska on the northeastern border of the ghetto, to the Transavia, DEA, and Oxaco workshops

---

64 Walewski, *Jurek*, 74.

in the northwestern section of the ghetto, and to the building housing the *Werterfassung* on Niska, where the Germans had stored valu-
ables they had stolen from the Jews in the ghetto. Earlier ZZW fighters had set fire to the Brauer workshop on Nalewki. In effect, the
German workshops and facilities in the northern part of the ghetto,
including their equipment and stores, had been destroyed.[65]

After his men had been continuously attacked and after the
losses they had suffered, Stoop began to sense a breakdown of discipline among his troops, and he saw among them the first signs of
fear. He decided that rather than continuing to let his troops come
into close contact with the Jewish fighters, he would take advantage
of his long-range weapons – The tank mounting a 37-mm gun, the
100-mm howitzers, and the 20-mm anti-aircraft guns, and direct
them directly against the buildings in which the Jewish fighters had
established themselves. After consulting with Hahn and Krueger,
and making contact with Berlin, Stroop ordered that houses in the
ghetto be set on fire. Shortly flames and smoke enveloped the houses
in the ghetto.[66]

Himmler, who had been receiving continuous reports of the
fighting in the Warsaw ghetto, sent a telegram to Krueger in Krakow
on April 22, with instructions that "the clearing out of the Warsaw
ghetto is to be carried out with all firmness and thoroughness, without mercy. It is best to act aggressively. The events in Warsaw prove
how dangerous these Jews are."[67]

---

65 Yehuda Helman, *Al goralam shel sridei ha-lohamim shel "Hairgun Hatsvai
Hayehudi" be-Varsha* [On the fate of the surviving fighters of the "Jewish
Military Union" in Warsaw] (Haifa: Haifa University, ha-Machon le-Heker
Tekufat ha-Shoah, 1966), 314. These are the reminiscences of ZZW fighter
Pawel Besztimt, written in Warsaw at the behest of Yitzhak Zuckerman
shortly after he left the ghetto.

66 Stroop's second report for April 22, 1943; and MacLean, *The Ghetto Men*,
167.

67 Blumental and Kermish, *Ha-meri ve-ha-mered be-Geto Varsha*, 367.

That evening Frenkel decided to transfer the second contingent of his fighters from the ghetto to the Michalin Forest in the Otwock region so as to establish there a partisan base, according to an arrangement that had been made with the Polish underground. When David Landau reported that evening to ZZW headquarters at Muranowska 7, he found fifty ZZW fighters, together with Polish instructors, making last-minute preparations to descend into the tunnel leading to the house on Muranowska 6 outside the ghetto wall. Close to midnight, Landau saw the weary fighters go down with their weapons, one after another, into the bunker that led to the entrance to the tunnel. Frenkel was the last to go down to see them safely to the other side. Then he returned to the ghetto.[68]

On that day three ZZW fighters from the Toebbens-Schultz Workshop area, led by Natan Shultz, left the ZZW headquarters at Karmelicka 5 carrying explosives, crawled through the sewers toward the German command center, the *Befehlstelle*, at Zelezna, just outside the ghetto wall, and attempted to blow it up. But their attempt was not successful.[69]

Stroop lost three men that day – SS Untersturmfuehrer Dehmke and two Ukrainians – and one SS-Police sergeant was wounded. He reports that over 6,000 Jews were caught and sent off for deportation, over 200 Jews were killed, and fifteen bunkers were blown up. ZZW lost forty of its fighters in the battle that day.[70] At the end of the day Stroop assumed that the heaviest fighting was behind him and released 150 of the 335 Ukrainians among his forces for duty on the eastern front.[71]

---

68 Landau, *Caged*, 211–13. Also Helman, *Al goralam*, 314.
69 Korngold's diary, Yad Vashem Archives O33/1566.
70 Eisner, *The Survivor*, 183–97.
71 Stroop's operational report for April 23, 1943.

That day, the *New York Times* carried a report about the fighting in the Warsaw ghetto on the front page. It quoted a broadcast by a secret Polish radio that was picked up in Stockholm, which said: "The last 35,000 Jews in the ghetto at Warsaw have been condemned to execution. Warsaw again is echoing to musketry volleys. The people are being murdered. Women and children defend themselves with their naked arms. Save us..."[72] This broadcast by the Polish underground radio was based on communiqués issued by Yitzhak Zuckerman and Adolf Berman, who were in "Aryan" Warsaw, outside the ghetto walls, listening to the sounds of fighting inside the ghetto. Zuckerman was the representative of ZOB and Berman represented the Jewish National Committee (ZKN) in their contacts with the Polish underground. The Polish underground radio broadcast some of the communiqués that they received from them.

Based on fragmentary information reaching them from the embattled ghetto, and from what could be seen and heard from outside the ghetto, Berman and Zuckerman composed battle communiqués that purported to report on the ongoing battles there. The first three communiqués were issued by Berman and Zuckerman on April 19 and 20. Bulletin No. 1 states: "Today, on Monday, April 19, the Germans started a new, deadly action in the Warsaw ghetto. By four o'clock in the morning, intensive rifle and machine gun fire, as well as the bursting of shells, were heard in the vicinity of the ghetto walls. Armored cars and tanks moved into the ghetto. The action is being carried out by German military police under the command of the SS.... The Jewish Fighting Organization [ZOB], which encompasses all active elements of the Jewish community, is putting

---

72 New York Times, April 22, 1943. The same story was carried the following day, April 23, by the Histadrut daily Davar in Palestine, under the banner headline: "The Remnants of the Jewish Diaspora Are Fighting for Their Lives – Resistance in Warsaw."

up strong resistance in many buildings. Violent battles are going on between the Jewish fighters and the Germans...."

In Bulletin No. 2, issued on April 20, they reported: "The struggle between the Jewish Fighting Organization [ZOB] and the Germans in the Warsaw Ghetto continues in full force...." Bulletin No. 3 was also issued on April 20, and reported: "...The Jewish fighters have hoisted two flags on the roof of a building in Muranowska Street: one red and white, the other blue and white." The Polish underground radio broadcasts were picked up by German intelligence and transmitted to Berlin. On May 1, 1943, Joseph Goebbels made the following entry into his diary: "...exceptionally sharp fighting in Warsaw between our police, and in part even the Wehrmacht, and the Jewish rebels. The Jews have actually succeeded in putting the ghetto in a condition to defend itself. Some very hard battles are taking place there, which have gone so far that the Jewish top leadership publishes daily military reports. Of course this jest will probably not last long. But it shows what one can expect of the Jews if they have arms. Unfortunately, they also have some good German weapons, particularly machine guns. Heaven only knows how they got hold of them."[73]

The reports issued by Berman and Zuckerman were the only announcements describing the fighting in the ghetto. They created the impression that a single Jewish fighting organization was resisting the Germans, and that organization was ZOB. ZZW had no representatives in "Aryan" Warsaw, and no alternate "ZZW version of events" appeared at the time. Although Berman and Zuckerman were fully cognizant of the participation of ZZW in the fighting, and must have known that it was ZZW that had raised the Zionist and Polish flags

---

73 Blumental and Kermish, *Ha-meri ve-ha-mered be-Geto Varsha*, 212. And Louis P. Lochner, ed., *Goebbels Tagebuecher aus den Jahren 1942–1943 mit anderen Dokumenten* (Zurich, 1948), 318.

over a building near Muranowski Square – knowing full well that the Bund would not have agreed to raise the Zionist flag as a symbol of the uprising – they naturally were interested in giving the world the impression that Jewish resistance in the ghetto was being conducted by a single fighting organization.[74] It was the beginning of the development of a narrative of the Warsaw Ghetto Uprising that tended to ignore the role of ZZW in the fighting.

During those days Zuckerman was desperately trying to obtain the cooperation and assistance of the Polish underground for the fighters in the ghetto. Representatives of the left-wing Polish underground, the Armija Ludowa (AL), promised to supply him with twenty-eight rifles, but they were not available immediately. And how was he going to get them into the ghetto, which was cordoned off night and day? They never reached the ghetto fighters.

Next he went to meet a representative of the right-wing Polish underground (AK). In a large room in a private apartment, a man standing at a desk was waiting for him. It was Major Janiszowski of the AK – a tall, broad man with a big, bald head. The AK representative told him that they were aware of what was going on in the ghetto, and that they knew it was a Communist uprising and that the Communists were serving the interests of Moscow. Zuckerman's assurances that most of the fighters were Zionists or members of the Bund and that the commander was a Zionist were of no avail. Janiszowski repeated the AK proposal that the fighting be stopped and that the fighters should be moved out of the ghetto to a partisan unit. Then he stood up and in parting told Zuckerman that if the ghetto proved to be a Moscow base and continued to fight, not only would they not help the Jewish fighters, but would actually fight against them. That dashed any hope of obtaining assistance from them.[75]

---

74 Zuckerman, *A Surplus of Memory*, 371.
75 Ibid., 353 and 359.

On April 22, a battle took place between the ZZW fighters who had established themselves in the Michalin Forest near Otwock and German gendarmes who discovered their presence there, with heavy losses to the ZZW fighters.[76]

---

76 B. Mark, *Tsum tsenten yortog*, 190.

Chapter 10

The Ghetto in Flames

April 23–April 28, 1943

Friday, April 23, 1943 – the fourth day of Passover, the fifth day of the uprising

At 7 a.m. that morning, ZZW fighter Jack Eisner was at his post next to the flags on the roof of Muranowska 17 when he saw German troops enter the ghetto through the Dzika Street entrance and arrange themselves in an arc in the streets around Muranowski Square. They had brought with them a tank, armored cars, and artillery, but fewer foot-soldiers than the previous day. He assumed that it was Stroop's intention to subject the buildings around Muranowski Square to heavy artillery fire and level the buildings there. When the situation was reported to Frenkel and Rodal, they gave the order to their fighters to pull out of the buildings. When the shelling began, buildings in the area began to collapse, and flames and smoke enveloped everything. By midday, the buildings around the square were on fire.[1]

Stroop sent search parties into the Central Ghetto with orders to discover bunkers, ferret out the Jews hiding in them, and blow them up. He reported that they had discovered forty-eight bunkers and demolished them with explosives, captured 3,500 Jews, and killed 200. The ZZW fighters who had left Muranowski Square had taken up positions in the northern part of the ghetto and fired on the

---

1   Eisner, *The Survivor*, 183–97.

Germans from these positions. Stroop ordered that every building from which shots were fired be set on fire, and that Jews escaping from these buildings be hunted down.[2] Stroop withdrew some of his troops for two hours during the day, hoping that Jews who were in hiding would come out into the open, but when his forces returned they found that ZZW fighters had returned to their previous positions on Muranowski Square.[3]

In the Toebbens-Schultz area, sporadic firing at German and Ukrainian troops by ZOB and ZZW fighters continued, although the situation of these fighters became more and more precarious as attacks against their positions continued.[4]

At 10 p.m., Stroop withdrew his forces from the ghetto. ZZW had suffered heavy losses in dead and wounded. The flags had been shot to pieces and the area of Muranowski Square had to be abandoned. Reserves of ammunition were being exhausted. Stroop's losses that day were three members of the 3rd Battalion of the 22nd SS Police Regiment wounded and one Ukrainian wounded.[5]

On this day, Mordechai Anielewicz, from his hideout in the bunker at Mila 29, managed to get a letter to Yitzhak Zuckerman on the "Aryan" side. The letter was brought out of the ghetto by workers of the Pinkert Burial Society, which had continued its pre-war occupation of conducting burials in the Jewish cemetery even after the ghetto was established. The Jewish cemetery, although adjacent to the ghetto, was outside the ghetto walls, which gave the gravediggers the opportunity to leave the ghetto and return to it. During the initial days of the uprising, the Germans ordered the "Pinkert men" to bring the corpses of dead Jews in the ghetto to the cemetery. One

---

2 Stroop's operational report of April 23, 1943.
3 Moczarski, *Gespraeche mit dem henker*, 182.
4 Simha Korngold's diary, Yad Vashem Archives O33/1566. Also Carmi and Frimmer, *Min ha-dlikah ha-hi*, 120.
5 MacLean, *The Ghetto Men*, 168.

of Anielewicz's men had entrusted the letter to them for transmittal to someone who was in contact with Zuckerman.

In the letter, written in Hebrew, dated April 23, 1943, Anielewicz wrote:

Dear Yitzhak,

I don't know what to write to you. I will skip personal details. There is only one expression to describe my feelings and the feelings of my comrades: something has happened that is beyond our wildest dreams. The Germans ran away twice from the ghetto. One of our units held out for forty minutes, and the second for more than six hours. The mine that was buried in the area of the Brushmakers exploded. We have lost only one fighter – Yehiel, a hero who fell next to his submachine gun.

When we received the news yesterday that members of PPR attacked the Germans and that the radio station "Swit" broadcast the wonderful news about our self-defense, I had a feeling of fulfillment. We still have much work ahead of us, but all that was done so far has been done perfectly.

From this evening we are moving over to partisan tactics. At night three of our units go out. They have two tasks: armed reconnaissance and acquisition of arms. And you should know, the pistol is of no value, we almost did not use it. We need grenades, rifles, automatic weapons, and explosives.

I cannot describe to you the conditions under which Jews are living. Only very few will be able to hold out. All the rest will die sooner or later. Their fate is sealed. In all the bunkers in which our comrades are hiding it is impossible to light a candle because of the lack of air....

Of all the units in the ghetto only one is missing: Yehiel. That is also a victory. I don't know what else to write you. I imagine that there is no end of questions. But for now this will have to do.

The general situation: all the workshops in the ghetto have been closed, except for the *Werterfassung*, "Transavia," and "Doering." As for the situation at Schultz and Toebbens I have no information. The contact has been broken. The Brushmakers' shop has been in flames for the past three days. I have no contact with the units. Many fires in the ghetto. Yesterday the hospital was burning. Blocks of buildings are in flames. The police force has been disbanded, except for the *Werterfassung*. Szmerling has appeared again. Lichtenbaum has been released from the *Umschlag*.[6] Not many people were taken out of the ghetto. This is not the case for the workshops. I have no details. During the day we are in hiding – be well my friend. Perhaps we shall meet again. The most important thing: my dream was realized. I lived to see Jewish defense in the ghetto in all its greatness and glory.

Mordechai[7]

---

6   Mieczyslaw Szmerling was an officer in the Jewish police and Marc Lichtenbaum was head of the *Judenrat*.

7   Zuckerman, *A Surplus of Memory*, 357. The original letter, written in Hebrew, did not survive; what has been found is Zuckerman's Yiddish translation of the letter. Actually ZOB had suffered by then the loss of another of its fighters, Michael Klepfisz, who fell in the Brushmakers' Workshop area. Anielewicz at this point had not yet had any contact with the ZOB fighters who had come over to the Central Ghetto from there. The attack by members of PPR mentioned in the letter is a reference to the attack by the leftist Polish underground AL on Stroop's anti-aircraft batteries that were firing at the Brushmakers' area from positions outside the ghetto on April 20. Anielewicz's reference to the ZOB tactic of remaining in the bunkers during daylight hours is confirmed by the reminiscence of other ZOB fighters, such as Borzykowski (*Bein kirot noflim*, 61).

That day, contact was made between the ZOB fighters in the bunker at Mila 29, ZOB fighters in the bunker at Nalewki 36, and the ZOB fighters who had escaped the burning Brushmakers' Workshop area and were now in the bunker at Franciskanska 20.[8]

Saturday, April 24, 1943 – the fifth day of Passover, the sixth day of the uprising

Stroop returned with his forces to the Central Ghetto at 10 a.m., sending twenty-four search parties in all directions with orders to search for bunkers. In the late afternoon, they ran into heavy resistance from ZZW fighters in the northeastern part of the ghetto, in the block of houses occupied by the *Werterfassung*. This developed into an eight-hour battle. When Stroop saw that his troops were unable to overcome the resistance and his forces were suffering casualties, he ordered that the entire block of buildings be burned down. Moving his troops back to a safe distance, he had flamethrowers set fire to the buildings. Shortly a sea of flames engulfed the buildings, walls collapsed, and the whole area was lit as if it were daylight. Only at 2 a.m. did Stroop order his forces to withdraw from the ghetto. They had destroyed 26 bunkers, shot 330 Jews, and captured over a thousand for transportation to Treblinka or the workshops at Trawniki and Poniatowa. Two soldiers of the Waffen-SS and one Ukrainian were wounded in the fighting that day.[9]

The flames spreading through the northern part of the Central Ghetto reached the building at Mila 29. The bunker was by now crowded with additional men, women, and children who had fled burning houses. The many ZOB fighters who had taken shelter in

8   Rotem, *Memoirs of a Warsaw Ghetto Fighter*, 40.
9   Stroop's operational report of April 24, 1943. Also Moczarski, *Gespraeche mit dem henker*, 183–84; and MacLean, *The Ghetto Men*, 168.

this bunker, together with hundreds of others who had found refuge there, were forced to leave it, as flames began to consume the entire building and the heat became unbearable. Hoping to hold out until nightfall, they nevertheless were forced to abandon the bunker at 7 p.m., two hours before dusk, as the fire reached the ground floor of the building. Shepherded by the ZOB fighters, they all made their way up Mila Street, past burning buildings, assembling in the three courtyards of Mila 9.

At this point ZOB decided that the time had come to evacuate their fighters from the ghetto. Four fighters who had an "Aryan" appearance were charged with finding a way out of the ghetto in order to seek help to evacuate the ZOB fighters from the ghetto.[10]

Sunday, April 25, 1943 – the sixth day of Passover, the seventh day of the uprising

It was Easter Sunday and the weather was fine. Poles had come to celebrate the holiday in the Krasinski Garden, just outside the ghetto wall, next to the Brushmakers' Workshop area, now in flames. Czeslaw Milosz, the Polish poet, watched the people who had come to celebrate in the shadow of the burning ghetto and wrote in the poem "Campo dei Fiori" the following lines:

I thought of the Campo dei Fiori
In Warsaw by the sky-carousel
One clear spring evening
To the strains of the carnival tune.
The bright melody drowned
The salvos from the ghetto wall,

---

10 Borzykowski, *Bein kirot noflim*, 48–51.

And couples were flying
High in the cloudless sky.
At times wind from the burning
Would drift dark kites along
And riders on the carousel
Caught petals in midair.
That same hot wind
Blew open the skirts of the girls
And the crowds were laughing
On that beautiful Warsaw Sunday.

On that Easter Sunday, Stroop decided to delay the entry of his troops into the ghetto until 1 p.m. Knowing that thousands were hiding in bunkers, he split his forces into seven search parties of seventy men, each led by one officer, with orders to search the Central Ghetto, find the bunkers, and blow them up; if they were to meet resistance or if the bunkers could not be reached, they were to set fire to the building. Shortly flames and smoke enveloped the entire ghetto. Based on reports Stroop received from his subordinates, he assumed that by now all the leaders of the Jewish resistance in the Warsaw ghetto had been killed, and he hastily cabled Krueger in Krakow this mistaken information. But as prisoners taken by the Germans were interrogated it became clear to Stroop that he had been mistaken, and he had to cable a correction to his superiors. Himmler remarked to him caustically that he evidently still had a lot to learn about Warsaw.

At the end of the day, Stroop reported that his forces had caught 1,960 Jews, killed 274, and that an uncounted number of Jews had been burned alive. Four of his troops were injured that day – a member of the Panzer Training and Replacement Battalion, a member of the Cavalry Replacement Battalion, a member of the Gestapo, and a Ukrainian.

When Stroop withdrew his troops at 10 p.m. he returned, tired, from the burning ghetto to his luxurious quarters on the Aleja Roz, and fell into bed without taking his nightly bath. He ordered his adjutant not to wake him the next morning before 7 a.m., unless he were to receive a call from Himmler or unless blue-white and white-red flags were to again appear over the ghetto.[11]

That day, Borzykowski, Halina, and Yirmiyahu of Hashomer Hatzair, and Dorka Goldkorn of the Communists, all chosen for their "Aryan" appearance, went down into the sewers seeking a way out of the ghetto, in an attempt to find a means to evacuate the remaining ZOB fighters from the burning ghetto. In the sewers they found tens of men, women, and children mired in the refuse flowing through the underground system, hoping to find refuge from the inferno that was raging above ground. People were fainting and dying right there. After many hours of advancing through the muck and opening two manholes, which they found were still in the confines of the ghetto, they finally reached one that was just outside the ghetto wall.

As Halina and Dorka climbed out of the sewer they were im-mediately apprehended by the Polish police standing guard there and turned over to the Germans. As Yirmiyahu climbed out he was shot and killed, while Borzykowski just managed to descend back into the sewer and to return to the ghetto to report to his comrades at Mila 5 that his mission had failed. He and his comrades then made their way past burning buildings from Mila 5 to Mila 7, and after dark, when the German troops had withdrawn from the ghetto, they reached the ZOB bunker at Mila 18, where the ZOB command headed by Anielewicz was now located.

The bunker at Mila 18 was well hidden and camouflaged, hav-ing been built under the rubble of three buildings that had been

---

11 Stroop's operational report of April 25, 1943. Also Moczarski, *Gespraeche mit dem henker*, 186–88.

destroyed by German bombs during the siege of Warsaw. It covered a large area, included a number of chambers and cellars, contained a kitchen, water, and electric facilities, and was outfitted with a large store of food. It had been built by members of the Warsaw Jewish underworld who had continued their activities in the ghetto, amassing considerable wealth. The king of this underworld group, Shmuel Ishachar, "Asher," ruled this domain, assigning places and distributing food to those who had found shelter in his bunker.

Anielewicz had been joined in this bunker by members of his Command. As the news spread that the ZOB commander was in the bunker at Mila 18, many more ZOB fighters came to join him, until the bunker housed about 120 ZOB fighters. The "boss" of the bunker welcomed Anielewicz and his fighters into their midst. They, in turn, were joined by others fleeing the Germans and the flames, those who had tagged after the ZOB fighters, until the bunker became crowded and stuffy. The number of people who found shelter in this bunker grew quickly from a few tens to 300.[12]

Evacuating its fighters from the ghetto had been much easier for ZZW because of the two tunnels that had been prepared months earlier, which provided an exit beyond the ghetto wall. The tunnel from Muranowska 7 led to the cellar of the building at Muranowska 6, outside the ghetto, and ZZW had established a base on one of the upper floors of that building. That Sunday, the group of armed ZZW fighters who had left the ghetto through the tunnel the previous Thursday and had established themselves at Muranowska 6, left for the Michalin Forest near Otwock, some distance from Warsaw, with orders to begin partisan activity against the Germans there. They unobtrusively left the building posing as mourners and corpses in caskets in a number of funeral processions that were supposedly on

---

12 Borzykowski, *Bein kirot noflim*, 51–58. Also Lubetkin, *Biymei chilayon u-mered*, 134–35.

their way to the cemetery. They were led by Leon Rodal. A base of operations had been prepared for them in a house in the forest by ZZW fighters who had left the ghetto a few days earlier.[13]

Monday, April 26, 1943 – the last day of Passover, the eighth day of the uprising

That day Stroop continued to hunt the ghetto's Jews. Beginning at 10 a.m. Stroop had yesterday's search parties continue to comb through the districts of the Central Ghetto that had been assigned to them. On discovering bunkers his forces encountered occasional resistance, which they overcame by returning fire or setting fire to the house and letting the heat force the bunker's residents out into the open. According to him 1,700 Jews were killed, 16 bunkers were discovered, and 30 Jewish metal workers were sent to the Poniatowa workshops. Stroop withdrew his troops from the ghetto at 9:45 p.m. One soldier of the SS Cavalry Replacement Detachment was wounded.[14]

Tuesday, April 27, 1943 – the ninth day of the uprising

At 9 a.m. Stroop's forces reentered the ghetto. Frenkel had used the hours of darkness to redeploy his forces in the vicinity of Muranowski Square, thus assuring his access to the Muranowska 7 tunnel and his

---

13 Helman, *Al goralam*, 314–15. It contains the reminiscences of Pavel Besztimt, a ZZW fighter who found refuge in "Aryan" Warsaw after the uprising in the ghetto. Also David Klein, *Mitn Malach ha-Mavet untern orem* [With the Angel of Death under the arm] (Tel Aviv: I.L. Peretz Publishing House, 1968), 224–25.

14 Stroop's operational report of April 26, 1943; and MacLean, *The Ghetto Men*, 168.

connection to the world outside the ghetto. A group of armed ZZW fighters had gone through the tunnel during the night and taken up positions in the building on the other side, at Muranowska 6.

When Stroop, to his surprise, came up against ZZW fighters in the vicinity of Muranowski Square, he assigned a special combat group composed of 320 officers and men to engage the ZZW forces that had returned to the area. His tactics had by now become routine. First his attacking forces advanced and engaged in initial exchanges of fire with the Jewish fighters. Then Stroop brought up his artillery and began blasting away at the buildings being defended. As soon as he suffered the first casualties among his soldiers, he sent the flamethrowers ahead. While his machine guns kept hammering away, flames began to lick at the buildings. Then he ordered his forces to advance and seek out moving targets.

The ZZW fighters were outgunned and outnumbered. Their single advantage was their intimate acquaintance with the buildings in the area and their ability to move from building to building, using interconnected attics and cellars, without exposing themselves to the enemy's fire. After a battle that lasted until 10:30 p.m., Stroop ordered his forces in the Central Ghetto to withdraw from the ghetto.[15]

But that afternoon Stroop had received the second shock of the day. An anonymous letter had been received in the afternoon by SS-Obersturmbannfuehrer Ludwig Hahn, commander of the Security Police and Security Service, informing him that "outside the ghetto wall, on the northeastern side, Jews and Aryans were gathering, who had evidently obtained weapons from some hiding place, and that their number is constantly growing." These were a group of ZZW fighters, accompanied by a few Polish instructors, who had estab-

---

15   Stroop's operational report of April 27, 1943; and Moczarski, *Gespraeche mit dem henker*, 193.

lished themselves in the building at Muranowska 6, expecting to move from there to the Michalin Forest to take up partisan activity.

Stroop, on being informed by Hahn of this development, promptly dispatched a special combat group under the command of SS-Obersturmfuehrer Diehl of the 22nd SS Police Regiment to attack the building. Stroop believed he had chosen the right man for the task, as Diehl had a reputation as a "daredevil." Diehl's unit ran into strong opposition from the Jewish fighters in the building, who suddenly found themselves encircled and attacked by Diehl's unit. They returned the German fire with fire from pistols, rifles, submachine guns, and hand grenades. "Our soldiers fight, but the enemy is strong," Stroop recalled. Hahn saw to it that Diehl's unit immediately received reinforcements.

But Stroop's major concern was that he might be witnessing a partial mobilization of the Polish' resistance movement. Dr. Ernst Kah, Hahn's deputy, counseled that the fighting should be kept as unobtrusive as possible, to be continued into the night, while encircling the building and blocking off the neighborhood. The important thing, he said, was not to incite the Poles to acts of desperation, which might extend the flare-up beyond the ghetto to all of Warsaw, which could result in the greatest difficulties.

When Diehl reported that among the encircled fighters there were members of the Wehrmacht, Stroop panicked and notified Berlin. He realized that overcoming the resistance at Muranowska 6 was now his first-priority mission. Krueger in Krakow, as well, ordered Hahn to deal exclusively with overcoming the difficulties the Germans had encountered at Muranowska 6. Hahn and Kah, using "police methods" of interrogation, beatings, and shooting, worked through the night until the following noon. Some of the Polish police in the area, whom Kah suspected of having assisted the Jewish fighters, were shot by him on the spot.

Twenty-five ZZW fighters fell in this battle. Others succeeded in getting away. Some of the ZZW fighters used German uniforms and German helmets, and therefore were initially mistaken by Diehl for Wehrmacht soldiers. SS-Obersturmfuehrer Diehl was recommended for the first-class Iron Cross decoration for his action that day.

In his daily report Stroop wrote that "the external appearance of the Jews caught shows that it is now the turn of those who were the leaders of the resistance movement." To Moczarski he confided: "These were not anymore weak-willed masses, but rather the Zionist elite. These people knew exactly why and for what they were fighting.... Well educated and well armed, tough and cunning – and determined to die if necessary."

"That Tuesday, the 27th of April, 1943, was a busy day and difficult on the nerves," Stroop told Moczarski, when recalling the events of the day. Stroop claimed to have caught 3,000 Jews and killed 1,000 that day.[16]

Two soldiers of the SS Panzer T&R Battalion and one Ukrainian were injured.[17]

Wednesday, April 28, 1943 – The tenth day of the uprising

At 10 a.m. Stroop moved his forces into the ghetto. They again encountered strong resistance around Muranowski Square. After the interrogation of some of the fighters apprehended in yesterday's battle at Muranowska 6, Stroop had become aware that he was up against ZZW fighters. His report states that he continued "to attack the nest of the Jewish Military Organization [ZZW] situated at the border of the ghetto." And his report for that day continues: "Again today we

---

16 Stroop's operational report of April 27, 1943. Also Moczarski, *Gespraeche mit dem henker*, 193–95; and Kaczynska, *Obok Piekla*, 72–73.
17 MacLean, *The Ghetto Men*, 168.

encountered very strong resistance in many places and broke it. It becomes clearer every day that we now encounter the real terrorists and activists, because the action takes longer than expected." It was the last major battle of the uprising in the Warsaw ghetto.

Stroop claimed to have discovered a number of bunkers that day and to have pulled 335 Jews from these bunkers, to have killed ten Jewish fighters and arrested nine, and to have captured arms, munitions, and other military equipment. One soldier of the SS Panzer T&R Battalion and three soldier of the SS Cavalry Replacement Detachment were wounded in the fighting.[18]

---

18 Stroop's operational report of April 28, 1943. Also Moczarski, *Gespraeche mit dem henker*, 195; and MacLean, *The Ghetto Men*, 168. Three years later, in Wiesbaden on May 1, 1946, Stroop prepared a report at the behest of his American captors regarding the Warsaw Ghetto Uprising. In the report he refers to the Jewish fighters as "people organized in a movement known as Halutzim, that I believe was also called Betar."

Chapter 11

Escaping from the Ghetto

April 22–April 30, 1943

Confronted with Stroop's tactics of burning down the ghetto, both ZZW and ZOB found it increasingly difficult to engage Stroop's forces in battle. Both organizations began planning the evacuation of their fighters from the ghetto. Whereas Frenkel had made provisions for this eventuality – the two tunnels under the ghetto's wall at Muranowska 6 and Karmelicka 5, allowing ZZW fighters access to the world beyond the ghetto – ZOB had not made any plans for this eventuality. During the planning stages of the uprising, they had even negated the possibility of their fighters leaving the ghetto. Now that the reality on the ground forced them to plan for an evacuation of their people, they were dependent on the sewer system to get them out. But the sewers were a dark, filthy, and narrow labyrinth that was almost impossible to navigate without acquaintance with its complicated network. ZOB's first attempt to find a way out of the ghetto through the sewers, by sending Borzykowski and his three comrades on April 25 to explore that possibility, had ended in failure.

Frenkel planned to redeploy the ZZW fighters who survived the fighting in the ghetto to an area outside the ghetto, where they would begin partisan activity against the Germans. The tunnel at Muranowska 7 in the Central Ghetto, and the tunnel leading out of the ghetto at Karmelicka 5 in the Toebbens-Schultz Workshop area, would permit his fighters to leave the ghetto safely. He had arranged with members of the Polish underground that when the time came, they would assist the ZZW fighters who left the ghetto, transport them to an agreed location, and help set them up as a partisan unit. The area that had been chosen was in the forests near Otwock, about thirty kilometers southeast of Warsaw.

The first group, which included some of those wounded in the fighting at Muranowski Square, had left the Central Ghetto through the Muranowska tunnel on the night of April 20. As planned, they were transported to the forests near Otwock. There they were discovered by German forces on April 22, and in the ensuing battle they suffered heavy losses. Unaware of this, Frenkel sent the second group of ZZW fighters through the tunnel on the night of April 22. After establishing themselves in the building outside the ghetto wall, at Muranowska 6, they awaited their Polish contacts, who were supposed to transport them to the Otwock area. After waiting a few days and attempting to contact their Polish connections in Warsaw to no avail, they finally made their own arrangements to get to the Otwock area. Posing as mourners accompanying a number of funeral processions, they left Muranowska 6 and arrived safely in the Michalin forest near Otwock.[1]

When a group of ZZW fighters that had moved through the tunnel to Muranowska 6 found itself surrounded and attacked by German troops on April 27, there was good reason to suspect that the Germans had received prior information from Polish informers, who might have come from the ranks of ZZW's Polish contacts. The reliability of this connection, on which Frenkel had based his plans for the continuation of ZZW's combat against the Germans outside the ghetto, had now become questionable.

By April 26, 1943, the leaders of the ZZW unit in the Toebbens-Schultz Workshop area had concluded that the time had come to

---

1   Helman, *Al goralam*, 314–15.

evacuate their forces from the ghetto. Natan Shultz, joined by another fighter, entered the tunnel from the ZZW bunker at Karmelicka 5 that led to the building at Karmelicka 6 outside the ghetto wall, but discovered that there was a substantial presence of German forces in the courtyard of Karmelicka 6.

The following night, the fighters standing guard at the entrance to the sewer pipe that connected to the Karmelicka tunnel heard approaching footsteps. When asked to identify himself the man gave the agreed-upon password. On coming up from the sewer pipe he was recognized as "Tadek," the Polish liaison to the Betar group in the area. He said that he had been sent by the Betar leadership with orders that the group at Karmelicka 5 was to leave the ghetto at once because the Germans intended to set fire to the buildings in the area the following morning. Tadek was to lead them through the sewers to a prearranged location in Warsaw where members of ZZW and the Polish underground were awaiting them.

Thirty-one men and five women, carrying their weapons, descended into the tunnel at Karmelicka 5, and from the tunnel they entered the Warsaw sewer system.

Simha Korngold describes this tortuous journey through the sewers:

> One behind the other, there is not enough room for two to stand side by side. In a long line, each holding on to the hand of the one ahead of him, we are wallowing in mud. Sometimes the stream of water increases and each of us holds on more tightly, so as together to withstand the rising stream which threatens to drag us with it. The sewer pipe becomes narrower and we are crawling on all four, only our heads above the water. Our bodies struggle against the stream. When the water level decreases our shoulders and hips rub against the rough concrete.... We are making our way through the dampness

and the darkness…. Suddenly we see lights – the beam of light from searchlights. "Tadek" advances to investigate. He returns to report to us that there are German guards there. We must find another way. We go back. We seem to get lost. Nobody knows the way.

They find themselves again underneath the ghetto area, but unable to lift the manhole cover so as to leave the sewers.

Our strength is drained from the endless crawling in the sewers. Here the stream of water rises, and we have to escape it. Nobody thinks anymore about the direction we are going in, we only have to escape the rising water…. It is now 3 p.m. We have been crawling for thirteen hours. Will this be our end in these narrow filthy pipes? We decide to stay where we are…. We are lost in a dark labyrinth.

At 5 p.m. after having stayed in place for two hours, we hear steps, and two beams of light from searchlights approach us. Our hands reach for our weapons…somebody asks for the password, and two approaching men respond – Polish sewage workers. They are ours! A moment of happiness at the bottom of hell. They tell us that they waited for us at the Krolakowa 2 exit, as was agreed. Since we did not arrive and hours passed, they were given the task of going down into the sewers to search for the lost group. Now we cannot go out at Krolokowa 2, they had waited there for too long and possibly somebody noticed the commotion. Now we are being awaited at the Grzybowska 13 exit among the ruins of bombed-out houses. There members of the Polish underground and one member of ZZW await us. We again line up. The two Poles walk ahead of us and we drag our feet with the last of our strength after them. We were told to wait while our two guides check to see if the way is clear....

Finally they return. We have to wait until it is completely dark. Be patient, they tell us. Out there everything is ready for us to go out. We have no choice, so we continue to wait. Finally we move. We are told that as soon as the manhole cover is lifted we are to move out one by one into the house of the janitor of Grzybowska 13. Among the ruins there is a member of the Polish underground and he will direct us to the janitor's house. We have all assembled near the manhole. We count our people. Nobody is missing, what a miracle![2]

In the evening of April 28, 1943, they had arrived at the end of their seemingly endless journey through the sewers. It was supposed to be their first station on the way to joining their comrades in the forests near Otwock and begin partisan activity. Two members of the Polish underground and one member of ZZW met them and brought them food and water. They took their weapons and told them to go to sleep. The wooden floors felt like soft beds to them after spending almost twenty-four hours in the sewers.

At 5 a.m. on April 29, they were woken. Their weapons were returned to them and they were told to disperse among the ruined buildings, and stay there, each one in a different corner, until somebody came to take them to Miendzylesie on the Otwock railroad line.

By 12 noon they were getting hungry and nobody had yet come to take them. Four of them decided to get to Miendzylesie on their own, meet their comrades in the Michalin Forest, and then return for those who were staying behind. They commandeered a horse-drawn carriage and ordered the driver to take them to the railway

---

2   Simha Korngold's diary, Yad Vashem Archives O33/1566, pp. 258–67.

station. The ensuing altercation drew the attention of two Polish policemen and German gendarmes in the vicinity. They found themselves surrounded, jumped from the carriage, drew their weapons, and fired and hurled grenades at the Germans and the Polish policemen. There were losses on both sides but all four ZZW fighters fell in this encounter.

By evening the members of the Polish underground who had promised to transfer the group to the Michalin Forest had still not shown up. Natan Shultz and Pinhas Toib, who had been in contact with the Poles in the past, had by now concluded that they had been betrayed by them and there was no point in continuing to wait for them.[3]

On April 29, the ZOB Command, hiding out with many of their fighters in the bunker at Mila 18, decided that their fighters should be evacuated from the ghetto. Nineteen-year-old Simha Ratajzer (Rotem), nicknamed "Kazik," of Akiva and thirty-two-year-old Zygmunt Fryderych of the Bund were assigned the mission of leaving the ghetto, contacting "Antek" Zuckerman in Warsaw, and organizing the escape of the ZOB fighters from the ghetto. The two had found the ZZW tunnel under Muranowska Street. That night, accompanied to the tunnel entrance at Murannowska 7 by Lutek Rotblat and Adolf Hochberg, they crawled through it and entered the building at Muranowska 6 on the other side. There they hid in an attic until morning.

It was the third day after the battle between ZZW fighters and the Germans at Muranowska 6, and "Kazik" and Fryderych could still see clear signs of the battle that had taken place there – bodies

---

3   Ibid., 271–73. Stroop's operational report for May 2 includes mention of a battle with Jews that took place outside the ghetto in which four Germans and three Polish police were wounded. It is likely that this refers to this incident, which took place a few days earlier.

on the roof, bullet casings, holes in the walls. The two made their way to the home of Anna Wachalska in Warsaw, the widow of a PPS (Polish Socialist Party) activist, who had met Fryderych in the past in their contacts with the Bund. There they got themselves cleaned up and ate. The next day they went on to meet Feigl ("Wladka") Peltel, a Bund courier in "Aryan" Warsaw. At her home in the afternoon they met Antek Zuckerman, accompanied by Franya Beatus, who was serving as Zuckerman's courier. To Zuckerman they described the desperate situation in the ghetto and the urgent need to save their comrades.

Kazik had assumed that he would find Zuckerman prepared for a rapid rescue operation – guides to move into and out of the ghetto through the sewers, transportation from the exit from the sewers, and apartments in which the rescued ZOB fighters could be lodged and hidden in "Aryan" Warsaw. To his great disappointment he found that this was not the case, and he, Fryderych, and Zuckerman set to work in an attempt to make the necessary arrangements. It turned out that the preparations were going to take more than a week. In the meantime the ghetto was burning, and Stroop continued his daily search for the bunkers in the ghetto.[4]

The ZOB fighters in the Toebbens-Schultz Workshop area had no contact with the ZOB Command in the Central Ghetto. They had to make their own decisions. Like the ZZW fighters operating from this area, they saw the buildings around them going up in flames, and, like them, they concluded that they had no choice but to try to escape from the ghetto through the sewer system. In the evening of April 27, Eliezer Geller, the ZOB commander in the Toebbens-Schultz Workshop area, after attempting to contact his units, an-

---

4   Rotem, *Memoirs of a Warsaw Ghetto Fighter*, 43–47; and Zuckerman, *A Surplus of Memory*, 366.

nounced that a way had been found to get out of the area and that they would leave the ghetto that night.

Regina (Lilit) Fuden, a member of Hashomer Hatzair, who in recent months had been working as a ZOB courier in "Aryan" Warsaw purchasing arms and ammunition, had since the uprising served as the contact with the outside world for the ZOB forces in the Toebbens-Schultz area. Now she had established contact with members of the Polish underground who were prepared to evacuate Jews coming out of the ghetto through the sewers. A tunnel leading into the sewers had been found in the cellar of the building at Leszno 56. Geller and Lilit wanted to concentrate the ZOB forces in the area in that building and from there lead them through the sewers out of the ghetto. Geller was prepared to take along others who had shared bunkers with the ZOB fighters and were eager to leave the ghetto.[5]

Aharon Carmi, a member of Gordonia, and one of the ZOB fighters in Yaacov Feigenblat's unit, described years later how they moved over rooftops and attics from Leszno 76 through the burning ghetto, evading German guards, toward Leszno 56:

> The departure was scheduled for 11 p.m. We carefully wrapped rags around our shoes, and posted lookouts and guards. Yatsek [Feigenblat] together with others went to inform those who had been close to us that if they wanted to leave, they could join us. And some of them came and we instructed them how to behave silently while walking.
>
> At the designated hour we started out. A number of houses were in flames and we advanced. Shadows in a long line, we were ordered to hold onto each other and watch out for holes and cracks in the roofs. The sky seemed red against the ruined

5 Carmi and Frimmer, *Min ha-dlikah ha-hi*, 146–47; and Putermilch, *Ba-esh u-va-sheleg*, 102–103.

buildings and walls, and this redness lit our way. Thus we arrived at the building opposite Leszno 74, which was burning. From here we could not proceed anymore through the rooftops and we had to descend into the street, to bypass the burning building and climb up the next building. We ran past the building on the street, one by one, and when six of us had assembled on the other side of the building we continued."[6]

When they finally arrived at Leszno 56, Geller was waiting for them. The tunnel, which had been been dug by smugglers in the past, led from Leszno 56 to the sewers, and from the sewers they could reach the world outside the ghetto. On the morning of April 28, forty ZOB fighters began the journey. They had to part from a number of wounded comrades who had to be left behind in the care of one of the girlfighters.

And so, on the very same day, two groups of fighters from the Toebbens-Schultz Workshop area, one belonging to ZZW and the other belonging to ZOB, unaware of each other, entered the sewers at points about 200 meters' distance from each other in an attempt to reach safety outside the ghetto. One group was led by Pinhas Toib and Natan Shultz, the other by Eliezer Geller. Ten days earlier, just before the outbreak of the uprising, an initial contact between the two groups had been made. An offer of grenades made by ZZW was accepted by a ZOB unit in the area, and ZOB fighters went to the ZZW headquarters at Karmelicka 5 and carried the grenades back to their unit. But for the following ten days, throughout the battles of the uprising, they kept apart. Their commanders had decided to leave the ghetto at the same time through the sewers. They entered them at different points and were not to meet again.

---

6   Carmi and Frimmer, *Min ha-dlikah ha-hi*, 147.

Years later, Yaacov Putermilch, one of Geller's fighters, described the journey:

> At 9:15 a.m. Lilit and her companion were ordered to descend into the sewer, to reconnoiter it and inform us if the way was clear. We were divided into groups. The excitement was great. We were tired and worn out. For some days we had not slept or eaten, but no one complained.
>
> A few minutes before 10, Lilit returned and informed us that the way was clear. In the pre-arranged order we began descending into the tunnel, which was about 15 meters long. We had to get in feet first and crawl on all fours backwards. We saw how Lilit entered and we followed her example. Everyone pushed himself forward and allowed the one who followed him to descend. The sewer at this point was narrow and low. We stood, bent over, and awaited instructions. The sewage water reached our knees, and our clothes became wet. The smell was stifling and rats were jumping over our heads. From time to time the sewage water reached up to our heads.
>
> Around us total darkness. Instructions were passed from one to the other by whisper, because we did not want to be heard outside, since the echo was very strong in the sewer. The sewer pipe was narrow; we could advance only in the order in which we entered. If one of us wanted to advance, he could do so only if he passed between the legs of those standing ahead of him, through the filth.
>
> After an hour's wait in the sewer we were ordered to advance. The noise made by the movement of forty pairs of feet in the water was deafening. From time to time someone lit a candle to light the way, but they went out immediately because of the stale air.

The bends in the sewer pipe were covered by filth and rubbish. After walking about fifty meters we were suddenly ordered to stop. We knew that we had to get to Ogrodowa 27 on the "Aryan" side, where we were going to be received. It was 12 noon. At that hour it was impossible to leave the sewer. The street was full of Poles, and the danger of meeting them was no less than meeting up with Germans. Standing bent over to await the evening was beyond our strength. Our comrades found near the sewer entrances, which were usually near the middle of the streets, dry areas about 20 to 30 centimeters above the sewage water; these were used by the sewage workers in their work. The length of such an area was about a meter and a half, and its width about 70 to 80 centimeters. Pressed against each other we placed ourselves on these dry islands. There were those who stood with one foot on the entrance ladder while they leaned on the opposite wall. All of us crowded onto three of these entrances, and we maintained contact through liaisons who moved between the groups. Our legs were stuck to each other; we could not move. We were wet, trembling from the cold, and tortured by hunger. We did have our iron rations, which contained pieces of sugar and a biscuit, but we did not touch them. It took a great effort to make sure that our weapons did not get wet and dirty....

Suddenly we sensed a sharp smell. Hayka Spiegel, who sat next to me, complained of being unable to breathe. Others, as well, complained of feeling stifled. A smell of disinfectant of a sweetish taste spread among us. Somebody said that this was surely gas that the Germans had injected into the sewers. Eliezer sent Lilit and Shlomo Bachinski to check the rest of the way, and they had not yet returned. Eliezer consulted with Feigenblat. It was difficult to hold out, and people began getting up. Eliezer gave the order to return to the bunker. Worn out, exhausted, and filthy, we started back. At the entrance from the sewer to the tunnel somebody was stationed to await the return of Lilit and Shlomo Bichanski.

In the bunker we lay down on the dry floor and stretched our bodies. From the inhabitants of the bunker we received water, and Eliezer permitted us to eat our iron rations.

At 5 a.m. Lilit and Shlomo returned. She related: when they arrived at one of the sewer junctions they met two sewer workers. They were about to close one of the dams. Since that would mean blocking our way to Ogrodowa, they opposed it. But the sewer workers claimed that they had to carry out a disinfection. 'We could not convince them with words, so we pulled our guns. Only thus did we convince them,' Lilit added. From the sewer workers we learned that the disinfect-ant was an injurious gas. So it became clear that the return to the bunker had saved our lives....

At 9 p.m. we left the bunker for the second time and en-tered the tunnel. Again we began to wander in the sewers. After walking a few tens of meters we stopped and sent out scouts to check the area. At 1 a.m. we arrived at Ogradowa Street....[7]

Aharon Carmi, who was in the group that had wandered through the sewers, relates how they finally emerged above ground:

Only at 2 a.m. the manhole cover was opened and we were told that we were coming out. Our exit from the sewers was not as originally planned. According to the plan, a car was supposed to have been waiting for us to take us out of the city. The car did not arrive. To return to the ghetto was impossible. Also to

---

7 Putermilch, *Ba-esh u-va-sheleg*, 109–111.

remain in the sewers for another day was unbearable. We were hungry, depressed, and exhausted. So we improvised: to leave the sewer and to hide in one of the attics in the neighborhood. We came out one by one as we helped each other climb onto the street.

The picture we had imagined when we were told yesterday that we were leaving the ghetto was completely different from the reality. Yesterday we imagined many people coming to assist us, people who were armed from head to toe, guarding the place, providing us with food, and a large truck waiting for us to take us to the forest. And what we saw now was so pale and disappointing – not a living soul awaited us. A black night and hunger eating our guts, and we are in the middle of the street. Not far from here, at the corner of Zelezna-Ogrodowa, there stood a German guard, but they did not notice us. Our leaders took us to the entrance of Ogrodowa 27.[8]

Lilit, who had guided the group out of the ghetto, exhausted like the rest of them, insisted on returning to the ghetto in order to bring out the remaining ZOB fighters of Geller's unit. She argued with Geller until he finally gave her permission to return to the ghetto. Back down she went into the sewer and back to the ghetto. There she succeeded in locating Shlomo Winogren's unit and brought them to the entrance to the tunnel. But while winding her way among the burning buildings, a German bullet hit her, and her comrades brought her wounded to one of the bunkers. She never made it out of the ghetto. Members of Hershel Kawe's Communist unit, which succeeded in leaving the ghetto through the sewers, brought with them the story of this heroic young girl: Regina Fuden, a member of Hashomer Hatzair – "Lilit."

8　Carmi and Frimmer, *Min ha-dlikah ha-hi*, 152.

Chapter 12

The Bunker War – Mila 18

April 29–May 16, 1943

The Warsaw ghetto was burning. The fighters would venture out at night while Stroop's troops were withdrawn from the ghetto, and stay in hiding in one of the bunkers during daylight hours. Tzivya Lubetkin described the ghetto in those days:

> With their last strength Jews sought refuge, running among the ruins and the flames. The fire chased them from hiding places and underground bunkers. Many were burned alive and suffocated by the smoke, but many – men, women, and children – emerged from the bowels of the earth, loaded down with remains of food, pots, and blankets. Babies at their mother's bosom and the bigger ones were dragged behind their parents, and their eyes – hollows of sadness and grief, sorrow and confusion, cried out for help. And they all moved around seeking refuge behind any wall, among ruins that could not burn anymore, in corners that the fire had not yet reached. Who can describe the intensity of sorrow, the great terror of the Jews among the flames!
>
> The ghetto burned. Days and nights it was in flames. The flames licked and consumed every building. Building after building, street after street were put to the stake. Columns of

smoke rose and sparks flew and the sky took on a terrifying red color.[1]

Most of the remaining Jews in the ghetto were hiding in the hundreds of underground bunkers that had been built in the past weeks and months in the hope of surviving the German manhunt. The bunkers were camouflaged so that their existence was impossible to discern by the uninitiated from the outside; only those acquainted with their location were able to find the entrances to the hideouts. Stroop realized that the Jews were hiding in the bunkers during daylight hours. His aim was now to find each and every bunker and extract the Jews hiding in them. He would wage war against the bunkers, using dogs that would pick up the trace of human habitation, acoustic equipment to sense the slightest noise, and soldiers sensitive to the smell of food that was being cooked. And above all, he tried to catch informers who, for the promise of food and their life, would be prepared to point out the location of well-camouflaged bunkers. Once they lost their usefulness, they were summarily shot.

Many of those who had invested money and great effort in preparing a bunker and a store of food and water, had also acquired pistols, grenades, and ammunition and were prepared to defend themselves if their bunker were to be discovered. Thus the discovery of bunkers was sometimes accompanied by an exchange of fire and injury or death to some of the German soldiers who tried breaking into the bunker, and the killing of the bunker's inhabitants.

On April 29, 1943, Stroop reported that he had discovered thirty-six bunkers, killed 109 Jews, and captured 2,539. One member of the SS Cavalry Replacement Detachment was wounded.[2] The fol-

---

1   Lubetkin, *Biymei chilayon u-mered*, 140.
2   Stroop's operational report for April 29, 1943.

lowing day Stroop reported that 179 Jews had been killed and 1,599 captured, with no losses to Stroop's forces.[3]

On May 1, 1943, the Germans discovered the existence of the large underground bunker, composed of a series of cellars, at Franciskanska 30. Among the many Jews who had found refuge in this bunker were some of the ZOB fighters who had fought in the Brushmakers' Workshop area and moved to the Central Ghetto after the Germans had set fire to the buildings there. They were led by Marek Edelman, who had commanded the ZOB forces in the Brushmaker's Workshop area.

The Germans began by surrounding the building under which the bunker was located. Then they broke into one of the openings to the bunker, fired into the bunker, and hurled grenades into it. ZOB fighters returned fire at that bunker entrance, while others escaped from the bunker through another opening that the Germans had not yet discovered. There were losses on both sides and the Germans withdrew. The Germans returned the following day and a battle ensued as they simultaneously attacked all the entrances to the bunker. Smoke bombs thrown by the Germans into the bunker immobilized the defenders. Only on the third day, May 3, did the Germans complete the clearing of the bunker. Two Germans were killed and two were wounded in the fighting. Eight ZOB fighters fell in the battle. Hanoch Gutman, the Dror unit commander from the Brushmakers' Workshop area, was seriously wounded in this battle and died of his wounds shortly thereafter. Edelman survived and joined his comrades in the bunker at Franciskanska 22.[4]

On May 2, 1943, SS-Obergruppenfuehrer Krueger arrived unexpectedly from Krakow to personally inspect the operation in the

---

3　Ibid., April 30, 1943.
4　Stroop's operational reports for May 1, 2, and 3. Also Borzykowski, *Bein kirot noflim*, 67; and Edelman, *The Ghetto Fights*, 41.

Warsaw ghetto and see why it was taking so long. Krueger had made a name for himself in the Nazi hierarchy as a great expert on racial matters, and was intent on exterminating all the Jews in the area under his control. He had been frequently calling Stroop since the *Grossaktion* began, trying to manage the operation in the Warsaw ghetto from Krakow. On arrival he entered the ghetto in full uniform, officiously inquired into everything, paid attention to every detail, and gave Stroop advice and instructions. He was concerned that the action was taking too much time. But after listening to Stroop's explanations and receiving reports from the Gestapo officers working with Stroop, Hahn, and Kah, he admitted that Stroop was facing a serious problem in the ghetto.

At the final situation review at Stroop's headquarters on Ujazdowskie Avenue, Krueger ordered that extensive photographs be taken of the ghetto operation. "This will provide invaluable historical material for the Fuehrer, for Heinrich Himmler, and for the future researchers of the history of the Third Reich, for our National Socialist poets and writers, as well as educational material for the SS. But above all, this material will document what great efforts had to be made and what heavy and bloody sacrifices the Nordic and Germanic races had to make in order to clear Europe and the whole world of the Jews," he explained.

As he parted he told Stroop, referring to the resistance the Germans were encountering, "I understand that considering the unexpected situation it was difficult to achieve rapid success. Continue the operation. It would be good if the operation could be formally completed on May 15. The completion of the operation must be signaled by fireworks. As the final accord, for political and propaganda purposes, I would suggest blowing up the great Warsaw synagogue.

The best explosive expert on my staff in Krakow has already worked out the detailed plan."[5]

The well-camouflaged bunker at Mila 18, to which Anielewicz and his comrades were welcomed on April 25 by the "owners" of this initially almost luxurious underground abode, contained bathrooms, kitchens, living rooms and bedrooms, electricity, and a plentiful supply of provisions. But it became crowded and stuffy during the following ten days, as 120 of ZOB's fighters joined their commander, and hundreds of others, fleeing the fires above ground and seeking safety, found their way into it. The accepted rule was that anybody who had succeeded in finding one of the entries into this bunker, located under the ruins of a large building, had to be admitted, so that knowledge of the bunker's location remain within the confines of the bunker.

As the fires above ground spread through the entire neighborhood, the heat began penetrating the bunker's many compartments and alcoves. Borzykowski, who had joined Anielewicz in the bunker, described conditions there:

> The crowding had become worse. The long corridor was already occupied, people were lying on the floor, and as one passed in the darkness he would step on them. There was filth everywhere and lice appeared.... As the number of people increased the amount of food each received decreased. And hunger made its appearance. The babies did not know what an emergency was and demanded their food. Their crying and screaming could bring a catastrophe on the bunker and its inhabitants, but there was no way to keep them quiet. There was no more bread or potatoes.... The hunger weakened the body

5   Moczarski, *Gespraeche mit dem henker*, 200–202.

and depressed the soul and made the spirit indifferent and apathetic. Even the reaction to the sound of explosions or the sound of the enemy's footsteps brought about no more than an instinctive reaction. Many already wished that, come what may, there would be an end to the suffering. They were certain that their fate was sealed, since the Germans were strong and had more patience than they. The news that reached them that the Germans daily discovered bunkers and killed those in the bunker using gas, only strengthened the feeling that the present torture was no more than a prelude to certain death.[6]

From May 1 to 3, Stroop reported that his forces had discovered forty-six bunkers, shot 575 Jews, and apprehended over 3,000. Two more SS soldiers were wounded on May 3 in the fighting around the bunkers. For the next three days, while continuing to set fire to the ghetto's buildings, Stroop pursued his search for bunkers, claiming in his daily reports to have discovered over a hundred bunkers, to have killed hundreds of Jews and apprehended for "shipment" thousands. His intelligence services informed him of the approximate location of the hide-out of what he assumed was the leadership of the Jewish resistance, and he was now intent on finding it.

On May 6 Stroop thought that he was beginning to come close to the "headquarters bunker" of the Jewish resistance. Two days earlier a Jewish informer, bribed with food by Stroop's Gestapo officers, Hahn and Kah, and as a bonus supplied with a pass that would allow him to move freely in the area of the *Generalgouvernement*, had directed them to what the informer claimed was the approximate location of this bunker. The bunker at this location, when stormed by the Germans, turned out to be a disappointment – it contained

---

6   Borzykowski, *Bein kirot noflim*, 58–59.

three corpses, one grenade, and one pistol. For this the informer was rewarded by a bullet in the head.[7] And the search continued.

Stroop had been proceeding systematically with his search of bunkers in the ghetto, and news reached those hiding in the bunker at Mila 18 that even well-camouflaged bunkers were being discovered every day. The ZOB fighters there concluded that they had to prepare for the discovery by the Germans of this bunker as well. Their only hope was that on discovering the bunker the Germans would not simultaneously discover all five entrances to it, and the fighters would be able to leave through one of the other entrances and attack the Germans from the outside. But there was little time for making plans. On May 7 at 3 p.m. they sensed much movement above the bunker. There was the sound of some instruments as plaster and sand began coming down from the bunker's ceiling. It seemed that the Germans were attempting to drill into the bunker from above. For three hours the sounds continued to reach the bunker, but at 6 p.m. it seemed that the Germans had left.[8]

In the evening of May 7 the ZOB Command at Mila 18 concluded that the Germans had located the bunker and would probably return the following morning to break into it. Appropriate preparations would therefore have to be made already that evening. The possibility of leaving the bunker was discussed. Based on information that had reached them, that on Smocza Street in the ghetto there existed an entry into the sewer system, a group of fighters was ordered to leave the bunker immediately to check the possibility of entering the sewer there. Should this turn out to be possible, some of them who had "Aryan" looks were to pass through the sewers out of the ghetto, contact Zuckerman in "Aryan" Warsaw, and obtain help

---

7   Moczarski, *Gespraeche mit dem henker*, 209–210.
8   Borzykowski, *Bein kirot noflim*, 70–71.

for the fighters and the remaining Jews in the ghetto. The rest were to remain in the sewer to await the results.

Borzykowski and a group of ZOB fighters left the bunker shortly after midnight to look for the entry to the sewers on Smocza Street. On the way they ran into German patrols. In the exchange of fire that followed, some of them were wounded, and it was decided that part of the group would return with the wounded to the bunker at Mila 18. Borzykowski, Mordechai Growas, who had commanded a Hashomer Hatzair unit at the Nalewki-Gensia intersection on the first day of the uprising, and Yisrael Kanal of Akiva, who had commanded the ZOB forces in the Central Ghetto, continued on in an attempt to fulfill the mission that had been entrusted to them and reach the sewer entrance on Smocza Street. After further encounters with German patrols during the night, they finally had to take shelter at daybreak in an abandoned bunker, where they spent the daylight hours. At 11 p.m. on May 8, they decided to abandon the search for the entry into the sewer system and began to make their way back toward Mila 18. When they finally arrived there they found nothing but ruins – the bunker was gone. The Germans had broken into it during the day and blown it up.[9]

Borzykowski described after the war what he experienced that night:

> We finally arrived at our destination, Mila 18 – but it was no more. As we came close we discerned immediately that a tremendous change had taken place here during the day. The whole shape of the ruins under which the bunker had been located had changed; mounds of bricks, sand, and stone had been torn from their original locations. The hidden paths which led to the entries to the bunker, that were known only

---

9   Ibid., 72–79.

to those in the bunker, had been completely wiped out. No one manned the guard posts; we repeatedly called out the password and there was no reply. Had we been mistaken? But a quick check made it clear that this was the place we had left twenty-four hours ago, but in the meantime it had changed beyond recognition.

We proceeded deeper into the labyrinth, from opening to opening, and from crack to crack, until we got to a corner and there discovered a group of seven or eight comrades, among them: Tosya Altman, Michael Rosenfeld, Yehuda Wengrower, Pnina and Menahem Beigelman – the only remnants of all the Jews and fighters who had been at Mila 18.

These were moments of inner turmoil for us. Twenty-four hours ago, when we left on our mission, we had comrades, Jews, an organization – we had a base of operation. And now – on our return – mounds of dirt and scattered bricks. And underneath them, our comrades, who had been our comrades in life and in battle. Until now we were kept going by the common ideal of resistance and the act of resistance itself; but now as we stood in the darkness of night at the grave of the organization, surrounded by fires, it was clear to us, the last observers of this melancholy scene, that it was all over, everything. Our world had disappeared and there was no sense anymore to our lives as individuals, isolated, depressed, and forgotten.[10]

The night that Borzykowski and his comrades left the bunker at Mila 18 on their mission, Tzivya Lubetkin and Haim Frimmer also left the bunker, attempting to reach Franciskanska 22, which was also rumored to have an entry to the sewer system. In that bunker, it was

---

10 Ibid., 79–80.

said, there was a man who knew his way around the sewers and might be able to lead the ZOB fighters out of the ghetto. On arriving at Franciskanska 22, they found their comrades in a very crowded bunker and met the man who claimed to know his way about in the Warsaw sewers. They decided to send a group out that night, May 8. They planned to exit the sewers at a designated manhole outside the ghetto; they would hide among the ruins of bombed-out buildings and send a few with "Aryan" appearance to make contact with Zuckerman. After two and a half hours, two of the group returned together with the guide and reported that after some members of the group had climbed out of the sewer, they had heard shots fired in the street. Those remaining in the sewer had returned to the bunker and were concerned about the fate of the group which had climbed out onto the street.

Rather than risking returning to Mila 18 during daylight hours, Lubetkin and Frimmer awaited the hours of darkness and then, together with Edelman, made their way to Mila 18. On arrival they found only ruins and destruction; the bunker at Mila 18 was no more. Among the ruins they ran into Borzykowski, Kanal, and Growas, together with a few survivors. From them they heard a description of what happened in the bunker that day: At about noon on May 8 the Germans had been heard in the vicinity of the bunker. They surrounded the bunker and broke through the five entrances. The ZOB fighters posted at the entrances fired on the Germans. The Germans began throwing smoke bombs into the bunker. When the Germans called for everybody to come out most of those in the bunker obeyed the call, except for the ZOB fighters. Arye Wilner was the first to urge the fighters to commit suicide and not fall alive into the hands of the Germans. Most of them shot themselves or took poison. Among those who perished in the bunker were the ZOB commander Mordechai Anielewicz and his companion Mira Fruchner. A large part of the ZOB fighting force in the ghetto was lost. A few succeeded in leaving the bunker through one of the openings after the Germans assumed that everyone had already come out and the rest were left for dead. One of the survivors was the Communist representative on the ZOB Command, Michael Rosenfeld.[11]

On May 7 Stroop had reported that "the location of the so-called 'select Party Directorate' is now known."[12] Stroop at the time had only nebulous ideas of just who were the leaders and members of the Jewish resistance in the ghetto. His intelligence had provided him information, based on the interrogation of Jews who had been caught, of the existence of two organizations – ZZW and ZOB – and that their fighters were members of what he later referred to as a so-called "Halutz-Movement, sometimes also called Betar." As a result of the heavy fighting at Muranowski Square during the first days of the uprising, he had reached the conclusion that ZZW "was the main Jewish combat group."[13]

In his daily reports Stroop had adopted the terminology, dictated by Berlin, Krueger, and Hahn, that depicted the uprising in the Warsaw ghetto as the work of Communists. He understood that propaganda considerations required this, even though he knew that it was not the case. The "headquarters bunker" that he thought he had now located had therefore to be labeled the "Party Directorate," but he assumed that it was the headquarters of ZZW. In his report of May 8 reporting on his discovery and breaking into the bunker at Mila 18, he proudly announced that he had apprehended "the

---

11 Lubetkin, *Biymei chilayon u-mered*, 152–62; and Borzykowski, *Bein kirot noflim*, 80–81.

12 Stroop's operational reports for May 4, 5, 6, and 7.

13 See report on the suppression of the Warsaw Ghetto Uprising prepared by Stroop on May 1, 1946, at the behest of the U.S. military authorities after he was captured by them in Wiesbaden. The full text appears in appendix 4. And see Stroop's final report on the *Grossaktion* in the Warsaw ghetto to Krueger of May 16, 1943, as it appears in appendix 3.

Deputy Leader of the Jewish Military Organization 'ZWZ' [sic] and his so-called Chief of Staff and liquidated them." In his daily report Stroop claimed that he had caught sixty Jews and killed 140 in the bunker at Mila 18. He emphasized that he was "resolved not to terminate the *Grossaktion* until every last Jew had been destroyed." In the fighting at the Mila 18 bunker, two German soldiers were killed and three wounded.[14]

It had taken Zuckerman and Rotem (Kazik) and the people working with them more than a week to organize for the rescue of the ZOB fighters in the ghetto. On May 8, the day on which the Germans discovered the bunker at Mila 18, Kazik finally set out on this precarious mission. He, Ryszek Musselman, who had served as liaison between the Communists in Warsaw and the ghetto, and two Polish sewer workers whom they had induced to lead them, entered the sewers on the "Aryan" side on their way to the ghetto. While walking through the filth and stench, from time to time the Poles would change their minds and had to be persuaded and even threatened at gunpoint to proceed. Finally, at 2 a.m. the Poles announced that they were now underneath the ghetto.

When Kazik climbed up the iron ladder and lifted the manhole cover, he found that he was a few meters away from the ghetto gate on Zamenhofa, between Stawki and Niska. To evade the searchlight from Dzika he crawled on his belly to Muranowska and from there to Franciskanska 30, where he knew there had been a bunker in which ZOB fighters had found shelter. There he found nothing but ruins. He continued to Franciskanska 22, the location of another bunker, but found none of his comrades there. Continuing his search he rushed to Nalewki, Mila, and Zamenhofa, finding nothing but ruins

---

14 Stroop's operational report for May 8, 1943. In the report Stroop got the initials of ZZW wrong and wrote instead "ZWZ." Also Moczarski, *Gespraeche mit dem henker*, 213.

and piles of corpses. He decided to return to the sewers. "Let's go! There's nobody there!" he shouted to Musselman and the two Polish sewer workers who had been waiting for him, as he climbed back into the sewer through the manhole. He had come too late.[15]

That night Edelman, Lubetkin, Frimmer, Kanal, and Borzykowski shepherded the few survivors of the Mila 18 bunker, who were exhausted and barely able to move, to the bunker at Franciskanska 22, arriving there after midnight. They had been expecting to rest and recover their forces there, but found the inhabitants of the bunker making preparations for leaving it. The presence of German troops in the vicinity of the bunker that day was taken as an indication by those in the bunker that the Germans were preparing to storm it on the following day. Now their only choice was to attempt to leave the ghetto through the sewers.

Not very optimistic about their chances, Borzykowski and seven other ZOB fighters climbed down into the sewers that night, hoping to find a path out of the ghetto for their comrades in the bunker. For Borzykowski it was the second descent into the filthy sewage water. Two weeks earlier he had participated in an unsuccessful attempt to leave the ghetto through the sewers, which had ended in disaster. His three comrades paid with their lives for the attempt, while he himself barely managed to return to the ghetto through the sewers. This time he thought it was a hopeless venture.

Crawling through the sewers on all fours, their journey became more and more difficult and began to seem endless. After two hours it seemed to them that they were still under the ghetto. They had lost all sense of direction, having to guess at each turn which way to go.

"Suddenly," Borzykowski wrote years later, "we were astounded and frightened. The bright light of a searchlight shone from a distance and approached us. We had only one explanation for this: the

---

15 Rotem, *Memoirs of a Warsaw Ghetto Fighter*, 50–52.

Germans were chasing the remnants of the Jewish fighters.... At first we instinctively moved backwards. But then we remembered that there was no way back. The ghetto is in ruins. Death awaits us wherever we go. It is best to stay where we are and let come what may. The tension was unbearable. We stare at the light getting larger and larger. Its rays are coming close to us, and we can see each other. But who is approaching us? We can't make it out. The light is blinding us. Each one of us can already see his life coming to an end, swept away by the filthy water, just like the corpse that floated between our legs a short while ago. It was the last moment between life and death."[16]

As Borzykowski and his comrades were trying to find their way through the sewers, Simha (Kazik) Rotem, convinced that all his comrades in the ghetto were dead, was making his way back through the sewers out of the ghetto, accompanied by Musselman and the Polish sewer workers.

"We started back," he writes. "As we walked I signaled with my flashlight, in case someone remained hiding here. Suddenly I heard a noise in a side sewer. I though I could make out a flickering light. Were they Germans or Jews? My nerves were stretched to the limit, my fingers caressed the trigger of my revolver. I was ready to shoot but something stopped me. I waited and repeated the password of the organization. The tension mounted. From the side sewer a group of ten fighters suddenly burst out. For a moment we were petrified. Was this a dream? Everyone wanted to hug me. A few minutes later I knew we had arrived only one day late."

Kazik told them that arrangements had been made for them to be picked up by truck as they came out of the sewer in Warsaw and taken to a safe location.

---

16 Borzykowski, *Bein kirot noflim*, 81–84.

Two of the group were sent back through the sewers to the ghetto to report to their comrades at the bunker in Franciskanska 22, as well as to Artstein and his fighters at the bunker in Nalewki 37, and guide them through the sewers to the agreed-upon exit at Prosta and Twarda streets, over two kilometers from the sewer entry at Franciszkanska 22. There they were all to leave the sewer and be taken to safety.[17]

After learning that Anielewicz and many of her comrades had been killed in the bunker at Mila 18, Tzivya Lubetkin had had trouble falling asleep that night. When she finally fell asleep she was suddenly wakened and told by the two who had returned from the sewers that they had met Kazik in the sewers that night, that he had made preparations to get them out of the sewers and to safety outside the ghetto, and that she and the others had to follow them immediately into the sewers. There was no time to search for Artstein and the others.

The fighters in the bunker at Franciszkanska 22 jumped into the filthy sewer water, one after the other, Lubetkin and Edelman taking up the rear. "A long line of people crawl through the narrow sewer, proceeding through the filthy waters," Tzivya wrote years later. "The back is bent, in one hand a lit candle. This is how we proceed, one behind the other, no one sees the other's face. Probing and moving forward in the darkness. Nothing to eat or drink, weak and exhausted.... The time passed. Every hour seemed like eternity. Thus we walked continuously."

Toward morning they arrived at the designated sewer exit – the Twarda-Proska intersection. They were told to wait; they decided to disperse and not remain concentrated in one group. Two of their comrades were sent back to the ghetto to bring back those who had stayed behind. However, they returned shortly reporting that the

---

17 Rotem, *Memoirs of a Warsaw Ghetto Fighter*, 52–53.

Germans had blocked the sewers leading to the ghetto. At midnight some soup and bread was passed down to them, and they were told that the following morning they would be taken out of the sewer. Only at 10 a.m. on May 10, after having spent two nights and a day in the sewers, they heard the manhole cover being lifted, and could see the sun of a beautiful spring day.

Kazik had planned to have a truck waiting at the manhole before sunrise but the arrangement had not worked out. He thought that his comrades in the sewer would not be able to survive another day down there, and when a truck that was passing in the street was commandeered at 10 a.m., he decided to take a chance and bring his comrades out in full daylight, a hundred meters from a German-Ukrainian guard position. Watched by hundreds of Poles who had assembled in the street and others looking out from the windows of nearby houses, out of the sewer climbed thirty filthy, mud-covered figures, looking more like ghosts than human beings.

After half an hour, Kazik, who had been expecting the arrival of all the surviving ZOB fighters, was surprised to see that no one else was leaving the sewer. He bent down into the sewer and called out, "Anybody inside?" When there was no reply he ordered the manhole cover returned, got into the truck, and ordered the driver to move off. When Tzivya saw that not all the ZOB fighters had left the sewer and gotten onto the truck, she ordered Kazik to stop the truck and wait for the others. Kazik, fearing that Germans would approach at any minute, insisted that he was in charge of the operation and that they had to move out immediately. Some fifty ZOB fighters were left behind in the sewers. Some of them climbed out of the sewers later and were killed in a pitched battle with German troops who had in the meantime surrounded the area.[18]

---

18 Rotem, *Memoirs of a Warsaw Ghetto Fighter*, 54–57; Lubetkin, *Biymei chilayon u-mered*, 169–76; Borzykowski, *Bein kirot noflim*, 85–89; and

Having reported to his superiors that he had eliminated the leadership of the Jewish resistance in the ghetto, Stroop now continued his war against the bunkers and what he thought were the remnants of the Jewish fighters. At night he sent special patrols into the ghetto in order to kill Jews who were moving around among the ruins in the darkness. During the following four days he reported to have discovered over 150 bunkers, caught over 3,000 Jews, and killed over 800. One German soldier was killed and six were wounded during this period. Systematically Stroop ordered the burning down of any buildings still remaining, until only a desert of rubble was left of the ghetto. Now he felt that he had completely fulfilled Himmler's orders to raze the ghetto. On May 13, after four of Stroop's SS soldiers were wounded in fighting in the ghetto and two of his SS soldiers were killed in a Soviet air raid on Warsaw that day, he and Krueger decided that from now on all Jews caught would be sent to the gas chambers in Treblinka.[19]

May 14 brought further battles with Jewish fighters in the ghetto. During the night Stroop's night patrols collided several times with what he referred to as "armed bandits," and three SS soldiers and one SS policeman were wounded. During the day another four SS soldiers were wounded in encounters with Jewish resistance fighters. On that day Stroop received an inspection visit from SS-Gruppenfuehrer Maximilian von Herff, the head of Himmler's personnel bureau. Himmler was checking up on him.

The following day, May 15, Stroop reported that a member of the 22nd SS Police Regiment had been wounded in an encounter

---

Frimmer's account in Carmi and Frimmer, *Min ha-dlikah ha-hi*, 239. Zuckerman's account of the action near the Prosta manhole appears in Zuckerman, *A Surplus of Memory*, 382–86. Also see Stroop's operational report for May 10, 1943.

19 Stroop's operational reports for May 9–13, 1943; and Moczarski, *Gespraeche mit dem henker*, 216.

with Jewish fighters. In preparation for "declaring victory" the next day, he now reported: "A special task force searched once more and subsequently destroyed the last block of buildings which were still intact within the ghetto. In the evening the chapel, mortuary, and all adjoining buildings in the Jewish cemetery were blown up and destroyed by fire. The sum total of Jews caught has risen to 55,885." Seemingly satisfied with these results, he announced that he would terminate the entire *Grossaktion* on May 16, 1943, at dusk "by blowing up the synagogue, which we did not succeed in accomplishing today, and will subsequently charge the 3rd Battalion, 23rd SS Police Regiment with continuing and completing the measures that still may be necessary."

On Sunday, May 16 Stroop submitted his last report for the *Grossaktion*, which had lasted twenty-eight days. The following is the text of this report:

> The operation began at 1000 hours. Altogether 180 Jews, bandits, and subhumans were destroyed. The former Jewish Warsaw ghetto is no longer standing. The action was terminated at 2015 hours by blowing up the Warsaw synagogue.
>
> All measures to be taken with respect to the established banned areas were handed over to the commanding officer of the 3rd Battalion, 23rd SS Police Regiment. I instructed him carefully. The total number of Jews dealt with was 56,065; this includes both those Jews we caught and those whose extermination can be proven. We had no friendly losses today. I will submit a final report to the Conference of SS and Police Commanders on May 18, 1943.[20]

---

20 Stroop's operational reports for May 14–16, 1943.

In accordance with Krueger's wishes Stroop had prepared to blow up the Tlomacki synagogue as the final accord of the *Grossaktion*. The preparations for this "operation" took ten days. The interior of the synagogue had to be cleared and a few hundred holes for the explosives had to be drilled into the foundations and walls, since the synagogue was built very solidly. Extensive work by electricians and explosives experts was required in order to blow it up in a single explosion.

While in Warsaw prison awaiting trial for war crimes committed in the Warsaw ghetto, Stroop described to his cellmates his victory celebration:

> What a marvelous sight it was – a fantastic piece of theater. My staff and I stood at a distance. I held the electric device that would detonate all the charges simultaneously. Jesuiter called for silence. I glanced over at my brave officers and men, tired and dirty, silhouetted against the glow of the burning buildings. After prolonging the suspense for a moment, I shouted "*Heil Hitler*" and pressed the button. With a thunderous, deafening bang and a rainbow burst of colors, the fiery explosion soared toward the clouds, an unforgettable tribute to our triumph over the Jews. The Warsaw ghetto was no more. The will of Adolf Hitler and Heinrich Himmler had been done.[21]

The German armies were in retreat before the Red Army in the Soviet Union, and the German forces had surrendered unconditionally to the Allied armies in Tunis. It was the beginning of the end for Hitler's Germany. But Stroop thought he had delivered Hitler and Himmler a victory over the Jews.

---

21 Moczarski, *Gespraeche mit dem henker*, 217–16.

In his summary report to the assembled SS Police Leaders in Krakow the next day, Stroop wrote: "Although the *Grossaktion* is completed, we have to reckon with the possibility of a few Jews still living in the ruins of the former ghetto; therefore this area must be firmly shut off from the Aryan residential area and be guarded.... In this way, it should be possible to keep the small remainder of Jews there, if any, under constant pressure and to exterminate them eventually."[22]

Nevertheless, some Jews continued to hold out in the ruins of what had remained of the ghetto area and there were occasional armed encounters with German troops throughout the rest of the year. Two illustrious fighters, one from ZOB and the other from ZZW, who were still roaming the ghetto ruins in June, had at this point no difficulty in overcoming past differences that separated their organizations. They were Zecharya "Zecharyash" Artstein, the ZOB fighter who had fired the first shot of the uprising at the Nalewki-Gensia intersection on April 19, 1943, and Yuzek Lopata, a ZZW unit commander from the Brushmakers' Workshop area. They had been hiding out together, and at the beginning of June, while attempting to establish contact with the "Aryan" side, they fell together in a firefight with German troops.[23]

On June 18, 1943, Stroop was decorated with the Iron Cross 1st Class by Field Marshal Wilhelm Keitel, Chief of the German High Command, in appreciation of his command over the *Grossaktion* in the Warsaw ghetto.

Proud of his accomplishment, Stroop had three copies of an elegant album prepared, which contained all his daily reports and his summary report, and some fifty photographs that were taken during

---

22 Stroop's summary report. See appendix 3.
23 Najberg, *Ha-aharonim*, 117.

the liquidation of the ghetto. The album was entitled: *Es gibt keinen juedischen Wohnbezirk in Warschau mehr* (The Jewish residential quarter in Warsaw no longer exists). It went on to list the names of soldiers who had fallen "For the Fuehrer and the Fatherland – In the battle for the annihilation of Jews and bandits in the former Jewish residential quarter of Warsaw." One copy was sent to Himmler, the second to Stroop's superior in Krakow, Krueger, and the third he kept for himself. One of the copies was eventually presented as evidence in the Nuremberg war crimes trials.

At the conclusion of the war Stroop was apprehended by the U.S. army in western Germany and later brought to trial in Dachau, where he was sentenced to death for the shooting of captured American airmen. At the request of the Polish government he was extradited to Poland. In Warsaw in 1951, he was tried for war crimes and sentenced to death by hanging. On March 3, 1952, he was hanged at the former site of the Warsaw ghetto.

Chapter 13

Outside the Ghetto

With the fighting in the ghetto essentially over, the leadership of ZOB and ZZW were faced with the decision of where to locate their fighters as they left the ghetto. Both organizations were dependent on the advice and assistance of their Polish contacts. As the ZOB fighters left the ghetto through the sewers, they were taken to a small wooded area near the village of Lomianki, seven kilometers northwest of Warsaw. ZZW fighters were directed to the Michalin Forest thirty kilometers southeast of Warsaw, where they planned to begin partisan activity against German targets.

Lomianki

In the early hours of the morning of April 30, the forty ZOB fighters from the Toebbens-Schultz Workshop area who had succeeded in leaving the ghetto through the sewers were lying in the attic of the building at Ogrodowa 27. Led by the ZOB Toebbens-Schultz area commander, Eliezer Geller, they had made the tortuous journey through the sewers to leave the ghetto, expecting to be met by trucks that would take them to safety. As they came out of the sewer they had been greatly disappointed to find that there was no one to greet them. Filthy and smelling from the sewer, feeling abandoned, they found refuge for the night in the attic, lying there in suspense not knowing what the next day would bring.

Suddenly they heard steps on the stairs. The man who appeared was unknown to them, but he knew the password. It was Krzaczek

(Wladisilaw Gajek), a Polish member of the Armia Ludowa (AL), the Communist-led Polish underground, who had been serving as liaison between Zuckerman and the AL. He had come with a truck, prepared to take them out of Warsaw. By 6 a.m. they had descended from the attic, under Krzaczek's direction, and had gotten onto the truck. To their surprise Geller did not join them. Wishing them good luck and good-bye, he said that he had much to do in Warsaw and had decided to stay behind.

The truck moved through the streets of Warsaw, crossed the bridge over the Wisla River, and continued into the country, finally stopping on a sandy mound. From there Krzaczek led them to a wooded area. They were now in a small fir wood near the village of Lomianki, seven kilometers northwest of Warsaw

The area was not suitable for an extended stay, and certainly not for partisan activity. There were a number of villages in the vicinity, and there was a German military base not far from there. The meager food rations they brought with them had almost run out; they had no water and were using the early morning dew from the vegetation in the area to slake their thirst. During the cold nights they shivered in their tattered clothes, unable to sleep. After sundown they could see in the distance the sky red from the fires that were burning in the ghetto.

Velvel Rozovski, who had an "Aryan" appearance, was sent to Warsaw in order to make contact with Zuckerman, but he was caught and killed by the Germans. From a nearby village, they managed to get some food and water that made it possible for them to survive. On May 9 a messenger arrived and told them that "Kazik" had succeeded in making contact with surviving ZOB fighters in the ghetto, that they were now assembled in the sewers waiting to be taken out the following day, and that they would then be brought to Lomianki. The next day, May 10, at 10:30 a.m., they could hear an approaching truck. When the truck stopped, Krzaczek and Kazik got off and, on being told that all was clear, told the rest of the group in the truck to get off. They were almost unrecognizable, emaciated and filthy from the many hours spent in the sewers.

Kazik and Krzaczek returned that day to Warsaw expecting to bring the rest of the group that had remained in the sewer, but shortly news arrived that that they had all been killed. Almost all the surviving ZOB fighters of the Warsaw ghetto – eighty in all – were now in the Lomianki woods. They were divided into groups, each group locating itself in a separate area, and using branches to provide a flimsy cover over their heads. The leadership, now composed of Tzivya Lubetkin, Marek Edelman, Yisrael Kanal, and Tuvia Borzykowski, stuck together in one area and were in continuous consultation about future plans.

There was no doubt that the location was unsuitable, that sooner or later the Germans would discover them there, and that they would have to move out as quickly as possible. Zuckerman was trying to make arrangements for a Polish partisan unit to accept the ZOB fighters but was having no success. In the meantime it was decided to transfer the leadership to Warsaw, to hiding places in apartments that had been arranged for them by Zuckerman. Tzivya Lubetkin, Tosya Altman, Marek Edelman, Abrasha Blum, and Tuvia Borzykowski were taken to Warsaw. The others continued to wait. Finally, they were notified that contact had been established with the Communists, and with their assistance they would be moved to a partisan unit operating near the Bug River, in the Wyszkow Forest, 55 kilometers northeast of Warsaw. On May 22 two trucks took them to the area.[1]

In time many of the surviving ZOB fighters from the Warsaw ghetto drifted to Warsaw looking for hiding places there. Money began arriving from the Jewish Agency and the Joint through AK chan-

---

1   Putermilch, *Ba-esh u-va-sheleg*, 115–33.

nels, which made it possible for many of them to survive until the end of the war.

Michalin

The first ZZW fighters to reach the Michalin area were a group of eight men and six women, some of them wounded during the fighting at Muranowski Square, who were evacuated with the help of Poles through the Muranowska Street tunnel on the night of April 20.[2] On April 22 they were discovered in Otwock by a German police unit and attacked. In the ensuing battle they were all killed.[3]

On that day the second group of ZZW fighters, led by Leon Rodal, left through the tunnel and established itself in the building at Muranowska 6. There they waited for their Polish contacts to arrive so as to take them to the Michalin area. After three days spent in trying to reach their Polish contacts, they finally decided to make the move on their own. On April 25, in the guise of a funeral procession, forty-four ZZW fighters made the trip from Muranowska 6 to the Michalin area where they installed themselves in one of the villas in the area. There they waited again for the arrival of the Poles.

At noon on April 30, they were fired on by Polish police who wounded the man standing guard. Exchanging fire with the Polish police, they moved into the forest, carrying their wounded comrade

---

2   Halperin, *Helka shel Betar ba-Mered ha-Geto*, 22.

3   Mark, *Tsum tsenten yortog*, 190. Mark quotes a report of the Warsaw gendarmerie district of April 23, 1943: "On April 22 at 6 o'clock in Otwozek, Warsaw district (24 kilometers southeast of Warsaw) during a clearing operation the gendarmerie attacked 14 Jews, 8 men and 6 women, and they were quickly dealt with by the usual means. Some of the Jews had been lightly wounded, wounds that were incurred during the night of the 20 to the 21 in the Warsaw ghetto occurrences. The Jews left the ghetto through underground passages that had been previously prepared. Signed by Major of the Gendarmerie."

with them. When crossing the Swider River they were attacked by a German police unit with automatic weapons. Twelve of their fighters fell in a battle that lasted five hours. For the following two days they were hunted in the area by the Germans. Five ZZW fighters who survived these battles decided to try to make it to Warsaw and go into hiding there.[4]

The group that had left the ghetto through the tunnel on the night of April 26 was discovered by Stroop's forces the following day, before they had a chance to move to the Michalin area, and attacked. In the ensuing battle many of them were killed.

Grzybowska 11

ZZW fighters who had left the ghetto and reached Warsaw decided to establish themselves at Grzybowska 11, a building outside the ghetto. The group included their commander Pawel Frenkel and his deputy Leon Rodal. Some of the fighters from the Toebbens-Schultz Workshop area who had left the ghetto through the sewers had established themselves in the next building at Grzybowska 13.

At this point Frenkel and Rodal decided to attempt to rescue Jews who were still in the burning ghetto and bring them to hiding places in Warsaw. A unit of eight fighters, headed by Rodal, was charged with the mission. Two of them reentered the ghetto through the sewers, while the other six were to receive those that were brought out and bring them to safety. On May 5 the first group was brought out of the ghetto. The following day, as the second group was being brought out of the ghetto, they were attacked by German troops and

---

4   Helman, *Al goralam:* This article contains the reminiscences of Pawel Besztimt, a ZZW fighter who managed to reach Warsaw and at Zuckerman's behest recorded his experiences. Also Klein, *Mitn Malach ha-Mavet untern orem,* 225. As he writes in his memoir, David Klein spent the war in hiding in Warsaw and met Besztimt when he reached Warsaw.

Polish police who were stationed outside the ghetto walls. In the ensuing battle Leon Rodal and his comrades fell.[5]

This battle is recorded in Stroop's report for May 6, 1943: "The Jews who had broken out of the ghetto seem to be returning with the intention of assisting the ghetto Jews either to help them fight or to liberate them."[6] According to the report, two men from the "external cordoning force" that guarded the ghetto walls were wounded in the battle with Rodal's unit.

Frenkel and his men continued hiding out at Grzybowska 11, but they lacked money for supplies to keep themselves going. According to Zuckerman, he was aware of their presence there and provided them with some assistance.

On June 19, two months after the beginning of the uprising, Frenkel and his men were discovered by the Germans. They defended themselves, and in the ensuing battle four Germans were killed and a number of Germans were wounded. Frenkel and six of his comrades fell. Three of them were caught alive by the Germans and later murdered by them. Zuckerman was told that when they were discovered, "they defended themselves and fell in battle on the 'Aryan' side of Warsaw."[7]

The battle did not go unnoticed. ZEGOTA, the underground Polish Council for Aid to Jews, announced on July 15, 1943, in its special bulletin no. 6: "Warsaw: The operation of searching and arresting Jews in hiding continues. Those caught are taken to Pawiak, and after a short period they are killed (men, women, and children). Group executions of Jews take place daily. In certain cases, the Jews

---

5   Halperin, *Helka shel Betar ba-Mered ha-Geto*, 25.

6   Stroop's operational report for May 6, 1943.

7   Zuckerman, *A Surplus of Memory*, 413. Zuckerman met Pawel Besztimt at the house of David Klein in Warsaw and heard from him that Pawel Frenkel and his men were hiding out on Grzybowska Street and were in need of financial support.

who are discovered resist. For example, on June 19, at Grzybowska 11, gendarmes killed a Jewish family that consisted of ten persons who had been living there officially as German citizens. The Jews were armed with grenades and revolvers. As a result of their resistance, four Germans were killed, seven Jews were killed, and three were taken away."[8]

ZEGOTA did not know at the time that a commander of the Warsaw Ghetto Uprising had fallen in battle that day. The presence of Jewish fighters who had participated in the Warsaw Ghetto Uprising in the building at Grzybowska 11 was known to some Jews who had left the ghetto and were hiding out in the neighborhood. They also heard the sounds of the battle that took place there.[9]

It was Pawel Frenkel's last battle, and the last battle of the Warsaw Ghetto Uprising.

---

8   Mark, *Tsum tsenten yortog*, 203.

9   In testimony given by Cesia Kolska, who had escaped the Warsaw ghetto, to her cousin in Israel, Joseph Komem, she related: "While she was hiding out at Ciepla 19, her husband, Arnold Walfisz, lived and worked in the building at Grzybowska 11, posing as a Pole. He told her that in one of the apartments in that building there was a group who had participated in the Warsaw Ghetto Uprising, which had in its possession a considerable quantity of arms. He himself served as an underground courier for this group. When the group was discovered, they resisted, and in the ensuing battle four Germans were killed and a number were wounded. Walfisz was arrested on the following day and killed." Stanislawa Kolska, Cesia Kolska's Polish sister-in-law, who lived at Grzybowska 22, also testified to Komem that she had heard the sounds of the battle. See also the videotaped testimony of Yosef Greenblatt, a ZZW fighter who survived the uprising, in the Jabotinsky Institute Archives 213/1- דו.

Chapter 14

Setting the Record Straight

The Warsaw Ghetto Uprising was one of the major events of World War II, the first act of organized resistance against the Germans in a large city under their control. It will go down in history as a battle between the few against the many, the sons of light against the sons of darkness, good against evil incarnate. In Jewish history it stands out as a heroic act of resistance against the German murder machine that brought death to six million Jews.

The uprising took place against a background of intense political rivalry in the Jewish world in the years before the war, a rivalry so deep that it carried over into the war years and even into the ghetto. It prevented unity between all those dedicated to resistance to the Germans in the Warsaw ghetto. The rivalry continued after the war and has not completely subsided to this day. It was therefore almost inevitable that political parties and youth movements would want to claim the major part of the credit for these acts of valor, to maintain that it was their adherents in the ghetto – youth from their ranks who had been educated in accordance with their ideology – who fought the battles against the Germans, and that their political rivals had no significant role in the uprising. And so the commonly accepted narrative of the Warsaw Ghetto Uprising bears the marks of political manipulation, putting the spotlight on some of the participants and attempting to obscure others.

Pawel Frenkel and all leading members of ZZW fell in battle against the Germans. The few members of ZZW who survived the fighting in the ghetto and thereafter the war years, were relatively

unknown and could not make their voices heard after their arrival in Israel. In any case, the Revisionist movement in Palestine in
the aftermath of the war was totally focused on supporting the IZL's
struggle against British rule in Palestine. On the other hand, some of
the members of ZOB who survived were well known to the Zionist
movement in Palestine, and all surviving ZOB fighters who arrived
in Israel were welcomed with open arms on their arrival by the official leadership of the Jewish community, who were at the time engaged in a confrontation with the IZL. Foremost among them were
Yitzhak Zuckerman and his life-long companion, Tzivya Lubetkin.
After the war they told and retold the story of the Warsaw Ghetto
Uprising, leaving little room for ZZW's part in the uprising. Their
descriptions of the events in the Warsaw ghetto form the core of the
generally accepted narrative of this historic event.

The first news of the uprising came out of "Aryan" Warsaw. There,
outside the ghetto walls, the emissaries of the Jewish National Committee (ZKN) that was established in the ghetto as the political representation of ZOB, Adolf Berman of Left Po'alei Zion and Yitzhak
Zuckerman of Dror, himself a member of the ZOB Command, could
hear the sounds of the battle going on behind the ghetto walls. They
had established contact with the Polish underground in their attempts to obtain weapons for ZOB.[1] Leon Feiner, the representative
of the Bund in "Aryan" Warsaw, constituted together with Berman
and Zuckerman the representation of the Jewish Coordinating Committee (ZKK), which had been set up so as to enable the Bund to join
ZOB.[2] Based on fragmentary information reaching them from the

---

1   Zuckerman, *A Surplus of Memory*, 298. Left Po'lei Zion was a Marxist
     Zionist party and Dror was a Socialist Zionist youth movement associated
     with the Socialist Zionist party Po'alei Zion, the precursor of the Israeli
     Labor party.
2   Ibid., 339 and 462. The Bund, a Jewish non-Zionist Socialist party, al-

embattled ghetto, and from what could be seen and heard from outside the ghetto, they composed battle communiqués that purported to report on the ongoing battles there.

The first four communiqués were issued by Berman and Zuckerman on April 19, 20, and 21. Thereafter the communiqués were issued on behalf of the Jewish Coordinating Committee, with the participation of Feiner. The communiqués were passed on to the Polish underground and some of them were broadcast over their clandestine radio station.[3]

Bulletin No. 1, issued by Berman and Zuckerman, states: "Today, on Monday, April 19, the Germans started a new, deadly action in the Warsaw ghetto. By four o'clock in the morning, intensive rifle and machine gun fire, as well as the bursting of shells, were heard in the vicinity of the ghetto walls. Armored cars and tanks moved into the ghetto. The action is being carried out by German military police under the command of the SS.... The Jewish Fighting Organization [ZOB], which encompasses all active elements of the Jewish community, is putting up strong resistance in many buildings. Violent battles are going on between the Jewish fighters and the Germans...." In Bulletin No. 2, issued on April 20, they reported: "The struggle be-

---

though prepared to join ZOB, was not prepared to be represented in the political committee (ZKN) that was to oversee ZOB's military activity with the other parties, and insisted on the establishment of a coordinating committee (ZKK) that would coordinate between ZKN and the Bund.

3   A fragment of such a broadcast was picked up in Stockholm and appeared on the front page of the *New York Times* on April 22, 1943, under the headline "Secret Polish Radio Asks for Help, Cut Off." The story, datelined Stockholm, April 21, 1943, read: "The secret Polish radio appealed for help tonight in a broadcast from Poland and then suddenly the station went dead. The broadcast as heard here said: 'The last 35,000 Jews in the ghetto at Warsaw have been condemned to execution. Warsaw again is echoing to musketry volleys. The people are murdered. Women and children defend themselves with their naked arms. Save us....'"

tween the Jewish Fighting Organization [ZOB] and the Germans in the Warsaw ghetto continues in full force...." Bulletin No. 3 was also issued on April 20, and reported: "The Jewish Fighting Organization [ZOB], which leads the fight in the Warsaw ghetto, has rejected an ultimatum of the Germans demanding the laying down of arms by ten o'clock Tuesday morning.... The Jewish fighters have hoisted two flags on the roof of a building in Muranowska Street: one red and white, the other blue and white." From April 22 the communiqués were issued by the Jewish Coordinating Committee (ZKK). A situation report on April 28 reported on the fighting of April 27: "In the area of the carriage station on Muranowska a unit of fighters carried out an attack on the Germans...."[4]

The reports issued by Berman, Zuckerman, and Feiner during the initial ten days of combat were the only announcements describing the fighting in the ghetto. They created the impression that a single Jewish fighting organization was resisting the Germans, and that organization was ZOB, and they ascribed actions of ZZW to ZOB. ZZW had no representatives in "Aryan" Warsaw and no alternate "ZZW version of events" appeared at the time. Although Berman, Zuckerman, and Feiner were fully cognizant of the participation of ZZW in the fighting, and knew that it was ZZW that had raised the Zionist and Polish flags over a building near Muranowski Square, they quite naturally were interested in giving the world the impression that Jewish resistance in the ghetto was being conducted by a single fighting organization. Zuckerman writes about that period: "...we issued propaganda communiqués in which truth and fiction were intermingled.... At the moment I wasn't thinking of historical precision. It was an appeal to the Poles designed to stir their feelings of sympathy for our struggle; and it didn't matter how that battle occurred, or how we were defending our lives.... They were typed up

---

4   Blumental and Kermish, *Ha-meri ve-ha-mered be-Geto Varsha*, 211–19.

in Polish (Berman did that). Things were collected from all kinds of sources and I always knew they weren't terribly precise."[5]

On April 26, 1943, a cable arrived in London from Warsaw, addressed to Yaakov Zerubavel, a leader of Left Po'alei Zion in Palestine, from Natan Buksbaum, Adolf Berman, and Emmanuel Ringelblum, members of Left Po'alei Zion, who were hiding out in Warsaw, asking for help for those fighting "for the honor of the remnants of our people" and sending "the fighters' greetings to the Jewish workers of Eretz Yisrael and the entire world." The text of the cable appeared in *Davar*, the daily of the Jewish Labor Federation (Histadrut) in Palestine, on April 30, 1943.[6] It was the first of many attempts that followed to depict the fighters in the uprising as representing the working class.

Continuing the description of the uprising as being carried out solely by ZOB, on May 5, 1943, Berman and Feiner cabled an appeal for help on behalf of the Jewish Coordinating Committee, through Polish underground channels, to Ignacy Schwartzbart and Shmuel Zygielbojm, the two Jewish members of the Polish government-in-exile in London. It included the following: "The heroic battle of the Warsaw ghetto still continues in a few defensive positions. Great is the spirit of sacrifice and the courage of the Jewish Fighting Organization [ZOB].... A similar cable describing "the heroic defense of the ghetto under the leadership of the Jewish Fighting Organization

---

5   Zuckerman, *A Surplus of Memory*, 371. From Zuckerman's contacts with ZZW before he left the ghetto, he knew that ZZW was defending the area of Muranowski Square. He and Berman knew that the Bund and the Communists would not have agreed to hoist the blue-white Zionist flag. Hashomer Hatzair and Left Po'alei Zion preferred the red flag to the Zionist flag.

6   Neustadt, *Hurban u-mered shel Yehudei Varsha*, 43; and *Davar*, April 30, 1943.

[ZOB]" and asking for help was signed by the Jewish National Committee [ZKN] – Warsaw.[7]

On May 24, 1943, *Davar* headlined a report received by Schwartzbard in London that had been sent from Warsaw on May 11 by the Central Committee of Polish Jewish Workers [Bund] and the Jewish National Committee. The report called for assistance and said "the resistance and defense of the Warsaw ghetto is accompanied by fierce fighting...the leader of the Jewish resistance, [Michael] Klepfisz, died a hero's death."[8] Actually, by May 11 the fighting in the ghetto had died down. Klepfisz was a member of the Bund who had fallen in the Brushmakers' Workshop area where the ZOB forces were led by Edelman, on April 20, 1943. He had done important work bringing arms into the ghetto, but he was not the leader of Jewish resistance in the ghetto. The Bund's claiming him as the leader of the resistance was one of a number of attempts by the Bund to emphasize their part in the uprising.[9]

In June, public meetings were held in Palestine and New York dedicated to the fighters of the Warsaw Ghetto Uprising, each movement emphasizing the part played by its own members in the uprising. In Kibbutz Yagur, a memorial meeting was held by the Kibbutz Hameuhad movement for Tzivya Lubetkin and Tosya Altman, who

---

7   Blumental and Kermish, *Ha-meri ve-ha-mered be-Geto Varsha*, 222. Schwartzbard, who was a General Zionist, represented the Zionists in the Polish government-in-exile, and Zygielboim represented the Bund. Zygielboim committed suicide on May 12, 1943, in despair over the fate of the Jews of Poland.

8   *Davar*, April 24, 1943.

9   In June 1943, the Bund monthly in the U.S., *Unzer Tsait*, reported that "Comrade Klepfisz, the leader of the resistance, fell in battle." In September 1943 *Unzer Tsait* published an obituary of Michael Klepfisz, hailing him as "the soul of armed resistance in the Warsaw ghetto."

had erroneously been reported killed. They were acclaimed as leaders of the Socialist Zionist underground in Poland.[10]

On June 15 Meilech Neustadt, a senior official of the Histadrut
and leading member of the Labor party (Mapai), published an article in *Davar* entitled "The resistance of the Polish Jews," in which
he wrote: "Clearly the full burden of the work in the underground,
and especially the actions in the revolt, fell on the Halutz youth
movements, on Socialist Zionism, and on the Polish Jewish workers'
movement. And not because they are more courageous and more devoted, but because in these movements was concentrated the young
element that was more prepared, that was educated to discipline
and sacrifice. Years of education stood the test in the days of difficult
trial."[11] These sentiments were echoed by Yitzhak Tabenkin, leader
of the Kibbutz Hameuhad movement, when he said at a meeting in
Tel Aviv on June 22: "Hehalutz in Poland stood the test."[12]

On June 19, the Jewish Labor Committee in the U.S., many of
whose leaders had their roots in the Polish Bund, sponsored a meeting to pay homage to the fighters of the Warsaw ghetto.[13] It was
the beginning of a campaign by the Socialist Zionist parties and the
Bund to embrace and adopt the Warsaw Ghetto Uprising and to
claim the major role in the uprising for their members. Little, if any,
credit was given to the fighters of ZZW.

On June 22, 1943, Zuckerman and his wife, Tzivya Lubetkin,
sent a cable to Palestine, using Polish underground channels, addressed to Eliyahu Dobkin, a member of the Jewish Agency Executive

---

10 *Davar*, June 6, 1943. The report of their death was erroneous. Tosya Altman, a leading member of Hashomer Hatzair in Poland, was hiding out in
Warsaw at the time. She was caught by the Germans and executed shortly
thereafter. Tzivya Lubetkin survived the war and settled in Israel.

11 Ibid., June 15, 1943.

12 Ibid., June 23, 1946.

13 *The New York Times*, June 20, 1943.

in Jerusalem; Meir Yaari, leader of Hashomer Hatzair; and Yitzhak
Tabenkin, leader of Hakibbutz Hameuhad. The cable included the
following: "The battles in the ghetto are over. Hundreds of our comrades fell. Tens decided to commit suicide. Hehalutz–Hashomer Hatzair were the backbone of the Jewish Fighting Organization [ZOB]."
In August contents of this cable appeared in *Davar*.[14]

At the same time a report was prepared by the Bund in Warsaw, which arrived after some delay abroad, and was published in
May 1944, in the monthly of the Bund delegation in the U.S., *Unzer
Tsait*. It contained the following: "The resistance was organized and
led by the Jewish Fighting Organization [ZOB], which played the
central role. This fighting organization was the operational arm of
the Coordination Committee, which was composed of representatives of the Bund and the Jewish National Committee. The Revisionists and the Aguda did not belong to it. The Revisionists set up a
small organization of their own, 'Nekamah,' which ceased its operations after two days of fighting. The members of ZOB were mainly
young workers...."[15]

A year after the uprising, a narrative describing the events as
reported from Warsaw was beginning to become generally accepted.
It was presumably a battle fought by the fighters of ZOB, while the
Revisionists had made a marginal contribution to the uprising during the first two days and had then left the ghetto. Whether the major credit for the uprising should go to the Zionist movements who
participated in ZOB or the fighters from the Bund became an issue
of dispute in the following years.

---

14 Neustadt, *Hurban u-mered shel Yehudei Varsha*, 43; and *Davar*, August 22,
    1943. The emphasis on the role of Hehalutz and Hashomer Hatzair in the
    uprising was designed to counter the claims of the Bund.
15 Neustadt, *Hurban u-mered shel Yehudei Varsha*, 169–72.

Party affiliations had remained firm throughout the war years, and Zionist party members who had escaped the ghetto and reached "Aryan" Warsaw felt the need to communicate with the leaders of their movements in Palestine and report on the respective party activities in the ghetto years and especially during the uprising. In November 1943, reports were sent to the leadership of Hehalutz, of the Labor party (Mapai), and of Left Po'alei Zion in Palestine. That month the Jewish National Committee (ZKN) in Warsaw sent to London a list of 224 ZOB fighters who perished, each name followed by his or her party affiliation. No Revisionists or members of Betar appeared on the list.[16]

Emmanuel Ringelblum, who had watched the flags waving over the heads of the ZZW fighters in Muranowski Square during the uprising, was hiding out in "Aryan" Warsaw in a crowded bunker with many other Jews at the time. When he saw the list he expressed concern about the absence of data regarding the fighters of the ZZW. "And why is there no data regarding ZZW? In the history we must leave their tracks, even though they are not sympathetic in our eyes," he wrote in a note to Berman on December 13, 1943. On December 28 he expressed his concern again in another note to Berman: "As for the Rev[isionists] I have no data on them...an effort should be made to complete the list. I have only two names: Rodalski [Rodal] and Frenkelowski [Frenkel]. The latter (brown hair)...was manager of the firm. One of them should be found or one of their comrades."[17]

---

16 Neustadt, *Hurban u-mered shel Yehudei Varsha*, 239. The list appeared in *Davar* on March 3, 1944.

17 Yisrael Gutman, ed., *Emmanuel Ringelblum: The Man and the Historian* (Jerusalem: Yad Vashem, 2006), p. 43. In an attempt to keep the names of ZZW's commanders secret in case the note was intercepted, Ringelblum had converted their names and referred to ZZW as the "firm." Ringelblum and his family were executed when their hiding place in Warsaw was discovered by the Germans in March 1944.

It was the historian in Ringelblum, a leading activist of the Left Po'alei Zion party, insisting that the truth about the participation of ZZW in the uprising not be buried. Berman and Zuckerman did not share his concerns, and no attempt was made to complement the list of ZOB fighters who perished with a list of ZZW fighters who fell. Moreover, Berman deposited Ringleblum's notes in his archives, without bothering to reveal their contents when he came to Israel. They were discovered only many years later.

In the following year, while the German army still occupied Poland, some of the ZOB fighters who had succeeded in leaving the ghetto and were hiding out in "Aryan" Warsaw, assisted by Zuckerman and Berman, wrote eyewitness accounts of their part in the uprising. These accounts were transmitted through the channels of AK to London. Mention of ZZW was omitted in these accounts. The leaders of ZZW, Frenkel, Rodal, and their chief lieutenants had been killed in the fighting. That had also been the fate of many of the ZZW fighters who had participated in the fighting in Muranowski Square. Others had been killed in encounters with the Germans after leaving the ghetto. The few who survived were unknown to the leadership of the Revisionist movement in Palestine and had no connections with the outside world. Zuckerman's, Berman's, and Feiner's connections with the Polish underground army, AK, which was under the authority of the Polish government-in-exile in London, made it possible for them to transmit cables and letters abroad and to receive financial support from the Jewish Agency in Palestine and the Joint. They were also known to the leadership of their organizations abroad. Thus it was their story that reached the outside world.

Less than a year after the revolt, still more than a year before the conclusion of hostilities in Europe, it had become generally recognized that the Warsaw Ghetto Uprising was a momentous occurrence during the Holocaust, and a major event in Jewish history. The political parties and movements whose members had participated in the uprising were now eager to attain recognition for their contribution, even if it meant belittling or erasing the part played by others. All the news about the uprising was coming out of Warsaw from members of ZOB or people associated with ZOB, and reinforced the narrative that had at first reached the outside world. In March 1944, *Davar* quoted from "a letter of November 1943 received from Poland: '...Despite everything we kept to the ideological-moral force that guides our actions. We did not draw this force from ourselves, but rather from those values that were imbued in us. It is from these values that stemmed the initiative for resistance and revolt, as part of the Eretz Yisrael Workers' Movement.'"[18]

On May 24, 1944, Zuckerman and Berman, on behalf of the ZKN, sent a number of dispatches to London. The dispatches included the battle reminiscences of three ZOB fighters – Shalom Grayek, Tuvia Borzykowski, and Simha Ratajzer (Rotem) – and a report on the history of the Warsaw ghetto, on the formation and organization of ZOB, and a detailed description of its combat in the revolt. The report completely ignored the existence of Revisionists and Betar in the ghetto and made no mention of the participation of ZZW in the uprising. Nor does ZZW appear in the reminiscences of Grayek, Borzykowski, and Rotem. It seems that Zuckerman and Berman, both well aware of the existence of ZZW in the ghetto and the combat of its fighters against the Germans, had decided to efface ZZW from the history of the uprising. From this point on, the narrative of the uprising that gave ZOB the major role and discounted the part played by ZZW, or at best relegated it to a marginal role, became for many years the generally accepted narrative of the uprising.

In addition, Zuckerman and Berman were at the time eager to emphasize that the Socialist Zionist youth movements, rather than

---

18 *Davar*, March 1, 1944.

the Bund, were the backbone of ZOB. The report on the activities
of the Jewish National Committee (ZKN), transmitted at the same
time, included a plea to counter the claims that the Bund was making regarding the role of their members in the uprising. It included
the following passage:

> But for truth's sake we want to mention a few points. Based
> on reports from abroad, it seems to us that the Bund abroad
> is trying to take the credit for the battles in the Warsaw
> ghetto, and if not all, then the major part. We let you know
> unequivocally that this is not consistent with the truth. For
> the sake of historical truth you have to uproot this incorrect
> and unjustified legend. The struggle in the Warsaw ghetto,
> and in other ghettos and camps, was initiated, organized, and
> carried out by our organizations, and first and foremost by
> the workers' movements and the youth movements of Labor
> Eretz Yisrael, Hehalutz, Dror, Hashomer Hatzair, Po'alei Zion
> ZS, and Left Po'alei Zion. These organizations carried out the
> battles, provided the major part of the fighters, and made the
> greatest sacrifice.
>
> The commander of the Jewish Fighting Organization [ZOB]
> was our hero comrade Mordechai Anielewicz, the leader of
> Hashomer Hatzair. In the Command we had four representa-
> tives, and the Bund – had one. Of the 22 fighting units of
> ZOB our organizations had 18, and the Bund four. Of the total
> number of fighters the Bund did not constitute more than 18%.
> The Bund units within the framework of the Jewish Fighting
> Organization fought courageously, as all the units fought, with-
> out exception. But it was not they that determined the spirit
> and the character of the battles. Now as well, it is our comrades
> who stand at the head of ZOB. We were very surprised that the
> [Polish] medal "Virtuti Militari" was only awarded to Michael

Klepfisz, a member of the Bund. The fighter Klepfisz fought courageously, but he was only one among hundreds of heroic fighters. If the intention was to make a symbolic award to the Jewish Fighting Organization, or to all the heroic fighters, we believe that it would have been appropriate to make the award to the Commander of the Jewish Fighting Organization.

We are also pained by the fact – and maybe we are mistaken – that the Bund has obtained a monopoly abroad in the propaganda among the workers' organization, especially in England and the United States, that it has taken over the Jewish Labor Committee of America. Don't Po'alei Zion and Left Po'alei Zion continue with the necessary propaganda among these workers' organizations? Let the workers' movements in the entire world know that the organizers and leaders of the Warsaw ghetto revolt was the Workers' Movement for Labor Eretz Yisrael, and that hundreds of fighters struggled and fell inspired by the ideal that their death will be one of the foundations for a Socialist future for the Jewish masses in Eretz Yisrael.[19]

Although claiming to establish the "historical truth" about the Warsaw Ghetto Uprising, while taking issue with the Bund "propaganda," the authors of this report deliberately ignored the important part of the Revisionist-led Jewish Military Organization (ZZW) in the uprising, although they were fully aware of it.

In January 1945 the Red Army liberated Warsaw. The Soviet-sponsored Polish government had earlier established itself in Lublin, and Lublin Radio began regular broadcasts in Yiddish, bringing

---

19 Neustadt, *Hurban u-mered shel Yehudei Varsha*, 140. The report was signed by Adolf Berman, Yitzhak Zuckerman, Shimon Gottesman of the General Zionists, and Yosef Sak of Po'alei Zion.

greetings from Jewish survivors in Poland to their relatives abroad.
Some quickly adjusted themselves to the spirit of the Communist
regime. In February 1945, Adolf Berman, speaking on the Lublin
Radio Yiddish broadcast, monitored in Palestine, about resistance
in the Warsaw ghetto, spoke not about ZOB, nor, of course, about
ZZW, but described the establishment in 1942 of the Anti-Fascist
Bloc (the precursor of ZOB) in the Warsaw ghetto.[20] The Anti-Fascist
Bloc had been initiated by Communists and included members of
Socialist Zionist parties, but not the Bund. Berman, now in Com-
munist-controlled Poland, considered it advisable to emphasize this
organization, even though it had fallen apart many months before
the Warsaw Ghetto Uprising.

On April 19, 1945, *Davar* devoted a long article to the second
anniversary of the Warsaw Ghetto Uprising. Based on the dispatches that had been sent from Warsaw in 1944 through Polish underground channels, the article described the formation of ZOB in July
1942 by "all the political parties and social organizations" in the
ghetto, and the appointment of Mordechai Anielewicz as commander and Yitzhak Zuckerman as his deputy. In the description of the
fighting during the uprising it made no mention of the part played
by ZZW. On that day Zuckerman, speaking on the Lublin Radio Yiddish broadcast, eulogized the fighters who fell in the Warsaw Ghetto
Uprising and their commander Mordechai Anielewicz. On April 21
and 22, Lublin Radio announced that sixty-seven Jews had been
awarded high military honors for their heroism during the Warsaw
Ghetto Uprising. Mordechai Anielewicz led the list, which did not
include any members of ZZW.[21]

Three months after Germany's surrender to the Allied powers,
the leaders of the Zionist movement met with two key members of

---

20 *Davar*, February 3, 1945.
21 Ibid., April 19 and 20, and May 14, 1945.

ZOB. On August 2, 1945, a Zionist Assembly opened in London. It was the first convocation of world Zionist leaders since the last Zionist Congress held on the eve of World War II in August 1939. It was attended by leading Zionist personalities, including Chaim Weizmann, David Ben Gurion, Stephen Wise, and Abba Hillel Silver, and a large delegation from Palestine. A delegation from Poland, which included Zuckerman and Berman, arrived on August 4. They were greeted emotionally by the assembled delegates. Zuckerman was acclaimed as commander of Jewish resistance in Poland. Before a meeting of Po'alei Zion delegates, in the presence of Ben Gurion, he spoke of the Warsaw Ghetto Uprising. Ben Gurion, greeting Zuckerman, spoke of his "role in the history of the Diaspora," and referred to him "as a symbol of the uprising."[22] Zuckerman met with many of the other leaders from Palestine. From him they heard his version of what happened during the uprising.

An opportunity to revise Zuckerman's description of the uprising came during the Nuremberg war crimes trials. In one of its reports on the trials, *Davar* reported that the American prosecutor, Major Walsh, read from Juergen Stroop's report that "the main Jewish combat group retreated to Muranowski Square and there they raised the Jewish and Polish flags."[23] Zuckerman, Berman, and all the survivors of the uprising knew that this was a reference to the major battle of the Warsaw Ghetto Uprising in which ZZW confronted Stroop's forces at Muranowski Square. All those in leading positions in the Zionist movement knew well that raising the Jewish (Zionist) flag could not have been an initiative of ZOB, which included the Bund and the Communists in its ranks. Nevertheless this report was studiously ignored in Palestine.

---

22 Ibid., August 6, 1945. See also Zuckerman's description of his participation in the Zionist Assembly in London in *A Surplus of Memory*, 596–601.

23 *Davar*, December 14, 1945.

The years 1944 and most of 1945 had been a period of violent opposition by the Jewish Agency leadership to the IZL's military actions against British rule in Palestine. The IZL, led by Menahem Begin, had declared a revolt against British rule in Palestine in February 1944, and its forces had begun attacking British military targets in Palestine. The end of 1944 and the spring of 1945 had been a period of active collaboration between the Jewish Agency, led by the Labor party (Mapai), and the British administration in Palestine – a cooperation which involved the forcible detention of members of the IZL by the military arm of the Jewish Agency, the Haganah, and handing the IZL fighters over to the British police. The period is referred to as the "season," that is, an open hunting season on IZL fighters. It was not a time when the official Zionist leadership was prepared to give any credit to Revisionist fighters in the Warsaw ghetto.

Not only was the role of the Revisionists in the Warsaw Ghetto Uprising generally ignored, but their activity there was frequently disparaged. In February 1946 the General Labor Federation (Histadrut) published a collection of documents received from Warsaw during the war years relating to the Warsaw Ghetto Uprising. The book was edited by Meilech Neustadt, a leading member of Mapai. In the foreword, written in December 1945, he wrote:

> The documents published in this book also clearly describe the public aspect of the events. The remnants of the Jews appeared then as a single body, unified and solid. In this Polish Jewry, with all its parties, movements, and internal friction, a common front was assembled at this hour, which all Jews supported and had full confidence in. Of course, it is tragic that this unity was arrived at only in those days, in the face of death that threatened everybody. But it is also the ultimate indication of what beat in their hearts. In these days of trial, the entire

spectrum of the Jewish political and social groups – from Agudat Yisrael to the Jewish Communists – united for action.[24]

Without referring to ZZW by name Neustadt goes on to deal with
fighting groups that were called "wild ones." "All kinds of people
belonged to them, those who believed in the fight and those who
wanted to use the support for the uprising for their own purposes.
ZOB did everything possible – by explaining and applying pressure –
to liquidate these groups and to assure a single fighting leadership.
And those who sincerely supported the uprising joined ZOB, and
the others were eliminated," he writes. It was the first of many books
and articles dealing with the Warsaw Ghetto Uprising that assigned
the ZZW a minor and sometimes even negative role in uprising.[25]

In June 1946 Tzivya Lubetkin, one of the leaders of ZOB, arrived in Palestine. A year later Yitzhak Zuckerman, her husband,
followed. In the years that followed, they told and retold the story
of the Warsaw ghetto revolt. In May 1947 Zuckerman appeared at
Kibbutz Na'an. In a long discourse on the Warsaw Ghetto Uprising,
this is what he had to say about ZZW:

> We then had to deal with an organization called Nekama (Re-
> venge). This was a Revisionist organization in the Warsaw
> ghetto. After the first liquidation, when we turned to all the
> movements to establish a united fighting organization, we also
> found a small group of Revisionists. As opposed to the other
> movements that worked during the war, published newspa-
> pers, educated a generation, ran underground activities, the

---

24   Neustadt, *Hurban u-mered shel Yehudei Varsha*, 36, 39.
25   A leading Revisionist, Abba Ahi-Meir, published in *Hamashkif* on Decem-
     ber 12, 1946, a scathing critique of Neustadt's book and of a review of the
     book that had appeared in *Davar*, in which he compared Neustadt to the
     writers of official Soviet history.

Revisionists did nothing. We knew that they still had some
youth, and we turned to them to join us. As is their way they
broke discipline. We built the foundations of [ZOB] on a movement basis, on the basis of people that had received their education in youth movements, or in youth movements where the
parties were responsible for them. We were concerned about
the possibility of the ZZW being infiltrated by Gestapo agents.
It must be emphasized that in the ZOB there was not a single
case of betrayal, and there was not a single informer or traitor.
At the beginning the Revisionists did not have any people, after a while they began opening their ranks and accepting people. Afterwards they also began buying arms on their own and
even tried to make connections with the "Aryan" side.... Their
pretensions made them want that they too should rule in the
ghetto. We used against them negotiations and also force, and
we overpowered them. We turned over to them a part of Muranowska Street and told them: from here you won't go out, if
you want to fight – fight here! And, actually, this group fought
bravely on April 19 and 20. But their people could not hold
out, on the second day of the battle they left the ghetto.[26]

The Jewish leadership in Palestine, led by Mapai, accepted
Zuckerman's version of events in the Warsaw ghetto. Zuckerman's
description of the Revisionists as "breakers of discipline" was in line
with the accusations leveled at the time against the underground
Irgun Zvai Leumi, led by Menahem Begin, who in their battle against
British rule in Palestine had refused to accept the discipline of
restraint the official leadership tried to impose. Mapai was in power
for the first twenty-nine years of Israel's existence. During this period,
Zuckerman's narrative of the Warsaw Ghetto Uprising, consistent

---

26 Zuckerman, *Ba-geto u-va-mered*, 146.

with the prevalent ideologies of the dominant Socialist Zionist parties and their disdain for the Revisionists and their successors, became embedded in the collective memory.

Years later Marek Edelman, who had been the Bund representative in the Command of ZOB and the commander of ZOB forces in the Brushmakers' Workshop area, referred to the ZZW as Fascists and "a gang of porters, smugglers, and thieves."[27]

To Revisionists and members of Betar in Palestine, it was inconceivable that the Polish Betar – the largest Zionist youth movement in pre-war Poland, whose members had received an indoctrination of militant Zionism as well as paramilitary and military training – had not actively participated in the Warsaw Ghetto Uprising. But where was the evidence? The leaders of ZZW, Pawel Frenkel and Leon Rodal, had fallen in battle. So had all senior commanders. The few surviving ZZW fighters who reached Israel had held no position of importance in the Revisionist movement, or else had not been affiliated with the movement, and consequently their voices were not heard.

Two Revisionist survivors of the Warsaw ghetto who did command recognition in the movement were Dr. David Wdowinski and Adam Halperin. The first had been one of the leaders of the Revisionist movement in Poland before the war; the second had been a leader in one of the local Betar branches in Warsaw before the war. Neither had been fighters in the ranks of ZZW, but both had been in contact with ZZW leaders, including Pawel Frenkel. Wdowinski had participated on behalf of ZZW in negotiations with representatives of ZOB in unsuccessful attempts to unite the two fighting organizations. On

---

27 Anka Grupinska, *Shor shor* [Round and round] (Tel Aviv: Hakibbutz Hameuhad, 2002), 214–15. Grupinska, a Polish journalist, interviewed Edelman in Lodz in 1999. He had remained in Poland after the war.

April 26, 1946, while still in a DP camp in Italy before going on to the U.S., Wdowinski published an article in the Revisionist daily in Palestine, *Hamashkif*, entitled "The Warsaw Ghetto Revolt," describing the existence of the two fighting organizations in the ghetto, ZZW and ZOB, and some of the encounters with the German forces during the uprising.[28] Halperin had survived the Warsaw ghetto, arriving in Palestine in 1946 as an "illegal immigrant." His recollections, "The Part of Betar in the Ghetto Revolt"[29] was published as part of a booklet issued in 1946 by the World Betar Executive in Tel Aviv, entitled "The Truth about the Warsaw Ghetto Revolt," which also included a chapter entitled "A reply to the falsifiers – history that was made but has not yet been written."[30] These publications had at best a marginal effect on the public. At this point the Revisionist party was completely overshadowed by the underground struggle of the Irgun Zvai Leumi against British rule in Palestine. *Hamashkif* had a circulation of only a few thousand, while the energies of Betar members in Palestine were dedicated to support of the IZL. Begin, who had been leader of the Polish Betar before the war, and might have been expected to lead a campaign for the recognition of the ZZW's part in the Warsaw Ghetto Uprising, was now commander of the IZL and fully committed to this Herculean task.

The powerful kibbutz movements, Hakibbutz Hameuhad and Hakibbutz Haartzi, whose members had played a leading part in ZOB, established museums, research institutes, and publications dedicated to resistance during the Holocaust. In 1949, at Kibbutz Lohamei Hagetaot, a kibbutz founded by former resistance fighters

---

28 *Hamashkif*, April 26, 1946.

29 Halperin, *Helka shel Betar ba-Mered ha-Geto*. Halperin described in some detail the ZZW's battles in the Central Ghetto, the Brushmakers' Workshop area, and the Toebbens-Schultz area.

30 In addition, a leading Revisionist, Abba Ahi-Meir, published in *Hamashkif* on December 12, 1946, a scathing critique of Neustadt's book.

from Europe that included Yitzhak Zuckerman and Tzivya Lubetkin, a museum and archives dedicated to transmitting the story of Jewish resistance in German-occupied Europe was established, called Beit Lohamei Hagetaot. Fourteen years later, the Mordechai Anielewicz Memorial Holocaust Studies and Research Center was established by members of Hashomer Hatzair, and it began the publication of a twice-yearly research journal, *Yalkut Moreshet*. These institutions benefited from support from the Israeli government and their own kibbutz movements. They, and the publication of a number of books by ZOB fighters who had settled in Israel, helped to propagate a narrative of the Warsaw Ghetto Uprising that left little room for ZZW. The Revisionist movement, by now replaced by Herut and led by Begin, did not have the resources to establish a comparable research institution, which might have balanced what quickly became the generally accepted version of the Warsaw Ghetto Uprising. Nor does the issue seem to have been anywhere near the top of Begin's political agenda.[31]

---

31 Begin, the leader of Betar in pre-war Poland, had been arrested by the NKVD while in Vilna in September 1940 and sentenced to eight years of penal servitude, convicted by the Communists of being a "dangerous element to society." After the German invasion of the Soviet Union, Stalin agreed to the enlistment of Polish citizens on Soviet soil in the Polish army led by General Wladyslaw Anders. Together with other Polish citizens, Begin was released from a work camp in Siberia, and as a soldier in Anders' army Begin arrived in Palestine in April 1942. In the fall of that year, while still in Polish army uniform, he assumed the position of leader of Betar in Palestine, but after six months found that his duties were incompatible with his status as a soldier in Anders' army. Efforts were made to have him demobilized from the Polish army, which were crowned with success in November 1943. Immediately on being discharged from the Polish army Begin assumed the position of commander of the IZL. After the establishment of the State of Israel, Begin led the Herut party and thereafter the Likud, becoming prime minister in May 1977.

The first extensive research into the Warsaw Ghetto Uprising was published by Ber Mark in Warsaw. Mark had been appointed the director of the Jewish Historical Institute in Warsaw in 1949. He had spent the war years in the Soviet Union, returning to Poland after the war. Upon his return he began research into the Warsaw Ghetto Uprising, publishing a number of books on the subject in Yiddish and Polish.[32] In Poland he had access to survivors of the Warsaw ghetto, as well as to some of the Polish archives containing documents of that period. In his books, which were the first books published devoted to research of the uprising, he gives almost equal emphasis to the parts played by ZOB and ZZW in the uprising, naming commanders and fighters in both organizations. Considering the fact that the book was published in Communist Poland, as might have been expected undue emphasis was given by him to the participation of Communists in the uprising.

Mark's publications did not bring about a reassessment of the generally accepted version of the Warsaw Ghetto Uprising, but did serve as an important source for Haim Lazar's book *Matzada shel Varsha*[33] published in Israel in 1963, in which Lazar established the important role of ZZW in the revolt. Lazar, who had left the Vilna ghetto to fight as a partisan against the Germans in the White Russian forests, immigrated to Israel after the war. He had been a member

---

32 *Churves dertseilen* [Ruins relate] (Lodz: 1947); *Tsum tsenten yortog* [On the tenth anniversary] (Warsaw: Jewish Historical Institute, 1953); *Der ofshtand in Varshaver geto* [The uprising in the Warsaw ghetto] (Warsaw: 1955); *Walka in zaglada warszawkiego getta* (Warsaw: 1959); *Powstanie w gecie warszawskim* (Warsaw: 1963). The last book appeared in an English translation, *Uprising in the Warsaw Ghetto* (New York: Schocken Books, 1975).

33 Haim Lazar Litai, *Matzada shel Varsha: Ha-irgun ha-Zvai ha-Yehudi be-Mered Geto Varsha, ZZW* [Masada of Warsaw: The Jewish Military Organization in the Warsaw Ghetto Uprising, ZZW] (Tel Aviv: Jabotinsky Institute, 1963).

of Betar in Vilna and continued his association with the Revisionist movement in Israel. He felt impelled to do justice to the fighters of ZZW, many of them fellow members of Betar. In the introduction to his book, Lazar wrote:

> It would have been better if this book, which relates the actions of the national movement founded by Jabotinsky, had not appeared; in other words if there had been no need for it. But what choice was there, when it had to be proven by testimonies and documents, that almost everything that has been written so far – and much was written in hundreds and thousands of books and articles – about the resistance of the Jews of Warsaw, is a deliberate falsification by those attempting to glorify themselves while ignoring others; or else was mistaken due to ignorance or trust in live "witnesses," who brought with them their biased tales and versions, which did not belittle their own actions while effacing the actions of others....
>
> After twenty years a picture has emerged in the public eye as it was described by one camp, and when there are memorials to the Warsaw ghetto revolt and to the Jewish fighting underground, they "of course" refer to the Jewish Fighting Organization that had the Polish initials ZOB, which was led by the Zionist organizations of the left, in cooperation with General Zionists and the Bund. And above all, ignoring deliberately and stubbornly the other fighting underground, the ZZW – Irgun Zvai Yehudi – founded by Betar and other organizations from the Jabotinsky movement. And I emphasize: the other fighting underground, and I do not say the second, even though for truth's sake as becomes clear from testimonies and documents, I should have said, and as every objective historian should say: the first Jewish fighting underground – the

first to organize, the first to warn, the first to train and arm, and the first to take action.[34]

Lazar was not alone in his conviction that the role of ZZW was being neglected. In 1963, the year of the publication of Lazar's book, Rahel Auerbach, a survivor of the Warsaw ghetto, who had been a collaborator of Emmanuel Ringelblum, the chronicler of the Warsaw ghetto, published her book, *Mered Geto Varsha*, in which she wrote: "A separate chapter, that unfortunately has as yet not at all been researched, is the existence of a parallel combat organization, which in some of the sources is called ZZW (Irgun Zvai Yehudi).... Unlike ZOB, ZZW had among its members expert military men, former officers in the Polish army. The ZZW also had weapons. It even had a machine gun, and that evidently accounts for the effectiveness of its combat actions during the first days of the revolt."[35]

Two years later, in 1965, Yosef Kermish, the head of archives at Yad Vashem at the time, wrote in his preface to *Ha-meri ve-ha-mered be-Geto Varsha*, a compilation of documents relating to the Warsaw ghetto revolt:

> As for the revolt itself and the actual preparations for it, the Jewish and Polish sources are regretfully not sufficiently adequate. They do not cover all the aspects of the revolt. A number of points, which if cleared would add greatly to research of the revolt, have been only dealt with in general terms.... Also the four-day battle in Muranowski Square (a heavy battle took place here on the fourth day of the revolt, on April 22, when the Germans captured the Jewish and Polish flags) was de-

---

34 Ibid., 11–12.

35 Rahel Auerbach, *Mered Geto Varsha* [The Warsaw Ghetto Uprising] (Tel Aviv: Menora, 1963), 21–22.

scribed in Jewish sources in a most minor way.... What is missing in the Jewish and Polish sources regarding the revolt must necessarily be complemented from German sources that were written by the enemy himself. The most important of the German documents regarding the revolt are the reports of SS Brigadefuehrer Juergen Stroop, which were written at the time of the events themselves.[36]

In this preface the historian Yosef Kermish made it clear that the reminiscences of ZOB fighters that had been published until this time, as well as the Polish sources that had become available, were inadequate to reconstruct the events of the Warsaw Ghetto Uprising. He implied that the generally accepted narrative of the Warsaw Ghetto Uprising was deficient in its description of the major role played by ZZW in the uprising, and that the best available source regarding the uprising were the operational reports of Juergen Stroop.

One might have expected that the books of Mark and Lazar, followed by the comments made by Rahel Auerbach in her book and then the remarks of Yosef Kermish, would have led to a revision of the Warsaw Ghetto Uprising narrative as sketched by Zuckerman. Or, at the very least, one would have expected these writings to have initiated historical research based on the many reports of Stroop, supplemented by the conversations with Stroop in his prison cell in Warsaw, as published by Moczarski some years later. But this was not the case.

The appearance of the books by Mark, Lazar, and Auerbach and the publication of Kermish's analysis of the available sources did not have a significant impact on the generally accepted narrative of the Warsaw Ghetto Uprising as it had been related by Yitzhak Zuckerman. In academic circles in Israel, Lazar's book was disparaged for

---

36 Blumental and Kermish, *Ha-meri ve-ha-mered be-Geto Varsha,* 23–24.

not providing adequate documentation for the events as described by him.

The academic confirmation for Zuckerman's version was provided by Yisrael Gutman, a professor at the Hebrew University in Jerusalem, himself a fighter in the ranks of ZOB in the Warsaw ghetto and a member of Hashomer Hatzair, in his book published in 1977.[37] About half of his book is devoted to the underground in the ghetto, preparations for the uprising, and the uprising itself. It came to be considered the most authoritative historical account of the uprising. His history of the uprising gives ZOB the central role. While not ignoring the ZZW, Gutman leaves it in the margin, thus essentially giving academic credence to the commonly accepted narrative of the uprising. He specifically takes issue with the following points appearing in Mark's and Lazar's books: the duration of the "battle of the flags" at Muranowski Square, and the renewal of the fighting there on April 27 and 28; he barely mentions the existence of ZZW fighting units in the Brushmakers' Workshop area and ignores the presence of ZZW units in the Toebbens-Schultz Workshop area.

The battle at Muranowski Square, Gutman writes, lasted one day and "ended with the destruction of ZZW's main force." Thereafter, according to him, the group of ZZW forces "left the ghetto through the tunnel." Consistent with this description, he makes no mention of the renewed battle against German forces conducted by ZZW in Muranowski Square on April 27 and 28, and of the battle ZZW fighters waged against German forces in the building, just outside the ghetto wall, at Mutanowska 6, on April 27. Gutman's description even detracts from Zuckerman's version that ZZW fought at Mu-

---

37 Yisrael Gutman, *Yehudei Varsha 1939–1943: Geto, mahteret, mered* (Jerusalem: Yad Vashem, 1976). An English translation of the book was published in 1989: Yisrael Gutman, *The Jews of Warsaw 1939–1943: Ghetto, Underground, Revolt* (Bloomington, IN: Indiana University Press).

ranowski Square for two days and then left the ghetto.[38] But from Stroop's daily operational reports, it is clear that the fighting with ZZW forces at Muranowski Square, which began in the afternoon of April 19, 1943, continued during the following three days until April 22, while Stroop's forces were attempting, on Himmler's orders, to remove the flags ZZW had hoisted over Muranowska 17. On April 22, Stroop reported that Unterstrumfuehrer Hans Dehmke had been killed in the fighting there that day.[39] As for the renewed fighting between ZZW fighters and German forces in Muranowski Square on the April 27 and 28, Stroop's operational report for the 28th of April includes the following: "We continued to attack the nest of the Jewish military organization (*das Nest der Juedischen militaerischen Organisation*), situated at the border of the ghetto.... Again today we encountered very strong resistance in many places and broke it. It becomes clearer every day that we now encounter the real terrorists and activists, because the action takes longer than expected."

There is no doubt that ZZW fighters fought in the Brushmakers' Workshop area and in the Toebbens-Schultz Workshop area. Their presence there is confirmed by the testimony of a number of eyewitness accounts, including members of ZOB.[40]

---

38 See Zuckerman's account of his appearance at Kibbutz Na'an in May 1947, in Zuckerman, *Ba-geto u-va-mered*, 145–146. For Gutman's version of the ZZW battle in Muranowski Square, see Gutman, *Yehudei Varsha 1939– 1943*, 376–77.

39 Dehmke's grave is located in the cemetery reserved for German soldiers in Joachim Mogily near Bolimow, about fifty kilometers from Warsaw, and bears the date of his death as April 22, 1943.

40 See the testimonies of Juta Hartman-Rutenberg (Lazar Litai, *Matzada shel Varsha*, 182–85, 258), Fella Shapchik-Finkelstein (Lohamei Hagetaot Archives 9648), and Simha Korngold (Yad Vashem Archives O33/1566). See also Carmi and Frimmer, *Min ha-dlikah ha-hi*, 119; and Putermilch, *Ba-esh u-va-sheleg*, 75.

Part three of Gutman's book, covering the period from mid-September 1942 to the end of the uprising, devotes far more space to the activities of ZOB than to those of ZZW. The inescapable conclusion from the book is that ZZW's part in the uprising, though not negligible, was secondary.

Since the publication of Gutman's book, two books have been published written by ZZW fighters: *The Survivor* by Jack Eisner,[41] and *Caged* by David Landau.[42] Eisner had joined ZZW shortly before the uprising, while Landau, affiliated with Betar, had been with ZZW for many months prior to the uprising. Both participated in the fighting in Muranowski Square, and their accounts, though written many years after the events, tend to confirm the central role of ZZW in the Warsaw Ghetto Uprising.

But the most important documentation regarding the uprising became public knowledge sixty years ago, shortly after the war – Juergen Stroop, the German general who suppressed the uprising, sent daily operational reports to his superior, the commander of police forces in the *Generalgouvernement*, Friedrich Wilhelm Krueger, and presented a summary report to an assembly of SS officers, headed by Krueger, in Krakow on May 18, 1943.[43] They confirm the central role of ZZW in the uprising. Nevertheless, the evidence, seemingly so clear in Stroop's reports, has been bypassed by the promoters of the accepted narrative. Nor, in the years that have passed since the publication of Eisner's and Landau's books, has there been

---

41 New York: William Morrow & Co., 1980.

42 *Caged: The Landau Manuscript*. Landau's book was published posthumously by his family in 1999. A second edition was published under the title *Caged: A Story of Jewish Resistance*, by Pan Macmillan Australia, 2000.

43 Kermish, *Mered Geto Varsha be-enei ha-oyev*. For the original in German, see Joseph Wulf, *Das Dritte Reich und seine Vollstrecker* [The Third Reich and its executioners] (Berlin: Arani Verlags GmbH, 1961), 74–81, 93–179.

a reexamination of the commonly accepted version of the Warsaw Ghetto Uprising.

The fratricidal rivalry that marked the relationship between the Socialist Zionist movements and Jabotinsky's Zionist Revisionist movement, ever since the murder of the Socialist Zionist leader Chaim Arlozoroff in Palestine in 1933, left its mark even in the ghetto of Warsaw. It kept ZOB and ZZW from uniting, and led to the attempt by the Socialist Zionist parties to claim the role of leaders and organizers of the resistance to the Germans and obscure the part of ZZW in the fighting against the Germans. This task was made easier by the fact that the commanders of ZZW, Frenkel and Rodal, as well as almost all of its leading members, fell in the fighting. The few surviving ZZW fighters were unknown and unable to make their voices heard. Zuckerman and Adolf Berman, well known to the Zionist leadership in Palestine, told and retold their version of the Warsaw Ghetto Uprising, a version that left almost no room for the fighters of ZZW. This version was eagerly embraced by the political leadership of the Jewish community in Palestine after the war under the aegis of the Socialist Zionists, and thereafter by the Labor party in Israel during the following twenty-nine years while they were in power. During those years the legend of Mordechai Anielewicz and the fighters of ZOB became enshrined in school textbooks, annual ceremonies, and the names of streets of Israel. In effect, the story of Jewish heroism in the Warsaw ghetto has been successfully politically manipulated.

The historians researching the revolt were not as successful in setting the record straight. Ber Mark's voice from Warsaw was hardly audible in Israel, while Haim Lazar's book was disparaged as not being the work of a serious historian. Gutman, a historian of high reputation, challenged a number of aspects of Mark's and Lazar's books and contributed to strengthening Zuckerman's version of the uprising.

There was one historian whose concern for historical accuracy took precedence over his political affiliation. It was Emmanuel Ringelblum, the chronicler of the Warsaw ghetto. He was a leading member in the ghetto of Left Po'alei Zion, a Marxist Zionist party, close in its positions to Hashomer Hatzair. He had no sympathy for the Revisionist-Zionists, but was aware of the existence of ZZW in the ghetto. In order to accurately record events in the ghetto, he had taken the trouble to visit the ZZW headquarters at Muranowska 7 shortly before the outbreak of the uprising and had left a report of this visit in his notes. He had watched the battle at Muranowski Square during the first days of the uprising, and was afterwards sent by the Germans to the SS work camp in Trawniki.

In an attempt to assure the survival of Ringleblum, efforts were made to rescue him from the work camp. Shoshana Kossower (Rosenzweig), who had passed the war years in Warsaw posing as a Pole and working as an AK courier, while maintaining contact with the ghetto and smuggling arms to ZZW and ZOB there, volunteered for this dangerous mission. The daring and courageous girl entered the camp under false pretenses and managed to spirit Ringelblum out of the camp and bring him to Warsaw in August 1943. There he and his family hid out in a bunker crowded with other Jews, but he continued working on his notes and was in contact with Berman.

When Ringleblum saw the list of ZOB fighters that had been assembled, he inquired about the ZZW fighters. Sitting in the bunker, in danger of being discovered at any moment, he repeatedly expressed his concern to Berman that the record of the participation of ZZW fighters in the Warsaw Ghetto Uprising might be lost. In March 1944, the bunker was discovered and those hiding there, including Ringelblum and his family, were executed.[44]

***

---

44 See Lazar Litai, *Matzada shel Varsha*, 192; and Zuckerman, *A Surplus of Memory*, 472.

For many years the history of the Warsaw Ghetto Uprising was manipulated for ideological and political reasons. Past political rivalries left their imprint on the generally accepted narrative of events, despite compelling evidence to the contrary. Now, decades after the uprising, the curtain is being raised on what really happened in those desperate days in the Warsaw ghetto. It is not the only case in modern history where the true course of events has been manipulated and obscured for political and ideological reasons. But reality can only be buried for so long, and it is only a matter of time before the truth is revealed.

Appendix 1

The Polish Connection

During the years of the post-war Communist regime in Poland, a number of Poles came forward claiming to have provided significant assistance to ZZW in the Warsaw Ghetto Uprising, including participation in the fighting in the streets of the ghetto. The most prominent among them was Henryk Iwanski, who claimed to have been instrumental in the founding of ZZW, to have provided it with its first batch of weapons, and to have led a group of Poles who entered the ghetto during the uprising and participated in the fighting against the Germans. In this battle, according to him, he lost his brother and son. His version of events was corroborated by another Pole, Wladyslaw Zarski-Zajdler, who claimed to have been one of the Poles who had been part of Iwanski's group during the fighting in the ghetto. These claims were put forth in notarized depositions and in newspaper articles in the Polish press. They were supported by Kalman Mendelson, a Jew living in Poland, who wrote that he had been one of the founders of ZZW and one of its commanders. Another Pole who claimed to have been in contact with ZZW and to have intimate knowledge of the activity of ZZW in the ghetto was Tadeusz Bednarczyk.

The claims, although not always consistent, were generally mutually supportive, and painted a picture of significant Polish support for the Warsaw Ghetto Uprising. They also added interesting details of the history, the organization, and functioning of ZZW in the ghetto. Coming from a number of sources and including much detailed information, they appeared at first hand to be credible. So much so that Iwanski was declared a "righteous among the nations" by Yad Vashem.

Since all of the senior ZZW commanders had fallen in battle, there was little information available after the war regarding ZZW, and the Polish testimony seemed to fill this void, supplying many details about ZZW, the organization that had played such an important part in the Warsaw Ghetto Uprising. The testimony of Iwanski and his associates was welcomed by many of those who wrote about the Warsaw Ghetto Uprising. The first to place trust in their testimony was Haim Lazar Litai in his book *Muranowska 7*,[1] devoted in large measure to ZZW. One of my earlier research papers[2] was based in part on these Polish claims.

A good part of the literature dealing with the Warsaw Ghetto Uprising includes references to the claims made by Iwanski, Bednarczyk, and their associates. The latest book based largely on this Polish testimony was written by Marian Apfelbaum.[3] Dedicated to Mieczyslaw David Apfelbaum, the author's relative, who according to the Polish sources had been the commander of ZZW, the book has also appeared in Hebrew, Polish, and English editions. The Hebrew edition was published by Yad Vashem and includes a preface by Laurence Weinbaum. Weinbaum in the preface refers to the articles published in Poland by Iwanski, Bednarczyk, and their associates during the period of Communist rule, which described cooperation between members of the Polish underground organization, KB, and ZZW, as "worthy of mention." He also refers to Kalman Mendelson as "the only surviving ZZW officer." Only Bednarczyk is singled out by

---

1   Haim Lazar Litai, *Muranowska 7: The Warsaw Ghetto Rising* (Tel Aviv: Massada P.E.C. Press, 1966).
2   Moshe Arens, "The Jewish Military Organization (ZZW) in the Warsaw Ghetto," *Journal of Holocaust and Genocide Studies* 19, no. 2 (2005).
3   Marian Apfelbaum, *Retour Sur Le Ghetto De Varsovie* [Return to the Warsaw Ghetto] (Paris: Editions Odile Jacob, 2002).

him because of his dubious activities after the war, but, nevertheless, he writes that "his testimony should not be rejected out of hand."[4]

The first to raise doubts about the veracity of the accounts of these Polish sources was Yisrael Gutman in his book about the Warsaw ghetto. "They are riddled with conflicting statements and exaggerated claims that cannot be taken seriously," he wrote.[5]

A detailed examination of their accounts and comparison with the accounts of Warsaw ghetto survivors reveals a glaring inconsistency. Whereas all survivors of the Warsaw ghetto who refer to ZZW point to Pawel Frenkel as the commander of ZZW and fail to even mention David Apfelbaum, the above Polish sources insist that it was David Apfelbaum who commanded ZZW. Emmanuel Ringelblum, as well, in one of his last notes refers to Pawel Frenkel as head of ZZW, making no mention of Apfelbaum. Moreover, Mendelson, who corroborated and supplemented the accounts of Iwanski and his associates, said that he had been commander of the ZZW unit at Karmelicka 5, in the Toebbens-Schultz Workshop area, whereas the testimony of survivors of that unit, Simha Korngold and Fella Shapshik-Finkelstein, do not mention him.

In a more recent publication Dariusz Libionka and Laurence Weinbaum state that declassified Polish secret-police documents "indicate that these Poles were associated to some degree with the security organs, and were regularly utilized to implement the agenda of the Interior Ministry."[6] It is possible that the Polish Communist government, in an attempt to create the impression that the Warsaw

---

4   Marian Apfelbaum, *Behazarah le-Geto Varsha: Hitkomemut ha-Igud ha-Tzvai ha-Yehudi* [Return to the Warsaw Ghetto: The Uprising of the Jewish Military Organization] (Jerusalem: Yad Vashem, 2004), 20–21.

5   Gutman, *The Jews of Warsaw 1939–1943*, 347.

6   Dariusz Libionka and Laurence Weinbaum, "Deconstructing Memory and History: The Jewish Military Union (ZZW) and the Warsaw Ghetto Uprising," *Jewish Political Studies Review* 18:1–2 (spring 2006).

Ghetto Uprising benefited from significant Polish assistance, encouraged these Poles to publish accounts that were in the realm of fiction. Utilizing the fact that, whereas a number of leading ZOB fighters had survived, all of the ZZW senior personnel had fallen in the uprising, the published accounts were limited to presumed Polish assistance to ZZW.

Appendix 2

Juergen Stroop's Daily Reports

The following is an official English translation of SS Brigadefuehrer Juergen Stroop's daily operational reports, written during the period of the destruction of the Warsaw ghetto. The complete document is retained in the U.S. National Archives.

Copy   SS Services Teletype Message
        From: The SS and Police Fuehrer in the District of Warsaw
                                        Warsaw, 20 April 1943

   Ref. No. I ab St/Gr 16 07 – Journal No. 516/43 secret
   Re: Ghetto Operation
   To: The Higher SS and Police Fuehrer East
      Cracow

Progress of Ghetto Operation on 19 April 1943:
   Closing of Ghetto commenced 0300 hrs. At 0600 order to Waffen-SS (strength: 16/850) to comb out the remainder of the Ghetto. Hardly had the units fallen in, strong concerted fire-concentration by the Jews and bandits. The tank used in this action and the two heavy armored cars pelted with Molotov cocktails (incendiary bottles). Tank twice set on fire. Owing to this enemy counterattack, we had at first to take the units back. Losses in first attack: 12 men (6 SS-men, 6 Trawniki-men).
   About 0800 hrs. Second attack by the units under the command of the undersigned. Although the counterattack was repeated, this time we succeeded in combing out the blocks of buildings according to plan. We caused the enemy to retire from the roofs and elevated prepared positions

into the cellars or dug-outs and sewers. During this combing-out we caught only about 200 Jews. Immediately afterwards raiding parties were directed to dug-outs known to us with the order to pull out the Jews and to destroy the dug-outs. About 380 Jews captured. We found out that the Jews had taken to the sewers. Sewers were completely inundated, to make staying there impossible. About 1730 hrs. We encountered very strong resistance from one block of buildings including machine gun fire. A special raiding party invaded that block and defeated the enemy, but could not catch the resisters. The Jews and criminals resisted from base to base, and escaped at the last moment across lofts or through subterranean passages. About 2030 hrs. the external barricade was re-enforced. All units were withdrawn from the Ghetto and dismissed to their barracks. Re-enforcement of the barricade by 250 Waffen-SS men.

Continuation of operation on 20 April 1943.

Units at my disposal:

SS-Panzer-Gren. Res. Batl.	6/400
SS-Cav. Res. Batl.	10/450
Police	6/165
Security Service	2/48
Trawniki-men	1/150

Wehrmacht:

1 10-cm Howitzer	1/7
1 Flame-thrower	1
Engineers	2/16
Medical detachment	1/1
3 2.28-cm A.A. guns	2/24
1 French tank of the Waffen-SS	
2 heavy armored cars of the Waffen-SS	
Total:	31/1262

I put Major of Police Sternagel in command of today's operations subject to my further instructions if necessary.

At 0700 hrs. 9 raiding parties were formed, each 1/36 strong, consisting of mixed units, to comb out and to search the remainder of the Ghetto intensively. This search is still in progress; its first objective will be completed by 1100 hrs. In the meantime it has been ascertained that in part of the Ghetto which is no longer inhabited but not yet released and which contains several armament factories and the like, there were several centers of resistance, which were so strong that the tank could not go through. 2 raiding parties defeated these centers of resistance and made a passage for the tank men. In this operation we already had two wounded (Waffen-SS).

Enemy is much more cautious than yesterday, since he has of course learned of the heavy arms at our disposal.

My intention is first to comb out completely the remainder of the Ghetto and then to clean out in the same manner the so-called uninhabited Ghetto, which so far has not been released. It has been ascertained in the meantime that the latter part of the Ghetto contains at least 10 to 12 dugouts, some of which are even in armament factories. The whole operation is made more difficult because there are still factories in the Ghetto which must be protected against bombardment and fire, because they contain machines and tools.

A further report will follow tonight.

> The SS and Police Fuehrer in the District of Warsaw
> signed: Stroop
> SS-Brigadefuehrer and Majorgeneral of Police

certified copy: SS-Sturmbannfuehrer

Copy   Teletype message

     From The SS and Police Fuehrer in the District of Warsaw
     Ref. No. I ab St/Gr 16 07 – Journal No. 517/43 secret
     Re: Ghetto Operation
     To: The Higher SS and Police Fuehrer East
        SS-Obergruppenfuehrer and General of Police
        Krueger – or deputy
        Cracow

Supplementing my teletype message of 20 April 1943 – Ref. St/Gr 16 07, re Ghetto operation. I beg to report as follows:

The resistance centers ascertained within the uninhabited but not yet released part of the Ghetto were crushed by a battle group of the Wehrmacht-Engineers and flame-throwers. The Wehrmacht had one wounded in this operation, shot through the lungs. Nine raiding parties broke through as far as the northern limit of the Ghetto. Nine dug-outs were found, their inmates crushed when they resisted, and the dug-outs blown up. What losses the enemy suffered cannot be ascertained accurately. Altogether the 9 raiding parties caught 505 Jews today: those among them who are able-bodied were kept ready for transport to Poniatowo. At about 1500 hrs. I managed to arrange that the block of buildings occupied by the Army Accommodation Office said to be occupied by 4,000 Jews is to be evacuated at once. The German Manager was asked to call upon the Jewish workers to leave the block voluntarily. Only 28 Jews obeyed this order. Thereupon I resolved either to evacuate the block by force or to blow it up. The A.A. Artillery – 3 2-cm. guns used for this operation had two men killed. The 10-cm howitzer, which also was used, expelled the gangs from their strong fortifications and also inflicted losses on them, as far as we were able to ascertain. This action had to be broken off owing to the fall of darkness. On 21 April 1943 we shall attack this resistance center again, as far as possible it will remain blocked off during the night.

In today's action we caught, apart from the Jews reported above, considerable stores of incendiary bottles, hand grenades, ammunition, military tunics, and equipment.

Losses: 2 dead (Wehrmacht)

              7 wounded (6 Waffen-SS, 1 Trawniki-man)

In one case the bandits had laid pressure mines. I have succeeded in causing the firms W.C. Toebbens, Schultz and Co., and Hoffmann to be ready for evacuation with their entire personnel on 21 April 1943 at 0600 hrs. In this way, I hope to get the way free at last for cleaning out the Ghetto. The trustee Toebbens has pledged himself to induce the Jews, numbering about 4 to 5,000, to follow him voluntarily to the assembling point for being resettled. In case this has as little success as was attained in the case of the Army Accommodation Office, I am going to clean out this part of the

Ghetto as well by force. I beg to acknowledge receipt of the order which the Obergruppenfuehrer communicated to me by telephone today, and of the powers granted to me.

Next report on 21 April 1943 at noon.

The SS and Police Fuehrer in the District of Warsaw
signed: Stroop
SS-Brigadefuehrer and Majorgeneral of Police

certified copy: SS-Sturmbannfuehrer

Copy   Teletype message
From: The SS and Police Fuehrer in the District of Warsaw
Warsaw, 21 April 1943

Ref. No. I ab St/Gr 16 07 – Journal No. 527/43 secret
Re: Ghetto Operation
To: The Higher SS and Police Fuehrer East
  SS-Obergruppenfuehrer and General of Police
  Krueger – or deputy
  Cracow

Progress of Ghetto Operation on 21 April 1943

Supplementing the report which I made today about 1400 hrs. by telephone, I beg to report:

Forces at my disposal as on 20 April 1943.

Start of Operation: 0700 hrs – the whole of the Ghetto has continued to be cordoned off since the start of the operations on 19 April 1943.

Inasmuch as the special operation concerning the block of buildings occupied by the Army Accommodation Office had to be interrupted yesterday because of darkness, one battle group reinforced by Engineers and heavy artillery was again sent into the block of buildings, which was found to contain an enormous quantity of dug-outs and subterranean passages firing from time to time. I resolved therefore to blow up those passages which we had discovered and subsequently to set the entire block on fire.

Not until the building was well aflame did screaming Jews make their appearance, and they were evacuated at once. We had no losses in this operation. Precautionary measures were taken in order to ensure that the conflagration remained localized.

The main body of our forces was detailed to cleanse the so-called uninhabited, but not yet released, part of the Ghetto by proceeding from South to North. Before we started this action, we caught 5,200 Jews who had been employed in enterprises under the supervision of the Commissioner for Armament (Rue Ko-Betrieben) and transported them under armed guard to the Railway Station which had been chosen for use in the resettlement. I formed 3 search-parties to which were attached special raiding parties who had the duty to attack or blow up the dug-outs which were known to us. This operation had to be interrupted when darkness set in, after one half of the area mentioned had been combed out.

Continued on 22 April 1943, 0700 hrs.

Apart from the Jews who were to be evacuated, 150 Jews or bandits were killed in battle and about 80 bandits were killed when their dug-outs were blown up. The enemy today used the same arms as on the previous day, particularly home-made explosives. Samples have been kept by the SS and Police Fuehrer. For the first time we observed the participation of members of the Jewish women's Battle Association (Chaluzin Movement). We captured rifles, pistols, hand grenades, explosive, horses, and parts of SS uniforms.

Own losses: 2 policemen, 2 SS-men, 1 Trawniki-man.
                (light wounds)

The SS and Police Fuehrer in the District of Warsaw
signed: Stroop
SS-Brigadefuehrer and Majorgeneral of Police
certified copy: SS-Sturmbannfuehrer

Copy   Teletype message
From: The SS and Police Fuehrer in the District of Warsaw
                                Warsaw, 22 April 1943

Ref. No. I ab St/Gr 16 07 – Journal No. 530/43 secret
Re: Ghetto Operation – Supplement to Par. 1 of letter of 21 April 1943
To: The Higher SS and Police Fuehrer of Police
    Krueger – or deputy
    Cracow

Our setting the block on fire achieved the result in the course of the night that those Jews whom we had not been able to find despite all our search operations left their hide-outs under the roofs, in the cellars, and elsewhere, and appeared at the outside of the buildings, trying to escape the flames. Masses of them – entire families – were already aflame and jumped from the windows or endeavored to let themselves down by means of sheets tied together or the like. Steps had been taken so that these Jews as well as the remaining ones were liquidated at once. During the whole night there were shots from buildings which were supposed to be evacuated. We had no losses in our cordoning forces. 2,300 Jews were caught for the evacuation and removed.

      The SS and Police Fuehrer in the District of Warsaw
      signed: Stroop
      SS-Brigadefuehrer and Majorgeneral of Police
certified copy: SS-Sturmbannfuehrer

Copy   Teletype message
      From: The SS and Police Fuehrer in the District of Warsaw
                   Warsaw, 22 April 1943

Ref. No. I ab St/Gr 16 07 – Journal No. 531/43 secret
Re: Ghetto Operation
To: The Higher SS and Police Fuehrer East
    SS-Obergruppenfuehrer and General of Police
    Krueger – or deputy
    Cracow

Progress of the Ghetto Operation on 22 April 1943 up to 1200 hrs.

One raiding party was dispatched to invade once more the block of buildings which for the greater part had burned out or was still aflame, in order to catch those Jews who were still inside. When shooting again started from one block against the men of the Waffen-SS, this block also was set on fire, with the result that a considerable number of bandits were scared from their hide-outs and shot while trying to escape. Apart from these, we caught about 180 Jews in the yards of the buildings. The main body of our units continued the cleansing action from the line where we terminated this action yesterday. This operation is still in progress. As on the proceeding days local resistance was broken and the dug-outs we discovered were blown up. Unfortunately there is no way of preventing part of the Jews and bandits from taking refuge in the sewers below the Ghetto, where we can hardly catch them since they have stopped the flooding. The City Administration is not in a position to frustrate this nuisance. Neither did the use of smoke candles or the candles or the introduction of Creosote into the water have the desired result. Cooperation with the Wehrmacht splendid.

> The SS and Police Fuehrer in the District of Warsaw
> signed: Stroop
> SS-Brigadefuehrer and Majorgeneral of Police

certified copy: SS-Sturmbannfuehrer

Copy   Teletype message
From: The SS and Police Fuehrer in the District of Warsaw
Warsaw, 22 April 1943

Ref. No. I ab St/Gr 16 07 – Journal No. 531/43 secret
Re: Ghetto Operation
To: The Higher SS and Police Fuehrer East
    SS-Obergruppenfuehrer and General of Police
    Krueger – or deputy
    Cracow

Progress of operation of 22 April 1943. Report on action up to 1200 hrs. has already been submitted by my message of today.

Continuing, I beg to report:

When the special raiding party searched the remainder of the blocks as already reported, they met with resistance at some places; they had the following success: 1,100 Jews caught for evacuation, 203 bandits and Jews killed, 15 dug-outs blown up. They captured 80 incendiary bottles and other booty. Units at my disposal: as reported by teletype message on 20 April 1943. Journal Nr. 516/43 secret.

> Our losses: SS-Untersturmfuehrer Dehmke (dead); enemy hit a hand grenade which he carried. (SS-Cav. Res. Batl.)
>
> 1 Sergeant of Police (shot through the lungs)

When the Engineers blew up the dug-outs, a considerable number of Jews and bandits were buried under the ruins. In a number of cases it was found necessary to start fires in order to smoke the gangs out.

I must add that since yesterday some of the units have been shot at time and again from outside the Ghetto, that is, from the Aryan part of Warsaw. Raiding parties at once entered the area in question and in one case succeeded in capturing 35 Polish bandits, Communists, who were liquidated at once. Today it happened repeatedly when we found it necessary to execute some bandits, that they collapsed shouting "Long live Poland," "Long live Moscow."

The operation will be continued on 23 April 1943, 0700 hrs.

> The SS and Police Fuehrer in the District of Warsaw
> signed: Stroop
> SS-Brigadefuehrer and Majorgeneral of Police

certified copy: SS-Sturmbannfuehrer

Copy   Teletype message
From: The SS and Police Fuehrer in the District of Warsaw
                                    Warsaw, 23 April 1943

Ref. No. I ab St/Gr 16 07 – Journal No. 538/43 secret

Re: Ghetto Operation
To: The Higher SS and Police Fuehrer East
    SS-Obergruppenfuehrer and General of Police
    Krueger – or deputy
    Cracow

Progress of Ghetto Operation on 23 April 1943.
    Start: 0700 hours.
    The whole of the former Ghetto had been divided for the purposes of today's combing-out operations into 24 districts. One reinforced searching party was detailed to each district with special orders. These assignments had to be carried out by 1600 hours.
    Result of this action: 600 Jews and bandits ferreted out and captured, about 200 Jews and bandits killed, 48 dug-outs, some of them of a quite elaborate character, blown up. We captured, apart from valuables and money, some gas masks.
    The units had been informed that we intended to terminate the operation today. In the morning the Jews had already become aware of this instruction. This is why a renewed search by the searching parties was undertaken after an interval of 1 to 1 1/2 hours. The result was, as always, that again Jews and bandits were discovered to be in various blocks. From one block shots were even fired against the cordoning units. An attack by a special battle group was ordered and in order to smoke the bandits out, every building was now set on fire. The Jews and bandits held out, every building was now set on fire.
    The Jews and bandits held their fire up to the last moment and then concerted their fire against the units. They even used carbines. A number of bandits who were shooting from balconies were hit by our men and crashed down.
    Furthermore, today we discovered a place said to have been the headquarters of the "PPR"; we found it unoccupied and destroyed it. It was on this 5th day of operations that obviously we found the worst of the terrorists and activists, who so far had always found ways and means to dodge every searching or evacuation action.

A racial German reported that again some Jews had escaped through the sewers into the Aryan part of the city. We learned from a traitor that there were some Jews in a certain house. A special motorized raiding party invaded the building and caught 3 Jews, 2 of them females. During this operation their motor-car was pelted with one incendiary bottle and one explosive; 2 Policemen were wounded.

The whole operation is rendered more difficult by the cunning way in which the Jews and bandits act; for instance, we discovered that the hearses which were used to collect the corpses lying around at the same time bring living Jews to the Jewish cemetery, and thus they are enabled to escape from the Ghetto. Now this way of escape also is barred by continuous control of the hearses.

At the termination of today's operation about 2200 hours, we discovered that again about 30 bandits had passed into a so-called armaments factory, where they had found refuge. Since the forces are storing goods of great value in this enterprise, this factory was requested to evacuate the building by noon on 24 April: This will enable us to cleanse that labyrinth of a building tomorrow.

Today 3,500 Jews were caught who are to be evacuated from the factories. A total of 19,450 Jews have been caught for resettlement or already evacuated up to today. Of these about 2,500 Jews are still to be loaded. The next train will start on 24 April 1943.

Strength as of 22 April 1943, without 150 Trawniki men; these have already been put at the disposal of the Eastern Command as reinforcement for another assignment.

Our losses: 2 Police corporals ("SS") wounded
1 Trawniki man wounded

The operation will be continued on 24 April 1843, 1000 hours. This hour was chosen so that Jews who may still be in the Ghetto will believe that the operation was actually terminated today.

The SS and Police Fuehrer in the District of Warsaw
signed: Stroop
SS-Brigadefuehrer and Majorgeneral of Police
certified copy: SS-Sturmbannfuehrer

Copy   Teletype message
               From: The SS and Police Fuehrer in the District of Warsaw
                                               Warsaw, 24 April 1943

   Ref. No. I ab St/Wdt 16 07 – Journal No. 545/43 secret
   Re: Ghetto Operation
   To: The Higher SS and Police Fuehrer East
      SS-Obergruppenfuehrer and General of Police
      Krueger – or deputy
      Cracow

Progress of operation on 24 April 1943, start 1000 hrs.

Contrary to the preceding days, the 24 searching parties which had again been formed did not start at one end of the Ghetto, but proceeded from all sides at the same time. Apparently the Jews still in the Ghetto were deceived by the fact that the operation did not start until 1000 hours into believing that the action really had been terminated yesterday. The search action, therefore, had especially satisfactory results today. This success is furthermore due to the fact that the non-commissioned officers and men have meanwhile become accustomed to the cunning fighting, methods and tricks used by the Jews and bandits and that they have acquired great skill in tracking down the dug-outs which are found in such great number.

The raiding parties having returned, we set about to clean a certain block of buildings, situated in the north-eastern part of the former Ghetto. In this labyrinth of buildings there was a so-called armaments firm which reportedly had goods worth millions for manufacture and storage. I had notified the Wehrmacht of my intentions on 23 April 1943 about 2100 hours, and had requested them to remove their goods by 1200 hours. Since the Wehrmacht did not start this evacuation until 1000 hours, I felt obliged to extend the term until 1800 hours. At 1815 hours a search party entered the premises, the building having been cordoned off, and found that a great number of Jews were within the building. Since some of these Jews resisted, I ordered the building to be set on fire. Not until all the buildings along the street and the back premises on either side were well aflame did the Jews, some of them on fire, emerge from these blocks, some of them endeavored to save their life by jumping into the street from windows and balconies, after having thrown down beds, blankets, and the like. Over and over again we observed that Jews and bandits, despite the danger of being burned alive, preferred to return into the flames rather than risk being caught by us. Over and over again the Jews kept up their firing almost to the end of the action: thus the engineers had to be protected by a machine gun when toward nightfall they had to enter forcibly a concrete building which had been very strongly fortified.

Termination of today's operation; on 25 April 1943 at 0145 hours. 1,660 Jews were caught for evacuation, 1,814 pulled out of dug-outs, about 330 shot. Innumerable Jews were destroyed by the flames or perished when the dug-outs were blown up. 26 dug-outs were blown up and an amount of paper money, especially dollars, was captured; this money had not yet been counted.

Our forces: as on the preceding day, minus 50 men of the Waffen-SS.

Our losses: 2 SS-men and one Trawniki man wounded.

Altogether there have now been caught in this action 25,500 Jews who lived in the former Ghetto. Since there are only vague estimates available of the actual number of inhabitants I assume that now only very small numbers of Jews and bandits still remain within the Ghetto.

Operation will be continued on 25 April 1943, 1300 hours. I beg to acknowledge receipt of teletype messages nos. 1222 and 1223 of 24 April 1943. As far as can be predicted, the present large-scale operation will last until Easter Monday inclusive.

Today large posters were affixed to the walls surrounding the Ghetto, announcing that everybody who enters the former Ghetto without being able to prove his identity will be shot.

> The SS and Police Fuehrer in the District of Warsaw
> signed: Stroop
> SS-Brigadefuehrer and Majorgeneral of Police
> certified copy: SS-Sturmbannfuehrer

Copy   Teletype message
              From: The SS and Police Fuehrer in the District of Warsaw
                                                Warsaw, 25 April 1943

    Ref. No. I ab St/Wdt 16 07 – Journal No. 549/43 secret
    Re: Ghetto Operation
    To: The Higher SS and Police Fuehrer East
        SS-Obergruppenfuehrer and General of Police
        Krueger – or deputy
        Cracow

Progress of operation on 25 April 1943, start 1300 hours.

    For today 7 search parties were formed, strength 1/70 each, each allotted to a certain block of buildings.

    Their order was: "Every building is to be combed out once more; dug-outs have to be discovered and blown up, and the Jews have to be caught. If any resistance is encountered or if dug-outs cannot be reached, the buildings are to be burnt down." Apart from the operations undertaken by these 7 search parties, a special operation was undertaken against a center of bandits, situated outside the wall surrounding the former Ghetto and inhabited exclusively by Poles.

    Today's operation of the search parties ended almost everywhere in the starting of enormous conflagrations. In this manner the Jews were forced to leave their hide-outs and refuges. A total of 1,960 Jews were caught alive. The Jews informed us that among them there are certain parachutists who were dropped here and bandits who had been equipped with arms from some unknown source. 274 Jews were killed. As in the preceding days, uncounted Jews were buried in blown-up dug-outs and, as can be observed time and again, burned. With this bag of Jews today, we have, in my opinion, caught a very considerable part of the bandits and lowest elements of the Ghetto. Intervening darkness prevented immediate liquidation. I am going to try to obtain a train for T II tomorrow. Otherwise liquidation will be carried out tomorrow. Today also, some armed resistance was encountered; in a dug-out three pistols and some explosives were captured.

Furthermore, considerable amounts of paper money, foreign currency, gold coins, and jewelry were seized today.

The Jews still have considerable property. While last night a glare of fire could be seen above the former Ghetto, today one can observe a giant sea of flames. Since we continue to discover great numbers of Jews whenever we search and comb out, the operation will be continued on 26 April 1943. Start 1000 hours.

Including today, a total of 27,464 Jews of the former Warsaw Ghetto, have been captured.

Our forces: as on the previous day.

Our losses: 3 members of the Waffen-SS and

          one member of the security police wounded.

Total losses up to date:

Waffen SS	27	wounded
Police	9	"
Security Police	4	"
Wehrmacht	1	"
Trawniki men	9	"
	50	"

and 5 dead:

Waffen SS	2	dead
Wehrmacht	2	"
Trawniki men	1	"
	5	"

       The SS and Police Fuehrer in the District of Warsaw
       signed: Stroop
       SS-Brigadefuehrer and Majorgeneral of Police
certified copy: SS-Sturmbannfuehrer

Copy   Teletype message

From: The SS and Police Fuehrer in the District of Warsaw

Warsaw, 26 April 1943

Ref. No. I ab St/Wdt 16 07 – Journal No. 550/43 secret

Re: Ghetto Operation – supplementary report

To: The Higher SS and Police Fuehrer East

   SS-Obergruppenfuehrer and General of Police

   Krueger – or deputy

   Cracow

1. The operation on 25 April 1943, was terminated at 2200 hrs.

2. General effects of the execution of this operation.

The Poles resident in Warsaw are much impressed by the toughness of our operations in the former Ghetto. As can be seen from the daily reports, the general situation has greatly calmed down since the beginning of that operation within the city area of Warsaw. From this fact one may conclude that the bandits and saboteurs resided in the former Ghetto, and that now all of them have been destroyed.

In this connection the fact may be of some interest, that an illegal ammunition store was seen to explode when we burned down a certain building in the dwelling area on which we were working at the time.

      The SS and Police Fuehrer in the District of Warsaw

      signed: Stroop

      SS-Brigadefuehrer and Majorgeneral of Police

certified copy: SS-Sturmbannfuehrer

Copy   Teletype message

    From: The SS and Police Fuehrer in the District of Warsaw

                   Warsaw, 26 April 1943

Ref. No. I ab St/Wdt 16 07 – Journal No. 551/43 secret

To: The Higher SS and Police Fuehrer East

   SS-Obergruppenfuehrer and General of Police

   Krueger – or deputy

   Cracow

Start of operation: 1000 hrs.

The whole of the former Ghetto was once more combed through today by the same search parties, each of them allotted to the same district as before. In this way I tried to bring about that the leaders of these parties work in thoroughfares, blocks of buildings, and courtyards which they know already and that thus they are able to penetrate deeper and deeper into the maze of dug-outs and subterranean passages. Almost every search party reported resistance, which however they broke either by returning fire or by blowing up the dug-outs. It becomes clearer and clearer that it is now the turn of the toughest and strongest among the Jews and bandits. Several times dug-outs have been forcibly broken open, the inmates of which had not come to the surface during the whole of this operation. In a number of cases the inmates of the dug-outs were hardly in a condition, when the dug-out had been blown up, to crawl to the surface. The captured Jews report that many of the inmates of the dug-outs became insane from the heat, the smoke, and the explosions.

Several Jews were arrested who had kept close liaison with the group of Polish terrorists and collaborated with it. Outside the former Ghetto we arrested 29 Jews. During today's operation several blocks of buildings were burned down. This is the only and final method which forces this trash and subhumanity to the surface. We again captured arms, incendiary bottles, explosive charges and considerable amounts of cash and foreign currency. Today I also arranged that several so-called armament and defense enterprises will evacuate their stores from the buildings at once, so that these buildings in which the Jews now have taken refuge, under the protection of the army of the German Wehrmacht and police, can be combed out. In one case we again discovered, as previously, that in a building which had been said to contain a giant enterprise there existed in fact almost no stores or goods. One factory was closed without further ado, and the Jews were evacuated.

Result of today's operation:

30 Jews evacuated, 1,330 Jews pulled out of dug-outs and immediately destroyed, 362 Jews killed in battle. Caught today altogether: 1,722 Jews. This brings the total of Jews caught to 29,186. Moreover, it is very

probable that numerous Jews have perished in the 13 dug-outs blown up today and in the conflagrations.

At the time of writing not one of the Jews caught still remains within Warsaw. The scheduled transport to T II had no success (note of translator: This probably means that no Jews were available for regular transport to the extermination camp.)

      Strength: as on preceding day.

      Our losses: none.

End of today's operation at 2145 hrs.; will be continued on 27 April 1943 at 0900 hrs.

          The SS and Police Fuehrer in the District of Warsaw

          signed: Stroop

          SS-Brigadefuehrer and Majorgeneral of Police

certified copy: SS-Sturmbannfuehrer

Copy   Teletype message

      From: The SS and Police Fuehrer in the District of Warsaw

                           Warsaw, 27 April 1943

      Ref. No. I ab St/Wdt 16 07 – Journal No. 555/43 secret

      Re: Ghetto Operation

      To: The Higher SS and Police Fuehrer East

        SS-Obergruppenfuehrer and General of Police

        Krueger – or deputy

        Cracow

Progress of operation on 27 April 1943. Start: 0900 hrs.

For today's operation I formed 24 raiding parties with the same task as on several days of last week; they had to search the former Ghetto in smaller groups. These search parties pulled 780 Jews out of dug-outs and shot 115 Jews who resisted. This operation was terminated about 1500 hrs.; some of the parties had to continue to operate because they had found more dug-outs.

At 1600 hrs. a special battle group, 320 officers and men strong, started cleansing a large block of buildings situated on both sides of the so-called Niska Street in the Northeastern part of the former Ghetto. After the search the entire block was set on fire, after having been completely cordoned off. In this action a considerable number of Jews were caught. As before, they remained in the dug-outs, which were either below the ground or in the lofts of the building until the end. They fired their arms to the last moment, and then jumped down into the street, sometimes from as far up as the fourth floor, having previously thrown down beds, mattresses, etc., but not until the flames made any other escape impossible. A total of 2,560 Jews were caught today within the former Ghetto, of whom 547 were shot. Moreover, Jews in a not ascertainable number perished when dug-outs were blown up or in the flames. The sum total of Jews, formerly residing in the Ghetto caught in this action, now amounts to 31,746.

We learned from an anonymous letter that there were a considerable number of Jews in a block of buildings adjoining the Northeastern part of the Ghetto, but outside of it. A special raiding party under the command of 1st Lt. of police Diehl was dispatched to attack these buildings. The raiding party discovered a gang of about 120 men, strongly armed with pistols, rifles, hand grenades, and light machine guns, who resisted. They succeeded in destroying 24 bandits in battle and arresting 52 bandits. The remainder could not be caught or destroyed, since darkness intervened. The buildings however, were surrounded at once, so that an escape will hardly be possible. This cleansing action will be continued tomorrow. Moreover we arrested 17 Poles, among whom 2 Polish Policemen, who should have been aware, among other things, of the existence of this gang. In this operation we captured 2 rifles, 12 pistols, partly of heavier caliber, 100 Polish "pineapple" hand grenades, 27 German steel helmets, quite a number of German uniforms, tunics and coats which were even furnished with the ribbon of the East medal, some reserve magazines for machine guns, 300 rounds of ammunition, etc. The leader of the raiding party had a difficult task because the bandits were disguised in German uniform. But despite this fact, he did his duty with great efficiency. Among the bandits who were caught or killed, there were some Polish terrorists who were identified with certainty. Today we succeeded furthermore in discovering and liquidating one of the founders and leaders of the Jewish-Polish resistance movement. The external appearance of the Jews whom we are catching now shows that it is now the turn of those Jews who were the leaders of the entire resistance movement. They jumped from the burning windows and balconies, abusing Germany and the Fuehrer and cursing the German soldiers.

SS-men who descended into the sewers discovered that a great number of corpses of perished Jews are being washed away by the water.

Our strength:

From 0700 to 1900 hrs.	288 German police	
	200 Trawniki-men	
	140 Polish Police	Cordoning Forces
From 1900 to 0700 hrs.	288 German Police	
	250 Waffen-SS	
	140 Polish Police	

Strength in the operation:	
	3/115 German Police
	4/400 Waffen-SS
	1/6 Engineering Serv.
	2/30 Security police
	2/21 Engineers

Our losses:	3 wounded:	2 Waffen-SS
		1 Trawniki-man

Termination of operation: 2300 hrs.

Will be continued on 28 April 1943 at 1000 hrs.

The SS and Police Fuehrer in the District of Warsaw
signed: Stroop
SS-Brigadefuehrer and Majorgeneral of Police
certified copy: SS-Sturmbannfuehrer

Copy   Teletype message
From: The SS and Police Fuehrer in the District of Warsaw
Warsaw, 28 April 1943

Ref. No. I ab St/Gr 16 07 – Journal No. 562/43 secret

Re: Ghetto Operation
To: The Higher SS and Police Fuehrer East
    SS-Obergruppenfuehrer and General of Police
    Krueger – or deputy
    Cracow

Progress of operation on 28 April 1943. Start 1000 hrs.

Today, 10 raiding parties were formed for combing out the whole of the Ghetto. These Raiding parties again discovered proceeding step by step, a number of dug-outs, which were found to have been prepared as long ago as the middle of last year for use in the resistance of the Jews. A total of 335 Jews were forcibly pulled out of these dug-outs. Apart from these operations, we continued to cleanse the resistance center used by the Jewish military organization, situated at the borders of the Ghetto. We succeeded in shooting 10 more bandits, and in arresting 9, beyond those caught yesterday, and in capturing more arms, ammunition, and military equipment. In the afternoon a battle group again was directed against a block of buildings which had already been combed out; the block was set on fire during this operation. As on previous days, masses of Jews emerged, forced out by the flames and the enormous clouds of smoke. At another point an Engineer Officer, attached by the Wehrmacht to the unite with great trouble opened a dug-out situated about 3 meters below ground. From this dug-out, which had been ready since October of last year and was equipped with running water, toilet, and electric light, we pulled out 274 of the richest and most influential Jews. Today again we encountered very strong resistance in many places and broke it. It becomes clearer every day that we are now encountering the real terrorists and activists, because of the duration of the operation.

Result of today: 1,655 Jews caught for evacuation, of whom 110 were killed in battle.

Many more Jews were killed by the flames; moreover, Jews in an un-ascertainable number were destroyed by the dug-outs being blown up. By the results of today the number of Jews caught or destroyed rises to 33,401 altogether. This number does not include the Jews who were killed by fire or destroyed in the dug-outs.

Our strength: as on the previous day.

Our losses: 3 wounded (1 Police, 2 Waffen-SS)

Termination of operation: 2200 hrs. Will be continued on 29 April 1943, 1000 hrs.

> The SS and Police Fuehrer in the District of Warsaw
> signed: Stroop
> SS-Brigadefuehrer and Majorgeneral of Police

certified copy: SS-Sturmbannfuehrer

Copy   Teletype message

From: The SS and Police Fuehrer in the District of Warsaw

Warsaw, 29 April 1943

Ref. No. I ab St/Gr 16 07 – Journal No. 566/43 secret

Re: Ghetto Operation

To: The Higher SS and Police Fuehrer East

  SS-Obergruppenfuehrer and General of Police

  Krueger – or deputy

  Cracow

Progress of large-scale operation of 29 April 1943. Start 1000 hrs.:

As on the previous day I formed search parties, who had the special task of searching those blocks of buildings which had been recently separated. A larger raiding party was detailed to clean a certain block of buildings (formerly the Hallmann concern) and to burn this block down. 36 more dug-outs used for habitation were discovered altogether, and from them and other hideouts and from the burning buildings 2,359 Jews were caught, of whom 106 were killed in battle.

Captured are 2 rifles, 10 pistols, 10 kilograms of explosives, and ammunition of various types.

When a large dug-out was blown up, the entire building collapsed and every one of the bandits perished. In the ensuing conflagration loud detonations and darting flames showed that the building must have contained large stores of ammunition and explosives. Some sewer entrances were blown up. Two exits discovered outside the Ghetto were also made unusable by blowing them up or walling them up. The depositions of some of the inmates of the dug-outs are to the effect that those Jews have been unable to leave the dug-outs for the last 10 days and that their food, etc., is now beginning to grow short because the large-scale operation has lasted so long. Furthermore, the Jews testify that bandits appeared at night who were Jews or sometimes Poles, wearing black masks, who walled the dug-outs up from the outside and admonished them not to give any signs of life, so that they could continue to live in the Ghetto when the action was finished. Some of the armaments factories are being evacuated very slowly. In several cases one gains the impression that this is done intentionally. Thus I discovered with regard to one firm, Schultz and Co., which I had visited on Easter Monday and then instructed to start evacuation at once and to have it completed within 3 days, that up till today, Thursday, nothing had been done.

      Our strength: as on the previous day.

      Our losses: none

Termination of operation 26 2100 hrs. will be continued on 20 April 1943, 0900 hrs.

      Total caught or destroyed: 35,760

          The SS and Police Fuehrer in the District of Warsaw
          signed: Stroop
          SS-Brigadefuehrer and Majorgeneral of Police
certified copy: SS-Sturmbannfuehrer

Copy   Teletype message
      From: The SS and Police Fuehrer in the District of Warsaw
                     Warsaw, 30 April 1943

      Ref. No. I ab St/Gr 16 07 – Journal No. 579/43 secret
      Re: Ghetto Operation
      To: The Higher SS and Police Fuehrer East

SS-Obergruppenfuehrer and General of Police
Krueger – or deputy
Cracow

Progress of large-scale operation on 30 April 1943, start 0900 hrs.

Combing out by search parties was continued. Although some giant blocks of buildings now are completely burned out, the Jews continue to stay in the dug-outs 2 to 3 meters below ground. In many cases we are not able to discover those dug-outs unless some Jew, whom we have already caught, gives us a hint as to their whereabouts. Repeatedly, during the last few days, Jews have testified that some armed Jews emerge at night from some hide-outs or dug-outs and threaten the other Jews with shooting if they give any signs of life. We were able to ascertain beyond all doubt that several dug-outs had been closed from the outside by these bandits, who tried in this manner to prove that they meant business. Altogether, 30 dug-outs were discovered, evacuated, and blown up today.

Again we caught a great number of bandits and subhumans. Apart from the bombing-out operation effected by small parties, two larger battlegroups were occupied with bombing out and destroying by fire several interconnected blocks of buildings.

A total of 1,599 Jews were caught today, of whom 179 were killed in battle. The sum total of Jews caught up to date thereby rises to 37,359. 3,855 Jews were loaded today. The number of Jews in possession of arms was much higher than before among the Jews caught during the last few days. Today, we again captured arms and particularly parts of German uniforms from them. The operation against Fort Traugutta did not have any positive results. Inasfar as we were able to discover subterranean exits, we either occupied them or blew them up. In attacking one of the blocks we had to use a gun today.

Our strength:
Used in the operation:

Police	5/133
Security Police	3/36
Waffen-SS	6/432
Engineer	2/40

Staff   3/7
Cordoning forces:
    Waffen-SS   3/316
    German Police   2/89
    Trawniki men   200
    moreover some Polish Police
Our losses: 1 wounded (Police)
Termination of today's large-scale action 2100 hours.
Will be continued on 1 May 1943, 0900 hours.

The SS and Police Fuehrer in the District of Warsaw
signed: Stroop
SS-Brigadefuehrer and Majorgeneral of Police
certified copy: SS-Sturmbannfuehrer

Copy   Teletype message
From: The SS and Police Fuehrer in the District of Warsaw
                            Warsaw, May 1, 1943

Ref. No. I ab St/Gr 16 07 – Journal No. 583/43 secret
Re: Large-scale Ghetto operation
To: The Higher SS and Police Fuehrer East
    SS-Obergruppenfuehrer and General of Police
    Krueger – or deputy
    Cracow

Progress of large-scale operation on 1 May 1943, start 0900 hrs.

Ten searching parties were detailed, moreover a larger battle group was detailed to comb out a certain block of buildings, with the added instruction to burn that block down. Within this block of buildings there exists a so-called armament factory which had not yet been entirely evacuated, although it had been enough time to do so. It was not exempted from the operation. Today's operation a total of 1,026 Jews were caught, of whom 245 were killed, either in battle or while resisting. Moreover, a considerable number of bandits and ringleaders were also caught. In one case a Jew who had already been made ready for transport fired three shots against a 1st Lieutenant of Police, but missed his mark. All the Jews caught today were forcibly pulled out of dug-outs. Not a single one gave himself up voluntarily, after his dug-out had been opened. A considerable part of the Jews caught were pulled out of the sewers. We continued systematically blowing up or blocking up the sewer entrances. In one case the Engineers laid a strong concentrated charge and had to proceed to an adjoining entrance where they had something to do. In the meantime a Jew from the sewer removed the fuse from the concentrated charge, and appropriated the charge. In the further course of this operation we succeeded in catching this Jew, still in possession of the concentrated charge.

In order to ascertain the movements of the Jews at night, today I used for the first time 5 scouting parties, each 1/9 strong, at irregular intervals during the night. In general, it has to be stated that our men need extraordinary diligence and energy to discover the Jews who are still in so-called dug-outs, caves, and in the sewerage system. It can be expected that the remainder of the Jews who formerly inhabited the Ghetto will now be caught. The sum total of Jews caught so far has risen to 38,385. Not included in this figure are those who died in the flames or in the dug-outs. One patrol discovered an unascertainable number of corpses floating in a main sewer under the Ghetto. Outside of the Ghetto, in the immediate vicinity of Warsaw, the gendarmerie has shot a total of 150 Jews who would be proved to have escaped from Warsaw.

Again we captured pistols and explosives.

Our strength:

Used in operation:

Police (German)	4/102
Waffen SS	7/350
Engineers (Wehrmacht)	2/38
Engineering Emergency Service	1/6
Security Police	2/1

Cordoning units:

Waffen SS	300
German Police	1/71
Trawniki	250

Our losses: 1 Policeman
                – wounded yesterday, died from wounds.
Termination of today's large-scale action: 2200 hours.
    Will be continued on 2 May 1943, 1000 hours.

          The SS and Police Fuehrer in the District of Warsaw
          signed: Stroop
          SS-Brigadefuehrer and Majorgeneral of Police
certified copy: SS-Sturmbannfuehrer

Copy   Teletype message
      From: The SS and Police Fuehrer in the District of Warsaw
                           Warsaw, 2 May 1943

    Ref. No. I ab St/Gr 16 07 – Journal No. 584/43 secret
    Re: Large-scale Ghetto operation
    To: The Higher SS and Police Fuehrer East
        SS-Obergruppenfuehrer and General of Police
        Krueger – or deputy
        Cracow

Progress of large-scale operation on 2 May 1943, start 1000 hrs: 9 raiding parties combed out the whole area of the former Ghetto; moreover a larger detachment was detailed to clean out or destroy one block of buildings grouped around the two armament enterprises Transavia and Wischniewski. To find more dug-outs, the raiding parties took along with them some Jews caught on the previous day to act as guides. In these operations the raiding parties pulled out 944 Jews from dug-outs; 235 more Jews were shot on this occasion. When the block of buildings mentioned above was destroyed 120 Jews were caught and numerous Jews were destroyed when they jumped from the attics to the inner courtyards, trying to escape the flames. Many more Jews perished in the flames or were destroyed when the dug-outs and sewer entrances were blown up. The Jews were removed from two armaments concerns and the managers were requested to evacuate within a short time.

Altogether we caught today: 1,852 Jews.

The sum total of Jews caught thereby rises to 40,237 Jews. 27 dugouts were discovered, forcibly opened and destroyed, arms and ammunition captured. When the external barricade was shot at and when some Jews who broke out from a sewer entrance outside the Ghetto made an attack, we suffered 7 losses, 4 Policemen and 3 Polish Policemen. The scouting parties used during the night encountered armed resistance from some Jews who under the protection of darkness ventured to emerge from their holes and dug-outs. We did not suffer losses thereby. On the other hand, a considerable number of Jews were killed or wounded in this operation.

Our Strength:

Used in operation:

German Police	3/98
Engineering Em. Service	1/6
Security Police	3/12
Engineers (Wehrmacht)	2/37
SS-Gren.	11/409
SS-Cav.	3/7

Cordoning forces:

German Police	2/9
SS-Gren.	1/300
Trawniki	200

Our losses: 4 Policemen wounded

3 Polish policemen wounded

Present at today's large-scale operation was the Higher SS and Police Fuehrer East, SS-Obergruppenfuehrer and General of Police Krueger. Termination of operation: 2030 hours. Will be continued on 3 May 1943, 0900 hours.

> The SS and Police Fuehrer in the District of Warsaw
> signed: Stroop
> SS-Brigadefuehrer and Majorgeneral of Police
certified copy: SS-Sturmbannfuehrer

Copy   Teletype message
          From: The SS and Police Fuehrer in the District of Warsaw
                                        Warsaw, 3 May 1943

Ref. No. I ab St/Gr 16 07 – Journal No. 597/43 secret
Re: Large-scale Ghetto operation
To: The Higher SS and Police Fuehrer East
    SS-Obergruppenfuehrer and General of Police
    Krueger – or deputy
    Cracow

Progress of large-scale operation on 3 May 1943, start 0900 hrs. In the combing-out of the former Jewish Ghetto today 19 more dug-outs were discovered and the result was as follows:

Pulled out of dug-outs	1,392 Jews
Shot	95
Evacuated from former armament factories	177

The sum total of Jews caught thereby rises to 41,806 Jews. In most cases the Jews offered armed resistance before they left the dug-outs. We had two casualties (wounded). Some of the Jews and bandits fired pistols from both hands. Since we discovered several times today that Jewesses had pistols concealed in their bloomers, every Jew and bandit will be ordered, from today on, to strip completely for the search. We captured among other things, one German rifle, model 98, two 08 pistols and other calibers, also homemade hand grenades. The Jews cannot be induced to leave their dug-outs until several smoke candles have been burned. According to depositions made yesterday and today, the Jews were asked during the second half of 1942 to erect air raid shelters. At that time under the camouflage of erecting air-raid shelters, they began to build the dug-outs which they are now inhabiting, in order to use them for an anti-Jewish operation. Some of the scouting parties used in the Ghetto were shot at last night. One casualty (wounded). These scouting parties reported that groups of armed bandits marched through the Ghetto.

Strength: as on the previous day.

Losses: 3 SS-men wounded.

Termination of today's operation: 2100 hrs.

Will be continued on 4 May 1943, 0900 hrs.

3,019 Jews were loaded.

The SS and Police Fuehrer in the District of Warsaw

signed: Stroop

SS-Brigadefuehrer and Majorgeneral of Police

certified copy: SS-Sturmbannfuehrer

Copy   Teletype message

From: The SS and Police Fuehrer in the District of Warsaw

Warsaw, 4 May 1943

Ref. No. I ab St/Gr 16 07 – Journal No. 603/43 secret

Re: Large-scale Ghetto operation

To: The Higher SS and Police Fuehrer East

SS-Obergruppenfuehrer and General of Police

Krueger – or deputy

Cracow

Progress of large-scale operation on 4 May 1943, start 0900 hrs.

For mopping up the dug-outs a raiding party was used, 1/60 strong and reinforced by an Engineers' detachment provided by the Wehrmacht. This raiding party pulled 550 Jews out of dug-outs and killed in battle 188 Jews. Discovering the dug-outs becomes more and more difficult. Often they can only be discovered by betrayal through other Jews. If the Jews are requested to leave their dug-out voluntarily, they hardly ever obey; they can only be forced to do so by the use of smoke candles.

The main forces were detailed about 1100 hours to comb out, mop up, and destroy two large blocks of buildings containing the former firms Toebbens, Schultz and Co., and others. After these blocks had been completely cordoned off, we requested the Jews who were still within the buildings to come forward voluntarily. By this measure, we caught 456 Jews for evacuation. Not until the blocks of buildings were well aflame and were about to collapse did a further considerable number of Jews emerge, forced to do so by the flames and the smoke. Time and again the Jews try to escape even through burning buildings. Innumerable Jews whom we saw on the roofs during the conflagration perished in the flames. Others emerged from the upper stories in the last possible moment and were only able to escape death in the flames by jumping down. Today we caught a total of 2,283 Jews, of whom 204 were shot and innumerable Jews were destroyed in dug-outs and in the flames. The sum total of Jews caught rises to 44,089.

As is learned from depositions made by the Jews, today we caught part of the governing body of the so-called "Party." One member of the committee which leads the gang will be used tomorrow for mopping up some more fortified dug-outs with armed Jews inside. When the armament enterprises were moved it was again determined that instead of valuable military equipment, as had been pretended, trifles, like used furniture and other requisitioned items were moved. We took appropriate measures against this at once.

The scouting parties who patrolled during the night in the former Ghetto again reported movements of the Jews in the burned out and destroyed streets and courtyards. In order to be better able to take the Jews by surprise, the scouting parties at night tie rags and other stuff round their shoes. In skirmishes between the scouting parties and Jews, 30 Jews were shot.

We captured 1 carbine, 3 pistols, and some ammunition. During the conflagration a considerable amount of stored ammunition exploded.

Our strength:

Used in operation:

German Police	4/101	
Engineering Em. Service	1/6	
Security Police	2/14	
Engineers	2/41	
Waffen SS	11/407	
Cordoning forces:	Day	Night
German Police	2/87	1/11

Waffen SS	25	1/300
Trawniki	200	
Polish Police	1/180	1/180

Our losses: None.

Termination of operation: 2330 hours; will be continued on 5 May 1943, 1000 hours.

The SS and Police Fuehrer in the District of Warsaw
signed: Stroop
SS-Brigadefuehrer and Majorgeneral of Police
certified copy: SS-Sturmbannfuehrer

Copy   Teletype message

From: The SS and Police Fuehrer in the District of Warsaw

Warsaw, 5 May 1943

Ref. No. I ab St/Gr 16 07 – Journal No. 607/43 secret
Re: Large-scale Ghetto operation
To: The Higher SS and Police Fuehrer East
  SS-Obergruppenfuehrer and General of Police
  Krueger – or deputy
  Cracow

Progress of large-scale operation on 5 May 1943. Start 1000 hrs. In the beginning of today's operations the raiding parties seemed to have less results than on the preceding days. When the operation terminated, however, quite a number of dug-outs had again been discovered, owing to the tracking ability of the men and to betrayal; 40 of these dug-outs were caught (1070 altogether). The combing out patrols shot about 126 Jews. Today again the Jews resisted in several places until they were captured. In several cases the entrances (hatches) of the dug-outs were forcibly held or bolted from the inside, so that only by using a strong explosive charge could we force them open and destroy the inmates. Today, we again captured arms and ammunition, including one pistol. From one enterprise still in existence (so-called Prosta) 2,850 Jews were caught for evacuation. This figure was included in the sum total reported earlier, so that only 1,070 have to be added; the present sum total therefore is 45,159.

    Our strength: as on the preceding day.

    Our losses: 1 SS man wounded, 1 Policeman wounded.

    Sum total of losses to date: 8 dead, 55 wounded.

Termination of operation: 2200 hrs. Will be continued on 6 May 1943, 0900 hrs.

               The SS and Police Fuehrer in the District of Warsaw

               signed: Stroop

               SS-Brigadefuehrer and Majorgeneral of Police

certified copy: SS-Sturmbannfuehrer

Copy   Teletype message

       From: The SS and Police Fuehrer in the District of Warsaw

                          Warsaw, 6 May 1943

    Ref. No. I ab St/Gr 16 07 – Journal No. 614/43 secret

    Re: Ghetto large-scale operation

    To: The Higher SS and Police Fuehrer East

      SS-Obergruppenfuehrer and General of Police

      Krueger – or deputy

      Cracow

Progress of large-scale operation on 6 May 1943, start 0930 hrs.

    Today we combed especially these blocks of buildings which were destroyed by fire on 4 May 1943. Although it was hardly to be expected that any living person could still exist in these blocks we discovered quite a number of dug-outs in which a burning heat had developed. From those dug-outs which we discovered in other parts of the Ghetto, we pulled out 1,553 Jews. While resisting, and in a skirmish, 356 Jews were shot. In this skirmish the Jews fired from 08 pistols and other calibers and threw Polish "pineapple" hand grenades. One SS Unterscharfuehrer was wounded and a total of 47 dug-outs were destroyed.

Two men of the external cordoning forces were wounded. The Jews who had broken out from the Ghetto seem to be returning now with the intention of assisting the Ghetto Jews' force or liberating them. One Jew who had escaped from Lublin was caught just outside of the Ghetto wall. He was armed as follows: 1 08 pistol, ample reserve ammunition, 2 Polish "pineapple" hand grenades. It could not be reliably ascertained so far whether the so-called "Party Directorate" of the Jews ("PPR") have been caught or destroyed. We are on their traces. It is to be hoped that tomorrow we shall succeed in tracing down this so-called Party Directorate. In order to enable us to intercept more effectively the Jews and bandits who approach the Ghetto, covering detachments of the external barricade were shifted farther inside the Aryan part. The former miniature Ghetto "Prosta" was searched by raiding parties today. We caught some Jews who had stayed behind. The firm Toebbens was requested to evacuate this miniature Ghetto by noon on 10 May 1943. The so-called Library, situated outside the Ghetto, was put at their disposal for temporary storage of their raw materials, etc.

The sum total of Jews caught so far rises to 47,068. The Polish Police take pains to deliver to my office every Jew who turns up within the city, because they are eager to win such premiums as have been paid in earlier cases. The undersigned received some anonymous letters in which he was notified of the fact that some Jews are staying in the Aryan part of the city. One anonymous letter draws a parallel between Katyn and the large-scale action within the Ghetto.

Our Strength:

Used in operation:

German Police		4/101
Engineering Em. Service		1/6
Security Police		2/14
Engineers		3/72
Waffen SS		10/500
Cordoning forces:	<u>Day</u>	<u>Night</u>
German Police	2/87	1/11
Waffen SS	25	1/300

Trawniki	200	
Polish Police	1/180	1/180
Our Losses:	1 Policeman	dead
	1 "	seriously wounded
	1 SS Unterscharfuehrer	
		less seriously wounded

Termination of Operation: 2100 hours; will be continued on 7 May 1943, 0930 hours.

> The SS and Police Fuehrer in the District of Warsaw
> signed: Stroop
> SS-Brigadefuehrer and Majorgeneral of Police

certified copy: SS-Sturmbannfuehrer

Copy   Teletype message

From: The SS and Police Fuehrer in the District of Warsaw

Warsaw, 7 May 1943

Ref. No. I ab St/Gr 16 07 – Journal No. 616/43 secret

Re: Large-scale Ghetto operation

To: The Higher SS and Police Fuehrer East
  SS-Obergruppenfuehrer and General of Police
  Krueger – or deputy
  Cracow

Progress of large-scale operation on 7 May 1943, start 1000 hrs.

The combing-out parties today obtained the following results: 49 dug-outs discovered. Part of the Jews were caught. A considerable, not ascertainable, number of Jews who refused to leave the dug-outs and offered armed resistance were destroyed when the dug-outs were blown up. Altogether 1,019 Jews were caught alive today, 255 shot. The sum total of Jews caught so far rises to 48,342. Today we again encountered armed resistance in several cases, whereby we lost 1 SS man (wounded). We captured 4 pistols of various calibers and some stores of ammunition.

The location of the dug-out used by the so-called select "Party Directorate" is now known. It is to be forced open tomorrow. The Jews testify that they emerge at night to get fresh air, since it is unbearable to stay permanently within the dug-outs owing to the long duration of the operation. On average the raiding parties shoot 30 to 50 Jews each night. From these statements it was to be inferred that a considerable number of Jews are still underground in the Ghetto. Today we blew up a concrete building which we had not been able to destroy by fire. In this operation we learned that the blowing up of a building is a very lengthy process and takes an enormous amount of explosives. The best and only method for destroying the Jews therefore still remains the setting of fires.

Our strength: as on the preceding day.

Our losses: 1 Waffen-SS man wounded.

Termination of Operation: 2100 hours. Will be continued on 8 May 1943, 1000 hours.

> The SS and Police Fuehrer in the District of Warsaw
> signed: Stroop
> SS-Brigadefuehrer and Majorgeneral of Police

certified copy: SS-Sturmbannfuehrer

Copy   Teletype message
From: The SS and Police Fuehrer in the District of Warsaw
                                    Warsaw, 8 May 1943

Ref. No. I ab St/Gr 16 07 – Journal No. 624/43 secret
Re: Large-scale Ghetto operation
To: The Higher SS and Police Fuehrer East
    SS-Obergruppenfuehrer and General of Police
    Krueger – or deputy
    Cracow

Progress of operation on 8 May 1943, start 1000 hours.

The whole former Ghetto was searched today by raiding parties for the remaining dug-outs and Jews. As reported some days a number of subhumans, bandits, and terrorists still remain in the dug-outs, where heat has become intolerable by reason of the fires. These creatures know only too well that their only choice is between remaining in hiding as long as possible or coming to the surface and trying to wound or kill off the men of the Waffen-SS, Police, and Wehrmacht who keep up the pressure against them.

We continued today the operation against the dug-out of the so-called select "Party Directorate" which we had discovered yesterday, as reported in my teletype message yesterday. We succeeded in forcing open the dug-out of the Party Directorate and in catching about 60 heavily armed bandits. We succeeded in catching and liquidating Deputy Leader of the Jewish Military Organization "ZWZ" and his so-called Chief of Staff. There were about 200 Jews in this dug-out, of whom 60 were caught and 140 were destroyed, partly owing to the strong effect of smoke-candles, and partly owing to heavy explosive charges which were laid in several places. The Jews whom we caught had already reported that innumerable Jews had been killed by the effect of the smoke-candles. The fight of the first six days was hard, but now we are able to state that we are catching those Jews and Jewesses who were the ringleaders in those days. Every time a dug-out is forced open, the Jews in it offer resistance with the arms at their disposal, light machine guns, pistols, and hand grenades. Today we again caught quite a number of Jewesses who carried loaded pistols in their bloomers, with the safety catch released. Some depositions speak of 3 to 4,000 Jews who still remain in underground holes, sewers, and dug-outs. The undersigned is resolved not to terminate the large-scale operation until the last Jew has been destroyed.

A total of 1,001 Jews were caught today in dug-outs; about 2,800 Jews were shot in battle, innumerable Jews were destroyed in the 43 dug-outs which were blown up. The sum total of Jews caught has risen to 40,712. The buildings which had not yet been destroyed by fire, were set on fire today and we discovered that a few Jews were still hiding somewhere within the walls or in the staircases.

     Our strength:

        Used in operation:

           German Police   4/101

	Day	Night
Engineering Em. Service	1/6	
Security Police	2/14	
Engineers	3/69	
Waffen SS	13/527	
Cordoning forces:	Day	Night
German Police	1/87	1/36
Waffen SS	–	1/300
Trawniki	160	–
Polish Police	1/160	1/160

Our losses: 2 Waffen SS dead

2 Waffen SS wounded

1 Engineer wounded

A Policeman wounded on 7 May 1943 died today from wounds. We captured about 15 to 20 pistols of various calibers, considerable stores of ammunition for pistols and rifles, moreover a number of hand grenades, made in the former armament factories.

Termination of action: 2130 hours; will be continued on 9 May 1943, 1000 hours.

The SS and Police Fuehrer in the District of Warsaw

signed: Stroop

SS-Brigadefuehrer and Majorgeneral of Police

certified copy: SS-Sturmbannfuehrer

Copy   Teletype message

From: The SS and Police Fuehrer in the District of Warsaw

Warsaw, 9 May 1943

Ref. No. I ab St/Gr 16 07 – Journal No. 625/43 secret

Re: Large-scale Ghetto operation

To: The Higher SS and Police Fuehrer East

SS-Obergruppenfuehrer and General of Police

Krueger – or deputy

Cracow

Progress of large-scale operation on 9 May 1943, start 1000 hours.

The operation carried out today had the following result: The raiding parties at work today discovered 42 dug-outs. From these dug-outs we pulled out alive 1,037 Jews and bandits. In battle 319 bandits and Jews were shot, moreover an uncertain number were destroyed when the dug-outs were blown up. The block of buildings which formerly contained the "Transavila" concern was destroyed by fire; in this operation we again caught a number of Jews, although this block had been combed through several times.

Again we captured some pistols and hand grenades.

Our strength:

Used in operation:

German Police		4/103
Security Police		2/12
Engineers		3/67
Waffen SS		13/547

Cordoning forces:	Day	Night
German Police	1/87	1/36
Waffen SS	–	1/300
Trawniki	160	–
Polish Police	1/160	1/160

Our losses: none.

The total of Jews caught up to date has risen to 51,313. Outside the former Ghetto 254 Jews and bandits were shot. Termination of operation: 2100 hours; will be continued on 10 May 1943, 1000 hours.

The SS and Police Fuehrer in the District of Warsaw
signed: Stroop
SS-Brigadefuehrer and Majorgeneral of Police
certified copy: SS-Sturmbannfuehrer

Copy   Teletype message
From: The SS and Police Fuehrer in the District of Warsaw
Warsaw, 10 May 1943

Ref. No. I ab St/Gr 16 07 – Journal No. 627/43 secret
Re: Large-scale Ghetto operation
To: The Higher SS and Police Fuehrer East
    SS-Obergruppenfuehrer and General of Police
    Krueger – or deputy
    Cracow

Progress of large-scale action on 10 May 1943, start 1000 hrs.

Today raiding parties again combed out the area of the former Ghetto. As on preceding days we again pulled out of the dug-outs, against all expectations, a considerable number of Jews. The resistance offered by the Jews had not weakened today. In contrast to the previous days, it seems that those members of the main body of the Jewish battle group who are still in existence and have not been destroyed have retired into the ruins still within their reach, with the intention of firing from there against our men and inflicting casualties.

Today we caught a total of 1,183 Jews alive, 187 bandits and Jews were shot. Again a not ascertainable number of Jews and bandits were destroyed in the blown-up dug-outs. The total of Jews caught up to date has risen to 52,683.

Today at 0900 hours a truck drove up to a certain sewer in the so-called Prosta. Someone in the truck exploded two hand grenades, which was the signal for the bandits who were standing ready in the sewer to climb out of it. The bandits and Jews – there are always some Polish bandits among them – armed with carbines, small arms, and one machine gun, climbed into the truck and drove away in an unknown direction. The last man of the gang, who stood sentry in the sewer and had the duty of closing the sewer lid, was captured. It is he who gave the above information. He testified that most of the members of the gang, which had been divided into several battle groups, had either been killed in battle or had committed suicide because they had realized the futility of continuing the fight. The search for the truck, which was ordered at once, had no results. The bandits testified further that the Prosta is now the refuge for the still existing Jews because the Ghetto has become too hot for them. For this reason,

I resolved to deal with the Prosta in the same manner as with the Ghetto, and to destroy this miniature Ghetto.

Today, we again captured small arms and some ammunition. The Security Police yesterday succeeded in capturing a workshop outside the Ghetto which manufactured 10 to 11,000 explosive charges and other ammunition.

Our strength: as on the preceding day.

Our losses: 3 SS men wounded.

Owing to the excellent understanding between us and the Wehrmacht, the detachment of Engineers was reinforced. Moreover, a considerable amount of explosives was put at our disposal.

Termination of operation 2200 hours; will be continued on 11 May 1943, 0930 hours.

> The SS and Police Fuehrer in the District of Warsaw
> signed: Stroop
> SS-Brigadefuehrer and Majorgeneral of Police

certified copy: SS-Sturmbannfuehrer

Copy　　　　　　　　　　Teletype message
From: The SS and Police Fuehrer in the District of Warsaw
Warsaw, 11 May 1943

> Ref. No. I ab St/Gr 16 07 – Journal No. 629/43 secret
> Re: Ghetto large-scale operation
> To: The Higher SS and Police Fuehrer East
> 　SS-Obergruppenfuehrer and General of Police
> 　Krueger – or deputy
> 　Cracow

Progress of large-scale operation on 11 May 1943, start 0930 hours.

The scouting parties sent out last night again reported that there must still be some Jews within the dug-outs, since some Jews were seen in the ruined streets. The scouting parties formed raiding parties who in combing-out operations discovered, captured, and destroyed a total of 47 dug-outs. Today again we caught some Jews who had taken refuge in ruins which were still protected by a roof. The Jews and bandits are still seeking this new refuge, because staying in the dug-outs has become unbearable. One dug-out was discovered which contained about 12 rooms equipped with plumbing, running water, and separate bathrooms for men and women. Considerable amounts of food were captured or secured, in order to make it more and more difficult for them to get necessary food.

A total of 931 Jews and bandits were caught. 53 bandits were shot. More of them perished when dug-outs were blown up and when a small block of buildings was destroyed by fire. The total of Jews caught up to date has risen to 53,667. We captured several pistols, hand grenades, and ammunition. We have not been able to smoke out the sewers systematically, since we are short of smoke-candles. "OFK" is ready to provide new smoke-candles.

Our strength:

Used in operation:

German Police		6/126
Engineering Em. Service		1/6
Security Police		2/14
Engineers		4/76
Waffen SS		12/308
Cordoning forces:	<u>Day</u>	<u>Night</u>
German Police	1/112	1/80
Waffen SS	–	1/130
Trawniki	160	–
Polish Police	1/160	1/160

Our losses: 1 SS man wounded.

Total of losses up to date: 71 wounded, 12 dead.

Termination of today's operation: 2145 hours; will be continued on 12 May 1943, 0930 hours.

The SS and Police Fuehrer in the District of Warsaw
signed: Stroop
SS-Brigadefuehrer and Majorgeneral of Police
certified copy: SS-Sturmbannfuehrer

Copy   Teletype message
From: The SS and Police Fuehrer in the District of Warsaw
Warsaw, 12 May 1943

Ref. No. I ab St/Gr 16 07 – Journal No. 637/43 secret
Re: Large-scale Ghetto operation
To: The Higher SS and Police Fuehrer East
  SS-Obergruppenfuehrer and General of Police
  Krueger – or deputy
  Cracow

Progress of large-scale operation on 12 May 1943, start 0930 hours.

When the raiding parties combed out the area for remaining dug-outs, in which Jews were hiding, they succeeded in discovering 30 dug-outs. 663 Jews were pulled out of them and 133 Jews were shot. The sum total of Jews caught has risen to 54,463.

Furthermore today the units cordoning off the miniature Ghetto were reinforced and destroyed by fire. Probably a considerable number of Jews perished in the flames. No accurate information in this regard could be obtained since the fire was still burning when darkness set in. One concrete building in the Prosta, from which Jews have been removed, was heavily damaged by blowing-up operations in order to make it impossible for the bandits to use it as a base later.

It is noteworthy that the Poles, without having been warned, took appropriate measures for protecting their window-panes, etc., before the blowing-up started.

The transports of Jews leaving here will be directed to T.II beginning today.

Our strength:
  Used in operation:

German Police	5/126
Engineering Em. Service	1/6
Security Police	2/14

Engineers		4/74
Waffen SS		12/508
Cordoning forces:	<u>Day</u>	<u>Night</u>
German Police	1/112	1/86
Waffen SS	–	1/300
Trawniki	160	–
Polish Police	1/160	1/160

Our losses: 1 Waffen SS man wounded.

Termination of today's operation: 2100 hours; will be continued on 13 May 1943, 1000 hours.

> The SS and Police Fuehrer in the District of Warsaw
> signed: Stroop
> SS-Brigadefuehrer and Majorgeneral of Police

certified copy: SS-Sturmbannfuehrer

Copy   Teletype message

From: The SS and Police Fuehrer in the District of Warsaw

Warsaw, 13 May 1943

Ref. No. I ab St/Gr 16 07 – Journal No. 641/43 secret

Re: Large-scale Ghetto operation

To: The Higher SS and Police Fuehrer East

SS-Obergruppenfuehrer and General of Police

Krueger – or deputy

Cracow

Progress of large-scale operation on13 May 1943, start 1000 hours.

In combing out the Ghetto and the miniature Ghetto (Prosta) today we found 234 Jews. 155 Jews were shot in battle. Today it became clear that the Jews and bandits whom we are catching now belong to the so-called battle groups. All of them are young fellows and females between 18 and 25 years of age. When we captured one, a real skirmish took place, in which the Jews not only fired from 08 pistols and Polish Vis pistols, but also threw

Polish "Pineapple" hand grenades at the Waffen-SS men. After part of the inmates of the dug-out had been caught and were about to be searched, one of the females as quick as lightning put her hand under her shirt, as many others had done, and fetched from her bloomers a "Pineapple" hand grenade, drew the safety-catch, threw the grenade among the men who were searching her, and jumped quickly to cover. It is only thanks to the presence of mind of the men that no casualties ensued.

The few Jews and criminals still staying in the Ghetto have for the last few days been using the hide-outs they can still find among the ruins, retiring at night into the dug-outs whose location is known to them, to eat and get provisions for the next day. Lately we have been unable to extract information on the whereabouts of further dug-outs from the captured Jews. The remainder of the inmates of that dug-out where the skirmish took place were destroyed by using heavier explosive charges. From a Wehrmacht concern we evacuated 327 Jews today. The Jews we catch now are sent to T.II.

The total of Jews caught has risen to 55,179.

Our strength:

Used in operation:

German Police	4/182
Engineering Em. Service	1/6
Security Police	2/14
Engineers	4/74
Waffen SS	12/517

Cordoning forces:

	Day	Night
German Police	1/137	1/87
Waffen SS	–	1/300
Trawniki	270	–
Polish Police	1/160	1/160

Our losses: 2 Waffen SS man dead
3 Waffen SS wounded
1 Policeman wounded

The 2 Waffen SS men lost their lives in the air attack against the Ghetto.

33 dug-outs were discovered and destroyed. Booty: 6 pistols, 2 hand grenades, and some explosive charges.

Termination of today's operation 2100 hours, will be continued on 14 May 1943, 1000 hours.

My intention is to terminate the large-scale operation of 16 May 1943 and to turn all further measures over to Police battalion III/23. Unless ordered otherwise, I am going to submit to the conference of SS and Policefuehrers a detailed report of the operation, including an appendix containing photos.

The SS and Police Fuehrer in the District of Warsaw
signed: Stroop
SS-Brigadefuehrer and Majorgeneral of Police

certified copy: SS-Sturmbannfuehrer

———————————————

Copy   Teletype message
From: The SS and Police Fuehrer in the District of Warsaw
Warsaw, 14 May 1943

Ref. No. I ab St/Gr 16 07 – Journal No. 646/43 secret
Re: Large-scale Ghetto operation
To: The Higher SS and Police Fuehrer East
  SS-Obergruppenfuehrer and General of Police
  Krueger – or deputy
  Cracow

Progress of large-scale operation on 14 May 1943, start 1000 hours.

The raiding parties formed today went to work within the areas allotted to each of them under orders to force open further dwelling dug-outs and to catch the Jews. In this way a considerable number of bandits and Jews were caught, especially as some traces had been discovered during the night, which were now followed up with good results. The night patrols clashed with armed bandits several times. These bandits fired a machine gun and small arms. In this operation we had four casualties, 3 Waffen-SS men and 1 Policeman. Repeatedly, shots were fired from the Aryan part against the external barricade. In the skirmishes about 30 bandits were shot and 9 Jews and bandits, members of an armed gang, were captured. One dug-out was taken during the night, the Jews captured, and some pistols, among them one of 12 mm caliber, were captured. In one dug-out inhabited by 100 persons, we were able to capture 2 rifles, 16 pistols, some hand grenades and incendiary appliances. Of the bandits who resisted, some again wore German military uniform, German steel helmets and "Knobelbecher" [Jackboots]. Apart from the carbines, we captured 60 rounds of German rifle ammunition. One raiding party had a skirmish with a gang, 10 to 14 strong, on the roofs of a block of buildings at the border of the Ghetto (Aryan part). The bandits were destroyed; we suffered no losses.

The captured bandits repeatedly testify that still not all persons in the Ghetto have been caught. They confidently expect that the action will soon be over, and that they will then be able to continue to live in the Ghetto. Several bandits stated that they had long been in a position to kill off the leader of the action, the "General," as they call him, but that they would not do so, since they had orders to that effect to avoid the risk of a further intensification of the anti-Jewish measures.

Today again some concrete buildings in which the bandits find refuge time and again were blown up by the engineers.

In order to force the bandits in the sewers to come to the surface, 183 sewer entrances were opened at 1500 hours, and smoke-candles were lowered into them at an ordered x-time; thereupon the bandits, seeking escape from what they supposed to be poison gas, crowded together in the center of the former Ghetto, and we were able to pull them out of the sewer entrances there.

I shall come to a decision after tomorrow's operations regarding termination of the action.

Today SS Gruppenfuehrer and Lieutenant General of Waffen-SS von Horff was present during the operations.

Our strength:

Used in operation:

German Police	4/182
Engineering Em. Service	1/6
Security Police	2/16

Engineers		4/73
Waffen SS		12/510
Cordoning forces:	<u>Day</u>	<u>Night</u>
German Police	2/138	1/84
Waffen SS	–	1/300
Trawniki	270	–
Polish Police	1/160	1/160

Our losses: 5 wounded, 4 Waffen SS, 1 Police

A total of 398 Jews were caught today, furthermore 154 Jews and bandits were shot in battle. The total of the Jews caught has risen to 55,731.

Booty: rifles, pistols, and ammunition. Further, a number of incendiary bottles (Molotov cocktails).

Termination of action: 2115 hours; will be continued on 15 May 1943 0900 hours.

The SS and Police Fuehrer in the District of Warsaw
signed: Stroop
SS-Brigadefuehrer and Majorgeneral of Police
certified copy: SS-Sturmbannfuehrer

Copy   Teletype message
From: The SS and Police Fuehrer in the District of Warsaw
Warsaw, May 15th 1943

Ref. No. I ab St/Gr 16 07 – Journal No. 648/43 secret
Re: Large-scale Ghetto operation
To: The Higher SS and Police Fuehrer East
  SS-Obergruppenfuehrer and General of Police
  Krueger – or deputy
  Cracow

Progress of large-scale operation on 15 April 1943, start 0900 hours.

The 5 scouting parties who patrolled the Ghetto last night reported that they encountered Jews only sporadically. In contrast to the preceding night, they were able to shoot 6 or 7 Jews. The combing-out actions today also had little result, 29 more dug-outs were discovered; but part of them were no longer inhabited. A total of 87 Jews were caught today and 67 bandits and Jews were shot in battle. In a skirmish which developed around noon, and in which the bandits again resisted by using Molotov cocktails, pistols, and home-made hand grenades, the gang was destroyed; but subsequently a Policeman was wounded by a shot thought the right thigh. A special unit once more searched the last block of buildings which was still intact in the Ghetto, and subsequently destroyed it. In the evening the chapel, mortuary, and all other buildings on the Jewish cemetery were blown up or destroyed by fire.

The sum total of Jews caught has risen to 55,885.

Our strength:

Used in operation:

German Police		4/184
Engineering Em. Service		1/6
Security Police		2/16
Engineers		4/74
Waffen SS		12/510
Cordoning forces:	Day	Night
German Police	2/138	1/87
Waffen SS	–	1/300
Trawniki	270	–
Polish Police	1/160	1/160

Our losses: 1 Policeman wounded.

We captured 4 pistols of larger calibers, 1 infernal machine with fuse, 10 kilograms of explosives, and a considerable amount of ammunition. Termination of operation: 2130 hours. Will be continued on 16 May 1000 hours.

I will terminate the large-scale operation of 16 May 1943 at dusk, by blowing up the Synagogue, which we did not succeed in accomplishing today, and will subsequently charge Police Battalion III/23 with continuing and completing the measures which are still necessary.

The SS and Police Fuehrer in the District of Warsaw
signed: Stroop

SS-Brigadefuehrer and Majorgeneral of Police
certified copy: SS-Sturmbannfuehrer

Copy   Teletype message
From: The SS and Police Fuehrer in the District of Warsaw
                                        Warsaw, May 16th 1943

Ref. No. I ab St/Gr 16 07 – Journal No. 652/43 secret
Re: Large-scale Ghetto operation
To: The Higher SS and Police Fuehrer East
   SS-Obergruppenfuehrer and General of Police
   Krueger – or deputy
   Cracow

Progress of large-scale operation on 16 May 1943, start 1000 hours.

180 Jews, bandits, and subhumans were destroyed. The former Jewish quarter of Warsaw is no longer in existence. The large-scale action was terminated at 2015 hours by blowing up the Warsaw Synagogue.

The measures to be taken with regard to the established banned areas were handed over to the commander of police battalion III/23, whom I instructed carefully.

Total number of Jews dealt with 56,065, including both Jews caught and Jews whose extermination can be proved.

No losses today.

I will submit a final report to the Conference of SS Police Fuehrer on 18 May 1943.

The SS and Police Fuehrer in the District of Warsaw
signed: Stroop
SS-Brigadefuehrer and Majorgeneral of Police
certified copy: SS-Sturmbannfuehrer

Copy   Teletype message
              From: The SS and Police Fuehrer in the District of Warsaw
                                              Warsaw, 24 May 1943

Ref. No. I ab St/Gr 16 07 – Journal No. 663/43 secret
Re: Large-scale Ghetto operation
To: The Higher SS and Police Fuehrer East
    SS-Obergruppenfuehrer and General of Police
    Krueger – or deputy
    Cracow

I beg to reply to the above teletype message:

No. 1:   Of the total of 56,065 caught, about 7,000 were destroyed
in the former Ghetto during the large-scale operation. 6,029 Jews were
destroyed by transporting them to T.II; the sum total of Jews destroyed is
therefore 13,929. Beyond the number of 56,065 an estimated number of
5 to 6,000 Jews were destroyed by being blown up or by perishing in the
flames.

No. 2:   A total of 631 dug-outs were destroyed.

No. 3 (Booty):

                7 Polish rifles, 1 Russian rifle, 1 German rifle,
                59 pistols of various calibers,
                several hundred hand grenades, including Polish and
                home-made ones,
                a few hundred incendiary bottles,
                home-made explosive charges,
                infernal machines with fuses,
                large amounts of explosives, ammunition for all calibers,
                including machine-gun ammunition.

With regard to the bag of arms one must take into consideration that in
most cases we were not able to capture the arms themselves since the Jews
and bandits before they were captured threw them away into hide-outs
and holes which we could not discover or find. The smoke which we had
developed in the dug-outs also prevented our men from discovering and

capturing the arms. Since we had to blow up the dug-outs at once we were not in a position to search for the arms later on.

The hand grenades, explosive charges, and incendiary bottles captured were used at once against the bandits.

Furthermore, we captured:

> 1,240 used uniform tunics (partly with medal ribbons, Iron Cross and East medal),
>
> 600 pairs of used trousers,
>
> pieces of equipment, and German steel-helmets,
>
> 100 horses, 4 of them in the former Ghetto (hearse).

We counted up to 23 May 1943:

> 4.4 million Zloty. We captured moreover about 5 to 6 million Zloty, not yet counted, a considerable amount of foreign currency, including:
>
>> $14,300 in paper,
>>
>> $9,200 in gold,
>
> large amounts of valuables (rings, chains, watches, etc.)

<u>No. 4</u>:   With the exception of 8 buildings (Police barracks, hospital and accommodations for working parties) the former Ghetto has been completely destroyed. Where blowing-up was not carried out, only partition walls are still standing. But the ruins still contain enormous amounts of bricks and scrap material which could be used.

> The SS and Police Fuehrer in the District of Warsaw
> signed: Stroop
> SS-Brigadefuehrer and Majorgeneral of Police

certified copy: SS-Sturmbannfuehrer

Juergen Stroop's Summary Report

The following is an excerpt from SS Brigadefuehrer Juergen Stroop's summary report of the fighting in the Warsaw ghetto, dated May 16, 1943. The English translation of the document is retained in the U.S. National Archives.

It soon became clear, however, that not all dangers had been removed by this confining the Jews to one place. Security considerations required removing the Jews from the city of Warsaw altogether. The first large resettlement action took place in the period from 22 July to 3 October 1948. In this action 310,322 Jews were removed. In January 1943 a second resettlement action was carried out by which altogether 6,500 Jews were affected.

When the Reichsfuehrer SS visited Warsaw in January 1943 he ordered the SS and Police Leader for the District of Warsaw to *transfer to Lublin the armament factories and other enterprises of military importance which were insulated within the Ghetto, including their personnel and machines.* The execution of this transfer order proved to be very difficult, since the managers as well as the Jews resisted in every possible way. The SS and Police Leader thereupon decided to enforce the transfer of the enterprises in a large-scale action which he intended to carry out in three days. The necessary preparation had been taken by my predecessor, who also had given the order to start the large-scale action. I myself arrived in Warsaw on 17 April 1943, 0800 hours, the action itself having started the same day at 0600 hours.

Before the large-scale action began, the limits of the former Ghetto had been blocked by an external barricade in order to prevent the Jews from breaking out. This barricade was maintained from the start to the end of the action and was especially reinforced at night.

When we invaded the Ghetto for the first time, the Jews and the Polish bandits succeeded in repelling the participating units, including tanks and armored cars, by a well-prepared concentration of fire. When I ordered a second attack, about 0600 hours, I distributed the units, separated from each other by indicated lines, and charged them with combing out the whole of the Ghetto, each unit for a certain part. Without firing commencing again, we now succeeded in combing out the blocks according to plan. The enemy was forced to retire from the roofs and elevated bases to the basements, dug-outs and sewers. I ordered to construct a barrier dam below the Ghetto and fill it with water, but the Jews frustrated this plan to a great extent by blowing up the turning-off valves. Late the first day we encountered rather heavy resistance, but it was quickly broken by a special raiding party. In the course of further operations we succeeded in expelling the Jews from their prepared resistance bases, sniper holes, and the like, and in occupying during the 20 and 21 April the greater part of the so-called remainder of the Ghetto, to such a degree that the resistance [that] continued within these blocks could not longer be called considerable.

The main Jewish battle group, mixed with Polish bandits, had already retired during the first and second day to the so-called Muranowski Square. There, it was reinforced by a considerable number of Polish bandits. Its plan was to hold the Ghetto by every means in order to prevent us from invading it. The Jewish and Polish standards were hoisted at the top of a concrete building as a challenge to us. These two standards, however, were captured on the second day of the action by a special raiding party. SS Untersturmfuehrer Dohmke fell in this skirmish with the bandits; he was holding in his hand a hand-grenade which was hit by the enemy and exploded, injuring him fatally.

After only a few days I realized that the original plan had no prospect of success, unless the armament factories and other enterprises of military importance distributed throughout the Ghetto were dissolved. It was therefore necessary to approach these firms and to give them appropriate time for being evacuated and immediately transferred. Thus one of these firms after the other was dealt with, and we very soon deprived the Jews and bandits of their chance to take refuge time and again in these enterprises which were under the supervision of the Armed Forces. In order to decide how much time was needed to evacuate these enterprises, thorough inspections were necessary. The conditions discovered there are indescribable. I cannot imagine a greater chaos than in the Ghetto of Warsaw. The Jews had control of everything, from the chemical substances used in manufacturing explosives to clothing and equipment for the Armed Forces. The managers knew so little of their own shops that the Jews were in a position to produce inside these shops arms of every kind, especially hand grenades, Molotov cocktails, and the like.

Moreover, the Jews had succeeded in fortifying some of these factories as centers of resistance. Such a center of resistance in an Army accommodation office had to be attacked as early as the second day of the action by an Engineer's Unit equipped with flame-throwers and by artillery. The Jews were so firmly established in this shop that it proved to be impossible to induce them to leave it voluntarily; I therefore resolved to destroy this shop the next day by fire.

The managers of these enterprises, which were generally also supervised by an officer of the Armed Forces, could in most cases make no specified statements on their stocks and the whereabouts of these stocks. The statements which they made on the number of Jews employed by them were in every case incorrect. Over and over again we discovered that these labyrinths of edifices belonging to the armament concerns as residential blocks, contained rich Jews who had succeeded in finding accommodations for themselves and their families under the name of "armament workers" and were leading marvelous lives there.

Despite all our orders to the managers to make the Jews leave those enterprises, we found out in several cases that managers simply concealed the Jews by shutting them in, because they expected that the action would be finished within a few days and that they then would be able to continue working with the remaining Jews. According to the statement of arrested Jews, women also seem to have played a prominent part. The Jews are said to have endeavored to keep up good relations with officers and men of the Armed Forces. Carousing is said to have been concluded between Jews and Germans.

The number of Jews forcibly taken out of the buildings and arrested was relatively small during the first few days. It transpired that the Jews had taken to hiding in the sewers and in specially erected dug-outs. Whereas we had assumed during the first days that there were only scattered dug-outs, we learned in the course of the large-scale action that the whole Ghetto was systematically equipped with cellars, dug-outs and passages. In every case those passages and dug-outs were connected with the sewer system. Thus, the Jews were able to maintain undisturbed subterranean traffic. They also used this sewer network for escaping subterraneously into the Aryan part of the City of Warsaw. Continuously, we received reports of attempts of Jews to escape through the sewer holes. While pretending to build air-raid shelters they had been erecting dug-outs within the former Ghetto ever since the autumn of 1942. These were intended to conceal every Jew during the new evacuation action, which they had expected for quite a time and to enable them to resist the invaders in a concerted action. Through poster, handbills, and whisper propaganda, the communistic resistance movement actually brought it about that the Jews entered the dug-outs as soon as the new large-scale operation started. How far their precautions went can be seen from the fact that many of the dug-outs had been skillfully equipped with furnishing sufficient for entire families, washing and bathing facilities, toilets, arms and munition supplies, and food supplies sufficient for several months. There were differently equipped dug-outs for rich and for poor Jews. To discover the individual dug-outs was difficult for the units, as they had been efficiently camouflaged. In many cases, it was possible only through betrayal on the part of the Jews.

When only a few days had passed, it became apparent that the Jews no longer had any intention to resettle voluntarily, but were determined to resist evacuation with all their force and by using all the weapons at their disposal. So-called battle groups had been formed, led by Polish-Bolshevists; they were armed and paid any price asked for available arms.

During the large-scale action we succeeded in catching some Jews who had already been evacuated and resettled in Lublin or Treblinka, but had broken out from there and returned to the Ghetto, equipped with arms and ammunition. Time and again Polish bandits found refuge in the Ghetto and remained there undisturbed, since we had no forces at our disposal to comb out this maze. Whereas it had been possible during the first days to catch considerable numbers of Jews, who are cowards by nature, it became more and more difficult during the second half of the action to capture the bandits and Jews. Over and over again new battle groups consisting of 20 to 30 or more Jewish fellows, 18 to 25 years of age, accompanied by a corresponding number of women, kindled new resistance. These battle groups were under orders to put up armed resistance to the last and if necessary to escape arrest by committing suicide. One such battle group succeeded in mounting a truck by ascending from a sewer in the so-called Prosta, and in escaping with it (about 30 to 35 bandits). One bandit who had arrived with this truck exploded 2 hand grenades, which was the agreed signal for the bandits waiting in the sewer to climb out if it. The bandits and Jews – there were Polish bandits among these gangs armed with carbines, small arms, and in one case a light machine gun – mounted the truck and drove away in an unknown direction. The last member of this gang, who was on guard in the sewer and was detailed to close the lid of the sewer hole, was captured. It was he who gave the above information. The search for the truck was unfortunately without result.

During this armed resistance the women belonging to the battle groups were equipped the same as the men: some were members of the Chaluzim movement. Not infrequently, these women fired pistols with both hands. It happened time and again that these women had pistols or hand grenades (Polish "pineapple" hand grenades) concealed in their bloomers up to the last moment to use against the men of the Waffen SS, Police, or Wehrmacht.

The resistance put up by the Jews and bandits could be broken only by relentlessly using all our force and energy by day and night. *On 23 April 1943 the Reichs Fuehrer SS issued through the Higher SS and Police Fuehrer East at Cracow his order to complete the combing out of the Warsaw Ghetto with the greatest severity and relentless tenacity.* I therefore decided to destroy the entire Jewish residential area by setting every block on fire, including the blocks of residential buildings near the armament works. One concern after the other was systematically evacuated and subsequently destroyed by fire. The Jews then emerged from their hiding places and dug-outs in almost every case. Not infrequently, the Jews stayed in the burning building until, because of the heat and the fear of being burned alive, they preferred to jump down from the upper stories after having thrown mattresses and other upholstered articles into the street from the burning buildings. With their bones broken, they still tried to crawl across the street into blocks of buildings which had not yet been set on fire or were only partly in flames. Some of the Jews changed their hiding places during the night, by moving into the ruins of burnt-out buildings, taking refuge there until they were found by our patrols. Their stay in the sewers also ceased to be pleasant after the first week. Frequently from the street, we could hear loud voices coming through the sewer shafts. Then the men of the Waffen SS, the Police or the Wehrmacht Engineers courageously climbed down the shafts to bring out the Jews, and not infrequently they then stumbled over Jews already dead, or were shot at. It was always necessary to use smoke candles to drive out the Jews. Thus one day we opened 183 sewer entrance holes and at a fixed time lowered candles into them, with the result that the bandits fled from what they believed to be gas to the center of the former Ghetto, where they could then be pulled out of the sewer holes there. A great number of Jews, who could not be counted, were exterminated by blowing up sewers and dug-outs.

The longer the resistance lasted, the tougher the men of the Waffen SS, Police and Wehrmacht became; they fulfilled their duty indefatigably in faithful comradeship and stood together as models and examples of soldiers. Their duty hours often lasted from early morning until late at night. At night, search patrols with rags wound round their feet remained at the heels of the Jews and gave them no respite. Not infrequently they caught and killed Jews who used the night hours for supplementing their stores from abandoned dug-outs and for contacting neighboring groups or exchanging news with them.

Considering that the greater part of the men of the Waffen-SS had only been trained for three to four weeks before being assigned to this action, high credit should be given for the pluck, courage, and devotion to duty which they showed. It must be stated that the Wehrmacht Engineers, too, executed the blowing up of dug-outs, sewers, and concrete building with indefatigability and great devotion to duty. Officers and men of the Police, a large part of whom had already been at the front, again excelled by their dashing spirit.

Only through the continuous and untiring work of all involved did we succeed in catching a total of 65 Jews whose extermination can be proved. To this should be added the number of Jews who lost their lives in explosions or fires but whose numbers could not be ascertained.

During the large-scale operation the Aryan population was informed by posters that it was strictly forbidden to enter the former Jewish Ghetto and that anybody caught within the former Ghetto without a valid pass would be shot. At the same time these posters informed the Aryan population again that the death penalty would be imposed on anybody who intentionally gave refuge to a Jew, especially lodged, supported, or concealed a Jew outside the Jewish residential area.

Permission was granted to the Polish police to pay to any Polish policeman who arrested a Jew within the Aryan part of Warsaw one third of the cash in the Jew's possession. This measure has already produced results.

The Polish population for the most part approved the measures taken against the Jews. Shortly before the end of the large-scale operation, the Governor issued a special proclamation which he submitted to the undersigned for approval before publication to the Polish population; in it he informed them of the reasons for destroying the former Jewish Ghetto by mentioning the assassinations carried out lately in the Warsaw area and the mass graves found in Catyn; at the same time they were asked to assist us in our fight against Communist agents and Jews (see enclosed poster).

The large-scale action was terminated on 16 May 1843 with the blowing up of the Warsaw Synagogue at 2015 hours.

Now, there are no more factories in the former Ghetto. All the goods, raw materials, and machines there have been moved and stored somewhere else. All buildings, etc., have been destroyed. The only exception is the so-called Dzielna Prison of the Security Police, which was exempted from destruction.

III.

Although the large-scale operation has been completed, we have to reckon with the possibility that a few Jews are still living in the ruins of the former Ghetto; therefore, this area must be firmly shut off from the Aryan residential area and be guarded. Police Battalion III/23 has been charged with this duty. This Police Battalion has instructions to watch the former Ghetto, particularly to prevent anybody from entering the former Ghetto, and to shoot immediately anybody found inside the Ghetto without authority.

The Commander of the Police Battalion will continue to receive further direct orders from the SS and Police Fuehrer. In this way, it should be possible to keep the small remainder of Jews there, if any, under constant pressure and to exterminate them eventually. The remaining Jews and bandits must be deprived of any chance of survival by destroying all remaining buildings and refuges and cutting off the water supply.

It is proposed to change the Dzielna Prison into a concentration camp and to use the inmates to remove, collect and hand over for re-use the millions of bricks, the scrap-iron, and other materials.

Warsaw, 16 May 1943

        The SS and Police Fuehrer in the District of Warsaw

        SS Brigadefuehrer and Majorgeneral of Police

Appendix 4

The Wiesbaden Report

Toward the end of World War II, Juergen Stroop was apprehended in west Germany by the American Armed Forces and told to write a report relating his actions in the Warsaw ghetto. The report was dated May 1, 1946. The following is the part of the report dealing with the Warsaw Ghetto Uprising.[1]

In the Warsaw ghetto, which was surrounded by an outer wall, were situated a large number of military industries, each of which was enclosed by an inner wall. These industries were run by German professional staff, who were under the (military) supervision of the German Army. These factories turned out every possible item of German military equipment, supplies and uniforms, and contained huge stores, even of explosives and materials for the manufacture of munitions. The ghetto laborers were furnished with work cards which entitled them to reside in the ghetto and obtain rations. As it later transpired, however, not all bearers of work cards actually went to work. Many of them went into hiding in the ghetto and actually lived well: for one could get practically anything for money – from the finest flour to women's silk stockings. The whole of the Warsaw black market was kept constantly supplied by the ghetto.

---

1   Reprinted with permission from Lazar Litai, **Muranowska 7: The Warsaw Ghetto Rising**.

The fact that the main sewer ducts ran under the ghetto area out to the river Vistula made it extremely difficult to seal off the ghetto completely; for it was by means of these sewers that contact was maintained with the other parts of the city.

In the autumn of 1942, the Jewish authorities ordered the population to build air raid shelters. The people admittedly used the cellars for this purpose, but at the same time they also excavated secret hide-outs underneath the cellars. These hide-outs were joined up by a system of passageways from house to house and leading under the streets, thus forming an extensive communications network that was hidden from the knowledge of the supervisory German authorities. These hide-outs were reinforced and fitted out with sleeping and living quarters, toilets and washrooms. So as to be independent of the city electricity grid, their owners installed their own generators, which in some cases were operated manually. As it later transpired, the underground leaders shared in the planning of these hide-outs with a view to future communications. Large supplies of food, enough to last for as long as six to eight months, were stowed away – thousands of eggs, tins of meat (some produced in Germany), sacks of white flour and dry peas. Some of the hide-outs, particularly those built of concrete, were converted into fortified positions. Home-made bombs, metal pipes filled with explosive charges and Molotov cocktails (incendiary bottles) were manufactured in huge quantities. At a later time German uniforms were used: these were easily obtainable since they were produced in large quantities in the ghetto itself.

We knew nothing of all this till the ghetto operation actually commenced. To my mind the Warsaw revolt was planned inside the ghetto walls. The cooperation of the underground movement is attested to by the fact that during the operation the Polish and Jewish flags were hoisted from time to time on the insurgents' positions. As far as I remember, blue-and-white colors were hoisted, some of them bearing the Star of Zion.

I had only been in Warsaw once before, having stayed there overnight on my way to the East, so that I was unfamiliar with the terrain. In the course of a conversation with the SS and Police commanders of the *Generalgouvernement*, headed by the Commander-in-Chief of SS and Police, Obergrupppenfuehrer Krueger, I learnt that the SS commander in Warsaw, Oberfuehrer Ferdinand von Sammern-Frankenegg, had been ordered by Himmler to evacuate the ghetto completely and liquidate it.

Two days before the commencement of the 1943 operation, I was ordered by General Krueger (whose headquarters were in Krakow) to proceed to Warsaw immediately and take over command of the operation from von Sammern. Upon my arrival in Warsaw, von Sammern told me what it was all about, especially Himmler's orders to liquidate the ghetto and, once it was completely evacuated, to lay out parks and lawns there as quickly as possible. Von Sammern had already drawn up the necessary plans in conjunction with all the authorities concerned. Out of comradeship, I left the commencement of the operation in his hands, on the understanding that I was to take over at some time during the first day.

Hardly had the operation commenced, however – at 8:30 in the morning of the first day – when von Sammern appeared with his adjutant, Hauptmann Kloska (whom I later took as my own adjutant), and reported that the operation could not possibly be carried out as planned. The assault troops, he told me, had retreated from the ghetto with heavy losses, and he proposed asking Krakow for aerial support (low-flying aircraft). I asked von Sammern to wait for me outside the ghetto, leaving Hauptmann Kloska to show me the way about the ghetto, where I had never been before. On my arrival there, I saw the assault forces stationed just outside the ghetto gate; two tanks and two armored vehicles were in flames. On the strength

of the operational plans (details of which had become public knowledge though they were to have been a closely-guarded secret) and
the reports of the unit commanders I was able to form some picture and size up the situation. The request for air support was not
put through. I immediately gave orders that the *Judenrat*, whose
members had remained in the ghetto, be contacted and requested
to send people to all the houses in order to persuade the population
to present themselves at the assembly station (*Umschlagplatz*). Von
Sammern had already instructed the *Judenrat* to this effect, but the
Judenrat had replied that the people no longer were amenable since
they were subject to external influences.

The factory managers were also urged to take part in this operation; they were ordered to transfer all their stocks, machinery and
personal effects of their workers to the railway station adjoining the
assembly point. The manager of the Toebbens plant (I believe that
was the name) was given special authority for the rail transport of
freight that did not come under the jurisdiction of the commander
of the operation.

I deployed the operational forces (for their strength, see the supplement annexed to this report) along either side of the main street,
so as to capture at least this as an initial measure. However, no sooner had they entered through the main gate, than they immediately
came under extremely well-placed and directed fire. This fire came
from every window, cellar and aperture without our being able to see
who was firing. Casualties were immediately reported. The armored
vehicle went up in flames. Bombs and incendiary bottles blocked
any possible advance. As soon as we started mopping up one block
of buildings, they (the insurgents) took up positions in the adjoining buildings. Against some of the positions we were forced to use
anti-aircraft guns. It was only now that we discovered the subterranean defense posts. These underground positions gave the rebels the
decided advantage of remaining invisible to us and of being able to

move about freely from one position to the other, as the need arose, without our observing this. It was two days before we were able to take one particular position – it was here that there appeared the flags I have previously mentioned.

We were now able to determine beyond any shadow of a doubt, that not only were the men armed, but also some of the women, mainly those between the ages of eighteen and thirty. They were dressed in riding breeches and wore helmets, but some wore ordinary clothes. These people were organized in a so-called Chalutz movement, which, I believe, was also called Betar. Many of the women carried loaded pistols hidden in their drawers. In this manner the fighting proceeded till the very end, the battles raging from cellar to rooftop of each house. It was only now that we discovered the huge stores of food.

On the commencement of the operation, SS Reichsfuehrer Himmler had sent me a teletype message instructing me to carry out his orders ruthlessly and destroy the ghetto without fail. But the bombardment carried out by the assault troops proved that it would take years to destroy all the buildings by shelling. In order to prevent the return of undesirable elements and to speed up the demolition process, all the blocks of buildings were set on fire immediately after they were taken, and thus the operation was completed at the end of twenty-eight days. I left a small garrison of police in the ghetto to maintain the situation that had been gained. This force, together with the Polish police, closed down the ghetto.

I feel bound to point out that it was particularly the Polish police forces that performed the duties with which they were charged faultlessly and without reserve. I must further observe that in the course of the operation new military positions were discovered (and also lists of combat units and a plan of defense posts). The inmates of the ghetto repeatedly declared that they would have reported to the assembly stations of their own accord, had not outsiders forced them to resist, frequently at pistol point.

On the completion of the operation, I was appointed SS and Police Commander of the Warsaw district, and ipso facto Chief of Police. I performed my duties stringently but justly.

Brigadefuehrer Major-General Kutscherer, who took over my post in Warsaw, was murdered shortly after he assumed his new duties.

I have compiled this report after three years crammed with outstanding events, from memory alone, and I beg this to be taken into account in case of any errors or omissions.

[Signed] Juergen Stroop

Glossary

Agudat Yisrael. Ultra-orthodox non-Zionist party.

Ahdut Ha'avodah. Zionist Socialist activist political party.

AK, Armia Krajowa. Polish underground army operating under the authority of the Polish government-in-exile.

AL, Armia Ludowa. Polish Communist-dominated underground army.

Akiva. General Zionist youth movement.

Betar-Brith Trumpeldor. The Revisionist Zionist youth movement led by Vladimir Jabotinsky.

Bund. Jewish Socialist anti-Zionist movement in Poland and Lithuania.

Dror. "Freedom"; Socialist Zionist youth movement associated with Hakibbutz Hameuhad in Palestine.

General Zionists. Non-Socialist Zionist party.

Gordonia. Socialist Zionist youth movement associated with Hever Hakvutzot in Palestine.

Hanoar Hatzioni. General Zionist youth movement.

Hashomer Hatzair. Socialist Zionist youth movement with Marxist ideology, associated with Kibbutz Artzi in Palestine.

Hehalutz. Roof organization of Zionist youth movements, not including Betar, in the Histadrut.

Hever Hakvutzot. Kibbutz movement associated with the Labor Party.

Histadrut. General Labor Federation in Palestine dominated by Socialists.

IZL, Irgun Zvai Leumi. "National Military Organization"; military underground in Palestine headed by Jabotinsky.

Kibbutz Artzi. Kibbutz movement of Hashomer Hatzair.

Kibbutz Meuhad. Kibbutz movement associated with the Ahdut Ha'avodah party.

Left Po'alei Zion. Marxist Zionist Socialist political party with orientation toward the Soviet Union, which split from Po'alei Zion.

Masada. Zionist Revisionist youth movement of highschool students in Poland.

Mapai. Labor party of Eretz Yisrael.

PLAN, Polska Ludowa Akcja Niepodoleglosciowa. Polish military underground.

Po'alei Zion. Socialist Zionist party.

PPS, Polska Partia Socjalistyczna. Polish Socialist party.

Revisionists. Zionist party led by Jabotinsky.

ZKN, Zydowski Komitet Narodowy. Jewish National Committee, set up to oversee activity of ZOB.

ZKK, Zydowski Komisja Koordinacyjna. Jewish Coordinating Committee, set up to coordinate between the Bund and ZKN.

ZOB, Zydowska Organizacja Bojowa. Jewish Fighting Organization, led by Mordechai Anielewicz during the uprising.

ZZW, Zydowskie Zwiazek Wojskowi. Jewish Military Organization, led by Pawel Frenkel during the uprising.

Bibliography – Books

Adler, Stanislaw. *In the Warsaw Ghetto 1940–1943*. Jerusalem: Yad Vashem, 1982.

Ainsztein, Reuben. *Jewish Resistance in Nazi-Occupied Eastern Europe*. London: Paul Elek, 1974.

———. *The Warsaw Ghetto Revolt*. New York: Holocaust Library, 1979.

Apfelbaum, Marian. *Retour sur le Ghetto de Varsovie* [Return to the Warsaw Ghetto]. Paris: Editions Odile Jacob, 2002.

Arad, Yitzhak. *Vilna ha-Yehudit be-maavak u-ve-khilayon* [Jewish Vilna in struggle and destruction]. Jerusalem: Yad Vashem, 1976.

Auerbach, Rahel. *Mered Geto Varsha* [The Warsaw Ghetto Uprising]. Tel Aviv: Menora, 1963.

Bader, Yohanan. *Darki le-Tzion 1901–1948* [My road to Zion 1901–1948]. Jerusalem: Jabotinsky Institute, 1999.

Banai, Yaakov. *Hayalim almonim* [Unknown soldiers]. Tel Aviv: Yair Publications, 1989.

Bartoszewski, Wladislaw, and Zofia Lewin, eds. *Righteous among the Nations*. London: Earlscourt Publications, 1969.

Begin, Menahem. *White Nights: The Story of a Prisoner in Russia*. New York: Harper & Row, 1979.

Bender, Sara. *Mul mavet orev: Yehudei Bialystok bemilhemet haolam hashniya.* [Facing death: The Jews of Bialystok in the Second World War]. Tel Aviv: Am Oved, 1997.

Ben-Yeruham, Ch. *Sefer Betar* [The book of Betar]. Tel Aviv: Havaad Lehotzaat Sefer Betar, 1975.

Berlinski, Hersh. *Zichroines* [Remembrances] in *Drei* [Three]. Tel Aviv: Ringelblum Institute, 1966.

Berman, Adolf-Avraham. *Mi-yemei ha-mahteret* [From the days of the underground]. Tel Aviv: Menora, 1971.

Blumental, Nahman, and Yosef Kermish, eds. *Ha-meri ve-ha-mered be-Geto Varsha* [The uprising and the revolt in the Warsaw Ghetto]. Jerusalem: Yad Vashem, 1965.

Borzykowski, Tuvia. *Bein kirot noflim* [Between falling walls]. Tel Aviv: Hakibbutz Hameuhad–Beit Lohamei Hagetaot, 1964. Published in English as *Between Tumbling Walls*. Tel Aviv: Hakibbutz Hameuhad, 1972.

———. *Unter einstuerzenden Mauern* [Yiddish]. Warsaw, 1949.

Carmi, Aharon, and Haim Frimmer. *Min ha-dlikah ha-hi* [From that blaze]. Tel Aviv: Hakibbutz Hameuhad, 1961.

Cohen, Raya. *Bein "sham" le-"khan"* [Between "there" and "here"]. Tel Aviv: Am Oved, 1999.

Czerniaków, Adam. *The Warsaw Diary of Adam Czerniaków*. Edited by Raul Hilberg, Stanislaw Staron, and Josef Kermisz. New York: Stein & Day, 1979.

Donat, Alexander. *The Holocaust Kingdom*. New York: Holocaust Library, 1978.

Dror, Levi, and Yisrael Rosenzweig, eds. *Sefer Hashomer Hatzair* [The book of Hashomer Hatzair]. Vol. 1, 1913–1945. Merhavia: Sifriat Hapoalim, 1956.

Edelman, Marek. *The Ghetto Fights*. New York: American Representation of the General Jewish Workers' Union of Poland, 1946.

Eldad (Sheib), Yisrael. *Ma'aser rishon* [The First Tithe]. Tel Aviv: Hamatmid, 1950.

Eisner, Jack. *The Survivor*. New York: William Morrow & Co., 1980.

Engelkind, Barbara, and Jacek Leociak. *Getto Warszawskie Przewodnik Po Nieistniejacym Miescie* [The Warsaw Ghetto: A guide to a non-existing place]. Warsaw: IFiS PAN, 2001.

Eshkoli, Hava. *Ha-Yishuv ha-Yehudi be-Eretz Yisrael nochah ha-Shoah* [The Jewish Community in the Land of Israel facing the Shoah]. Jerusalem: Yad Yitzhak Ben Zvi, 1993.

Friedman, Philip. *Martyrs and Fighters*. New York: Lancer Books, 1954.

Goldstein, Bernard. *Five Years in the Warsaw Ghetto*. New York: Doubleday and Company, 1961.

———. *The Stars Bear Witness*. New York: Viking Press, 1949.

Gotesfurcht, David, Aharon Richman, and Haim Harari, eds. *Sefer Dror* [The book of Dror]. Ein Harod: Hakibbutz Hameuhad, 1947.

Grayek, Shalom-Stephan. *Shloshah yemei krav* [Three days of combat]. Maarahot, 1972.

Grinshpan-Frimer. *Yameinu hayu haleilot* [Our days were the nights]. Tel Aviv: Hakibbutz Hameuhad–Beit Lohamei Hagetaot, 1984.

Grossman, Hayka. *Anshei ha-mahteret* [The people of the underground]. Tel Aviv: Moreshet and Sifriat Hapoalim, 1965.

Grupinska, Anka. *Shor shor* [Round and round]. Tel Aviv: Hakibbutz Hameuhad, 2002.

Gutman, Yisrael, ed. *Emmanuel Ringelblum: Ha-adam ve-ha-historion*. English ed. *Emmanuel Ringelblum: The Man and the Historian*. Jerusalem: Yad Vashem, 2006.

———. *The Jews of Warsaw 1939–1943: Ghetto, Underground, Revolt*. Bloomington, IN: Indiana University Press, 1989. Originally published as *Yehudei Varsha 1939–1943: Geto, mahteret, mered*. Jerusalem: Yad Vashem, 1976.

———. *Resistance: the Warsaw Ghetto Uprising*. Boston: Houghton Mifflin, 1994.

Gutman, Yisrael, and Shmuel Krakowski. *Unequal Victims: Poles and Jews during World War Two*. New York: Holocaust Library, 1986.

Habas, Bracha. *Michtavim min ha-geta'ot* [Letters from the ghettos]. Tel Aviv: Am Oved, 1943.

Halperin, Adam. *Helka shel Betar ba-Mered ha-Geto* [Betar's part in the Ghetto Uprising], in *Ha-emet al Mered Geto Varsha* [The truth about the Warsaw Ghetto Uprising]. Information Department of Betar Headquarters in Eretz Yisrael, 1946.

Kaczynska, Alicja. *Obok Piekla* [Facing hell]. Gdansk: Marpress, 1993.

Kaplan, Chaim. *Scroll of Agony: The Warsaw Diary of Chaim A. Kaplan*. New York: Collier Books, 1973.

Karski, Jan. *Story of a Secret State*. Boston: Houghton Mifflin, 1945.

Katz, Shmuel. *Jabo*. Tel Aviv: Dvir, 1993.

Kermish, Joseph, ed. *Mered Geto Varsha be-einei ha-oyev: Ha-dochot shel Juergen Stroop* [The Warsaw Ghetto Uprising in the eyes of the enemy: The Juergen Stroop reports]. Jerusalem: Yad Vashem, 1966.

————, ed. *To Live with Honor and to Die with Honor! Selected Documents from the Warsaw Ghetto Underground Archives "O.S." (Oneg Shabbat)*. Jerusalem: Yad Vashem, 1986.

Klein, David. *Mitn Malach ha-Mavet untern orem* [With the Angel of Death under the arm]. Tel Aviv: I.L. Peretz Publishing House, 1968.

Korchak, Reyzel. *Lahavot ba-afar* [Flames in the ashes]. Merhavia: Moreshet and Sifriat Hapoalim, 1965.

Krakowsky, Shmuel. *Lehimah Yehudit be-Polin neged ha-Nazim*. Tel Aviv: Sifriat Hapoalim, 1977.

Kulski, Julian Engeniusz. *Dying, We Live*. New York: Rinehart and Winston, 1979.

Kunert, Andrzej Krzysztof, ed. *Polcy-Zydzi 1939–1945* [Poles-Jews 1939–1945]. Warsaw: Instytut Dziedzictwa Narodowego, 2001.

Kurzman, Dan. *The Bravest Battle: The Twenty-Eight Days of the Warsaw Ghetto Uprising*. New York: G.P. Putnam's Sons, 1976.

Landau, David J. *Caged: The Landau Manuscript*. Australia: The Landau family, 1999. Also published as *Caged: A Story of Jewish Resistance*. Pan Macmillan Australia, 2000.

Lapidot, Yehuda. *Lidata shel mahteret* [Birth of an underground]. Tel Aviv: Brit Hayalei Etzel, 2001.

Lazar Litai, Haim. *Hurban u-mered*. Tel Aviv: Beit Jabotinsky, 1988.

————. *Matzada shel Varsha: Ha-irgun ha-Zvai ha-Yehudi be-Mered Geto Varsha, ZZW* [Masada of Warsaw: The Jewish Military Organization in the Warsaw Ghetto Uprising, ZZW]. Tel Aviv: Jabotinsky Institute 1963.

————. *Muranowska 7: The Warsaw Ghetto Rising*. Tel Aviv: Massada P.E.C. Press, 1966.

Levin, Avraham. *Mipinkaso shel ha-moreh mi "Yehudiya"* [The journal of the teacher from "Yehudiya"] Tel Aviv: Hakibbutz Hameuhad–Beit Lohamei Hagetaot, 1969.

Lewin, Abraham. *A Cup of Tears: A Diary of the Warsaw Ghetto*. New York: Basil Blackwell, Inc., 1989.

Lubetkin, Tzivya. *Biymei chilayon u-mered* [In the days of destruction and revolt]. Tel Aviv: Hakibbutz Hameuhad–Beit Lohamei Hagetaot, 1979.

MacLean, French L. *The Ghetto Men: The SS Destruction of the Jewish Warsaw Ghetto, April–May 1943*. Atglen, PA: Schiffer Publishing, 2001.

Mark, Ber. *Churves dertseilen*. Lodz: 1947.

————. *Der Oifshtand in Varshaver Getto*. Warsaw: 1955.

————. *Powstanie w getcie warszawskim. Czesc druga, Dokumenty i materialy* [The Revolt of the Warsaw Ghetto. Also second part: Documents and materials]. Warsaw: 1963.

————. *Uprising in the Warsaw Ghetto*. New York: Schocken Books, 1975.

————. *Walka in zaglada warszawkiego getta*. Warsaw: 1959.

Mark, Ber, ed. *Tsum tzenten yortog* [On the tenth anniversary]. Warsaw: Jewish Historical Institute, 1953.

Mazor, Michel. *La Cite Engloutie*. Paris: 1955.

Meed, Vladka. *On Both Sides of the Wall*. Beit Lohamei Hagetaot, 1972.

Moczarski, Kazmierz. *Gespraeche mit dem henker* [Conversations with the executioner]. Dusseldorf: Droste Verlag, 1978; also, Frankfurt am Main: Fischer Taschenbuch Verlag, 1982.

Najberg, Arye. *Ha-aharonim* [The last ones]. Tel Aviv: Sifriat Poalim, 1958.

Neustadt, Meilech. *Hurban u-mered shel Yehudei Varsha: sefer eduyot ve-azkarot* [The destruction and revolt of the Jews of Warsaw]. Tel Aviv: The General Federation of Jewish Labor in Palestine, 1947.

Niv, David. *Ma'arachot ha-Irgun ha-Zvai ha-Leumi* [The battles of the Irgun Zvai Leumi]. Part 2. Tel Aviv: Mosad Klausner, 1965.

Porat, Dina. *Hanhagah be-milkud* [A leadership entrapped]. Tel Aviv: Am Oved, 1986.

————. *Me'ever la-gashmi* [Beyond the physical]. Tel Aviv: Am Oved, 2000.

Porat, Dina, and Yehiam Weitz, eds. *Bein Magen David la-tlai ha-tzahov* [Between the Star of David and the yellow badge]. Jerusalem: Yad Vashem, 2002.

Putermilch, Yaakov. *Ba-esh u-va-sheleg* [In fire and in snow]. Tel Aviv: Hakibbutz Hameuhad–Beit Lohamei Hagetaot, 1981.

Rafaeli, Alex. *Dream and Action.* Jerusalem: Private publication, 1993.

Raviv, Yitzhak (Isaac). *Keshet be-anan* [Rainbow in the Cloud]. Jerusalem: Hamercaz Lemoreshet Yerushalayim, 2001.

Reznik, Nisan. *Nitzanim Miafar* [Buds from the ashes]. Jerusalem: Yad Vashem, 2003.

Ringelblum, Emmanuel. *Ktavim aharonim* [Last documents], *Jan. '43–April '44.* Jerusalem: Yad Vashem, 1994.

———. *Notes from the Warsaw Ghetto.* New York: 1958.

———. *"Oneg Shabbat" Selected Documents.* Jerusalem: Yad Vashem, 1987.

Rotem, Simha (Kazik). *Memoirs of a Warsaw Ghetto Fighter.* New Haven, CT: Yale University Press, 1994.

Scheffler, Wolfgang, and Helge Grabnitz. *Der Ghetto-Aufstand Warschau 1943* [The Warsaw Ghetto Uprising 1943]. Munich: Goldman Verlag, 1993.

Schechtman, Joseph. *Fighter and Prophet: The Vladimir Jabotinsky Story.* New York: Thomas Yoseloff, 1961.

Seidman, Hillel. *Yoman Ghetto Varsha* [Warsaw Ghetto Diary]. New York: The Jewish Week, 1957.

Shilansky, Dov. *Hashekhah le-or ha-yom* [Darkness in the light of day]. Jerusalem: Yad Vashem, 2006.

Shpielman, Anshel. *Anshel: Adam ve-lohem* [Anshel: Man and fighter]. Tel Aviv: Yair Publications, 1995.

Shulman, Abraham. *The Case of Hotel Polski.* New York: Holocaust Library, 1982.

Stroop, Juergen. May, 1943. Report on the destruction of the Warsaw Ghetto. Document RG 238/1060 PS. College Park, MD: National Archives and Records Administration.

————. *The Stroop Report: The Jewish Quarter of Warsaw Is No More!* Edited by Sybil Milton. New York: Pantheon Books, 1979.

Tennenbaum-Tamaroff, Mordechai. *Dapim min ha-dlikah* [Pages from the fire]. Jerusalem: Yad Vashem and Beit Lohamei Hagetaot, 1987.

Turkow, Jonas. *Azoi iz es gevehn: churban Varsha* [That is how it was: The destruction of Warsaw]. Buenos Aires: 1948.

————. *In Kamf Farn Leben* [In the battle for life]. Buenos Aires: Central-Farband of Polish Jews in Argentina, 1949.

Walewski, Ryszard. *Jurek.* Tel Aviv: Moreshet and Sifriat Poalim, 1976.

Wdowinski, David. *And We Are Not Saved.* New York: Philosophical Library, 1963.

Weinbaum, Laurence. *A Marriage of Convenience.* New York: Columbia University Press, 1993.

Wood, Thomas A., and Stanislaus M. Jankowski. *The Man Who Tried to Stop the Holocaust.* New York: John Wiley & Sons, 1994.

Wulf, Joseph. *Das Dritte Reich und seine Vollstrecker* [The Third Reich and its executioners]. Berlin: Arani Verlags GmbH, 1961.

————. *Vom Leben, Kampf, und Tod im Ghetto Warschau* [Of life, combat, and death in the Warsaw ghetto]. Bonn: 1958.

Yellin-Mor, Natan. *Shnot ba-terem* [The preceding years]. Tel Aviv: Kinneret, 1990.

Zuckerman, Yitzhak (Antek). *Ba-geto u-va-mered* [In the ghetto and in the revolt]. Tel Aviv: Hakibbutz Hameuhad–Beit Lohamei Hagetaot, 1985.

————. *A Surplus of Memory.* Berkeley, CA: University of California Press, 1993. Published in Hebrew as *Sheva ha-shanim ha-hen 1939–1946* [Those seven years]. Tel Aviv: Hakibbutz Hameuhad–Beit Lohamei Hagetaot, 1990.

Zuckerman, Yitzhak, and Moshe Basok, eds. *Sefer milhamot ha-getaot* [The book of ghetto wars]. Tel Aviv: Hakibbutz Hameuhad, 1956.

Bibliography – Articles

Ahi-Meir, Abba. "This is how history is written." *Hamashkif*, Dec. 5, 1946.

Ben-Arieh, Katriel. "Politics and the Warsaw Ghetto Revolt," *Dapim le-Heker ha-Shoah* 12 (1955).

Berman, A. *"Oruchu oporu w getscie Warszawskiem (Refleksje)."* *Biultyn ZIH* (Warsaw, 1959).

Donat, Alexander. "Our Last Days in the Warsaw Ghetto." *Commentary*, May 1963.

Goldman, Baruch. *"75 dni w plonancym getsie warszawskim."* *ZIH Bulletin* 42 (1962).

Jaworski, Michal. *"Plac Muranowski 7."* *ZIH Bulletin* (1974).

Lasker, Peretz. *"Ha-Irgun ha-Zvai ha-Leumi herim rishon et nes ha-mered be-Varsha* [The Irgun Zvai Leumi was the first to raise the banner of revolt in Warsaw]." *Herut*, April 24, 1962.

Libionka, Dariusz, and Laurence Weinbaum. "Deconstructing Memory and History: The Jewish Military Union (ZZW) and the Warsaw Ghetto Uprising." *Jewish Political Studies Review* 18, no. 1–2 (Spring 2006).

Porat, Dina. "The Vilna Proclamation of January 1, 1942 in Historical Perspective." *Yad Vashem Studies* 24 (1996).

Smakowski, Jakub. "Diaries and Reminiscences of Jakub Smakowski." *ZIH Bulletin* 94, no. 2 (1975).

Rolirad, Henryk. Testimony in Yad Vashem Archives O3/3068.

Shilton. "Ha-emet al Mered Geto Varsha." *Betar be-Eretz Yisrael – Mahleket ha-hasbara*, 1946.

Stroop, Juergen. *"Bleter far Geshichte."* *ZIH Bulletin* 1, nos. 3–4 (1948); 6, nos. 1–2 (April 1953); 3, nos. 1–2 (1950).

Yelin, Dina. *"Ha-tnuah ha-revizionistit u-Veitar be-hanhagah u-va-mered ba-getaot Varsha, Lodzh, Vilna, ve-Kovna."* M.A. thesis, Tel Aviv University, 1983.

Index

About the author

Moshe Arens was born in 1925 in Kaunas, Lithuania, and immigrated to the United States with his family in 1939. As a youth, Arens became a leader in the Betar youth movement. After Israeli independence in 1948, he made *aliyah* and joined the Irgun forces. He has served as Israel's Minister of Defense and Minister of Foreign Affairs, as well as Israel's ambassador to Washington and chairman of the Israel Knesset's Foreign Affairs and Defense Committee.

A graduate of Massachusetts Institute of Technology and the California Institute of Technology, Arens was associate professor of Aeronautical Engineering at the Technion and vice president for engineering at Israel Aircraft Industries, where he received the Israel Defense Prize. He has been awarded honorary degrees from Yeshiva University, the Technion, and Ben Gurion University.

Arens has served on the board of a number of Israel's high-tech companies. He was a founding partner of Elron Electronic Industries, Israel's flagship high-tech company; vice-chairman of the board of the Israel Corporation, one of Israel's largest investment companies; and chairman of the board of ZIM, Israel's shipping company.

He is the author of two books: *Broken Covenant*, published by Simon & Schuster (1995), and *Flags over the Warsaw Ghetto: The Untold Story of the Warsaw Ghetto Uprising*, published in Hebrew by Yediot (2009), in Polish by Austeria of Krakow (2011), and in English by Gefen Publishing House (2011).